Democratic Backsliding and Public Administration

Liberal democracy is at risk. Its hallmark institutions – political pluralism, separation of powers, and rule of law – are coming under pressure, as authoritarian sentiment is growing around the globe. While liberal-democratic backsliding features prominently in social science scholarship, especially the branches concerned with political parties and political behavior, public administration research lags behind. However, without considering illiberal approaches towards the executive, efforts of actual and aspiring authoritarians remain only partly understood. State bureaucracies are, after all, important instruments of power. This timely and important volume addresses the administrative implications of liberal-democratic backsliding. It studies public administrations as objects and subjects in the context of illiberal dynamics. For this purpose, the volume brings together an international group of scholars to analyze authoritarian tendencies in several countries. The contributions combine theoretical with empirical work, providing the first comparative perspective on an overlooked aspect of one of the most important contemporary political trends.

MICHAEL W. BAUER is the Chair of Public Administration at the School of Transnational Governance of the European University Institute, Florence.

B. GUY PETERS is Maurice Falk Professor of Government at the University of Pittsburgh and founding President of the International Public Policy Association.

JON PIERRE is Professor of Political Science at the University of Gothenburg, Sweden, and Adjunct Professor at the University of Pittsburgh.

KUTSAL YESILKAGIT is Professor of Public Administration at University of Leiden.

STEFAN BECKER is Researcher at the Thünen Institute of Rural Studies, the Federal Research Institute for Rural Areas, Forestry and Fisheries, Germany.

Democratic Backsliding and Public Administration

How Populists in Government Transform
State Bureaucracies

Edited by

MICHAEL W. BAUER
European University Institute, Florence

B. GUY PETERS
University of Pittsburgh

JON PIERRE
University of Gothenberg

KUTSAL YESILKAGIT
University of Leiden

STEFAN BECKER
Thünen Institute of Rural Studies

Shaftesbury Road, Cambridge CB2 8EA, United Kingdom

One Liberty Plaza, 20th Floor, New York, NY 10006, USA

477 Williamstown Road, Port Melbourne, VIC 3207, Australia

314–321, 3rd Floor, Plot 3, Splendor Forum, Jasola District Centre, New Delhi – 110025, India

103 Penang Road, #05–06/07, Visioncrest Commercial, Singapore 238467

Cambridge University Press is part of Cambridge University Press & Assessment, a department of the University of Cambridge.

We share the University's mission to contribute to society through the pursuit of education, learning and research at the highest international levels of excellence.

www.cambridge.org
Information on this title: www.cambridge.org/9781009010412

DOI: 10.1017/9781009023504

First published 2021
First paperback edition 2024

A catalogue record for this publication is available from the British Library

Library of Congress Cataloging-in-Publication data
Names: Bauer, Michael W., editor.
Title: Democratic backsliding and public administration : how populists in government transform state bureaucracies / edited by Michael W. Bauer, B. Guy Peters, Jon Pierre, Kutsal Yesilkagit, Stefan Becker.
Description: Cambridge, United Kingdom ; New York, NY : Cambridge University Press, 2021. | Includes bibliographical references and index.
Identifiers: LCCN 2021010093 (print) | LCCN 2021010094 (ebook) | ISBN 9781316519387 (hardback) | ISBN 9781009010412 (paperback) | ISBN 9781009023504 (ebook)
Subjects: LCSH: Public administration. | Organizational change – Political aspects. | Administrative agencies – Management. | Bureaucracy. | Populism. | BISAC: POLITICAL SCIENCE / General | POLITICAL SCIENCE / General
Classification: LCC JF1525.O73 D46 2021 (print) | LCC JF1525.O73 (ebook) | DDC 351–dc23
LC record available at https://lccn.loc.gov/2021010093
LC ebook record available at https://lccn.loc.gov/2021010094

ISBN   978-1-316-51938-7   Hardback
ISBN   978-1-009-01041-2   Paperback

Contents

Figures

Tables

Contributors

Michael W. Bauer holds the chair of Public Administration at the School of Transnational Governance of the European University Institute, San Domenico di Fiesole.

Stefan Becker is a researcher at the Thünen Institute of Rural Studies, Germany.

Zsolt Boda is research chair and Director General of the Centre for Social Sciences – Hungarian Academy of Sciences Centre of Excellence as well as a part-time professor of political science at the ELTE University of Budapest.

Héctor Briceño is a PhD candidate in Political Sciences, at Rostock University, Germany, and researcher at the Center for Development Studies at the Central University of Venezuela (CENDES-UCV).

Fabrizio Di Mascio is Associate Professor at the Interuniversity Department of Regional and Urban Studies and Planning, University of Turin, Italy. He is also President of the Observatory on Regulatory Impact Assessment (Osservatorio AIR).

Eliška Drápalová is a Vinnova postdoctoral fellow at the University of Gothenburg and the QoG Institute, and Principal Investigator of her project on determinants of administrative capacity building in Southern and Eastern European Local Government (CAPA-City).

Mauricio I. Dussauge-Laguna is Professor-Researcher at the Public Administration Division of the Centro de Investigación y Docencia Económicas (CIDE) in Mexico City.

João Victor Guedes-Neto is a PhD student at the University of Pittsburgh.

György Hajnal is Professor at the Corvinus University of Budapest, and Director of the University's Institute of Economic and Public Policy. He also holds a part-time position of Research Professor of Public Policy and Governance at the Centre for Social Research, Hungarian Academy of Science Centre of Excellence.

Stanisław Mazur is Professor at the Cracow University of Economics, Rector of the Cracow University of Economics, former Dean of the College of Economy and Public Administration, and Head of the Department of Public Policies.

Donald Moynihan is the inaugural McCourt Chair at the McCourt School of Public Policy at Georgetown University, and is a visiting professor at Oxford University and Aarhus University.

Wolfgang Muno holds the Chair for Comparative Government at the University of Rostock.

Alessandro Natalini is Associate Professor of Political Science at the Department of Law at Parthenope University in Naples.

Edoardo Ongaro is Professor of Public Management at The Open University, UK.

B. Guy Peters is Maurice Falk Professor of Government at the University of Pittsburgh, and founding President of the International Public Policy Association.

Jon Pierre is Professor of Political Science at the University of Gothenburg, Sweden, and Adjunct Professor at the University of Pittsburgh.

Gerry Stoker is Chair in Governance at the University of Southampton, UK.

Bastian Strobel is Project Manager of the Census 2022 in the Statistical Bureau of North Rhine-Westphalia and PhD candidate at the Chair for Public Management at the University of Kassel. He is Lecturer at the University of Kassel and Contract Researcher at Leibniz University, Hannover.

Sylvia Veit is Professor of Public Management at the University of Kassel in Germany.

Kutsal Yesilkagit is a full professor of public administration at Leiden University.

Preface

In 2018, Stefan and Michael began working on a paper about populism, backsliding, and public administration. They came across papers from Guy and Jon, as well as from Kutsal, that approached the topic from different angles. We decided to join forces and organize a workshop on the topic that was supported by the Robert Schuman Center for Advanced Studies and the new School of Transnational Governance of the European University Institute. This workshop took place on several cold, snowy days in late January 2019. The workshop brought together junior and senior colleagues from all over the discipline and from many parts of the world – and the discussions we had were both theoretically and empirically stimulating. This workshop, in the wonderful Capella of the Villa Schifanoia of the European University Institute, constituted the start of the intellectual journey that led to the present volume analyzing populists in government and how they attempt to transform their bureaucracies. We are indebted to all the participants of the Florence workshop, and we are happy that many of the original presentations have been transformed into chapters of the book. The process of moving from those papers to the current volume was longer and more taxing than any of us would have liked, but we believe it has definitely been worth the effort.

Apart from the financial support from the EUI, we are grateful for the encouragement given to us by Professor Brigid Laffan, director of the Robert Schuman Center, as well as by Professor Miguel Poiares Maduro, then director of the School of Transnational Governance. Other colleagues at the EUI, as well as at the German University of Administrative Sciences, Speyer, including Alix Weigel, Mia Saugman and Andrea Arendt, contributed to the success of the workshop. We are extremely grateful to Nora Wagner for invaluable help in managing the production of the volume, and to John Haslam from Cambridge University Press for his encouragement to engage in an edited volume.

We are also indebted to the reviewers who provided apt and useful comments on earlier drafts.

The topic of this book is one of great importance in contemporary democracies, and we hope that, at least in some small way, we are contributing to maintaining and improving democratic governance. The process of producing this volume has been a learning experience for us all, but also a highly gratifying personal experience of working with great colleagues.

Michael W. Bauer, B. Guy Peters, Jon Pierre, Kutsal Yesilkagit, and Stefan Becker.

1 | Introduction: Populists, Democratic Backsliding, and Public Administration

MICHAEL W. BAUER, B. GUY PETERS, JON PIERRE, KUTSAL YESILKAGIT, AND STEFAN BECKER

Liberal democracy is at risk. Its ascent since the Second World War has recently come to a halt. Once considered to be the only political game in town, the fate of liberal democracy is growing more uncertain as actual and aspiring authoritarians have begun to undermine its hallmark institutions. Political pluralism, separation of powers, and rule of law are increasingly called into question. The "end of history," implying the exhaustion of viable systematic alternatives to Western liberalism (Fukuyama 1989; 2006), has failed to come closer in recent years. Instead, liberal democracy is contested as it has not been since 1945.

Two trends contribute to liberal democracy's current stagnation. On the one hand, many authoritarian regimes – China above all, but also many Middle Eastern and African states – have not faltered, as modernization theories once predicted. Rather, they have proven resilient, even in the face of external and internal pressure. On the other hand, many democracies, both old and new, have seen authoritarian backlashes. While almost complete collapses of democracy, such as in Venezuela, remain exceptions, governments in countries such as Turkey, Hungary, and Poland have implemented far-reaching illiberal reforms – hollowing out their democratic institutions. Even the United States, one of the most robust liberal democracies, has witnessed authoritarian dynamics with President Trump. In many other Western states, too, liberal democracy is under siege, as authoritarian-minded parties shift political discourses and thereby influence policies, or even enter government and implement illiberal reforms.

Many of these current processes of liberal-democratic backsliding are driven by populism. A rather controversial term in political practice, populism can be understood as "a thin-centred ideology that considers society to be ultimately separated into two homogeneous and antagonistic camps, 'the pure people' versus 'the corrupt elite,' and which argues that politics should be an expression of the [general will] of the people" (Mudde and Rovira Kaltwasser 2017, p. 6). The relationship between populism and liberal democracy is complex; in some circumstances, such as in autocratic regimes, populist movements can boost democratic politics by opening the political playing field for actors formerly excluded or underrepresented. Ultimately, however, populism is incompatible with modern notions of liberal democracy. As Müller (2016a, pp. 19–20) argues, populism is a "a particular moralistic imagination of politics, a way of perceiving the political world that sets a morally pure and fully unified . . . people against elites who are deemed corrupt or in some way morally inferior." Following this logic, populist ideologies are not only anti-elitist, but also anti-pluralist and, as such, illiberal. Some also see explicitly authoritarian elements increasingly blended into many, if not most, forms of contemporary populist ideologies (Norris and Inglehart 2019).

Liberal-democratic backsliding and the role of populism have attracted much scholarly attention in recent years (see, e.g., Galston 2018; Krastev 2017; Levitsky and Ziblatt 2018a; Luce 2017; Manow 2018; Mounk 2018; Zielonka 2018). However, while knowledge on the sources, variants and consequences of backsliding processes is accumulating, one central aspect of policymaking remains neglected: public administration. Much scholarship focuses on populist politicians breaking rules of political discourse, attacking the media and, if they enter government, obstructing the courts and interfering with elections. Yet how they approach the state bureaucracy features less prominently. This omission creates a peculiar void in the debate on liberal-democratic backsliding and populism, for bureaucracies are crucial in preparing and implementing policies. As Max Weber (1978, p. 220) wrote, "the exercise of authority consists precisely in administration."

Against this empirical and theoretical background, this volume addresses the administrative dimension of liberal-democratic backsliding with a focus on populist governments. It studies public administrations as both objects and subjects in the backsliding process. For this purpose, the volume brings together country case studies and cross-cutting analyses. The contributions combine theoretical and empirical work, providing the first truly comparative perspective on liberal-democratic backsliding, populism, and public administration.

The rationale for this undertaking is twofold. First, as already indicated, the volume fills an empirical void. We currently know little about administrative policies of populist governments, although there are ample hints that the recent wave of populism also involves transforming public administration. Many populists, for instance, are currently engaging in the rewriting of the "operational manual" of the state (Müller 2016a). These efforts cannot stop short of the state bureaucracy. Furthermore, in those cases where populists must still face credible elections, they seek to deliver on policy promises – an effort that is doomed to fail without the backup of the administrative machinery. Much dynamism is therefore to be expected when incoming populist politicians interact with established state bureaucracies, but most studies focus on alterations in the systems of checks and balances and tend to neglect public administration. This volume thus explores an overlooked aspect of one of the most important contemporary political trends – that is, democratic backsliding.

Second, the volume builds bridges between different strands of scholarship, which have remained rather insulated so far. It complements the debate on system transformation and democracy with administrative aspects, which it has long neglected. While there is a rich body of literature that deals with the causes, conditions, and consequences of liberal-democratic ascent and breakdown, most research has focused on macrolevel associations. It has thus paid little attention to the extent to which bureaucracies were objects and subjects in transformation processes. This volume offers one path to integrate public administration aspects in system transformation research by eliciting the role of bureaucracies in reform projects of populist governments. At the same time, it brings questions of democracy back to the Public Administration community, which has long favored studying issues of management and efficiency. It addresses the place and role of bureaucracy in democracy through the lens of recent backsliding dynamics. Also, the gathered knowledge on strategies and pathways of illiberal public administration policies employed by populist governments can offer advice on how to make the bureaucracy less penetrable to authoritarian tendencies.

This introduction lays the theoretical and conceptual groundwork. It first reviews broader debates on system transformation and public administration, showing that the repertoire to study the administrative dimensions of liberal-democratic backsliding is currently meager. It then identifies three areas of inquiry, outlining expectations and propositions for the empirical case studies. These areas are the general governance concepts of populist politicians, their strategies for administrative reform and the potential reactions of the bureaucracy. Taken together, these areas provide a comprehensive framework for studying the administrative dimensions of liberal-democratic backsliding.

Background: System Transformation, Democracy, and Public Administration

Understanding the conduct of populist governments in liberal-democratic settings could, in theory, greatly benefit from system transformation research, which has generated plenty of knowledge on democratic ascent and breakdown. Most of this research, however, focuses on macrolevel associations, building on Lipset's (1959) insights on modernization theory, and perhaps best exemplified by the study of Przeworski et al. (2000). It thus pays little attention to state administrations. Some studies have illuminated administrative issues, such as the phenomenon of bureaucratic authoritarianism as a variant of autocratic rule (Collier 1979) or the bureaucracy's role in the transition of Eastern European states after the fall of the Iron Curtain (Baker 2002). Yet these studies hardly add up to a comparative perspective on bureaucracies.

With a limited recognition of public administration, system transformation research follows the path of much thinking on democracy, wherein civil liberties, political competition, and fair elections lie at the core. The historical trajectory of system transformation research may explain this narrow view. The focus has long been on the shift away from authoritarian regimes and toward democratic rule. Democratization starts with greater societal organization, freer political competition, fairer elections, and so forth. These processes happen far from the bureaucracy, which instead remains dominated by an authoritarian executive until democratic transition in the other arenas has been successful. It follows that the bureaucracy is usually the natural stronghold of the autocratic leadership in power, and it is of little concern to transformation theorists interested in regime change *toward* democracy. However, analyzing transitions *from* democracy to authoritarianism is likely to need a more bureaucracy-centered perspective, as modern democracies feature highly entangled politico-administrative relations. It is also plausible that democratic public administration is among the first institutions subject to backsliding pressures from authoritarian-minded politicians. For these reasons, a stronger focus on the state bureaucracy could benefit transformation research.

If scholars were to direct their attention toward bureaucratic aspects, they would have difficulty finding appropriate concepts and operationalizations for their purposes, however. Whereas literature on democratization has mostly disregarded the bureaucracy, much scholarship on public administration has avoided issues of democracy. These research strands thus implicitly agree that such issues belong to the "political" rather than the "administrative" domain. Indeed, for much public administration literature, threats of democratic backsliding regarding the bureaucracy are irrelevant; by contrast, they perceive the hierarchical character and culture of bureaucratic organization as an impediment to democratic governance. The bureaucracy's comprehensive power is feared as being susceptible to escaping political control and turning citizens into underlings to anonymous rule (Durant and Ali 2012, p. 278), or perceived as overproducing public goods for its own organizational aggrandizement (Niskanen 1971). From this perspective, political control of the bureaucracy has utmost priority, and elected politicians should determine the direction according to which the bureaucracy must act. The underlying dichotomy of politics and administration remains a prominent analytical anchor, in particular for model-based, quantitative political science scholarship (Shepsle and Bonchek 2007), which focuses on idealized control and applies formal principal–agent analysis (Weingast 1984).

Other approaches, however, challenge this view. They apply bottom-up perspectives based on case studies to disentangle what undergirds the conduct of bureaucracy (Meier and O'Toole 2006, p. 12). This research strand perceives interactions between politicians and the bureaucracy as multifaceted and complex; regularly, they are more a matter of negotiation or collaboration than of top-down command and control. This approach does not render questions of political control irrelevant, but it emphasizes the democratic quality of the bureaucracy itself. As public administration constitutes a component of modern government, it must also be organized along some democratic guidelines. In the words of Dwight Waldo, who advocated this point of view, it is just not credible to claim that "autocracy during working hours is the price to be paid for democracy after hours" (Waldo 1952, p. 87).

Studies on bureaucracies provide empirical evidence as to why disregarding the bureaucracy renders discussions about democracy incomplete. The policymaking impact of administrations has been elicited in studies about implementation (Pressman and Wildavsky 1984), street-level bureaucracy (Lipsky 2010), representative bureaucracy (Meier 1993), coproduction (Bovaird 2007), networks, governance and bureaucratic interest intermediation (Lehmbruch 1991; O'Toole 1997), and administrative input in the preparation of laws – to name only a few prominent examples. Furthermore, the link between administrative capacities and the legitimation of the state (Suleiman 2013) suggests a much more complex relationship between public administration and democracy than system transformation debates and standard political science have hitherto acknowledged (Denhardt and Denhardt 2002). However, while these and other contributions have generated much systematic knowledge on many bureaucratic phenomena, they have hardly addressed issues of system transformation – regarding neither democratization nor democratic backsliding. Furthermore, they have barely been translated into democratic terms at all. While studies on accountability, citizen participation, and corresponding topics soared, they have rarely benefited debates on either democracy or system transformation.

The study of administrative dimensions of liberal-democratic backsliding can therefore build on a broad literature base, but it must still develop its own conceptual repertoire. System transformation research and Public Administration provide elements that must be ordered and synthesized, before being put to the empirical test.

Agenda: Studying the Administrative Dimensions of Liberal-Democratic Backsliding

Liberal-democratic backsliding is a complex, multidimensional process that can be approached from many different viewpoints. This section develops a framework for studying its administrative dimensions. It first discusses the broader governance concepts of recent illiberal sentiment, particularly in the guise of populism, before reflecting on its repertoire of specific reforms to transform the bureaucracy. Because administrations are no mere objects of political initiatives, this section also discusses concepts to capture the reactions of the civil service toward the new populist leadership. First, however, a few clarifications on the term "democratic backsliding" are in order.

Democratic Backsliding

Democratic backsliding has become a fashionable topic of debate in the last decade, but its precise meaning is often unclear. This volume follows Bermeo's (2016) use of the concept that captures, as coups d'états and revolutions become rarer, the more clandestine ways of undermining democracy. This backsliding includes harassment of the opposition, censorship of the media, and subversion of horizontal accountability, but it also shows itself in "executive aggrandizement" (Bermeo 2016, p. 10; see also Coppedge et al. 2018). This specific use of the concept has been criticized on normative and analytical grounds. As to the former, the concept implicitly defines democracy as liberal. Many understandings of democracy are more nuanced (see, e.g., the five dimensions of the *Varieties of Democracy* project (Lührmann et al. 2020): deliberative, egalitarian, electoral, liberal, participatory), and the broad notion of liberalism itself has drawn plenty of criticism. Accordingly, debates on what counts as democratic backsliding are often heated. While acknowledging different interpretations of democracy, this volume restricts its analysis to the liberal one, which takes a negative view of the concentration of political power and emphasizes the importance of civil rights and the rule of law, as well as checks and balances (see Coppedge et al. 2018). The normative premise is that, without some liberalism, other dimensions of democracy will also suffer, whereas the pragmatic reasoning is that, in a vast field of empirical developments, the analysis must start somewhere. The initial focus on liberal democracy can and should later be expanded.

The concept of democratic backsliding has also been criticized on analytical grounds: for its imprecision, implicit automatism and missing agency (who or what drives this process); its subjective starting point (deteriorations in authoritarian regimes do not seem to be included); and its lack of measurement strategies and reliable data.

These analytical problems lend weight to suspicions that the empirical phenomenon might not be as relevant as portrayed. The existence of a "third wave of autocratization" (Lührmann and Lindberg 2019) has, however, been empirically substantiated. While claims of the end of liberal democracies (Diamond 2016; Runciman 2018) appear exaggerated, "the deterioration of qualities associated with democratic governance, within any regime" is apparent (Waldner and Lust 2018, p. 8). This volume thus acknowledges the conceptual problems associated with the concept of democratic backsliding, but still uses it as a starting point, hoping to contribute to its further development by bringing in administrative factors.

General Approaches to the Bureaucracy

As acknowledged earlier, the voting of populist parties and politicians into government does not represent democratic backsliding; rather, it depends on their conduct in office. While governing always entails randomness and situational activity, governments, no matter their outlook, face a few general choices on how to govern. Their answers precede any specific policy preferences; they define how politicians in government see their role in relationship to other institutions. These governance concepts are crucial in understanding the dynamics after a new government enters office – and all the more so in cases of illiberal governments winning elections in liberal settings, given the presumably stark difference in governance approaches. Regarding the institution of interest here – public administration – politicians have three general choices after entering government: sidelining, ignoring or using the bureaucracy (see also Peters and Pierre 2019). Each of those can, however, entail unintended side effects.

In the first scenario, the government is reluctant to use the established bureaucracy. This unwillingness is, for instance, in line with the general populist dichotomy of the virtuous elite versus the corrupt elite. The public bureaucracy is, very clearly, part of the elite in capital cities, and therefore is a natural target for rejection and avoidance on the part of populist politicians. The sidelining of the bureaucracy may come through various forms of patronage (for options, see Peters 2013). Depending upon the nature of the administrative system, an incoming president or prime minister may be able to appoint hundreds, sometimes even thousands, of officials to replace incumbent officials. While this may be common practice, the style of patronage appointments may change: the appointments may move from being largely technically qualified individuals who can work easily with a qualified public bureaucracy to more politicized officials with few qualifications other than their political connections to the leadership.

Another option for populist politicians attempting to "occupy" the state is to construct alternative structures that complement or substitute for the work of the career public service. The Executive Office of the President in the United States is, for instance, a ready-made opportunity for this approach, and only needs to be occupied by populist loyalists to have a parallel structure to the bureaucracy. But other political systems that have had a more respected senior civil service have had leaders create such advisory structures for their political leadership. The Trump administration in the United States has made several moves to undermine the independence of the civil service and to politicize appointments in the federal government. These have included a gradual downsizing of the service through attrition, removing some protections against dismissals, and significantly undermining the powers of labor unions at the federal level.

A third alternative for sidelining the established bureaucracy is to adopt a technocratic solution to governing. Somewhat paradoxically, although populists may argue that elites are inherently corrupt, at least some American populists have attempted to involve experts, whether from within the bureaucracy or from outside. For example, Charles Postel (2007) has pointed to a "populist vision" of governing in which professional, businesslike solutions would substitute for the presumed incompetence of the politicians. This version of sidelining the bureaucracy tends to assume that more than being venial, the public bureaucracy fits the familiar stereotype of bureaucracy as lazy and incompetent. This leads to a vision of governing through creative, innovative and committed employees brought in from outside the "system." The recommendations of populist political leaders for the professionalization were roughly coterminous with the progressive movement's similar recommendations for improving governance. This vision of technocratic governance has been very evident in Latin American governments, especially those with relatively low levels of party system institutionalization (Mainwaring, Bizarro, and Petrova

2018). In these cases, the absence of expertise within government has led to the use of experts, often tied to individual political leaders, but in other cases with strong ties to a political party (Panizza, Peters, and Ramos 2019).

The second option for incoming governments is to ignore the established bureaucracy. Their rationale could stem from different reasons. One the one hand, political leaders coming into office may simply not be interested in governing; on the other hand, as in the case of Donald Trump (and many other populists), they may think they can govern more personally and with their cronies rather than through the apparatus of government. Many populist leaders tend to assume (often quite rightly) that the establishment is opposed to them and revert to governing through a smaller coterie of friends and advisers.

Paradoxically, this governance approach is likely to empower the bureaucracy. Despite the politicians' indifference, government will have to go on somehow. The absence of effective leadership and direction from the top may enable some form of "bureaucratic government" to appear, in direct contradiction to the intentions of politicians who wanted to "drain the swamp." This is analogous to the observations made at the time of extreme political instability in France and Italy that left the bureaucracy effectively in charge (Diamant 1968). Populist politicians may focus on a few policy domains, such as immigration and environmental regulation, and leave much of the rest of government unattended. Some civil servants may even engage in "guerilla government" (O'Leary 2006; Olsson 2016). While this is the stereotype of the role of bureaucracies held by many populists (as well as by others on the extreme right and left), public servants may believe their only reasonable option is to resist in place. Thus, the lack of concern of many populists with the bureaucracy – other than to denigrate it – may undermine their agenda. Such undermining may not be so much outright sabotage as the continuing daily tasks of public administrators to administer the laws that are on the books already. Rhetoric and anger will be insufficient to tame the administrative state. Without a clear strategy for controlling and remodeling the bureaucracy, the governance capacity of any illiberal regime will be limited.

The third option for populist politicians entering government is to use the bureaucracy. Roberto Michels argued (1915) that when socialist parties won power in government they had in fact lost. His argument was that, once in power, the principles of equality and shared power that had been their political leitmotiv would necessarily be abandoned when the leaders of the party took office and had to govern. Even if not enamored by the trappings of power, these party leaders would be captured by the need to govern and would become different from other members of the socialist movement. The same sort of capture and oligarchic change may occur for populist politicians who gain office and then are confronted with fulfilling the promises for governance and policy they made while campaigning. Governance is not easily produced, especially when the agenda is to undo much of what has been done before, and the individuals attempting to make the transformation are themselves often inexperienced and lack knowledge about procedures, as well as about substance. Unlike the aforementioned sidelining scenario, however, their desire to govern may overcome their ideological distaste for the insiders of the public sector, so they will begin to rely on the career bureaucracy.

This scenario may appeal more to the strongly authoritarian versions of populism than to the more contemporary democratic versions from the political right. If authoritarians with a populist inclination also want to exert control over the society, they may well need the bureaucracy (including the uniformed bureaucracy in the form of the military) to have any success. The need to govern may especially place the electoral authoritarians in something of a dilemma, risking losing their electoral base either by failure to deliver or by being seen to be cooperating too much with the elites in the national capital. The attempts of a populist government to cooperate, and co-opt, the existing bureaucracy may put that bureaucracy into something of a dilemma also. On the one hand, those bureaucrats may want to maintain their control over the machinery of government, and may therefore be willing to go along with the program of the populist regime to maintain that power. They may also believe that it is their task to serve any government that is selected by legitimated means, even ones that appear to regard them, the permanent administrators, as anathema. But the populist ideal of more democratic recruitment to public office may not be entirely practical, given the demands of modern governing. If the administration wants an effective government, even one dedicated to dismantling much of government, it will need to draw on the same group of educated elites that are assumed to be the problem. Thus, finding some mode of accommodation between the antisystemic goals of populist rhetoric and the need to govern presents a major challenge for both the political and the bureaucratic aspects of government.

Understanding the administrative implications of liberal-democratic backsliding thus begins with understanding what politicians wish to accomplish in general, and what this entails for the state bureaucracy in particular. This task can be challenging. Many political agendas are complicated, with discourse often being different from behavior. Furthermore, recent populist surges are driven by new movements, parties, and actors, who often have not yet consolidated their agendas. Their conduct may therefore be contradictory. What may seem as a deliberate attempt to sabotage the state bureaucracy may, for instance, sometimes simply be a collective action problem on behalf of the government. The first step necessary in analyzing populist public administration initiatives is thus the careful estimation of governance concepts.

Strategies for Illiberal Administrative Reform

Depending on their general governance concepts, different administrative options materialize for incoming governments. If they seek to sideline the established bureaucracy, they may design new institutions from scratch. But even if they decide to use the established bureaucracy, they must not resign themselves to accepting its current organization. Rather, they can engage in molding the administration into new illiberal forms. The rise of fascism in Europe in the early twentieth century provides some insights on possible pathways. Admittedly, such retrospective accounts have limits in their comparability with current developments. Present-day populists are no fascists, and current democracies appear more solid than the young republics of the early twentieth century that succumbed to totalitarianism. Nevertheless, the shared disdain for pluralism makes the administrative policies of the fascist era relevant for current times. The following illustrations are drawn from authoritative works on Italy (Bach and Breuer 2010), Germany (Bracher, Sauer, and Schulz 1962; Caplan 1988; Reichardt and Seibel 2011), Portugal (Costa Pinto 2004; Madureira 2007; Schmitter 1975) and Austria (Tálos and Manoschek 2005). When these young democracies crumbled, fascist rulers also transformed public administration. Five main lines of action are evident.

First, incoming authoritarian rulers sought to alter administrative structures. A common attempt was to reduce autonomy in what was usually a vertically and horizontally differentiated system. In effect, the new rulers sought to centralize the bureaucracy. Because even authoritarian leaders cannot build new bureaucratic structures from scratch, at least not in the short-term, change was incremental. The new rulers sought to disempower established organizations by creating new ones, planting new units in traditional bureaucracies, and transferring power to parts of the administrative system more ideologically consolidated and responsive to the wishes of the new leadership. Second, organizational realignment could also be realized through redistributing resources. In this case, budget and personnel allocations reshuffled administrative powers, while the formal set-up remained intact. Third, the new rulers aimed at influencing administrative personnel. Purges of staff and top bureaucrats occurred eventually, albeit to different degrees. Following large-scale dismissals, the new rulers often inserted ideological supporters into positions of strategic importance to consolidate their nascent executive power. Such appointments went beyond normal spoils behavior in that the very rules and procedures of recruitment and career progression were often reformed to produce a lasting personnel effect. Fourth, the incoming authoritarian leadership sought to overhaul bureaucratic norms. They tried to establish an administrative culture that framed critique as disobedience and suppressed dissenting opinions. In effect, bureaucrats were expected to be loyal to the new, charismatic leadership, not to institutions or constitutions. Fifth, European fascist regimes famously manifested their antipluralism through extensive use of executive decree, which sidelined legislative bodies and representative deliberation. The effect of such measures was a reconfiguration of power that granted total authority to the executive and silenced external pressures.

These illiberal strategies are valid primers for what might be employed today. However, public administration has undergone some transformation in the last century. One important trend has been increasing openness and accountability. Institutionalized access for civil society organizations, consultations with citizens, transparency laws, and increased media scrutiny have put bureaucracies under stronger external control. Parliaments have also professionalized, allowing for better scrutiny of the executive branch.

The pluralist implications of these developments must trouble populist politicians in government. Bearing this in mind, the historical cues can be developed into five dimensions of populist public administration policies (see also Bauer and Becker 2020). In each dimension, different strategies are available to transform the bureaucracy:

- Structure: Centralizing formal power by strengthening top-down command and control in central government, reducing horizontal power dispersion and restricting lower-level and agency autonomy, where it constitutes a counterweight to central government.
- Resources: Steering administrative conduct through allocation of funds as well as administrative and informational resources – for instance, weakening specific units by reducing funds and staff numbers, leaving them out of information loops, or impairing their work by imposing excessive administrative demands.
- Personnel: Ideological cleansing of staff by intensifying patronage in recruitment and career progression beyond "normal" spoils behavior, while weakening meritocratic and representative factors in personnel policy through excessive exhaustion of available or introduction of new politicization instruments.
- Norms: Completely committing the administrative culture to the new ideological order by undermining the official neutrality of the bureaucracy or emphasizing its instrumental character through, for instance, exercising informal pressure on staff.
- Accountability: Reducing the societal participation and responsibilities of service agencies vis-à-vis the parliament and other external controls, cutting back transparency and exchange of information with third parties, and restricting media access.

These are strategies populist politicians can use to transform public administration according to their needs. Neither the dimensions nor the strategies must necessarily be exhaustive, but they do provide plausible anchors for studying the administrative implications of liberal-democratic backsliding. By understanding specific administrative reform strategies, we then know more about populist politicians' conduct in government. However, modern bureaucracies are not passive, permeable structures; they are actors in policymaking. Bureaucratic reactions are, therefore, crucial for the fate of populist initiatives.

Reactions of the Bureaucracy

Conceptualizing bureaucracies as partly autonomous actors in policy-making goes against some conventional notions. Some argue that bureaucracies are not political entities. Indeed, the notion that politics and administration should be treated as separate spheres is not new. Wilson (1887, p. 212) portrays the latter as the "detailed and systematic execution of public law," and therefore apolitical. But, as Peters (2018a, p. 164) argues, it is exactly "this presumed separation of administration and politics [that] allows them [public administrators] to engage in politics." This means that once bureaucrats are not directly accountable to the public, they use their technical and legal knowledge to influence policymaking. Brehm and Gates (2002) offer three paths which bureaucrats may use to influence policies: working, shirking, or sabotage. Their premise is that government employees are moved by functional preferences – that is, the feeling that they are accomplishing something important. They may thus be interested in taking part in the policies they are supposed to implement. Take, for instance, Lipsky's (2010) suggestion that teachers are the street-level ministers of education. These civil servants have at least two strong motivations: the education of cocitizens, and representation of the state to the population. Problems can arise when bureaucrats do not believe that their efforts are being dedicated to something desirable.

The literature offers some insights into what happens then. Gailmard and Patty (2007, p. 874), for instance, divided bureaucrats into two types: "policy-motivated ('zealots') or policy indifferent ('slackers')." Although the motivation of slackers is also important for bureaucratic conduct, zealots are more crucial when it comes to ideological conflicts. If they hold the same ideological preferences of the principal, it should be a win–win situation. However, if they hold different policy preferences than the principal, zealots may use their expertise to guide the policy process along a different path than the one expected by the principal (Downs 1965). Such opposition could be mediated by a more general public service motivation (see Perry, Hondeghem, and Wise 2010), which, for instance, includes the "desire to do the job" (Wilson 1989, p. 159). However, public service motivation should not be overestimated. By way of example, a recent study has failed to identify its predictive power on measures of job attendance, and in-role and extra-role performance (Wright, Hassan, and Christensen

2017). Furthermore, a bureaucratic zealot facing an ideologically opposed government is starkly different from civil servants underperforming. In the former case, shirking and sabotage are likely outcomes.

Yet shirking and sabotage must not be the only outcomes. The administration of Ronald Reagan in the United States serves as a good example. He implemented reforms that aimed at reducing the size of the government. The civil servants' rational behavior should have been to either shirk or sabotage, if they were intent on protecting their institution. Whereas Aberbach and Rockman (2000) confirm that serious conflicts indeed took place during this administration, Golden (2000, p. 163) says that "compliance was the predominant [bureaucratic] response." Indeed, the general suspicion of bureaucratic shirking appears exaggerated (see Peters and Pierre 2017; Pierre and Peters 2017). Even Brehm and Gates have rejected it: "the assumption that subordinates necessarily prefer shirking over working is unnecessarily simplistic ... Workers will prefer producing some outputs over other outputs; they don't necessarily shirk at every opportunity" (Brehm and Gates 2002, p. 43).

When populist politicians come to power in established democracies, however, this is different from a regular transfer of power. They often enter office with a transformative agenda. Should we expect bureaucrats to work, shirk, or sabotage? Different dynamics are conceivable. Cost–benefit calculations may differ from normal transfers of power, and bureaucratic reactions may vary in temporal, sectoral, or hierarchical dimensions. Analyses should refrain from ascribing specific reactions, be they bureaucracies acting as bulwarks or bulldozers of democracy, but carefully examine them. In combination with the populist leaders' overarching governance concepts and their specific reform strategies, these reactions are crucial for eventual outcomes.

A Framework to Study Democratic Backsliding and Public Administration

Taken together, the three areas discussed yield an analytical framework to study liberal-democratic backsliding and public administration in a comprehensive manner (see Figure 1.1). It first touches upon the general governance concepts of governments. What do they want to accomplish regarding the state bureaucracy? We have proposed three options: sidelining, ignoring, and using. Depending

Political level

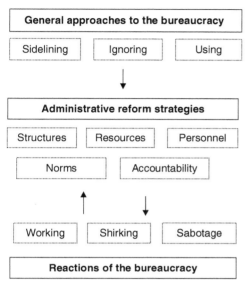

Figure 1.1 Analytical framework
Source: own compilation.

on the choices at this macro level, the analytical framework addresses the strategies populist politicians can pursue to reform the state administration. We have identified different options regarding administrative structure, personnel, resources, norms, and accountability. The analytical framework further includes the reactions of the bureaucracy. Will civil servants shirk, work or sabotage, and under what conditions?

This analytical framework serves as a heuristic that identifies, based on scientific literature and empirical cues, potentially important factors for studying the administrative dimensions of liberal-democratic backsliding. It guides the contributions to this volume, which represent the first systematic venture into the relationship between liberal-democratic backsliding, populism, and public administration. The remainder of this chapter briefly introduces the contributions.

Outline of the Volume

Liberal-democratic backsliding is a topic of current importance; however, it is hardly a new phenomenon. Lessons can be drawn from plenty of historical examples, even if circumstances differ. Before looking at present cases, the volume thus offers a retrospective. As argued earlier, the rise of fascism in Europe in the early twentieth century reveals some insights into the role of public administration in the transition from democratic rule. Bastian Strobel and Sylvia Veit (Chapter 2) analyze how the state bureaucracy in Germany was approached and eventually transformed by illiberal politicians in the late Weimar Republic and then under Hitler. They show that despite being a professional Weberian bureaucracy with strong barriers against politicization, the civil service did not function as a safeguard of democracy. Many civil servants even welcomed the rollback of democratic principles and facilitated the radical transformation and politicization of the bureaucracy in a short time. The case study underlines that democratic values must also be institutionalized in the civil service in order to strengthen its resilience against attempts to erode liberal-democratic institutions.

After this retrospective, the volume turns to recent cases of liberal-democratic backsliding. This change in perspective also brings populism – one the most important drivers of current backsliding dynamics – into focus. In the first case study, Fabrizio Di Mascio, Alessandro Natalini, and Edoardo Ongaro (Chapter 3) provide an account of administrative change and bureaucratic resilience under populist governments in Italy during the first two decades of the 2000s. They show that political parties in Italy have displayed quite radically different forms of populism, both left-wing and right-wing, and have also changed their stance over time. At the same time, however, the level of administrative continuity has proved significant. Their main argument is, therefore, that populist governments in Italy have displayed a marked chasm between the level of talk and the level of action when it comes to public administration reform.

Such a chasm is hardly evident in the two subsequent case studies, which examine recent dynamics in Hungary and Poland. These two countries represent the most drastic instances of liberal-democratic backsliding in the European Union, and, in both cases, public administration has been a central object of reform. As György Hajnal and Zsolt Boda show (Chapter 4), Viktor Orbán and his governments have implemented a wide and deep array of changes in the state bureaucracy in their quest for turning Hungary into an "illiberal" democracy. They consider this country an extreme case of backsliding, made possible by the fragility of Hungarian democracy, Orbán's personal governing style, based on an uncompromising use of power, and the length of his tenure. They further observe an almost complete absence of bureaucratic resistance, which they attribute to Hungary's autocratic traditions and the government's sweeping implementation of its illiberal transformation agenda. In Chapter 5, Stanisław Mazur takes a look at the changes in Polish public administration that have occurred since the 2015 elections, when the so-called United Right came to power. The following illiberal and populist drift has resulted, inter alia, in the expansion of central government powers, increased involvement of the state in the economy, state capture, colonization of the administrative apparatus and its politicization, and a weaker position of local governments. Here, too, historical legacies, including the precedence of personal ties over institutional mechanisms, loyalty to the ruling party over allegiance to the public interest, and political patronage over substantive competencies, appear to have facilitated dynamics of liberal-democratic backsliding.

In Chapter 6, Eliška Drápalová concludes the European case studies with an examination of technocratic populism at the local level in Barcelona, Prague, and Rome. The premise is that many cities with populist mayors may become laboratories for experiments of populist strategies, given that respective parties often govern at first – and sometimes only – at the local level. The chapter investigates how technocratic-populist parties and leaders in cities interact with the bureaucracy and combine different strategies of democratic backsliding. In so doing, the chapter also examines the role of ICT tools and innovations within populist strategies. The empirical analysis shows that technocratic populists in the three cities employ, with varying success, strategies to transform public administration, but there are considerable differences that point to heterogeneity within the populist camp.

With the next three contributions, the volume shifts its attention from Europe to the Americas. The case study by Donald Moynihan (Chapter 7) addresses the ways in which the Trump administration has exemplified and accelerated a long-term trend toward democratic backsliding in the United States. While previous administrations

looked for ways to exert closer control over parts of government they
were ideologically at odds with, the Trump administration has gone
further. It has sidelined administrative expertise and scientists in many
areas, selecting senior leaders whose lack of qualification is frequently
matched only by their disdain for their organizational mission, and
shown a willingness to push the boundaries of the law beyond its
breaking point. The Trump administration has also sought to weaken
the ability of public sector unions to negotiate for benefits, punished
individuals and units deemed not to be politically loyal, and weakened
oversight bodies. All of this has been accompanied by a rhetoric of
delegitimization, wherein the president and his supporters frequently
invoke conspiratorial theories of deep state plots.

The US neighbor to the south, Mexico, plays a central role in Donald
Trump's populist rhetoric and policies. In 2018, Mexico elected its own
populist leader: Andrés Manuel López Obrador. In Chapter 8,
Mauricio I. Dussauge-Laguna discusses how the Mexican public
administration has been affected by a backsliding process since then.
He argues that Mexico is experiencing a case of "doublespeak populism." In the administrative sphere, the centralization of decision-
making and the use of new executive controls have been described as
efforts to fight inefficiency, waste, and corruption, but in practice they
have been used to undermine the independence of institutions and
regulators. The portrayal of a so-called "golden" bureaucracy has
served to advance budgetary and salary reductions, only to provide
funding for presidential pet projects. As a result, López Obrador's
reforms have further deteriorated bureaucratic institutions and public
services, thus adversely affecting the overall welfare and basic rights of
the people they are supposed to help.

Moving to South America, the final case study deals with perhaps the
most drastic case of liberal-democratic backsliding in recent history:
Venezuela. Wolfgang Muno and Héctor Briceño (Chapter 9) show that
it has been a, more or less, functioning democracy since 1958. Then,
after Hugo Chávez became president in 1998, and especially under his
successor, Nicolás Maduro, Venezuela experienced a severe decline of
democracy, nowadays clearly being an authoritarian regime. A general
objective of Chavismo–Madurismo has been to expand and co-opt all
state institutions, including public administration, to subordinate it to
the revolution. In this process, Muno and Briceño identify three main
strategies to sideline the established bureaucracy, which was seen as

affiliated to the old regime: repression and firing; circumventing and neglecting, which means creating a "parallel state"; and militarization of the "civil" service.

Following the empirical case studies, João Victor Guedes-Neto and Guy Peters (Chapter 10) take a deeper look into reactions of the civil service in the face of democratic backsliding. They ask whether civil servants would be willing to act as veto players by refusing to implement policies that undermine democratic institutions. Their contribution provides preliminary answers based on a set of survey experiments conducted with Brazilian bureaucrats. Using the triad "working, shirking, and sabotage," their results confirm that civil servants are willing to shirk and sabotage if assigned to implement policies that are perceived to restrict democratic rights, such as the freedoms of press and expression. Furthermore, they demonstrate that different individual characteristics affect the bureaucrats' behavioral intentions in these situations.

In the final two chapters, the volume widens its perspective while also seeking to look ahead. Gerry Stoker (Chapter 11) first reminds us that the relationship between populism and public administration maybe more complex than is often presumed. Public administration may be a victim of populist-inspired backsliding, but also may have been an unwitting harbinger of the populist surge. Administrative reforms in vogue over the last two decades helped to create the conditions for populism. Performance management, citizen consultation, and evidence-based policymaking were popular managerial tools, but they may have encouraged a loss of public trust by the way they were put into practice. The threat of democratic backsliding, driven by populism, should stimulate public administration not to hunker down but to search for better ways of operating in order to rebuild public trust. Stoker finds some positive signs of new thinking and practice.

The final chapter synthesizes and reflects on the volume's most important findings. It starts with the drivers behind the populist surge as indicated in the case studies, before outlining the main lessons on the populist approach toward the bureaucracy, including their reform strategies and the reaction of the bureaucracy. It concludes by advancing recommendations on how to foster administrative resilience in times of populist threats.

2 | Incomplete Democratization, System Transformation, and the Civil Service: A Case Study on the Weimar Republic and the Nazi Regime in Germany

BASTIAN STROBEL AND SYLVIA VEIT

Introduction

A professional bureaucracy is considered a cornerstone of liberal democracy. There is, however, not *one* single model on how to organize political-administrative relations in liberal democracies. In Westminster systems, for instance, political-administrative relations are characterized by a rather strict formal division of both spheres (Hustedt and Salomonsen 2014), whereas many continental European states tolerate a much higher degree of formal politicization (Meyer-Sahling and Veen 2012; Veit, Fromm, and Ebinger 2018). Regardless of this variation, in all liberal democracies a "blurred area [exists], in which there is a degree of indeterminacy about the roles and relationship between the two domains [i.e., the political and the administrative sphere]" (Alford et al. 2017, p. 752). This intermingling of politics and bureaucracy occurs in particular in central government departments, where civil servants are deeply involved in policymaking by providing policy advice and assisting their political superiors in coordinating and negotiating policies. In this context, bureaucrats are expected to show responsiveness (to the minister) and, at the same time, to be critical of the minister when necessary (e.g. when constitutional or core democratic values are at stake) to safeguard the public interest and public integrity (Ebinger, Veit, and Fromm 2019).

Processes of liberal-democratic backsliding threaten the established delicate balance between, on the one hand, political responsiveness of the bureaucracy and, on the other hand, the adherence to professional standards and liberal-democratic values. Liberal-democratic backsliding processes are often accompanied by administrative reforms that attempt to enforce profound changes in political-administrative relations and lead to an increasing politicization (and restructuring) of the bureaucracy. As all governments and political leaders depend on the bureaucracy to enforce public policies as well as to exercise power, the civil service plays a key role in processes of liberal-democratic backsliding: it can support these processes by working loyally for illiberal politicians or oppose them with shirking or even sabotage (Bauer et al., Introduction, this volume; Guedes-Neto and Peters, Chapter 10, this volume). Under which conditions and for what reasons civil servants choose to work loyally for illiberal politicians or to oppose their attempts to hollow out liberal-democratic institutions is an important and only poorly investigated research question, and will be addressed in this case study on the transition process from the Weimar Republic to the Nazi regime in Germany in the 1930s as a historical example of liberal-democratic backsliding.

We first describe the material and data we used for the case study. We then outline the history of political-administrative relations in Germany from Prussia to the Weimar Republic and the political developments in the Weimar Republic as important framework conditions. Subsequently, we present our case study. Following the analytical framework described in the introduction to this book, we distinguish three analytical dimensions: governance concept, strategies for illiberal administrative reform and bureaucratic reactions. The chapter concludes with a reflection on the learnings from this historical case for contemporary incidents of liberal-democratic backsliding in different countries.

Data and Methods

We apply a mixed-methods approach relying on a review of findings from historical scholarship and an analysis of documents, as well as on prosopographical analysis of top civil servants. Historical scholarship has conducted several case studies on single ministries over time. More general historical publications covered public administration specifically in the Weimar Republic and the Nazi regime. Both forms of publication were included in the analysis. Furthermore, a document analysis of civil service regulations and other important regulations and legislative documents (e.g. the federal budget) was used to trace the formal patterns of political-administrative relations and the distribution of resources in the Weimar Republic and under the Nazi regime. Additionally, organizational charts of all Reich-ministries were drawn from the "Handbooks of the German Reich" and supplemented by information found in files from the Federal Archive. Together with findings from the literature, this data was used for the analysis of changes in the administrative structure.

The prosopographical method aims at investigating common characteristics of a distinct (often historical) group through the collective study of their biographies. We applied this method for the study of top civil servants. Top civil servants are not only in central positions of the politico-administrative system, but also make relevant decisions which are important for the strategic orientation of the ministry. They are influential actors in the policy process and with regard to internal management decisions, for instance concerning recruitment and promotion decisions at lower hierarchical levels. Due to their prominent position, they act as culture carriers (Schröter 1993) who represent and influence a ministry's organizational climate and culture. Characteristics of top civil servants reveal much insight on political-administrative relations: for instance, if many top civil servants have a background in party politics, this indicates a high degree of party politicization.

The prosopographical analysis presented here is based on an original dataset compiled by the authors.[1] Our research population is defined by the positional approach of elite identification (Hoffmann-Lange 2018). The dataset we used for this case study includes all officeholders in the two highest administrative ranks – that is, administrative state secretaries (level 1) and directors general (level 2) – in German central state ministries (*Reichsministerien*) at five different points of time during the Weimar Republic (1920, 1927) and the Nazi regime (1934, 1939, 1944) (see Table 2.1). In total, the analysis includes 376 individuals.

Table 2.1 *Number of cases for the five points of observation*

	1920	1927	1934	1939	1944
State Secretaries	19	16	21	35	38
Directors General	44	52	78	105	112
Total	63	68	99	140	150

Source: own data.

Data collection was based on personnel files from the German Federal Archive and other archives, official biographies, press releases/articles and preexisting own research. It included information on the top civil servants' time in office, party affiliation(s), political mandates, and memberships in different organizations and associations supporting or opposing the political system. Information was only added to the dataset when it was doubtlessly confirmed by the sources.

To measure the reactions of the civil service to political change (see section "Reactions of the Civil Service"), we apply two standardized additive indices: the formal systems reference index and the material systems reference index. Formal affinity or distance is measured by gathering data on formal memberships in important organizations of each political system – such as, for example, the paramilitary organizations SA (*Sturmabteilung*) and SS (*Schutzstaffel*) during the Nazi regime. For the formal systems reference index, we add up all organizational memberships in the three systems. Organizations supporting the system are assigned positive values; opposing organizations are assigned negative values. Material affinity to or distance from a political system are measured by analyzing statements and actions for or against each system. For the material systems reference index, we summarized all statements and actions for and against each system. Affine statements or actions are assigned positive values; negative statements or actions are assigned negative values (for an overview of all variables used for the index, see Appendix). For both indices, the sum of all values is divided by the number of used variables. Thus, the values of both the formal systems reference index and the material systems reference index range from −1 to 1.

Political-Administrative Relations from Prussia to the Weimar Republic

The Weberian bureaucracy of today's Germany is coined by its long-standing history and tradition. In Germany – in contrast to, for example, the United States – bureaucracy is much older than democracy, which had strong implications for the administrative culture and civil servants' role perception in the Weimar Republic and the Nazi regime. As early as the eighteenth century, the fundamental characteristics of the German bureaucracy were established in Prussia. This included, in particular, the core role perception of bureaucrats as servants of the *state* who are characterized by "Prussian virtues" such as loyalty, diligence and incorruptibility (Caplan 1988). This system was further institutionalized during the German Empire in the late nineteenth and early twentieth centuries, where bureaucrats considered themselves loyal servants of the reigning Emperor and a *counterpart* to political parties and trade unions (Rebentisch 1989).

After the German Empire was dissolved with the abdication of Wilhelm II on November 9, 1918, the first democracy in Germany, the *Weimar Republic*, evolved. Economic crises, in particular the hyperinflation until 1923 and the Great Depression from 1929 onwards, as well as political crises fostered political instability in the Weimar Republic. Especially in the early years, both right-wing and left-wing paramilitary forces tried to overthrow the government in a coup, the most famous one being the failed Hitler coup of 1923.

The Weimar Republic was governed by its president and coalition governments, which relied on both a majority in parliament (*Reichstag*) and the confidence of the president. Parliamentary stability was low, which caused a correspondingly high instability of governments during the Weimar Republic: from its foundation in 1918 to its end in 1933, there were twenty-one different governments. One important reason for this instability was the polarization and fragmentation of the party system. On the extreme right, the NSDAP (National Socialist German Worker's Party) and the DNVP (German Nationalist People's Party) and, on the extreme left, the Independent Social Democratic Party and the Communist Party polarized the party system and fought the republic from the inside. To form majority governments, multiparty coalitions with up to five political parties had to be established.

In this politically and economically unstable system, the bureaucracy was an anchor of stability and continuity (Middendorf 2015) as the traditional features of the German civil service were upheld: The main legal foundation for civil servants in the Weimar Republic, the *Civil Service Law* (*Reichsbeamtengesetz*), dated back to 1873 and was last amended in 1907. In the *Reichsbeamtengesetz*, life tenure (§ 2), a special loyalty to the state (§ 3), a salary based on position (§ 4), diligence and adherence to rules (§§ 10, 13), and incorruptibility (§ 15) were determined as core professional standards for civil servants. Almost all civil servants of the German Empire continued to work as civil servants in the Weimar Republic (Caplan 1988; Gössel 2002). Also, the newly appointed top civil servants in the Weimar Republic were mainly recruited from the established civil service and, thus, had a long tenure in the German Empire's bureaucracy (Scholz-Paulus et al. 2020). This high level of continuity through the process of a fundamental system transformation is striking, given the traditional role of the monarchistic civil service as antagonist to political parties and the parliament in the Empire.

In awareness of the prevalence of antidemocratic attitudes in the civil service, the constitution of 1919 extended the loyalty obligation of civil servants from the *Reichsbeamtengesetz* to loyalty to the new democratic constitution. In 1922, the parliament passed the *Law on the Duties of Civil Servants to Protect the Republic*. Its main intention was to undermine any attempts from within the civil service to reintroduce a monarchy: civil servants were obliged to support the republican form of government when fulfilling their duties (§ 10a). This included prohibiting them from speaking out against the government or the republican system in public or in front of subordinates. Although there was no formal prohibition of party membership for civil servants, Article 130 of the constitution that underlined civil servants' obligation to serve the public interest and *not* single political parties was interpreted as a de facto prohibition (Gössel 2002, p. 96 *ff.*). Also, it was considered inappropriate for civil servants to run for or hold a seat in parliament (Kordt 1938, p. 176). To sympathize with political parties from the entire democratic political spectrum was, however, explicitly permitted (Mommsen 2010, p. 24).

Despite the fact that the Weberian ideal of an impartial, rule-oriented and professional civil service was deeply anchored not only in the relevant legal provisions in the Weimar Republic but also in practice, the right of ministers to intervene in personnel decisions was not fully constrained: ministers had the right to hire and dismiss so-called "political civil servants" – that is, civil servants in the two highest hierarchical ranks in national ministries that could be sent into "temporary retirement" at any time – at their discretion (§ 25, *Reichsbeamtengesetz*). At lower levels, following the Weberian conception, the merit principle was the main recruitment standard for civil servants (Kordt 1938, p. 178 *f.*). In many respects, the bureaucratic system of the Weimar Republic was very close to the ideal type of a Weberian bureaucracy, which is considered a role model for liberal-democratic systems.

In the sections on "Governance Concepts," "Administrative Reform Strategies," and "Reactions of the Civil Service," we analyze the development and role of the bureaucracy in the process of liberal-democratic backsliding and the system transformation that started in 1930 after another collapse of a government coalition in the Weimar Republic. On March 28, 1930, President Paul von Hindenburg appointed Heinrich Brüning as chancellor of the first so-called presidential cabinet, a minority government composed of the three conservative parties, the Liberal party, the nationalist-right DNVP, and some splinter parties. Diverging from earlier minority governments, the presidential cabinets – the last four cabinets in the Weimar Republic (chancellors Brüning I and II, Franz von Papen, Kurt von Schleicher) – were characterized by a particularly strong position of the president (von Hindenburg), who initiated the use of the so-called emergency legislation following Article 48 of the constitution. The emergency legislation allowed the chancellor and the government to pass and implement laws without consulting parliament. This concentration of power in the hands of the executive is a typical characteristic of liberal-democratic backsliding (Bermeo 2016).

When Adolf Hitler was first appointed chancellor on January 30, 1933, he took over the government with a coalition of the NSDAP, the DNVP, and some nonpartisan politicians mainly connected to the *Stahlhelm*, a right-wing paramilitary organization of former soldiers. Just two days after Hitler came to power, he convinced his coalition partners and the president to dissolve parliament and schedule general elections in March 1933, which resulted in a majority for the NSDAP and the DNVP. In the months to come, Hitler and the NSDAP transformed the democratic Weimar Republic into an authoritarian dictatorship.

Governance Concepts

According to Bauer et al. (Introduction, this volume), illiberal politicians entering government can apply three different general governance concepts to control the civil service and enforce their power: sidelining, using, and ignoring. *Sidelining* occurs when the bureaucracy is reduced to its implementation functions, whereby its role in the policy-formulation process is taken over by other, more politicized actors. *Using* is applied when illiberal politicians use the capacities of the existing bureaucracy for policy formulation and implementation in order to accumulate and keep control over the public. The third governance strategy, *ignoring*, refers to the fact that most illiberal politicians are interested in only a very limited number of topics (e.g. immigration or terrorism), which therefore receive high levels of political attention and are increasingly politically controlled by a small coterie of loyal followers. In less salient policy areas, ignoring might even empower the bureaucracy, as political control of administrative action is widely lacking. These three governance concepts are not mutually exclusive, as different governance strategies can be applied across jurisdictions and agencies. Furthermore, governance concepts can vary over time.

Our analysis reveals that in the process of liberal-democratic backsliding from 1930 to 1933, the governance strategy of *using* the bureaucracy dominated. Especially cabinets of President Brüning (1930–1932) used the capacities of the existing bureaucracy to enforce a concentration of power in the hands of the executive by means of the emergency legislation. This was possible because many civil servants welcomed and supported this shift of power, which was considered appropriate to achieve more political stability and capacity to act for the government (see "Reactions of the Civil Service") (Bracher, Sauer, and Schulz 1962, p. 485; Middendorf 2015, p. 340).

After Hitler came to power, the governance concept of *sidelining* started to play a prominent role. It was applied particularly in the first phase of the Nazi regime in order to implement its totalitarian agenda, which meant first and foremost the "cooptation" (*Gleichschaltung*) of all parts of German society. The strategy of *sidelining* was observable at both the organizational and the individual levels. At the organizational level, it was reflected in the creation of new, highly politicized organizations and units (Gotto 2006). At the individual level, the sidelining strategy was reflected both in the creation of new positions (mainly within the newly created ministries and agencies) and in a large number of politically motivated replacements within the established bureaucracy, especially at the top level. The underlying rationale was mainly to ensure effective governance and to control the bureaucracy through patronage practices.

An opaque system was shaped wherein loyal top civil servants (and politicians) often held several positions at the same time: one example of this common practice is Konstantin Hierl, who was not only head of the fatigue duty (*Reichsarbeitsdienst*) but also director general for labor policy in the Ministry of the Interior and administrative state secretary in the Ministry of Labor. This combination of positions enabled Hierl to transfer key responsibilities, which had originally resided in the Ministry of the Interior and the Ministry of Labor, to the *Reichsarbeitsdienst*. The accumulation of power at the individual level was a strategic choice made to support Hitler. The emerging entanglement of state and party bureaucracy and the coexistence of competing organizations/actors with equal or similar competences (Bracher, Sauer, and Schulz 1962, p. 600) at all levels of society, and particularly within the politico-administrative system, is termed *polycracy* (Hüttenberger 1976, p. 422 *f.*). The polycratic system strengthened the position of Hitler as monocratic leader: his key position was based on the confusing coexistence of and competition between different actors, groups, and institutions and a strong reliance on personal relations and networks. An increasing access to Hitler simultaneously meant a rise in power for single actors in the system. This helped Hitler strengthen his position as an omnipotent leader (Thamer 1992, p. 340).

The polycratic system led to a decreasing influence of civil servants and an increasing influence of NSDAP leaders and SS officers over time (Hüttenberger 1976, p. 428 ff.). Thus, although *sidelining* was presumably the most obvious and prominent governance concept of the National Socialists, especially in the years after they first came to power, over time this concept was increasingly supplemented by the concept of *ignoring*. The most important reason for this was the distrust of the National Socialists toward civil servants of a Weberian type: they feared that the bureaucratic inclination toward legalism and bureaucratic control mechanisms would hinder the effective implementation of their own policy agenda (Hachtmann 2011, p. 36).

All this does, however, not mean that the established bureaucracy did not play any role in the Nazi regime. While the National Socialists came to power with a strongly antibureaucratic attitude – as early as in the 1920s, Hitler proclaimed that the civil service had to be "revaluated," which meant nothing other than a purge of democrats, opponents and non-Aryans from the bureaucracy (Mommsen 1973) – they soon realized that they needed the civil servants' capacities, competences, and experience to implement their political agenda. The extent to which the governance concept of *using* the bureaucracy was applied under Hitler was dependent on the salience of the policy area in question. In ideologically highly salient policy fields such as "Jewish" policy, "racial" policy or education policy, powerful new organizations were built up, sidelining the existing ministries and agencies to a considerable extent, whereas in more technical fields, such as the postal service and transport, the old bureaucracies remained rather influential actors (Hehl 2001, p. 11).

Administrative Reform Strategies

The five dimensions of illiberal administrative reforms described in the introduction to this book (accountability, structure, resources, personnel and norms) serve as a heuristic for the analysis of the administrative reforms that were implemented under Hitler.

Accountability

On the *accountability dimension*, reducing societal participation in policymaking, diminishing parliamentary control of the government and its bureaucracy, cutting back transparency and controlling the media are typical reform measures (Bauer et al., Introduction, this volume). All of these illiberal reforms have been pursued by the National Socialists. Comprehensive measures aiming at breaking veto powers and control mechanisms were implemented immediately after Hitler came to power ("cooptation policy"). All unions, parties and other societal associations were forbidden and replaced by Nazi organizations with obligatory memberships for its target groups, such as the Hitler Youth or the German Labor Front.

After dissolving parliament at the beginning of February 1933, Hitler governed for six weeks without an organized opposition, and used this time to initiate preliminary changes toward a totalitarian regime (Thamer 1992). With the *Decree of the Reich President for the Protection of the German People* and the *Reichstag Fire Decree* in February 1933, the government de facto destroyed the Communist

Party and abolished fundamental rights. With the *Enabling Act* of March 1993, the separation of power between the legislative and the executive branch was abolished and legislative competence was handed over completely to the government (Article 1). The *Enabling Act* explicitly allowed the government to pass laws that violated main principles of the Constitution of 1919 (Article 2).

The "cooptation" of the federal states – that is, the elimination of major veto players in German politics – started on March 31, 1933, with the *Preliminary Law for the Cooptation of the States with the Reich*. With this law, all *Länder* parliaments were dissolved and recomposed based on the proportional result of the national election of March 5, 1933. Only one week later, on April 7, 1933, the *Second Law for the Cooptation of the States with the Reich* put the state governments under the control and supervision of *Reich* Governors (*Reichsstatthalter*), which reported directly to Hitler. The *Reichsstatthalter* had the competence to nominate and dismiss the *Länder* minister presidents and dissolve state parliaments. In a last step, all rights of the *Länder* were transferred to the central government with the *Law on the Reconstruction of the Reich* on January 30, 1934.

In the same period, all newspapers, journals, and broadcasting services were brought under the control of Joseph Goebbels and his Ministry for Propaganda, which means, in essence, the NSDAP, as most of the positions in this ministry had been filled with loyal party members (Fischer and Wittmann 2015). After the death of President von Hindenburg in August 1934 and the amalgamation of the posts of the president and the chancellor in the person of Hitler, all influential veto players were eliminated, the "cooptation" of all major societal actors (e.g. unions, the media) was completed and democratic mechanisms of accountability abolished.

Structure

On the *structural dimension*, illiberal administrative reforms typically aim at centralizing the bureaucracy and abolishing or weakening regional/state and local administrative structures in order to increase centralized (political) control of the bureaucracy (Drápalová, Chapter 6 this volume). Another typical strategy is to create parallel structures. As was pointed out earlier, both strategies were applied by the National

Socialists. In addition to administrative centralization by eliminating federalism, the structure of government bureaucracy was subject to comprehensive changes during the Nazi era.

Especially in politically/ideologically salient policy fields such as race policies, education, and health, new organizations were established and responsibilities were shifted from the established bureaucracy to these new organizations. In total, eleven new ministries and another eleven new state agencies, which were subordinated directly to Hitler, were created at the federal level. The new ministries and agencies were highly politicized and strongly linked with NSDAP organizations, which mirrored important sections of the state bureaucracy. The NSDAP party bureaucracy monitored the state bureaucracy and competed with it over responsibilities and power. While many civil servants in the newly created organizations, which were led by NSDAP leaders, had considerable leeway in decision-making, their counterparts in the inherited state bureaucracy were often strictly politically controlled and far less autonomous in their work (Hachtmann 2011).

The analysis of organizational charts and archive files reveals that the changes at the political level were reflected in a growing total number of directorates in ministerial departments: while there were 89 directorates in 1934, their number grew to 118 in 1939 and 153 in 1944 (own data). The growing number of ministries was, however, not the only reason for the increase in the number of directorates: in addition, new directorates within the inherited ministries were created to fulfil an ideological mission and to exercise political control. For example, in several ministries, directorates for Germanity (*Deutschtum*) with a broad spectrum of competences were established. These directorates were mostly headed by young party loyalists (own data from prosopographical analysis). In total, one third of the newly created directorates was established to sideline the established directorates. Two thirds can be attributed to the newly created ministries (own data from the analysis of organizational charts).

Summing up, the creation of parallel structures (NSDAP-dominated organizations controlling the inherited bureaucracy) – both at the macrolevel of organizations and intra-organizationally (i.e. within the inherited bureaucracy) – was characteristic of the National Socialists' approach to administrative reform.

Resources

Data on the redistribution of financial and personnel *resources* during the Nazi regime is widely lacking. There are, however, some indications of an extensive redistribution of resources. The growth of the number of bureaucratic organizations and organizational units under Hitler, as described in the previous section, constitutes the growing demand for financial resources for the politicized bureaucracy and the described redistribution of existing personnel and increased recruiting of new personnel. The increasing demand for financial resources is reflected in the national budget: In 1929, the budget was 20.87 billion Reichsmark and decreased, due to diminishing inland revenue during the Great Depression, to 14.54 billion Reichsmark in 1933 (Statista 2019). From 1934 onward, the budget was not published. However, figures for some single ministries are available. They indicate that the budget must have increased tremendously. In 1934, the Ministry for Aviation and the Ministry for Defence, for example, each had a budget of 1.95 billion Reichsmark and the Ministry for Labor a budget of 2.5 billion Reichsmark (Buchheim 2008, p. 402 *f.*).

Personnel

The fourth dimension comprises administrative reforms focusing on changes in the bureaucratic *personnel*: "purging" the staff and implementing a system of patronage is a typical strategy of illiberal administrative reforms. Patronage policies indeed played an important role under Hitler.

In February and March 1933, the dismissal of civil servants who were followers or sympathizers of democratic parties started (Mommsen 1973, 2010; Thamer 1992, p. 239, 251 ff.). On April 7, 1933, parliament passed the *Law for the Restoration of the Professional Civil Service* and legalized the dismissal of a large group of civil servants, namely members of democratic parties, non-Aryans, women and allegedly "unreliable" civil servants. All civil servants had to fill in forms which were designed to test their loyalty to the new government. Moreover, they needed a certificate of "good character," issued by the NSDAP (Caplan 1988; Gössel 2002; Rebentisch 1989).

This policy led to a wave of dismissals. Analyzing time in office shows the extent of replacements at the top level during this period of time:

while the top civil servants in 1927 held their position on average for
67.6 months, average time in office was three times shorter (20.3
months) in 1934. As the Nazi regime was stabilized, average time in
office rose again (own data). This reflects that the replacement of top
civil servants as a means to control the bureaucracy was particularly
important in the transition period. For 81 out of 99 top civil servants in
1934, it was their first appointment into an elite position. Only 16 out of
68 top civil servants in 1927 still held a similar position in 1934. Figure
2.1 shows that 81 top civil servants in 1934 were newly appointed. In
1944, 23 of them were still in office.

Replacement of personnel also occurred at lower hierarchical levels.
The extent of dismissals beyond the top level varied considerably across
departments and jurisdictions. A well-investigated example for

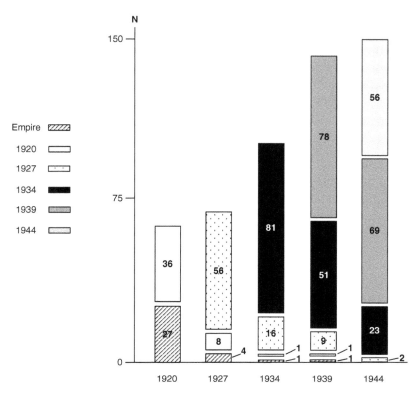

Figure 2.1 Replacements of top civil servants 1920–1944
Source: own data.

a jurisdiction with a rather low overall replacement rate is the financial administration of the Reich. Between January 1933 and August 1934, 1,732 out of 73,000 civil servants (2.4 percent) were replaced (Kuller 2013, p. 49 f.). Patronage policies not only referred to the "purge" of staff, but also included a policy of favoring the *old fighters* (i.e. individuals who entered the NSDAP before 1930) over other civil servants in recruitment and promotion: old fighters had easier entry exams and were promoted sooner than others (Mommsen 2010, p. 70).

Two final steps of the civil service reforms were executed in the years 1937 and 1942, starting with the *German Civil Service Law* from January 27, 1937. Originally, this law was meant to be enacted far earlier, but Hitler and the party chancellery had blocked the legislative procedure for more than two years as they interpreted the legal text as a threat to the *Führerprinzip*, which put the Führer's word above the written law. In practice, this principle was meant to protect the autonomy not only of Hitler but of all party leaders at the local, regional, and federal levels of the state, as Hitler instructed these leaders to act on his behalf in certain fields (Gössel 2002; Gotto 2006). The new law facilitated the possibility to dismiss "unreliable" civil servants and exacerbated the definition of unreliability. The smallest hint of a non-Nazi attitude – e.g. the incorrect performance of the Nazi salute – was sufficient for a dismissal (Majer 1987, p. 229). On April 26, 1942, the Reichstag, which had convened since September 1940, decided in its last meeting during the Nazi regime to abolish all remaining civil service rights until the end of the war, which led to the total implementation of the *Führerprinzip* in all parts of the public sector. Framed as an act of budget-saving, this further increased political control of the civil service (Mommsen 2010, p. 106 f.).

Norms

The fifth analytical dimension refers to administrative reforms intending to modify bureaucratic norms and values, i.e. to substitute neutrality, impartiality, and incorruptibility as the main professional standards, with strict loyalty to the new government as the most important norm. The politicization of the civil service during the Nazi regime was not only realized through dismissals, replacements, and patronage policies, as outlined earlier, but also through measures that aimed at the values and norms of civil servants and their families. Civil servants had to join

Table 2.2 *Party memberships for the five points of observation*

	1920		1927		1934		1939		1944	
	N	%	N	%	N	%	N	%	N	%
No Party	57	90.5	65	95.6	37	37.4	17	12.1	9	6.0
NSDAP	0	0.0	0	0.0	48	48.5	111	79.3	135	90.0
Other Party	6	9.5	3	4.4	0	0.0	0	0.0	0	0.0
Unknown	0	0.0	0	0.0	14	14.1	12	8.6	6	4.0

Source: own data.

Nazi organizations, had to send their children to the Hitler Youth and (after the death of President von Hindenburg in August 1934) had to swear their oath of office directly on the person of Adolf Hitler instead of swearing it on the constitution (Bracher 1983). Already in 1934, 48.5 percent of all top civil servants in German ministries were members of the NSDAP. The share of NSDAP members among top civil servants increased to 79.3 per cent in 1939 and 90.0 per cent in 1944 (Table 2.2) (own data). Whereas there were no former or actual politicians in top civil service positions during the Weimar Republic, this changed considerably after Hitler came to power: in 1934, 16.2 percent of the top civil servants held a mandate in a state parliament[2] or the Reichstag parallel to their top civil service position. This share further increased to 17.9 percent in 1939 and 20.7 percent in 1944 (own data).

Summing up the administrative reforms, we can state that the National Socialists used all policy options presented earlier, although administrative reform policy under Hitler was pursued with varying intensity over time. In spring 1933, the main focus was on the purge and exchange of civil servants. Later, the National Socialists tried to change the norms and values of the civil service into a value-system characterized by loyalty and obedience, which resulted in the new oath of office on the person of Adolf Hitler in August 1934. Simultaneously, the National Socialists restructured the civil service and redistributed budget, personnel, and competences between state and party organizations. The main reforms came to an end in summer 1934. With the German Civil Service Law of 1937 and the decision of the Reichstag in 1942, the formal conversion of the civil service ended.

Reactions of the Civil Service

Civil servants are basically given three different options (Brehm and Gates 2002): the first option is to *work loyally* for the new leaders just as they would after a "regular" change in government. The second option is *shirking*. Civil servants pretend to be to be loyal but try to circumvent direct orders of their superiors. The third option is to *sabotage* the new government by acting deliberately. These three ideal-typical reactions correspond to different degrees of loyalty/opposition to the new government.

The attitudes in the civil service changed during the process of democratic backsliding: while the majority of civil servants were loyal to the democratic governments at first, many of them eventually welcomed Hitler's rise to power in 1933. During the Nazi regime, there was no structural resistance in the civil service – that is, most civil servants worked loyally for the Hitler regime. Resistance from within the civil service – shirking or even sabotage – was constrained to single groups of civil servants, such as a few railway officials who refused to transport people to the concentration camps (Gottwaldt and Bartelsheim 2009). The (non-)reactions of the civil service during the process of democratic backsliding and system transformation can be explained by first, the historical roots of the civil service in the German Empire and its development during the Weimar Republic; second, their antidemocratic attitude; and third, the active monitoring of the civil service through the party bureaucracy.

As described earlier, the transformation from the German Empire to the Weimar Republic left the civil service mostly unchanged. Aversion to democracy was widespread in the civil service (Föllmer 2001; Gössel 2002) and was strengthened by economic crises and political instability. When the phase of liberal-democratic backsliding started in 1930 with the use of the emergency legislation, many civil servants welcomed this step as it promised stability and strengthened their influence on the development of new laws (Middendorf 2015, p. 340; Mommsen 1973, p. 151 *f.*; Rebentisch 1989, p. 128; Sontheimer 1999, p. 70). Between 1930 and 1932, the attitude of civil servants toward the two minority governments of Chancellor Brüning changed. In the 1920s and early 1930s, wage cuts and dismissals in the civil service led to frustration with the government (Föllmer 2001, p. 63; Mommsen 1973, p. 154 ff.). In the early 1930s, many civil servants therefore set their hopes on the

National Socialists, because they promised to "recover and revaluate" the civil service. In reality, the National Socialists had the opposite in mind, but the claim of revaluation was essential to convince the civil servants (Föllmer 2001, p. 66–67; Mommsen 1973, p. 165). Many civil servants became politicized in this period and protested openly against Brüning's policies. They started to shirk and even to sabotage the democratic government: despite the nonexistence of a right to strike, many civil servants participated in strikes, and some even refused the implementation of the civil service laws which were designed to enforce further wage cuts in the civil service (Mommsen 1973). In this situation, both politicians and civil servants urged the president to dismiss the chancellor (Föllmer 2001, p. 66 f.). Ultimately, Chancellor Brüning had to resign from office in Mai 1932.

When Hitler came to power in January 1933, many civil servants accepted and even welcomed this development and its consequences (Gössel 2002). Most civil servants were willing to work with the new government. According to the literature, this was due to three main reasons: first, many of the bureaucrats welcomed the new system because it suited their antidemocratic attitude. Second, with the principle of loyalty to the state per se and not to democratic principles or democratic parties, civil servants saw their duty in loyally serving the new leader of the state. Third, many civil servants accepted the policies and civil service reforms of the new government to save their own position in the system and to secure their economic status (Mommsen 2010, p. 67; Rebentisch 1989, p. 143). A distinct example of this "Nazification process" is the case of the Ministry of Economy. In spring 1933, the new minister Alfred Hugenberg assigned the director general of the personnel directorate, Fritz Freiherr von Massenbach, the task of purging the ministry's staff and the staff of the subordinated agencies. Massenbach, who had a background as a career civil servant in the ministry and had no affiliation with the National Socialist movement, not only fulfilled this task willingly but also used his new power to settle old scores with other civil servants of the ministry (Abelshauser, Fisch, and Hoffmann 2016).

Later in 1933, the inherited civil servants showed early signs of disappointment. The expected "revaluation" of the civil service had not happened. Rather, party officials strengthened the claim that the civil service still had to prove its worth (Mommsen 2010, p. 67). To control the state bureaucracy, the party bureaucracy implemented a monitoring system at every level of the state. Civil servants who did not comply with the National Socialist ideology were reported to the party chancellery by colleagues (mostly old fighters) who acted as snitches. Those nonconformists lost their job or even went to prison. Combined with the Weberian tradition of neutrality and submission to the reigning government, this led to a high level of conformity.

However, many civil servants were unsatisfied with the violations of the merit principle in recruitment and promotion as a consequence of patronage policies. With the enactment of the *German Civil Service Law* in 1937, therefore, an increasing amount of shirking became visible. In particular, § 71 of the *German Civil Service Law* was met with strong reservations. It stated that civil servants who acted against the National Socialist ideology were to be removed from the civil service. In many cases, civil servants who were accused by the NSDAP according to § 71 were protected by colleagues who, for instance, delayed the transfer of files and thus prolongated lawsuits (Mommsen 2010, p. 104 f., 106). This strategy of shirking was quite successful until the decision of the Reichstag on April 26, 1942, to abolish all remaining civil service rights (see section on "Norms").

Procedual shirking was first and foremost observable when the National Socialists tried to cut the rights and privileges of the civil servants (Mommsen 2010), whereas shirking with regard to policy implementation in other areas was restricted to scattered groups of civil servants and single cases (Guedes-Neto and Peters, Chapter 10 this volume). An example can be found in the Ministry of Foreign Affairs (*Auswärtiges Amt*), where a group of civil servants tried to oppose the policies of the political leadership. The group that formed around Ernst von Weizsäcker, Erich Kordt, and Eduard Brücklmeier attempted to prevent the attack on Poland and the subsequent war. The members of this group contacted foreign diplomats and warned them of the National Socialist intentions. By the end of 1939, the Minister of Foreign Affairs, Joachim von Ribbentropp, shattered this resistance by retiring or transferring the resisters into subordinate agencies (Conze et al. 2010). In other ministries, comparable isolated cases can be found.

Despite this fact, the civil service was far away from being the "rebelling institution" which some civil servants tried to present after 1945 (see, e.g., the testimonies of accused civil servants in the

Ministries Trial of 1947). Several independent boards of inquiry installed by federal ministries between 1998 and 2016 conclude that there is no evidence that a large number of civil servants sabotaged the regime or protested openly against the policies of the National Socialists (Abelshauser, Fisch, and Hoffmann 2016; Conze et al. 2010; Görtemaker and Safferling 2014; Nützenadel 2017). Rather, the civil service has been one core element in stabilizing the Nazi regime (Mommsen 2010, p. 121).

The prosopographical analysis of top civil servants supports this. In order to investigate the extent to which the top civil servants supported or refused the two political systems (the Weimar Republic and the Nazi regime), we distinguish formal and material affinity to or distance from each system (see section on "Data and Methods"). The *formal system reference index* (Figure 2.2) reveals that top civil servants in the Weimar Republic had no formal affiliation with organizations that supported or opposed the Weimar Republic, which reflects the Weberian tradition of party-political neutrality. After the transition to the Nazi regime, formal affiliation to Nazi organizations increased and formal affinity to the Weimar Republic decreased (i.e. top civil servants in the Nazi regime had often been members of organizations which opposed the Weimar Republic in the 1920s, such as the SA, the SS, or other right-wing paramilitary organizations).

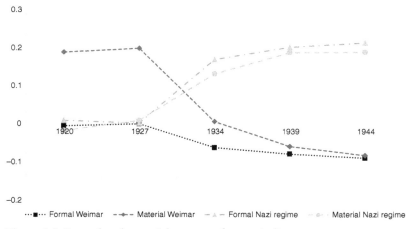

Figure 2.2 Formal and material system reference indices
Source: own data.

Analyzing the *material system reference index* (Figure 2.2), it becomes apparent that the top civil servants in the Weimar Republic had a positive attitude toward the Weimar Republic. For the top civil servants of 1934 a different picture emerges, as many of them openly sympathized with the Nazi regime. Between 1934 and 1939, the index for the Weimar Republic veers toward negative values, which reflects the hostile stance toward the democratic system. In 1939, the index for the support of the Nazi regime is at its peak level and remains stable until 1944, whereas the Weimar index slightly decreases.

Summing up this section, three findings should be highlighted. First, the top civil servants in the Weimar Republic did not uphold democratic values in the long term but, rather, identified themselves with the monarchy and, thus, supported tendencies of democratic backsliding. The democratic integration of the monarchic civil servants failed. Second, over time distrust toward democratic values and institutions (in particular, parliamentary decision-making) increased, which led to the welcoming of Chancellor Brüning in 1930, who started the erosion of liberal democracy and thus laid the foundation for the transformation process that followed. Civil servants were eager for a rollback to a system in which an autocratic leader makes decisions without a lengthy parliamentary process, which explains why they worked with the presidential cabinets of the early 1930s and finally with Hitler as autocratic leader. Third, in the Nazi regime, shirking or even sabotage was restricted to single cases.

Discussion and Conclusion

The transition from the Weimar Republic to the Nazi regime was a process of democratic backsliding. The bureaucracy played a significant role in this process by supporting the erosion of liberal-democratic practices and institutions in the early 1930s before the National Socialists came to power. In order to draw lessons for contemporary processes of liberal-democratic backsliding, it is instructive to shed light on the reasons for this development, and in particular on the history of public administration in Germany.

Even though a professional and meritocratic civil service is often associated with good government in liberal democracies (e.g. Boräng et al. 2018; Dahlström, Lapuente, and Teorell 2012; Nistotskaya and Cingolani 2016), our case study underlines that a highly developed

Weberian style per se does not determine administrative resilience in processes of liberal-democratic backsliding and in system transformations to authoritarian regimes. The literature on the politicization of bureaucracy shows that in liberal democracies, political responsiveness of the bureaucracy, on the one hand, and the adherence to professional standards and democratic institutions, on the other, have to be balanced (Ebinger, Veit, and Fromm 2019; Shaw and Eichbaum 2018; Veit, Fromm, and Ebinger 2018). In the Weimar Republic, this delicate balance was violated as the institutionalization of democratic values as professional standards of administrative action (next to technical competence and compliance with the law) was not accomplished. The attitudes of civil servants in the late Weimar Republic (see section on "Reactions of the Civil Service") underline this lacking institutionalization of democratic values.

The "incomplete democratization" of bureaucracy in the Weimar Republic can be interpreted as a result of inappropriate governance concepts and strategies of administrative reform in the process of system transformation *toward* democracy (from the German Empire to the Weimar Republic). What was missing in the Weimar Republic was a systematic anchoring of democratic values in the civil service. The attempt to regulate civil servants' values through the law did not lead to substantial changes in the civil servants' political attitudes and value systems, although the civil servants formally complied with the legal regulations. This confirms what we know from new institutionalism theory: in order to institutionalize regulations (i.e. to deeply anchor formal rules in the civil service in order to achieve compliance with the rules without the threat of sanctions), additional efforts and measures are necessary. In the case of the Weimar Republic, it would have been helpful to (1) replace more personnel in the civil service in order to weaken the power and the "esprit de corps" of the group of "monarchist" civil servants, (2) deliberately fill leadership positions in the civil service with competent civil servants with a high ideological affinity to the democratic system and (3) systematically offer political education and training for civil servants in order to "democratize" the civil service.

With regard to the transition process *from* democracy toward the Nazi regime, our case study reveals that the National Socialists applied not one single governance concept and reform strategy, but a mixture of governance concepts and reform strategies with variation over time and across jurisdictions. On the one hand, the bureaucracy under Hitler was highly politicized, fragmented and characterized by unclear hierarchies and overlapping responsibilities of agencies and office-holders (Bracher, Sauer, and Schulz 1962; Gössel 2002); on the other hand, the Weberian tradition was strong, and in many areas the bur-eaucracy operated smoothly and efficiently (Reichardt and Seibel 2011). These contradictory characteristics reflect the basic features of a *polycracy*. From a Weberian perspective, a polycratic system seems chaotic; from an authoritarian leader's point of view, it is productive and offers manifold opportunities for political control, efficient deci-sion-making and action through personalization, informalization, intransparency and network-building (on the latter see Reichardt and Seibel 2011, p. 12). Such a complex, polycratic system strengthens the position of a monocratic political leader and hampers external control and opposition.

This study reveals that the (by and large) nonresistance of the civil service to the illiberal/authoritarian turn in the German case cannot be fully explained in terms of active administrative reform policies undertaken by the Nazi regime. The "incomplete democratization" within the German bureaucracy during the Weimar Republic which implicated the persistence of antidemocratic attitudes and reactionary convictions in the civil service provided a fertile ground not only for the successful implementation of these reforms but also for the pro-cess of liberal-democratic backsliding that culminated in the fascist takeover.

The lesson to be drawn is that preventing liberal-democratic backsliding within the civil service with a regulative design only works if it is combined with a concept of democratic integration. Therefore, democratic values have to be anchored within the profes-sional civil service in order to reinforce its stabilizing function in democratic systems. Democratic politicization of bureaucracy is one approach to strengthen administrative resilience – that is, the demo-cratic quality of bureaucracy. Thus, an important lesson for modern liberal democracies that can be learned from this case study is that the Weberian approach only works in a system where officials are committed to the public interest as well as to liberal-democratic principles and values. Without these standards, liberal-democratic backsliding is hard to prevent.

Appendix

Variables used for the formal systems reference index and the material systems reference index. Each variable is marked in bold letters.

Variables	Description
Formal Affinity to the Weimar Republic (2 Variables)	Has the individual been a member of **a democratic paramilitary organization** or the **Jungdeutsche Orden**?
Material Affinity to the Weimar Republic (4 Variables)	Did the individual actively support the Weimarian system through **speeches, supportive actions,** or **violent acts**? Did the individual **profit economically** from the Weimarian system?
Formal Distance to the Weimar Republic (3 Variables)	Has the individual been a member of **a right-wing** or **left-wing paramilitary organization** or of **organized resistance**?
Material Distance to the Weimar Republic (8 Variables)	Did the individual actively oppose the Weimarian system through **speeches, opposing actions** or **violent acts**? How many **months** has the individual been **in prison** in the Weimar Republic? Did the individual go into **exile**? Has the individual been a **victim of violence** or **economic sanctions**? Has the individual been a **victim of systematic prosecution**?
Formal Affinity to the "Nazi Regime" (46 Variables)	Which societal **NS organizations, NSDAP party organizations,** and **mirror organizations** of the party has the individual been member of? What was his/her **highest rank in a military** (Wehrmacht) or **paramilitary organization** (e.g. Sturmabteilung SA, Schutzstaffel SS)?
Material Affinity to the "Nazi Regime" (4 Variables)	Did the individual actively support the NS system through **speeches, supportive actions** or **violent acts**? Did the individual **profit economically** from the NS system?

(cont.)

Formal Distance to the "Nazi Regime"? (1 Variable)	Has the individual been a member of **organized resistance?**
Material Distance to the "Nazi Regime"? (8 Variables)	Did the individual actively oppose the NS system through **speeches, opposing actions** or **violent acts?**
	How many **months** has the individual been **in prison** in the NS?
	Did the individual go into **exile?**
	Has the individual been a **victim of violence** or **economic sanctions?**
	Has the individual been a **victim of systematic prosecution?**

Notes

1. Data was collected in the research project "New Elites – Established Personnel? (Dis-)Continuities of German Ministries in System Transformations" (2017–2021). We thank the Federal Commissioner for Culture and Media for the generous funding of this research project. In the project, a wide range of data on socio-demographics, education, career paths and political affiliations of both top civil servants and politicians in the twentieth century was collected. For the purpose of this case study, only some selected variables and a selected group of individuals from this larger dataset were analyzed.
2. During the Nazi regime, the state parliaments and state governments still existed but had no legislative powers.

3 Resilience Without Resistance: Public Administration Under Mutating Populisms in Office in Italy

FABRIZIO DI MASCIO, ALESSANDRO
NATALINI, AND EDOARDO ONGARO

Introduction

This chapter describes the dynamics of administrative change and bureaucratic resilience under populist governments in Italy, focusing on the first two decades of the 2000s, which have been characterized by the intermittent presence of populist parties in government. Our key explanandum is the effect on public administration of populist governments in office, and the main traits of bureaucratic reactions in these circumstances. Our main argument throughout this chapter is that populist governments in Italy have displayed a marked chasm between rhetoric and deeds, between the level of talk and the level of action (Brunsson 1989), when it comes to public administration and the reforming of the bureaucracy, and that the level of administrative continuity has been significant. This has been due partly to populist governments having not attached great priority to administrative reforms in the governmental agenda, and partly to bureaucratic resilience.

The central proposition of this chapter is a qualified statement about bureaucratic resilience under populist government: the empirical datum is one of administrative continuity and resilience, albeit with qualifications. First, "resilience" is not synonymous with "resistance," although we have plenty of anecdotal evidence about civil servants torn about how to reconcile stewardship to the democratically elected government of the day with upholding constitutionally enshrined public values. Adaptation and preservation by the bureaucracy of the acquired status and power is an equally apt interpretation of the nature of bureaucratic resilience in Italy.

Second, and crucially, resilience by the bureaucracy and continuity in administrative arrangements have been facilitated by the manifest lack of an administrative reform agenda by all Italian populist governments. In other words, populist governments displayed limited interest in prioritizing administrative reforms. The basic strategic stance of these governments may have oscillated between an attempt to "capture" and one of "reforming" the administrative apparatus (Bauer and Becker 2020), but it has never either climbed to the top of the governmental agenda or been pursued by marshaling the required resources and deploying political capital to attempt convincingly to overcome bureaucratic resilience. At most, the administrative policy undertaken by populist governments can be qualified as piecemeal (with the partial exception of a populist government in office during the 2008–2011 period, but then the impact of the financial crisis took precedence over any other business).

We should add that transforming the public sector requires time (Pollitt and Bouckaert 2017), and hence the relatively short term of office of two of the three populist governments considered in this chapter partly explains why the magnitude of real change does not live up to the magniloquent talk. Short-lived cabinets explain why reforming the public sector in Italy requires coping with political instability and for would-be policy entrepreneurs of administrative reform to be equipped with a combination of skills (delineated by Mele and Ongaro 2014) which were not apparent in the governments we are examining.

The underpinnings of bureaucratic resilience do remain the factors identified by the literature (and summed up, with a normative thrust, by Bauer et al., Introduction, this volume; see also Skocpol 1985): the relatively high level of bureaucratic autonomy in the Italian state (Ongaro 2008; 2009), the intensive and extensive web of ties to international bodies and transnational networks, and a high level of supranational and international integration. Additionally, the civil service in Italy is mostly a career system, and the bureaucracy maintains a range of ties with large swathes of society (e.g. via the still-powerful unions). In sum, the basic conditions for expecting bureaucratic resilience are all in place in the case of Italy.

Our account of the dynamics of administrative change and bureaucratic resilience under populist governments in Italy proceeds as follows. First, we present the background of this study – namely, the institutional patterns of the Italian bureaucracy. Second, we provide more detail on the multiple forms of populism, which interacted with each other over the observed time span, and on government policy toward the bureaucracy. Third, we structure the empirical analysis by drawing on the analytical framework sketched in the introductory chapter of this book: first touching upon the general governance concepts of populist governments; and then addressing the different options for reform regarding administrative structures, personnel, resources, and accountability. We then examine bureaucratic reactions. The concluding section discusses the impact of populist governments and the resilience of the administrative order.

Analytically, this chapter focuses on Italy over the first two decades of the 2000s, which are characterized by the intermittent presence of populist parties in government. These are, in our classification, the governing coalitions consisting of Berlusconi-led *Forza Italia* (or "Go Italy," hereafter FI), together with *Alleanza Nazionale* (AN, which later in the observation period merged with FI to form the *Popolo della Libertà* [People of Freedom] party) and the *Lega Nord* (Northern League [LN]), which governed Italy first over 2001–2006 and then in 2008–2011; and the "yellow–green" coalition supported by the *Movimento Cinque Stelle* (Five Star Movement [FSM]) and the same LN in 2018–2019. These parties displayed radically different forms of populism, and also changed their stance over time, which is why we qualify Italian populism as "mutating" (Verbeek and Zaslove 2016). Notably, the FSM entered in a governmental coalition in 2019 with the Democratic Party (second Conte Government) forming a government which does not meet the qualification of populist. Later in 2021, both the LN and the FSM entered a nonpopulist government led by Mario Draghi, former Governor of the European Central Bank (2011-19) and a staunch pro-EU, antipopulist figure. The Draghi government features as many as three (former?) populist parties in its supporting parliamentary coalition, alongside other nonpopulist parties. This evidence reinforces our qualification of populism in Italy as mutating.

The reason why we distinguish between the governing periods 2001–2006 and 2008–2011 – although the same coalition was in government – is due both to the different composition of the cabinet (legislative elections were held both in 2006, won by a center-left coalition, and in 2008, won once again by the Berlusconi-led coalition) and, especially, to the different economic conditions: 2008 marked the beginning of the transformation of the financial crisis into an economic and then fiscal crisis in Europe (Kickert and Ongaro 2019). The main demarcation between these two periods and the period 2018–2019 is the different composition of the populist governing coalition: in 2018–2019, Italy had two populist parties simultaneously in government, and a combination of radical right and radical left elements: the right-wing populism of the LN combined with the somewhat left-wing populism of the FSM.

Features of the Italian Bureaucracy

The Italian administrative system is patterned in its fundamental traits on the French, "Napoleonic" model of state (Peters 2008; 2020): a career civil service, with a distinctive regulation of public employment, an ample body of administrative law, an emphasis on regulations and the administrative courts for oversight and accountability (Ongaro 2009, 2010, and 2018; Ongaro et al., 2016). Whilst the institutions are inspired by the French model, Italian public administration has also long displayed features typical of what has been labeled the Southern European bureaucratic model: clientelism in the recruitment of low-ranking officials; an uneven distribution of resources, institutional fragmentation, and insufficient mechanisms for policy coordination; formalism and legalism complemented by informal shadow governance structures; and the absence of a typical European administrative elite (Sotiropoulos 2004).

Another distinctive historical feature of the Italian bureaucracy is its "southernization," meaning that public administration was used as a social buffer to reward the loyalty of southern clienteles via the particularistic distribution of selective benefits, including jobs. Many public employees bring with them the attitudes typical of southern regions, meaning – among other things – that appreciation for job stability is prized over influence on decision-making. A possessive attitude toward public office has also been exhibited by senior executives. They constituted an "ossified world" (Cassese 1999), elderly and with a relatively low level of professionalism, in which promotions were rewards for age and length of service, with limited horizontal and vertical mobility.

The sclerotic tendencies of the higher civil service have been cemented by the pact of reciprocal self-restraint formed between political and administrative elites: the senior civil service renounced an autonomous and proactive role in the policymaking process, while politicians refrained from interfering in career management (Cassese 1999), although they did intervene in the administrative process on a case-by-case basis, in exchange for job stability, which was part of the bargain (Ongaro 2009).

The lack of integration between political and administrative elites made governments reluctant to use the established bureaucracy, as revealed by the subordination of senior civil servants to the Minister in the postunification history of the Italian administration (Mattei 2007). The general approach to the bureaucracy has been to "sideline" it, meaning that governments filled ministerial cabinets with hundreds of loyal party officials, setting up a parallel advisory structure. Thus, "sidelining" was a strategy utilized in Italy well before the age of populist governments. Ministerial cabinets were a substitute for the ordinary bureaucracies and exercised executive tasks, thus also blurring the lines of accountability between politics and the administration. The legalism typical of the Napoleonic administrative tradition led to the preferential appointments of magistrates, recruited from professional corps such as the Council of State and Court of Accounts, as top ministerial advisers (Di Mascio and Natalini 2016).

Traditionally, governments also sought to manipulate administrative structures. Ministerial bureaucracies had been disempowered by the development of a complex galaxy of public agencies and public corporations marked by a large variety of organizational models. This parallel structure of public bodies came under the full control of the then governing parties' networks, which, until the collapse of the traditional party system in the mid-1990s, were in Italy very tightly organized and bound together by a strong ideological glue. The quest for support also led the government of the day to leave most aspects of personnel administration and management to the consultation and negotiation processes with the then very powerful trade unions – a factor that in hindsight proved to be a source of bureaucratic resilience.

Mistrust toward the bureaucracy reinforced legal mechanisms for the sake of control: to reduce the discretion exerted by bureaucrats, laws had progressively regulated every aspect of administrative procedures, thereby enhancing the monitoring powers of bodies such as the Council of State, the Court of Accounts, and the General Accounting Department in the Ministry of Finance. The increasing legalism implied greater rigidity in management, which was circumvented by the rise of informal arrangements (Di Palma 1979). Political connection with governing parties was the main route of access to the bureaucracy for civil society organizations, as transparency and participation did not feature on the governmental agenda at the time. The emphasis on bureaucratic secrecy was consistent with the administrative legacy that the new Italian democracy had inherited from the fascist regime.

The Italian bureaucracy had thus been sidelined well before the advent of populist governments, and strategies for controlling it focused on multiple areas (structure, resources, personnel, norms, openness) to secure support for the ruling parties, combined with patterns of favoritism in the distribution of public resources. The "porosity" of public sector organizations to private interests led to a fragmentation of decisions and a loss of coordination, which made it difficult to guide them toward far-reaching change, ultimately reducing the Italian state's policy capacity (Ongaro 2008). Since public sector organizations were often utilized by political elites to cultivate their clienteles, no government was able or willing to undertake a reform of the bureaucracy (Tarrow 1977). These dynamics further exacerbated the lack of deference that was displayed by the Italian citizens toward the public sector (Cassese 1993).

Thus, it is not surprising that no breakthrough legislation had been formulated in the field of public management reform until the early 1990s, when globally circulating doctrines started to reshape the public debate on administrative reforms. Between 1992 and 1994, the party system underwent a major transformation, following an economic crisis (when the Italian currency was forced off the European Monetary System), a nationwide judicial investigation which decapitated the leadership of most political parties, and new electoral laws providing majoritarian arrangements. Most of the political parties participating in the 1994 election were either brand new or were the products of major leadership and organizational change; alternation in government between pre-electoral coalitions became the new predictable configuration of political competition.

The collapse of the traditional parties, which had been unwilling to modify a dysfunctional bureaucratic machine, opened a window of opportunity for public management reforms (Capano 2003). The formal autonomy of the higher civil service was conceived as the point of departure for administrative modernization in the 1990s (Di Mascio and Natalini 2014; see also Borgonovi and Ongaro 2011). In 1993, the technocratic government led by Ciampi introduced the formal distinction between the political and the managerial spheres, and management by objective was interposed between the two spheres (Ongaro 2011). This meant that managers were in charge of making decisions about the utilization of resources for achieving the objectives set by the political principals, and new specialized advisory bodies were introduced to appraise their results. The traditional subordination of senior civil servants to ministers was definitely eliminated in 1998, when a second major reform occurred under the center-left Prodi government, which abolished any prerogative of the ministers to override acts of senior public managers. All appointments to the positions of manager became temporary, in the attempt to link the confirmation and promotion of incumbents with performance evaluation.

The process of European integration imposed growing constraints on the irresponsible particularistic distribution of public resources. Fiscal pressures prompted a repertoire of cutback measures complemented by reforms that were inspired by New Public Management (NPM) doctrines (Di Mascio, Natalini, and Stolfi 2013; Ongaro 2009). However, a significant percentage of reform initiatives launched in this period suffered from an "implementation gap" (Ongaro and Valotti 2008) originating from the high level of political instability that determined a lack of political incentives to implement reforms and required reform champions endowed with a very rare mix of skills (Mele and Ongaro 2014). The implementation gap of administrative reforms contributed to the persistent deficit of economic competitiveness throughout the 1990s. This has kept budgetary pressures intense, contributing to relatively poor public services, which, together with continued widespread corruption and cumbersome administrative procedures, have probably contributed to fueling the rise of populist parties in the extremely fluid political landscape created by the collapse of the previous party system.

Italy: A Case of Mutating Populism

Unique in Europe, Italy witnessed three coalition governments dominated by populist parties in the first two decades of the 2000s. We qualify Italy as a case of "mutating populism," whereby diverse populist parties emerged (FI, LN, and FSM) as different incarnations of an antiestablishment ethos (Verbeek and Zaslove 2016). By mutating populism we mean that populist actors in Italy have reacted and responded to the success and the institutionalization of fellow populist actors. In particular, the continued presence of populist parties in government contributed to the rise of new populist forces. As populist parties entered coalition governments, new populist actors reacted to the inefficacy of governments torn by antagonism and paralysis stemming from the incoherence of policy positions of populist government coalition members and their nonpopulist allies.

The success of populist parties can be traced back, inter alia, to certain long-term determinants of political dissatisfaction characterizing the fragile Italian democracy. The shortcomings of the Italian administrative system (corruption, cumbersome administrative procedures, poor quality of public services) paved the way for the rise of populism that has come to the fore in full force since the early 1990s, when the magnitude of the unsolved economic and social problems and the scarcity of resources made dissatisfaction with public services a key issue of concern (Morlino and Tarchi 1996). In this sense, it can be hypothesized that dissatisfaction with the bureaucracy also played a role in propelling populist parties to power – a finding which may be interesting to develop further in a comparative perspective.

The austerity imposed by the Eurozone governance on the Italian budget has been another target of populist campaigning, which has fed the perception of the Euro as a painful constraint afflicting the stagnating economy (Badell et al. 2019). Lack of commitment to fiscal discipline turned into outright opposition to EU fiscal rules under the Conte I government (2018–2019) that was formed by two populist parties sharing virulent Eurosceptic rhetoric. Eurozone governance has been both a blessing and a curse for populist actors: on the one hand, austerity helped fuel dissatisfaction; on the other hand, it left limited space to introduce any major change in macroeconomic policy.

As shown in Table 3.1, which summarizes the programs of the populist parties that have been in government during the period under investigation (2001–2019), administrative simplification and reducing the burden on businesses and citizens (cutting red tape) have been mantras in populist campaigns. While administrative simplification has been a unifying feature, populist parties differed on the emphasis that should be given to different areas of reform.

Table 3.1 *Populist parties in government (Italy, 2001–2019): Policy positions on themes of public management reform*

PERIOD	GOVERNMENTS	POPULIST PARTIES IN GOVERNMENT	COALITION PARTNERS
2001–2006	Berlusconi II–III	**Go Italy:** personal party calling for deregulation and efficiency gains associated to a vaguely defined managerial reform of public administration; Emphasis put on "open politicization" that relies on the influx of outsiders to senior ranks of civil service **Northern League:** regionalist party calling for deregulation and major devolution of powers to regional and local governments to untie the productive Northern Italy from the inefficient central administration	**National Alliance:** postfascist party that did not support devolution and was sympathetic to civil service **UDC:** Christian-Democrat party that did not support devolution while practicing southernization of public employment by means of clientelistic recruitment
2008–2011	Berlusconi IV	**People of Freedom:** personal party calling for deregulation and efficiency gains associated to public management reform introducing total disclosure and evaluation of individual performance; Emphasis put on curbing public sector	No junior coalition partners

Table 3.1 (*cont.*)

PERIOD	GOVERNMENTS	POPULIST PARTIES IN GOVERNMENT	COALITION PARTNERS
		workforce privileges; Imposition of limits on collective bargaining and strict policy on absenteeism in the public sector; Structural reforms focused on the abrogation of provinces; Lack of commitment to fiscal discipline imposed by the EU; Lack of commitment to delegation of powers to an independent anticorruption agency. **Northern League:** regionalist party calling for deregulation and major devolution of powers to regional and local governments; Opposition to any reorganization of provincial and local tiers of government; Lack of commitment to fiscal discipline imposed by the EU; Lack of commitment to delegation of powers to an independent anticorruption agency.	

2018–2019   Conte I

Five Star Movement: antiestablishment party calling for administrative simplification and better regulation; Commitment to delegation of powers to an independent anticorruption agency complemented by less politicized senior ranks of civil service; Opposition to fiscal discipline imposed by the EU; Opposition to higher levels of autonomy granted to northern regions.

Northern League: far-right nationalist party calling for deregulation; Opposition to the intrusiveness of the anticorruption agency in the field of public procurement; Strict policy on absenteeism in the public sector; Opposition to fiscal discipline imposed by the EU; Commitment to higher levels of autonomy granted to northern regions.

No junior coalition partners

The personal parties led by the media tycoon Silvio Berlusconi (Go Italy in 2001 and People of Freedom in 2008) prioritized civil service reform. The LN had traditionally been a regionalist populist party that prioritized autonomy for northern regions in various forms (federalism, devolution, and even independence) depending on varying political opportunities. The territorial cleavage upset the coalition government led by Berlusconi in the period 2001–2005 when the LN played the role of "opposition within government," given the poor relationship with the fellow junior coalition partners – the postfascist AN and the former Christian Democrats of the UDC – both perceived as being sympathetic to the south of Italy and its clientelistic ties with the public sector (Albertazzi and McDonnell 2005).

Populist parties that joined the center-right coalition government in 2001–2006 and 2008–2011 shared the call for a deregulatory approach, which was expected to boost the efficiency of small companies. The LN kept its focus on deregulation in 2018 when it joined a coalition supported by the FSM, a party that endorsed a more statist approach to public policy, alongside an emphasis on legality and emphasizing probity as the prime quality required of public administrators. This led to policy contradictions: the LN wished to reduce red tape for construction companies to help boost the stagnating economy, but the FSM was concerned about anticorruption controls, which entailed more rather than less red tape. While previous populist parties in government had displayed little commitment to delegating powers to an independent anticorruption agency (Di Mascio, Maggetti, and Natalini 2018), the FSM's political agenda included a strong anticorruption and transparency stance (Mosca and Tronconi 2019). Also, more traditional north–south divides arose, with the LN dominating in regional governments across the northern and richer part of Italy, while the FSM campaigned for more spending in southern regions.

The collapse of the first Conte government in the summer of 2019 confirmed the controversial relationship between populisms and the volatility of the fragmented Italian party system. On the one hand, populists benefited from the inefficacy of coalition governments, which provided opportunities for the rise of new movements. On the other hand, once in power populists encountered turbulence within cabinets originating from the incoherence of policy positions.

Empirical Analysis

In this section we examine the dynamics of administrative reforms in Italy under populist governments, following the framework adopted in this volume (Bauer et al., Introduction, this volume): after reviewing the general approach or stance by populist governments to reforming the bureaucracy, we discuss the changes (or absence thereof) to administrative structures, resources, personnel, and accountability. We finally examine the reaction of the bureaucracy, and show how this has been crucial for eventual outcomes of reform efforts.

General Approach to the Bureaucracy

Italian populist governments to some extent chose a combination of all three of the major approaches outlined in the introduction to this volume: sidelining, using, and ignoring. Whereas the salient and highly sensitive issues of policy formulation and coordination were entrusted to ministerial cabinets as parallel structures (*sidelining* – a trait of continuity with previous decades of governing Italy, as we have seen), the execution of most tasks remained within the bureaucratic apparatus, as populist actors pursued appointments internal to the ministerial bureaucracy, with at most a modest level of turnover (*using*). More broadly, the Italian bureaucracy has not been reshaped by populist actors, who likely entered government without the commitment, and surely without the requisite strategic and operational skills, required to reshape the State apparatus (*ignoring*); indeed, the administrative apparatus has remained quite unaltered.

In more detail, bureaucracy has been sidelined via the appointment of staffers within ministerial cabinets, in continuity with practices that date back decades. In Italy, ministerial cabinets are not part of the administrative hierarchy and represent an alternative structure that substitutes for the work of senior civil servants as a source of policy advice. Populist parties in government recruited top officials for ministerial cabinets from the very same pool of technically qualified individuals who were members of the advisory structures inherited from the pre-1992 regime (in ways not much dissimilar to practices by governments that we do not label populist). It is worth highlighting the evolution of the approach to cabinet appointments of the LN, which, in the years when it first came to power, was the only party to appoint staffers with a party-political background in ministerial cabinets, as a result of the lack of ties with the professional corps; later, it emphasized appointees recruited from the three dominant professional corps at the core of the state (Council of State, Court of Accounts, State General Attorney). As for the FSM, it initially displayed a lack of mutual trust vis-à-vis professional corps and it appointed staffers who had not served under previous governments from a more varied range of recruitment pools than the *grands corps* that usually dominated ministerial cabinets.

Populist actors also drew on reforms of managerial appointments enacted just before they came to power (Mattei 2007). Reforms enacted by the center-left government in 1996–2001 made top civil servants appointable by the council of ministers, and the politicization of the senior civil service was then further enhanced by the Berlusconi government, which enlarged the scope of political appointments to lower hierarchical levels, as well as abolishing the minimum length of their term in 2002. In the period 2001–2006, the emphasis was also placed on the recruitment of outsiders to top bureaucratic posts: this reflected the trajectory of Berlusconi, who was the first person in Italy to take the role of prime minister without having held any previous public appointment. However, populist parties lacked the capacity to manage the extensive politicization of the senior civil service that had been envisaged by public management reforms (Di Mascio and Natalini 2014; Ongaro 2011). In a context of governmental instability, there was no time left for new political parties to colonize the bureaucracy, as their shallow organizations dominated by populist leaders were unable to consolidate networks of loyal officials reaching deeply into the ministerial bureaucracy (Di Mascio 2014). Berlusconi's governments were unable to fill most vacancies by appointing new loyal officials from nonministerial settings. The Berlusconi government also co-opted most of the existing senior public managers by confirming their appointment and, under pressure from within the bureaucracy, eventually reintroduced the minimum length of their term in 2005.

Under the Berlusconi governments in 2001–2006, the processes of appointment did not utilize performance evaluation: on the one hand, this enhanced political discretion in the distribution of appointments; on the other hand, the lack of accountability for performance results elicited hostility in the general public toward public managers, who were perceived as controlled by political principals. The widespread dissatisfaction with political appointments was tackled by the subsequent Berlusconi government in 2009, by establishing procedural mechanisms ensuring transparency and competitiveness in the distribution of appointments. However, the inclusion of two provisions in the more comprehensive deficit reduction packages determined a gap between talk and action (throughout this book we follow Brunsson's [1989] distinction between different levels at which organizational change "occurs": whether this be in reform "talk" – legally binding formal decisions – or at the level of the actual "actions," since most administrative reforms do not simply flow from being enshrined in legislation but require the active contribution of many actors to make them happen). The procedural links between performance evaluation and appointment were removed (Law Decree 78/2010), meaning that, in practice, appointments could continue to ignore performance measures; and the minimum length of the appointment of senior executives was abolished (Law Decree 138/2011), meaning that senior managers could be removed on a discretionary basis regardless of their performance.

The FSM reacted to the persistent politicization of appointments by campaigning for stabilizing managerial positions. Given its short time in office, the 2018–2019 Conte government could only issue a draft framework law on the reform of civil service, which mentioned neither procedural constraints on ministerial discretion in the appointment process nor the extension of the minimum length of positions. Like the Berlusconi-led governments, the Conte government opted for using the bureaucratic apparatus: the turnover rate remained medium and appointments remained the preserve of insiders, picked from within the individual ministries.

Structure

The changes to the party system in the 1990s contributed to strengthening the steering role of the Prime Minister's Office, in a country where the head of government had traditionally been the mere facilitator of the policy choices adopted by political parties in unstable coalitions. This was clearly the case for the Berlusconi governments, in which the head of government was also the leader of the main party of the coalition and the foundation of its electoral success. However, even under Berlusconi the centrality of the prime minister was mitigated by the nature of coalition government and the extended negotiations with the junior coalition partners. Furthermore, the strengthening of European budgetary constraints increased the prominence of the Minister of the Economy who, especially following the global financial, economic, and fiscal crises since 2008, within the new EU governance ended up playing the role of guarantor of fiscal stability (Di Mascio et al. 2019; Ongaro and Kickert 2020).

The fragmentation of governing coalitions affected not only the horizontal dispersion of power but also the bureaucratic organizational design. In a context marked by heterogeneous coalitions facing uncertainty about their survival prospects, populist governments lacked commitment to altering administrative structures and focused on "maintaining" the organizational set-up (Pollitt and Bouckaert 2017). The response to the fiscal crisis did not translate into mergers or termination of public bodies (Di Mascio and Natalini 2015) and no major organizational realignment was sought, nor has further transfer of powers to semiautonomous agencies or independent administrative authorities that characterized the end of the 1990s and the early 2000s occurred (Ongaro 2006).

As for the vertical dispersion of power, fiscal pressures have unleashed centripetal forces within a quite decentralized, regional institutional framework. Under ever increasing fiscal pressures from the EU, fiscal management was centralized by reinvigorating the constraints on the subnational governments' autonomy to spend, which had been introduced in the late 1990s to make all levels of government coresponsible for respecting EU-agreed fiscal consolidation targets. Under the Berlusconi IV government, the LN did not challenge the centralized financial supervision of subnational governments, while it staunchly opposed any termination or reorganization of provincial governments, though this was part of the austerity agenda that the Italian government agreed with European institutions. Under the LN–FSM coalition government in 2018–2019, the LN upheld the rhetoric about enhancing the autonomy of regional governments in northern Italy (the Italian constitution provides for the possibility of differential autonomy) – an outcome which was vetoed, however, by the FSM. In sum, continuity with the past rather than discontinuity was the dominant note.

Resources

The populist governments operated under tight fiscal constraints, but even though austerity was a fixture over many years, it did not lead to the adoption of prioritized approaches to spending cuts. In other words, the fiscal crisis was not exploited to reshuffle administrative powers through budget allocations. Despite its campaign against waste in the public sector, the Berlusconi government of 2008–2011 responded to the sovereign debt crisis solely by reinforcing already well-institutionalized, across-the-board cuts: an approach which avoided a fragmented governing coalition having to make tough decisions over priorities (Di Mascio and Natalini 2014).

The sovereign debt crisis did not imply a shift toward spending reviews aimed at efficiency gains. Indeed, exercises labeled as "spending reviews" had been carried out as an experimental activity since the early 1980s, before being progressively institutionalized through establishing technical committees; these committees had always been set up on an ad hoc basis and were filled with external experts operating at a distance from the budgetary administration of the General Accounting Department. Public dissatisfaction with austerity measures, as well as EU pressures to identify efficiency savings, renewed discussions about spending review: the magic wand to make cuts less painful. To accommodate these domestic and supranational pressures, subsequent governments in the period 2011–2016, led by Monti, Letta, and Renzi, once again called in external experts to identify where cuts could be achieved with the least impact on service provision. Notably, Carlo Cottarelli, former Director of the Public Finance Department at the International Monetary Fund, was appointed as commissioner for the spending review by the Letta government in late 2013, enjoying more powers than his predecessors and a larger scope for his mission. The work of Mr. Cottarelli was extolled by the FSM, which campaigned for implementation of the ambitious plan for efficiency savings that had been formulated by the spending review before his resignation in October 2014. However, the plan produced by Cottarelli was not implemented by the Renzi government, nor was a new spending review commissioner appointed before the collapse of the Conte I government. Summing up, in this area too continuity with the past is the dominant note. Unlike the previous reform area, here we do not find any cleavage at the talk level as populist parties shared with mainstream parties the identification in spending review of a key tool to respond to public dissatisfaction with austerity measures. Populist actors also shared with nonpopulist parties the same reluctance to grant autonomy for action to external technicians.

Personnel and Norms

In the early 1990s, a reform increased the areas of public employment subject to private labor law. It also introduced a two-tier labor contract system: one negotiated at the national level, and a supplementary one at the level of each administration. A new autonomous agency (ARAN) was tasked with negotiating collective contracts with unions.

The electoral manifesto of the Berlusconi campaign in 2001 emphasized rewarding merit and cutting spending. Berlusconi's talk also exhibited aversion to trade unions, though the governments led by the tycoon during 2001–2006 substantially increased public personnel pay, very much in line with a long tradition in Italy of using public employment to build support. In particular, the junior allies in the governing coalition (the AN and the UCD, but also the FI) competed for the support of this social group (which at the time amounted to *c*.3.5 million people). However, civil servants later became the target of an opinion campaign that was initially launched by representatives of the Democratic Party, but which was then widely taken up by all the governments (populist and otherwise) that have led Italy since 2008 (Ichino 2006).

In response to this campaign, the Berlusconi IV government attempted to revitalize the implementation of previous waves of reforms focused on increasing productivity via the relaunch of NPM tools such as performance management. For the first time, a government led by Berlusconi launched a major package of public management reform (Legislative Decree 150/2009), introducing a new performance management system: performance-related pay was reinstated by means of a forced-ranking logic focused on individual results whereby only one-quarter of civil servants could get the highest bonus, and one-quarter would not get any bonus, with a lower bonus to the remaining 50 per cent (Ongaro and Bellé 2010). The reform was launched as a crusade against the *fannulloni* (slackers) allegedly thriving in the Italian public workforce, and it was complemented by measures against absenteeism, which reduced sick leave pay and increased monitoring. The Berlusconi government also focused on reducing the scope of collective bargaining, which was meant to reduce the influence of trade unions over public employment regulations.

The reform was still under way when the effects of the global financial crisis of 2008 started to be felt, leading policymakers to hollow out the implementation of performance-related pay entirely, depriving the reform of the budgetary resources to support it, as public employment underwent massive cutbacks following the 2010 "emergency fiscal consolidation" package. The gulf between talk and action was further exacerbated by the combination of replacement rates and cuts to temporary jobs: on the one hand, this combination proved to be the more politically viable tactic as it enabled political executives not to face the resistance of unionized tenured workers who opposed any hypothesis of selective dismissals; on the other hand, it produced a dramatic aging of the public sector workforce (Di Mascio et al. 2017).

If NPM doctrines were still a core part of the toolkit in the last Berlusconi government, they were dumped in favor of a "pragmatic approach" by the Conte I government, thus reducing the incoherence between talk and action. Minister for Public Administration Giulia Bongiorno emphasized a more tailored approach to administrative reform, replacing previous NPM-inspired packages with a three-year Plan of "Concrete Actions," to be prepared annually by a self-styled "Unit for Concreteness" at the Ministry for Public Administration. The Conte I government also intervened on absenteeism by introducing biometric detection tools and cameras to monitor access of public employees to the workplace (Law n. 56/2019).

Accountability and Transparency

The four governments led by Berlusconi at different times between 1994 and 2011 did not tackle the conflict of interests resulting from the presence of a media mogul in government. Furthermore, a number of measures were passed to restrain and weaken the impact of judicial investigations on corruption and economic crimes involving Berlusconi, who denounced the excessive autonomy of the courts and its intrusion into the political sphere (Della Porta and Vannucci 2007).

The first Italian anticorruption agency was established in 2003 as a reaction to concerns from the OECD about the flaws in Italy's existing anticorruption policy, which had traditionally been restricted to criminal investigations. The scarcity of resources, complemented by the narrow scope of the agency's mandate and its termination in 2008, highlighted the lack of commitment to credible anticorruption efforts by the Berlusconi governments (Di Mascio, Maggetti, and Natalini 2018).

To address a new round of concerns from the OECD and Council of Europe-Group of States against Corruption (GRECO) the fourth Berlusconi government introduced a new under-resourced body, the Commission for the Evaluation, Transparency and Integrity (CIVIT), guiding the implementation of transparency reform (Legislative Decree n. 150/2009). Transparency was enhanced through the compulsory disclosure of data about public sector organizations and the salaries of civil servants, a measure that had been identified by the Berlusconi government as a key response to popular dissatisfaction with public services. Yet, this was mostly a public relations exercise to reap reputational benefits, and relevant stakeholders were in fact not engaged in selecting the information to be published. As a result, public bodies were obliged to publish data that the general public did not consider to be most useful (Di Mascio, Natalini, and Cacciatore 2019).

Since 2009, the FSM has campaigned for further proactive transparency measures as a key topic of its broader approach to unmediated popular sovereignty via implementation of digital tools for accountability. These pressures influenced the agenda of grand-coalition governments in the period 2012–2014. A new set of transparency obligations was introduced, providing for the unprecedented publication of information on political representatives, including income and asset declarations. The former CIVIT was reconfigured as the National Anticorruption Agency (ANAC), introducing an unprecedented anticorruption approach focused on prevention, which had been advocated by international organizations.

Since spring 2014 the ANAC has been led by Raffaele Cantone, a former anti-Mafia prosecutor. The lack of political affiliation and his reputation made Cantone a highly suitable candidate for the post. The FSM welcomed the new appointment, and also backed the call for more powers and further delegation of competences to the ANAC, notably supervisory and regulatory functions in public procurement. However, the ANAC became the target of reform efforts by the FSM–LN populist government. The coalition agreement (termed as a "contract"), envisaged the consolidation of the anti-corruption authority, but a provision pushed by the LN curbed the regulatory powers of the ANAC, in an attempt to accelerate procurement procedures, particularly in the area of public works, with the declared objective to deregulate and boost growth. Cantone highlighted the higher corruption risks resulting from this change before his resignation in the summer of 2019.

The areas of anticorruption and transparency are probably the areas in which populist governments have been most active in reforming, and in which they displayed the largest decoupling of talk and action. They are possibly also the areas in which efforts to "tame the bureaucracy," including attempting to curb its autonomy (autonomy of the courts, notably, in the Berlusconi governments) and ultimately to reduce its role as an institution of pluralism (see Bauer et al., Introduction, this volume; and Bauer and Becker 2020) took place.

As highlighted in Table 3.2, which provides a relatively stylized representation of our empirical analysis, populist governments largely did not pursue a distinctive agenda in matters of administrative reform: we found more talk than action, but we also found that most of the talk was quite similar to that of mainstream parties in respect of administrative reforms.

Perhaps the most noticeable element in populist governments in Italy, notably in their 2018–2019 incarnation, is an abandonment of NPM recipes in favor of interventions perceived as simpler and more direct. There is, however, an emphasis on both "taming the bureaucracy" (allegedly potentially hostile, given its acquaintance with the previous regime) and contemporaneously "befriending the bureaucracy," also as part of a quest for legitimation by antisystem parties aiming to become established. In light of these considerations, it is now time to consider the bureaucracy not as an object of intervention but rather as a subject of agency – that is, to discuss how the bureaucracy reacted to populist governments' attempts to intervene in its structure and functioning.

Bureaucratic Reactions

There has been no overt reaction from the higher civil servants to the precariousness of appointments. The established pattern of a bargain between political power and job security was reproduced: once again, higher civil servants were deprived of an autonomous role in policy-making, while politicians refrained from practicing a major turnover in top posts. Furthermore, higher civil servants were compensated by the soaring growth of their pay in the late 1990s and early 2000s (Gualmini

Table 3.2 *Populist parties in government (Italy, 2001–2019): Talk and action in selected dimensions of public management reform*

Dimensions	Berlusconi II and III (2001–2006)	Berlusconi IV (2008–2011)	Conte I (2018–2019)
General approach to the bureaucracy	**Talk** Open politicization of the civil service via the appointment of technically qualified outsiders **Actions** "Sidelining" of the bureaucracy via the appointment of ministerial cabinets; "Using" the bureaucracy via the distribution of temporary appointments	**Talk** Linkage between performance evaluation and distribution of appointments **Actions** "Sidelining" of the bureaucracy via the appointment of ministerial cabinets; "Using" the bureaucracy via the distribution of temporary appointments	**Talk** Stability of managerial positions and drastic cut of compensation of top officials **Actions** "Sidelining" of the bureaucracy via the appointment of ministerial cabinets; "Using" the bureaucracy via the distribution of temporary appointments; Stability of top officials' compensation
Structure	**Talk** Strengthening the Prime Minister's Office	**Talk** Abrogation of the provincial level of government	**Talk** More powers to northern regions

Actions	Reform was partially implemented in a context marked by fragmented and heterogeneous governing coalitions	Reform was staunchly opposed by the Northern League	Reform was vetoed by the FSM
Talk	Campaign against waste in the public sector	Campaign against waste in the public sector	Endorsement of technocratic spending review
Resources			
Actions	Across-the-board cuts; Lack of institutionalization of spending review	Across-the-board cuts; Lack of institutionalization of spending review	Lack of institutionalization of spending review
Talk	Call for recognition of merit	Campaign against trade unions; Reduction in the scope of collective bargaining; Link between performance evaluation and wages; Fight against absenteeism	"Concreteness" of reform measures; Fight against absenteeism
Personnel			
Actions	Increase of wages with no link to performance	Freezing of wages; implementation gap of performance evaluation	Biometric tools to detect personnel presence

Table 3.2 (*cont.*)

Dimensions	Berlusconi II and III (2001–2006)	Berlusconi IV (2008–2011)	Conte I (2018–2019)
Accountability and transparency	**Talk** Anticorruption controls are politically biased	**Talk** Proactive transparency as the only tool for corruption prevention	**Talk** Disagreement between FSM and LN on the simplification of anticorruption controls in the field of public works
	Actions Introduction of an under-resourced anticorruption agency	**Actions** Introduction of an under-resourced agency monitoring the implementation of transparency	**Actions** Deregulation of anticorruption controls in field of public works

2002). If we consider the antibureaucratic "talk" of the center-right coalition, it is rather surprising that the salary system of senior civil servants was not questioned by the Berlusconi government during the sovereign debt crisis. Conversely, the FSM campaigned for a significant reduction of senior civil servants' salaries, to lessen the burden of the sovereign debt crisis, but this issue was removed from its agenda when it entered government.

Public sector trade unions were framed as part of a major campaign against their allegedly excessive influence in the regulation of public personnel, which led to the split of their front when the largest confederation – the leftist Italian General Confederation of Labour (CGIL) voiced its opposition to austerity policies. This reaction proved to be ineffective since the other two major unions cooperated with the government, leading them to focus fiscal consolidation on temporary workers, who had a lower unionization rate (Di Mascio et al. 2017). Trade unions also benefited from the high level of regulation of the internal labor market in a legalist institutional context. This enhanced the veto power of actors such as the trade unions, who could threaten to report governments to the courts if they did not complement major reforms with a complex chain of implementing regulatory provisions (Di Mascio, Feltrin, and Natalini 2019).

Thus, the low level of politicization of higher civil servants and the legalist setting of the public labor market constitute factors that made the Italian public sector resilient by maintaining, or even reinforcing, the "iron triangle" among political elites, senior managers, and trade unions. It is also worth highlighting that the Europeanization process reinforced those bureaucracies that enjoy considerable credit in the eyes of the European technocracies; in particular, the State General Accounting Department emerged as a very powerful actor in the budget process, which keeps public spending under control.

The autonomy of the State General Accounting Department has been a constant source of tension within the executive, particularly under the Conte government. The FSM has shown considerable distrust toward the bureaucratic heads of the Ministry of Finance, but control over bureaucratic careers remained internal to the civil service, since lower-ranking officials were promoted to senior ranks. This reveals that populist governments took advantage of the competence of officials working in the financial administration, whose collaboration is essential to avoid being overwhelmed by speculative international financial operators and to maintain channels of dialogue with the EU concerning compliance with budgetary constraints.

Populist parties have also been forced to rely on policy advice provided by the professional corps of the Italian State, which continued to fill the top posts in ministerial cabinets and whose extensive personal networks are the glue holding together the inner workings of the public apparatus. It is also worth highlighting that the appointment of magistrates in ministerial cabinets has not meant any reduction of judicial independence. In fact, the lawfulness of decisions and actions made by populist cabinets has been frequently called into question by magistracies operating at all levels (Constitutional Court, Council of State, Court of Accounts, ordinary judiciary).

Conclusion

This chapter has investigated the impact of populism on the Italian public service, and has highlighted some traits marking its influence over bureaucracy and administrative reforms, as well as, albeit more indirectly, some features of Italian populism over the first two decades of the millennium. First, in Italy we should talk of *populisms* in the plural: a right-wing populism understandable through the lens of what seems to be an "international of populism" embodied by the LN and patterned on foreign models, such as France's Le Pen, to whose ideological positions the LN has come closer; this was after having begun as a regionalist/secessionist political force. Another right-wing populism had a neoliberal imprint and was shaped by the conflict of interests of its founder and *dominus*, Silvio Berlusconi. And, on the left-wing, there was the populism of the FSM, which started up as a radically antisystem party.

The key question is whether these differences led to these parties having different priorities for reshaping the bureaucracy. On the one hand, these parties focused their reform efforts on different targets: the LN focused on the structure of government, with a view to devolving competences and resources to regional governments (in line with its history as the regionalist party of the north); the FI focused on performance management, mostly as a way to tame the bureaucrats and tie them more closely to the steer of elected officials, but also displayed some elements of a "business-like government" (NPM) ideology, rooted not so much in international influences but rather in the personal biography of its founder and leader; the FSM focused on transparency and anticorruption as their flagship reforms. On the other hand, these parties shared a reluctance to apply NPM doctrines more widely, and this marked a departure from the course of action pursued by the governments in office in the 1990s. The dissatisfaction with the complexity of NPM, in doctrine and practices, is epitomized by the emphasis on "concrete" actions for raising the productivity of public employment displayed by the first Conte government.

Second, and the main finding, populist governments have displayed a marked chasm between rhetoric and deeds, between the level of talk and action (Brunsson 1989), and, in terms of the reform of the administrative system, they have hardly (if at all) walked the walk. The degree of administrative continuity is hard to overestimate, and indeed it is the main feature of re-*forming* under populist governing: there seem not to be alternative models or paradigms of public administration (Ongaro 2020, chapter 8) on display, and the fantasy about changing the administrative system seems to stop at removing certain high-fliers to replace them with others (not necessarily with different views, and, importantly, not necessarily less pliant than those who got dismissed) or introducing new checks on clock-in cheating and other practices of maladministration – a trait much in line with what happened elsewhere: "the rhetoric about undoing the administrative state has not been matched with much action or a strong and consistent emphasis on changing patterns of governance" (Peters and Pierre 2019, p.1522). This is also partly because reforming bureaucracy is not a priority, nor is any premium put for populist parties' staffers to develop in-depth knowledge about the functioning of the public sector and public services. Hence, people with the requisite skills are not available in the cadres of populist parties (Mele and Ongaro 2014). As a result, all populist governments faced the fiscal crisis by opting for reforms aimed at "maintaining" the administrative system – an approach that suits well the Italian context marked by fragmented governing coalitions hardly capable of setting priorities.

Third, the pattern of reaction of the bureaucracy was to 'react through nonreaction'. Shirking provided a simple ruse that often sufficed to defuse most of the attempts to change it (if ever those attempts were serious beyond the talk, and not just in Italy: see Guedes-Neto and Peters, Chapter 10, this volume). More broadly, throughout this chapter we assess the results of populist governments by considering the output of the interplay between populists and the other actors (senior civil service, policy advisers, oversight institutions, trade unions, etc.) who reacted to their initiatives. We interpret what we have observed as extensive continuity in the administrative practices, much like path-dependency. And, since our theoretical stance allows also for a logic of consequences in which individual agency does matter, we did find that individual actors' interventions did matter to trigger or defuse specific interventions. Overall, we observe that populist governments talked more than they acted, and that established institutions (and vested interests) shaped most of what happened – or, more precisely in this instance, what did *not* happen.

Fourth, in liberal-democratic regimes mainstream parties compete with populist ones by altering policy positions and the salience and ownership of issue dimensions. More specifically, mainstream parties can either dismiss populist parties' issues or they can address them by moving toward or away from the policy position adopted by populist parties (Heinze 2018). Our analysis revealed that mainstream parties did not actively try to win debates against populist parties by holding their policy position on administrative reform and communicating this more clearly. Rather, mainstream parties borrowed policy stances from populist parties, like the devolution of powers to subnational governments in the case of center-left government in the late 1990s in response to the "separatism" of the LN; or the anticorruption drive in the case of the Monti and Renzi governments, to stem the rise of FSM. In sum, establishment parties simply absorbed populist rhetoric. However, and crucially, we also found that populist parties did not pursue a distinctive agenda in matters of administrative reform beyond the loud tones: we found populist governments to be more about words than deeds, but we also found that most of the talk was quite similar to that of mainstream parties in terms of administrative reforms.

Fifth, and perhaps, the most noticeable element in populist governments in Italy, particularly in their 2018–2019 incarnation, is an abandonment of NPM recipes – probably deemed too complicated to implement (and possibly even too complicated to intellectually grasp), and replaced with solutions perceived as simpler and more direct. Combined with bureaucratic resilience, this may fully explain the very limited degree of administrative reforms under populist governments in Italy over the period of observation considered. More problematic is assessing whether the NPM-inspired reforms of the

1990s and the ways in which they were put into practice may have encouraged a loss of public trust, in turn spurring the rise of populist movements, as argued by Stoker in Chapter 11 of this volume, based on evidence from Anglo-Saxon countries. In light of the case of Italy, we are in no position to make statements about whether this has been the case for this Mediterranean country too: indeed, there simply seems to have been too little implementation of such reforms to attribute causality here.

Finally, an overly simplistic, yet possibly not unfounded, summary statement: we live in an age of populism in important regards even when we are not governed by a populist government. The administrative reform debate has slid out of the hands of the epistemic and policy community of the experts in public administration (academics, high-flier civil servants, and kindred spirits) and toward the spin doctors and media advisers of politicians; and, correspondingly, bureaucratic reforms – if and when prioritized on the governmental agenda – are no longer conceived for and driven by the traditional figure (possibly idealized) of the elected official practicing the ethics of responsibility (Weber 1949), but rather appropriated by the loquacious, media-obsessed, omnipresent – we might say pseudo-futurist, to cite an Italian artistic and doctrinal ideological movement of the first two decades of the twentieth century that is inspirational to some contemporary populist movements – politician.

4 | Illiberal Transformation of Government Bureaucracy in a Fragile Democracy: The Case of Hungary

GYÖRGY HAJNAL AND ZSOLT BODA

Introduction

Hungary represents perhaps the strongest example in the European Union of what the professional literature has termed, among other things, "democratic backsliding" or "illiberal regression" (Bermeo 2016; Levitsky and Ziblatt 2018a). In the early 2010s, the scholarly literature warned about the spread of populism, erosion of the rule of law, attacks against civil society and the media, widespread corruption, and patterns of "crony capitalism," especially in Hungary (Batory 2016; Bozóki 2011; Korkut 2012; Kornai 2015). In 2019, the European Union activated the "rule of law mechanism" under Article 7 against both Hungary and Poland, demonstrating that political recognition of these two countries' problems with liberal democracy had become more than academic.

Despite being – as we will shortly argue – an exceptionally strong case of what may be termed illiberal transformation, so far practically no scholarly attention has been devoted to the effects of this illiberal turn on Hungary's central government administration. Our initial proposition, however, is that these effects do exist, since consequences have been identified by previous studies at the level of territorial administration, and it is a safe assumption that these influences extend to the central administration (Hajnal and Rosta 2016). Additionally, ten years of illiberal politics and continuous, intense, and practically unbounded government reform in Hungary should be powerful enough to affect the structure and operations of central administration, even if one assumes that such institutions possess considerable inertia and resistance to change.

Comments and suggestions received with regard to earlier versions of this study from Prof. György Gajduschek (Corvinus University of Budapest and Centre for Social Research, Hungary) are hereby thankfully acknowledged.

Our overall ambition is to provide an in-depth description of how Hungary's system of governance has been transformed in the current illiberal (post-2010) era. In particular, we will examine, first, whether the analytical framework put forward in the introduction to this volume has sufficient descriptive power to characterize the illiberal transformation of Hungary's central government bureaucracy; and, second, whether the theoretical expectations regarding the direction and nature of this trans-formation are corroborated by the Hungarian case. In terms of its analytical focus, the study specifically explores the consequences of this illiberal turn in the political system. Empirically, the study concentrates on the central government's administrative machinery. Finally, insofar as data and method are concerned, our investigation endeavors to describe both the formal and informal elements of administrative changes. First, we provide a short overview of the Hungarian case. Then, we present our data and method. The fourth section details the empirical findings. Finally, we offer a discussion of our results and their implications, in order to understand better the nature of illiberal governance.

Before we proceed, we have a brief, mainly terminological, remark to make regarding one of our core concepts: illiberal transformation. Although we basically agree with the conceptual and terminological choices outlined in the introduction concerning democratic backsliding, autocratization, and illiberal democracy, when referring to the Hungarian case we use the term "illiberal transformation." We do so for two reasons. First, many other terms such as "recession" or "backsliding" imply a somewhat unintended and spontaneous process. As we will show, this is definitely not the case for the Hungarian transformation, which is long-term, carefully designed, and systemic. Second, "illiberal" (democracy, system, etc.) is a term used by the "reformers" themselves, such as Prime Minister Orbán.[1] The term thus reflects the systemic nature of the phenomenon in yet another way.

The Case of Hungary: Context and Background

In the late 1980s and early 1990s, Hungary was a leader in political and economic reforms on the road from communism to democracy and capitalism. Since 2010, the country's politics have taken a U-turn. In the relevant scholarly literature, it is largely undisputed that the quality of democracy has deteriorated while checks and balances have been weakened (Batory 2016; Bozóki 2011; Kornai 2015; Pap 2017). In the following, we provide a short overview of the main features of Hungary's illiberal turn, intended to offer a holistic view rather than a rigorous analysis of the transformation, and based primarily upon consensual claims in mainstream international academic discourse. We then turn to bureaucracy more specifically, and briefly present the contextual factors of its illiberal transformation, following the model set out the introduction to this volume.

In 2010, Viktor Orbán's center-right party, FIDESZ, won a landslide victory in the national elections, acquiring more than two-thirds of the seats in the parliament, which resulted in a constitutional "super-majority." The victory – arguably the defining moment and starting point of Hungary's illiberal transformation – was partly attributable to the deep economic and social problems caused by the 2007–2009 financial crisis, as well as to the previous Socialist-Liberal administration's weak performance, poor conflict management, and lack of integrity during that period.

In the run-up to the 2010 elections, a segment of the Hungarian public seemed apathetic and tired of the multiple economic and political crises, while another segment was, sometimes uncritically, enthusiastic about FIDESZ, the center-right opposition party, and its charismatic leader Viktor Orbán. Illustrative of the persistence of this public mood is that FIDESZ won the parliamentary elections with a supermajority, and this victory was followed by several additional wins in (local/regional and European) elections shortly afterwards. In the 2010s, gradual improvement in Hungary's economic situation, coupled with increasing structural funds from the EU, further strengthened Orbán's legitimacy. The political situation created an ideal context for unveiling his innovative and disruptive politics, frequently characterized as an ideal type of populism (Bartha, Boda, and Szikra 2020; Batory 2016). Orbán has been described as a political innovator who is constantly able to revise his style, his political objectives, and the means used to achieve them, thus surprising both the public and his opponents (Illés, Körösényi, and Metz 2018). Additionally, Orbán is frequently characterized as a populist leader who criticizes the liberal elites and institutions, including the European Union. He successfully constructs enemies to fight against, such as the International Monetary Fund, the philanthropic billionaire George Soros, and the "foreign" NGOs funded by the Soros Foundation, thus polarizing Hungarian polity along party lines while justifying his politics through majority support (Batory 2016; Korkut 2012).

In the first years of the illiberal, post-2010 era, FIDESZ passed a record high number of laws (Sebők, Kubik, and Molnár 2017), initiating large-scale policy reforms in the fields of education, energy, agriculture, and social policy, among others. A running theme of these reforms has been the "power grab" – that is, the radical strengthening and centralization of the central government's power and influence over other politico-administrative, societal, and business actors.

Moreover, the landslide reforms have fundamentally altered the system of checks and balances not only by vastly strengthening patronage, but also by introducing wide-ranging institutional reforms. FIDESZ has appointed prominent party loyalists to all important positions, including the President of the Republic, the justices on the Constitutional Court, and the Attorney General, as well as the heads of the Media Authority and of the State Tax Bureau. As for the institutional reforms, the administration enacted a new law regulating the media; put the body in charge of allocating funds for NGOs under the control of prominent government loyalists who make decisions in an increasingly politically and ideologically biased manner; set up a new authority to oversee the judiciary; modified the electoral system to their advantage; and, in 2011, even ratified a new constitution. In summary, the general direction of the institutional changes points, on one hand, toward a weakening of checks and balances on government power, and increasing government control over society and independent actors, on the other (Pap 2017).

In terms of the effects of the illiberal transformation on government administration, some investigations have been made. While not employing the terms "democratic backsliding" or "illiberalism," Hajnal and Csengődi (2014) account for the formal and informal means of increasing political control on public administration in post-2010 Hungary. They describe the trends of centralization at several levels: the weakening of legal protection for public servants, increased control and surveillance measures, patronage, and increased political interference through other means too. Hajnal and Rosta (2016) give an overview of selected transformative features from the 2010–2015 period that together constituted a deliberate shift in policy, weakening both the rule of law and input-side democratic legitimacy. These transformative features included the radical elimination of a career civil service (which still existed in a weak form), in addition to the drastic weakening of freedom of information legislation and institutions involved with interest reconciliation (Hajnal and Rosta 2016).

Whereas the above developments clearly make Hungary a case of illiberal transformation,[2] at the same time, it is debatable how far along Hungary is on the road from liberal democracy toward autocracy, and whether the Hungarian political system is "merely" a defective democracy or already a hybrid regime, if not an autocracy.[3] Importantly, in 2019 opposition parties won local elections in several major cities, including the capital, Budapest. This provided evidence for those who maintain that Hungary is still a democracy.

It is highly probable that the changes described here have been facilitated by Hungary being a relatively new and – apparently – fragile democracy. The country has no substantial democratic traditions, and during the seven decades prior to the 1989–1990 regime change, its political system vacillated between different forms of autocracy, limited democracies, and even totalitarian dictatorships.

The introduction to this volume suggests a number of contextual variables that presumably play a role in shaping the outcome which is our primary focus: the illiberal transformation of central government bureaucracy. International links between the central state bureaucracy and other, inter- or transnational actors and networks are relatively weak. Although being a member of the EU inevitably creates a broad range of functional connections between domestic and EU-level administrative actors, liaising with EU counterparts has traditionally been a strongly centralized and tightly overseen function within Hungarian administration. Such connections are restricted to a very limited set of insular administrative entities. Moreover, the Hungarian government has made conscious efforts to weaken existing links, a prime example of which was the Hungarian government's withdrawal from an important and highly visible international network, the Open Government Partnership, in 2016.[4]

Another feature moderating the process of illiberal transformation may be the prevalence of a specific type of bureaucratic expertise. Since at least the nineteenth century, Hungary's bureaucracy has been dominated by an almost exclusive focus on (positive) law and legalistic thinking (Hajnal 2016). This phenomenon may have even grown stronger after the system change of 1989/1990, creating conditions in which politicians' policy initiatives were frequently successfully halted by (senior) civil servants' monopolistic legal-

technocratic expertise. After the 2006 civil service reforms introduced by the second (Socialist-Liberal) Gyurcsány Cabinet under
the banner of "political governance," opportunities for such administrative discretion shrank to some extent. Nevertheless, (senior)
bureaucrats were able to retain significant power to change or
block undesired political actions. The institution of permanent state
secretaries – the central pillar of bureaucratic autonomy – was formally eliminated (Kovács and Hajnal 2017), although it must be
noted that it had long been a de facto political appointment (Ványi
2018). Many long-time and renowned senior administrators left
public service as a result. Thus, the 2010 transformation targeted
a bureaucracy already substantially weakened in terms of expertise
and capacity. Much of the remaining "old-school" administrative
expertise and many of the experts were swept from office shortly
after the administration changed in 2010, when the top four hierarchical levels of central government bureaucracy were almost
entirely purged (Hajnal and Csengődi 2014). Accordingly, instead
of a balanced relationship among government administration, sectoral interests, and socioeconomic actors, all sectors and segments of
governance and many of the socioeconomic arenas had, prior to
2010, been effectively "captured" by political parties, as Meyer-
Sahling and Jáger (2012) put it.

Among Central and Eastern Europe's post-Communist countries,
Hungary's civil service system was the first Western-style, merit-based
one in terms of its symbolic elements and formal components. (In
practice, it operated far less so.) Since its adoption in 1992, it has
been subject to frequent reforms. The stated goals and the rhetoric of
these reforms suggested (until at least 2006, but possibly even until
2010) that an important objective of the reforms was to increase the
merit-based, independent character of the civil service system.
However, careful observation of even these pre-2006 reforms suggests
that, behind the façade of merit-based reforms, increasing political
control by top politicians was subtly exercised and institutionalized
de facto. As mentioned earlier, the 2006 civil service reforms openly
departed from this trend, stressing the importance of a politically
instrumental and increasingly competitive, private-sector-spirited civil
service in several respects. This, presumably, had a direct impact on the
ethos and perception of the role of (in particular, senior) civil servants.
The   general   sentiment   among   practitioners   during   the

2006–2010 period was that experts and expertise no longer enjoyed the same clout.

In addition to the contextual features put forward in the introduction to this volume, we highlight an additional one: namely, the significance of personal relationships, which deserves particular attention since it may not be common to all illiberal regimes. Nonetheless, it was definitely important in Eastern European Communist regimes (Kulcsár 2001). Moreover, this deeply ingrained feature was shown to survive, to a significant extent, the system change and the first decades of democratic development afterwards (Staronova and Gajduschek 2013). Paradoxically, it was able to coexist with overregulation, giving rise to bureaucratic anarchy, since public servants are uncertain which rules or which officer to follow, thereby creating a "deviant bureaucracy" with limited effectiveness (Kulcsár 2001). (For somewhat similar conceptualizations in Western contexts, see Savoie 1999; 2008.)

In summary, Hungary constitutes an arguably exemplary case of an illiberal transformation – not only due to the extent of the change, which has pervaded the political arena and the political system's basic institutions, but also due to the unique set-up and operation of the bureaucratic machinery. It seems, therefore, a potentially insightful exercise to scrutinize the kinds of changes this illiberal transformation has brought to Hungary's central government bureaucracy. In the next section, we describe the empirical approach taken to accomplish this aim.

Data and Method

As explained in the introduction to this chapter, our aim is primarily descriptive and seeks to identify the implications of Hungary's illiberal transformation on its central government bureaucracy. The empirical basis of our study is a set of semistructured interviews conducted with key informants. Although the interviews were prepared as part of a broader research effort, they supplied relevant data for the current research, too. The interviewees were senior civil servants with substantive managerial experience in the central administration spanning the periods both before and after the onset of illiberal transformation (i.e. the pre- and the post-2010 years). We identified interviewees using the authors' personal network, supplemented by snowball sampling.

Note that, in terms of ideological leaning, the first selection criterion leads to a clear bias among respondents. Being a senior manager in the Orbán-era central administration means that the given manager must be (or, at least, must be perceived as) ideologically and politically in line with the governing party. However, given the ambition of our study – acquiring a deep insight into how Orbán-era government bureaucracy operates – we had to accept this bias as inevitable, since key informants with the information and attitudes we wish to uncover have to be in office. We conducted 22 interviews, each of which lasted between 1 and 2 hours. When quoting verbatim, we anonymized certain details in order to avoid exposing respondents' identities.

The descriptive-analytical framework informing our empirical work is slightly different from the one presented in the introduction of this book. More specifically, the interview guidelines inquired into changes regarding centralization, patronage, the role of expertise, external political interference, social dialogue and participation, bureaucratic anarchy, intragovernmental coordination, and bureaucratic resistance after 2010. Here we structure our findings along the analytical categories of the model put forth in this book. For the sake of convenience, we will briefly outline the main analytical categories in the empirical portion at the beginning of each subsection.

Findings

We structure and present our findings along the descriptive-analytical categories outlined in the introduction to this volume. First, we assess the general governance concept informing the illiberal transformation of bureaucracy. Then, we describe the strategy of administrative reforms in terms of structure, resources, personnel, norms, and accountability. Finally, we present how the bureaucracy has reacted to the measures of illiberal transformation.

General Governance Concept

The general governance concept of Bauer et al. (Introduction, this volume) refers to the question of "what the government wants to accomplish regarding the state bureaucracy." Three basic categories are proposed for this variable: sidelining, ignoring, or using bureaucracy. The overall findings of our study indicate that the government has both pursued sidelining and used the bureaucracy. We found hardly any evidence that they ignored it. As the following sections will show, politicization of bureaucracy has been a particularly dominant feature of the illiberal transformation in Hungary. It is mainly this dynamic which has led to the sidelining of bureaucracy and bureaucratic expertise, especially when it comes to policy formulation.

In contrast, the bureaucracy has been used especially for implementing, as opposed to designing, policies. Indeed, several of our respondents thought that the most significant emerging pattern of illiberal governance was the tight, top-down, command-style nature of government apparatuses, totally instrumental to their political masters' will. Note that some of the respondents saw this as a negative feature, while some of them viewed it as a clearly positive one, with yet another subset hesitant to make a choice on the evaluative spectrum.

The most important difference between bureaucracy pre- and post-2010 is the ability to act. I see several negative changes over the past years – nevertheless, this is a great difference. Before 2010, we didn't do anything. ... Once [after 2010] I mentioned to a State Secretary that I came back to the administration with great enthusiasm, but I was highly concerned by this new pattern of pushing everything through [the apparatuses] by sheer force. He replied that if they followed the professional standards and built the [new] system piecemeal, then there would be so many debates, so many chance events that it would tremendously slow down or even halt the process. Rather, he said, we should turn everything upside down and then continue correcting the mistakes afterwards. I do not agree with this – but still, there are many important and good things created this way. [Source 03]

Thus, the biggest virtue of the new emerging bureaucracy is, from a technical and operational perspective, that it is much quicker and operationally more effective:

Everything became much quicker. Many more regulations were created, but at the same time, implementation accelerated, too. If they said something should be done the next day, or some unit should move to another location – in the old days, that would have be impossible to fulfill. The volume of work has grown considerably. Nothing is impossible anymore. ... In the old days, at half past 4, everybody pissed off. Now this is rare; if you have to be there at

10 pm or on weekends, then you do it. Bureaucracy became more flexible, more like the private sector. [Source 05]

At the same time, as the data presented in the following sections will illustrate, the enhanced work ethic is based on fear rather than professional norms or a sense of duty. In 2011, in response to a Constitutional Court verdict that deemed it unconstitutional to fire civil servants without any justification, Parliament modified the law so that firing somebody was possible on such grounds as "lack of loyalty" or "nonconformance with the supervisor's value standards."

However, simultaneously sidelining bureaucracy (for policy formulation) and using it (for policy implementation) does not proceed without tensions. Expectations for bureaucrats to perform instrumentally and the pursuit of effective, military-like administrative operations implies the devaluation of bureaucratic expertise, the weakening of administrative autonomies, and increased political control. The latter phenomena lead to low staff morale and growing turnover (especially among seasoned experts) on the one hand, and uncertainty, lack of initiative, and bureaucratic anarchy on the other. It is far beyond the scope of this chapter to make a general evaluation of a decade of administrative operations in Hungary, but our respondents provided evidence for both patterns: increased effectiveness, especially in terms of implementing policies, and decreased quality of overall governance.

Strategies of Illiberal Administrative Reforms

Structure

Structural change is a key analytic dimension of illiberal reform strategies. We share the expectation that illiberal reforms may seek to strengthen "top-down command and control in central government, reducing horizontal power dispersion and restricting lower-level agency and autonomy" (Bauer et al., Introduction, this volume). Our actual findings corroborate this prediction. Our informants almost unanimously agreed that both formal and informal centralization has taken place within Hungary's central administration. Several sources emphasized, however, that this has been a long-term trend, having started well before 2010. Yet, even they mostly agreed that this tendency certainly received a boost in the past decade. Centralization occurred on several levels. The cabinet consists of a smaller number of ministries and ministers. "Super-ministries" were created by integrating several previously independent ministries. This centralization further strengthened the position of the prime minister: "Nowadays those closer to the political core – that is, the prime minister – can decide even against the sectorial [that is, ministerial] intentions" [Source 05].

Centralization happened not only among, but inside the administrative organizations, too: "Before, department heads had their own autonomy and even budget; but nowadays, this is unimaginable. This is the trend everywhere in the administration" [Source 05]. As this quote illustrates, one important aspect of centralization was controlling the budget and other resources. (We will elaborate more on this in the next section.) Other important motives of centralization seem to be a general distrust of bureaucracy and a desire for more control over the entire apparatus. "The real motive is that leaders want more control [over the bureaucracy], and greater distance means less control. This reflects a lack of trust" [Source 10].

Several respondents noted that centralization is not only a formal, top-down process, but also an informal, bottom-up process, in which lower administrative levels abandon the responsibility of making decisions.

It's probable that the department head does not dare to decide and passes the decision upward. The deputy state secretary does the same in turn ... in the old days, you didn't have this. If a mistake was made, the person wasn't finished. But now everyone is scared. If they do something improper, they will be fired. ... I cannot imagine Orbán saying, "Hey, I want to decide on everything." [Source 17]

Several respondents mentioned the fear of being laid off as a motive for risk avoidance, which in turn fuels informal centralization: "This is a tendency. If fear is part of the game, then decisions start to ride up the hierarchy, because everybody is taking precautions ... Before, people [working in the central administration] did not feel so vulnerable; they were not scared. Colleagues with expertise had high esteem, but today they are easily fired" [Source 13].

Respondents also see centralization as an instrument of effective governance: "They see this as a guarantee that political aims don't get halted by the apparatus. This is how you can control implementation the best. And it works, indeed. Look at the EKÁER [national system of road transport control], the case of online cash registers, the wall on the southern border [as examples of effective policy implementation]" [Source 01]. However, others are more skeptical concerning the effectiveness of centralization: "Everything is extremely centralized, even where it should not be. ... There is never enough information in the center" [Source 11]. Centralization often leads to an overload at the higher levels of the hierarchy: "I participated in a cabinet meeting where the agenda consisted of 400 items. That is insane, absurd. The prime minister has to decide over them whether he likes it or not" [Source 17].

Despite being a general trend, centralization is not uniform across policy areas and institutions:

It depends on the topic. Where there is strong political interest, it is very strong; where it is neither politically nor financially important, it is low. Still, in the end, it doesn't matter, since nothing happens in these areas, anyway. ... What is important is EU funds, transport, this migration bullshit – this is a political thing – and the media. What are not important are social affairs ... human policies in general, and rural policy. [Source 09]

This opinion illustrates that centralization is a deeply political process: "Important decisions have been extremely centralized" [Source 09]. However, some respondents held that centralization has depended to a great extent on the leaders (ministers and state secretaries) in question, some of whom were less prone to increase control over subordinates.

Resources
In terms of resources, the analytical framework expects illiberal changes to lead to "steering administrative conduct through allocation of funds as well as administrative and informational resources – for instance, weakening specific units by reducing funds and staff numbers, leaving them out of information loops, or impairing their work by imposing excessive administrative demands" (Bauer et al., Introduction, this volume).

Our main findings here – consistently pointing to the immense importance of resources in shaping the landscape of illiberal government bureaucracy – are twofold. First, politicians' quest to control resources is a crucial driver of the most visible change in government bureaucracy – namely, centralization, as described in the previous sub-section. Second, resource allocation decisions and patterns are, to a noticeable extent, driven by the intention to channel public funds to government-friendly economic and financial actors or circles.

As to the former finding, we have already highlighted the view held by several respondents that centralization is motivated by the urge to control the flow of money, especially the huge funds originating from the EU. The inflow of money has increased gradually since Hungary's accession to the EU (2004), but it sped up even more in later years. Centralization has followed that trend closely: "Till the accession to the EU, the dominant concepts were decentralization, subsidiarity, and MLG [multilevel governance]. Starting in 2006, the wind began to change, especially in the field of cohesion policy ... After 2010, a total breakthrough [of centralization] happened" [Source 16]. Centralization does not only affect EU funds and external contracts – that is, inward and outward flows of money. The financial autonomy of lower-level administrative units and their leaders have also been cur-tailed: "It is in the law that a deputy state secretary cannot decide over more than 3 billion forints without asking consent from the govern-ment. But before, that amount was 5 billion" [Source 12].

A peculiar feature related to resource allocation is that, contrary to the once-entrenched "traditions" of bureaucratic and political bargain-ing, decisions on resources are made with increasing ease, including those that affect funds and budgets: "In the old days it was impossible to imagine that the state secretary of the [core-of-government ministry] would receive ministers, one every 30 minutes, to agree about the budget plan" [Source 05].

Turning to the second finding on the role of channeling funds, we should keep in mind that Hungary is among the worst-performing countries in the EU in terms of corruption control.[5] In the past ten years, the overall trend in corruption has worsened. Patterns of corrup-tion, "crony capitalism," and the "predatory state" in Hungary have been addressed at length in the scholarly literature (e.g. Bozóki 2015; Scheiring 2019). Analyses highlight that the Hungarian government has effectively been able to channel large amounts of EU funds to businesses and business-people close to the governing party and to the Prime Minister himself (Becker 2017). These funds have been used to create a new economic elite which, in turn, has supported the political objectives of the government – for instance, by overtaking formerly independent media outlets and transforming them into pro-governmental media. Not surprisingly, our informants have similar views on how the government uses its power to strategically allocate resources to their allies: "The reasons [behind centralization] are manifold, like supporting the development of a 'national bourgeoisie' and channeling the funds where politics want" [Source 16].

A noteworthy mechanism of such channeling is "gray eminencies" or "consiglieri." These are trustees of powerful political or economic actors who possess no formal office or position; still, they are deeply involved in strategic and day-to-day decision-making. This was confirmed by several respondents: "The minister had an adviser who appeared in meetings. When he was there, everything happened as he wanted, regardless of whether state secretaries were present" [Source 10]; "What often happens is someone, an outsider, appears at the ministry and tells us what to do, giving orders to the leaders and disregarding administrative rules" [Source 05].

At the same time, most interviewees agreed that trustees of this sort have long existed, still, the number of respondents indicating a qualitative change is significant. Putting this together, our interpretation is that, from the perspective of bureaucratic operations, the change appears to be qualitative and twofold. Whereas the amount of influence exerted by economic and political "influencers," as perceived by respondents, might not have changed significantly, respondents perceive a merger of political and economic elites, an increased centralization in the network of "gray eminencies," as opposed to the pluralism of earlier years.

Personnel

Changes to civil service personnel refers to "ideological cleansing of staff by intensifying patronage in recruitment and career progression beyond 'normal' spoils behavior, while weakening meritocratic and representative factors in personnel policy through excessive exhaustion of available or introduction of new politicization instruments" (Bauer et al., Introduction, this volume). In terms of such personnel changes, we expected, in particular, a rise in the type of patronage based on personal confidential relations (as opposed to patronage based on ideological or political loyalty). Our sources corroborated both our expectations. Most respondents agreed that there was a sharp increase in patronage from 2010 on: "[The year]

2010 was the other turning point. Even I was fired, although I hadn't thought I had any reason to be scared. FIDESZ party cadres from the second and third ranks flooded the ministries" [Source 01]. An important point is that the strengthening of client-oriented networks in the 2010s is tied to the long incumbency of government: "After 12 years [i.e., from 2010 to 2022, three parliamentary cycles], it extends down to the level of schoolteachers. ... Not only the ministries, but the entire public sector. The situation is deteriorating, because earlier client-oriented networks were thrown out every four years, but now they can reach deep down" [Source 01].

Panizza, Peters, and Ramos Larraburu (2019) present a typology of patronage involving another dimension. In addition to the type of loyalty (partisan or personal), they consider the type of expected competence, where the possible categories are "professional" or "political." In terms of the former dimension, it seems that personal loyalty is becoming increasingly important:

It's rather personal – common past, common life experience, or economic and financial dependence. ... They went to school together, play football together. ... You can see the importance of personal loyalty by looking at how cadres move across organizations. If Boss X is placed somewhere, then all the people associated with Boss X also move and fill the lower-level positions. When the boss is moved to another place, then the subordinates go, too. [Source 01]

While personal loyalty is the dominant pattern, political loyalty is not irrelevant; rather, it is the bottom line: "It has clearly shifted to personal loyalty from 2010 on. Political loyalty is the starting point. At the very minimum, you should not be seen as rejecting it. When I hire someone, they check their Facebook profile; if the candidate likes opposition-type stuff, then forget it" [Source 10]. As for the second dimension, responses to our questions on the role and importance of expertise suggest that, apart from a limited set of technical areas, the role of professional competence has heavily declined: "[Politicians show] an emotional hostility toward expertise and institutions. It is forbidden for younger colleagues to learn from more seasoned ones. ... The very existence of independent experts is the problem" [Source 02]. Under such conditions, political competence – understood here as the ability to correctly perceive and identify with politicians' formal and informal expectations – became a gold standard:

[After 2010], you felt an unbridgeable rift between professionals and politicians. As civil servants representing professional knowledge, up to the level of deputy state secretary, we were unable to communicate to politicians what we considered important. Politicians, on the other hand, did not trust us. They deemed our proposals weak, politically pale … Distrust gradually grew. [Source 03]

Concerning the required competencies, our interviewees pointed to a contradiction, nevertheless. While, first and foremost, the bureaucracy is expected to deliver outcomes – which, in principle, requires expertise – obedience seems to be the most important expectation, which may run counter to technocratic considerations. As a consequence, the role of bureaucratic, legal, technical, and substantive policy expertise has clearly weakened since 2010. The downgrading of expertise is a means to substitute centralized and command-driven operations for autonomous and critical bureaucratic thinking and action: "Whereas, in 2003, a section head was a serious person with significant impact, by 2013 that person has become a manager of a group in charge of technical implementation" [Source 03]. Hostility to experts and expertise partly comes from the dominance of political considerations:

If you transform, say, the education system so that every single education expert criticizes it, then it's certain it's not OK. [But now] everything is subordinate to political benefits … An important element in overturning the rules of the game was that an MP could not hand in [to Parliament] a bill without first having it checked from the bureaucratic point of view. But after 2010, this oversight role of the bureaucracy ceased to exist. Somebody walks in with it [a legislative proposal], and next day it becomes law. In the old days, that couldn't have happened. There was, at least, some process to determine whether it conflicts with EU law or what the profession has to say about it. [Source 05]

Closely linked to the mechanisms described earlier, a new feature of central administration can be seen to be emerging. It is compounded by elements such as low esteem, low professional autonomy, and civil servants' low salaries: "Bureaucrats don't feel good. This is for sure. Everywhere. It is not an elevating experience to work here. Neither society nor the government respects them – so they don't feel they are empowered to make the decisions they are supposed to make ... They just don't care" [Source 15]. Not surprisingly, as a result the civil service faces recruitment problems and high turnover:

The prestige of being a civil servant is constantly deteriorating, and it is more and more difficult to find good professionals. Nowadays, it is mostly only young beginners we can hire, no seasoned experts. ... No matter how nice the [official] rhetoric is, the 30 percent yearly turnover you see in territorial administration is not healthy. But even here, in the Ministry of X, we have around 20 percent yearly turnover. [Source 07]

Norms

The analytical framework proposes to gauge changes to bureaucratic norms. Here, the expectation is that the administrative culture is committed "to the new ideological order by undermining the official neutrality of the bureaucracy or emphasizing its instrumental character through, for instance, exercising informal pressure on staff" (Bauer et al., Introduction, this volume). While we share this expectation, we add an additional one – namely, increasing bureaucratic anarchy. Taking into consideration the specifics of the Hungarian context, we assumed that downplaying expertise (in particular, bureaucratic expertise) while emphasizing extremely centralized, top-down policy and management style (in combination with an overload of tasks, informal political control mechanisms, and anti-institutional attitudes) would lead to frequent overstepping of formal rules and procedures that normally regulate the operations of bureaucracy. That is, we expected an erosion of traditional bureaucratic norms, a kind of anomie, and therefore an increase in bureaucratic anarchy. Again, these expectations were corroborated.

The norms governing expectations regarding political and personal loyalty to politicians constitute an important subset of bureaucratic norms. We have, however, already discussed these above. In addition, it seems that military-like discipline and execution of orders have gradually become the dominant norm in administration. Some respondents indicated that voicing any concerns or criticisms about decisions or plans has been construed as pettifogging, disobedience, or disloyalty: "In 2008, you could write down your point if you did not agree with a decision, but now this is not allowed. I had a disagreement with a deputy state secretary, and I asked him for permission to provide a written statement, but he said that my opinion was not needed" [Source 05].

Distrust from leaders has bred uncertainty and risk aversion in the lower ranks, while it has also reinforced the centralization tendencies that cause leaders to become overloaded. Although some of the respondents perceive the increasingly anarchic operations as a long-term trend rather than a feature of post-2010 changes, some of our sources' accounts resemble satirical depictions of bureaucracy:

It has gotten worse; it is increasingly unpredictable. And increasingly frustrating. They do this and that, and there are idiots all over. Deputy state secretaries are really like idiots. There is no work plan, and everybody deals with whatever happens to be the most critical issue to solve at that given second. They are all scared to death, that's why. They organize an interministerial coordination meeting. But there is no official invitation, no agenda, so there are twelve people talking all kinds of bullshit. After 45 minutes, two of them stand up and say, "Sorry, we think we came for another meeting," and they leave. This is an average working day at the ministry. [Source 06]

Accounts of bureaucratic operations similar to this were recurrent in the interviews. Ten out of the twenty-two respondents held that bureaucratic anarchy has increased since 2010. Anarchy, as the above quote suggests, is closely tied, in part, to civil servants' defensive, risk-avoiding behavior on the one hand, and superiors' want-it-all attitude on the other. In addition, however, anarchy is also tightly linked to the lack of expertise, as discussed earlier: "[As a result of the disregard for expertise], the policy process is increasingly hectic. Legal regulations change more frequently, and there is a general uncertainty in public administration. You suddenly receive the task of writing up a proposal within an hour. This kind of thing permeates the everyday life of bureaucracy" [Source 10].

Accountability

Changes in accountability patterns are to be expected, too, such as the reduction in "societal participation and responsibilities of service agencies vis-à-vis the parliament and other external controls, cutting back transparency and exchange of information with third parties, and restricting media access" (Bauer et al., Introduction, this volume).

Several of our respondents confirmed that there is a conscious move on the government's part to limit the scope of societal participation and to exclude "unfriendly" actors from the process:

The real change [since 2010] is that effective participation has decreased ... I do not involve the chamber of judges or public notaries in either policy formulation or implementation anymore. They create working groups, but this is more of a token gesture. I put the bill on the website, and there is a box to check [for public participation]. [Source 04]

Participatory features and social consultation have lost relevance, but they have not formally disappeared entirely. Rather, they have increasingly become a kind of ritual:

Previously it was like the apparatus announced that they want to consult the car industry. But now you cannot put forward any partner that does not enjoy strategic partner status. There is actually a list ... For example, at [Ministry X], a total of 150 partners were listed. In the education sector, however, you have only 20 organizations, and you can only consult with them. [Source 10]

Several respondents noted the new phenomenon of quasi-NGOs created by the government, in order to participate in the formalistic quasi-consultations mentioned earlier:

In order to demonstrate that basic requirements of the rule of law are met, they started to create, in every area, "appropriate" interest-representing actors. They do not have any influence on the decisions. Instead, they only legitimize the [government's] decisions. They know what they have to say. For example, it is the government who appoints the leader of body representing civil servant's interests. ... They only consult those that they know, in advance, will agree. [Source 05]

Even the government-friendly societal partners are constantly forced to support the government's cause due to the threat having their funding withheld:

It has happened, and it is happening nowadays, too, that the leaders [of two well-known NGOs advocating family policy issues] have to come to the fore when there is a political conflict. They have to formulate their opinions in public, since they are paid government grants. If they are not willing to participate, then we cut off their funding. ... In the old days, there was no state subsidy, so everyone could say what they wanted. Now you can only become a social partner if you are strongly committed to the government. [Source 15]

Reactions

In terms of bureaucratic reactions, the analytical framework identifies three possible reactions of the bureaucrats to the challenges of illiberal governance: working, shirking, or sabotage. Whereas our interviews did not address these strategies explicitly, we asked our interviewees about one particular aspect: bureaucratic resistance. Our expectation was that bureaucratic resistance has decreased or has even been eliminated. (Note our earlier discussion of drastically reduced labor rights and protections for civil servants.)

Our respondents see a decrease in the bureaucracy's ability to resist, let alone alter, their political masters' will. The elimination of bureaucratic resistance is closely intertwined with the elimination of expertise – bureaucracy's main resource to rely on when resisting – and the rise of patronage, the latter being the primary means of getting rid of bureaucratic experts:

In the old days, I used to know many more people who could offer some very stiff resistance. In the Ministry X, there are one or two of them left; however, these days, I just cannot imagine that you'd have a well-prepared, experienced old-timer who does not wholeheartedly support the official policy and still remains in a position of section head. No way, that person would be sacked. [Source 05]

In 2010, they started to eliminate the resistance … They brought in partisan loyalists. They are stupid as hell. They used to be out pasting up billboards [during the electoral campaign], but they execute the central orders they are given. [Source 06]

Our interviewees have not experienced instances of anything that could be considered direct sabotage. One respondent argued that resistance has always been very mild: "The bureaucracy has always known its place. It's been extremely rare that someone from the administration would have opposed the intentions of the government. I don't really see any change in this, because it's always been very sparse" [Source 14].

We could, however, identify signs of shirking in terms of bureaucrats' risk aversion and the bottom-up drive of centralization that we presented earlier. Since public servants are often uncertain when it comes to political expectations and do not dare to make mistakes, they tend to minimize their contribution, avoid showing any initiative, and delegate any responsibility to the higher levels of the administration.

The respondents indicated two dominant strategies of public servants: working (loyalty) or leaving (exit). As we presented earlier, since 2010, both the quantity and the pace of the work have substantially increased. Bureaucrats have been forced to adapt to the new conditions. However, the high rate of turnover signals that many were dissatisfied and chose to leave public service: "This is a change compared to previous times. Those who cannot adapt to the rhythm will sooner or later leave. This is new" [Source 13].

Summary of the Findings

In the foregoing sections, we presented our main findings on patterns and effects of illiberal transformation within Hungary's bureaucracy. Our data come from twenty-two interviews that we conducted among senior officers who have served in the central administration both before and after the start of illiberal reforms (2010). Although the interview guidelines we used were based on slightly different analytical categories than the model ones put forth in this book, for the purposes of this chapter we structured our findings according to the book's analytical categories.

We found that, out of the three general governance concepts proposed, ignoring bureaucracy does not apply to the case of Hungary. The general patterns that emerged are sidelining bureaucracy (especially with regard to policy formulation) and using it (during the implementation phase).

The main structural feature of the transformation is the extreme level of formal as well as informal centralization, both at all levels of government and inside the ministries. This is in line with the expectations of the model. Centralization was driven by a will to exert better control over the bureaucrats. Meanwhile, the perceived need to control was fueled by distrust toward the administration, the strengthened role of political considerations, and growing expectations of political loyalty, as well as the aim of enhanced efficacy. However, the results are mixed concerning the latter objective. Although implementation became more effective, the general quality of policies probably decreased. We also identified the mechanism of bottom-up centralization. Since lower-

rank bureaucrats are increasingly uncertain about political expectations, they tend to minimize initiatives, avoid responsibility, and
push decisions upwards.

Concerning the peculiarities of resource allocation, we found that
centralization was also driven by the quest to control resources better,
while the allocation of funds is affected to a large extent by the logic of
crony capitalism and the intention to channel those funds to "appropriate" recipients. In terms of personnel policies, the most important
pattern seems to be that of patronage – very extensive and strong, even
when compared to the pre-existing, already highly politicized civil
service. Patronage is based on personal loyalties, although political
loyalty is also important as a minimum condition. The expected competence is harder to identify. Apparently, the main expectation for
senior bureaucrats is a kind of political competence, in terms of being
able to recognize the formal and actual expectations of the political
masters and to execute them unquestioningly in minute detail. We also
found a general distrust for bureaucracy, especially in relation to its
expertise. These findings corroborate the expectations of the model.
Another feature of personnel under Hungarian illiberal governance is
the general discontent and frustration of public servants. This stems
from low esteem, low salaries, and the excessive workload. These features have led to high turnover in the ranks of the central administration,
especially among senior officers and experts, as well as an influx of
young, inexperienced recruits.

Concerning norms and bureaucratic culture, we identified the trend
of politicization suppressing the classic bureaucratic culture and ethos,
the decline of expertise, and the spread of military-type discipline.
Raising concerns or arguing against policy proposals by bureaucrats
has become unwelcome. Rising top-down expectations, coupled with
reduced autonomy and growing uncertainty at the bottom, lead to an
increase in bureaucratic anarchy.

We raised the issue of accountability in our interviews in relation to
public participation in the policy process. In line with the expectations
of the model, we found that participative venues have been eroded, on
the one hand, and consultations have become mere rituals with the
selective participation of progovernmental social actors, on the other.

Finally, in our interviews, we inquired about bureaucratic resistance
as a possible reaction of civil servants to illiberal governance. We found
that resistance was virtually nonexistent, and our respondents did not

give any accounts of sabotage. Although shirking is present – see, for instance, the aforementioned bottom-up centralization – the dominant pattern among public servants in Hungary seems to be either working (loyalty) or leaving (exit).

Conclusion

Hungary is a case of populist illiberal transformation. This affects the organization and operation of the central state administration, and our research seeks to shed light on the patterns emerging in government bureaucracy as a result of illiberal transformation. In this chapter, we presented our findings along the analytical categories of the model developed in the introduction to this volume. By applying the model to Hungary's case, our aim was to examine whether the model offers a useful and meaningful framework for studying the phenomenon of illiberal administrative reforms.

The results of our findings were rather reassuring in terms of the empirical relevance and descriptive power of the framework proposed in this book. The model offered a meaningful rubric for studying and interpreting illiberal administrative reforms in Hungary. Furthermore, the expectations based on the model were corroborated by our empirical data. However, two peculiarities of the Hungarian case certainly deserve attention when interpreting the results: first, the fact that Hungary is a new and fragile democracy with a strong autocratic historical legacy; and, second, the length, depth, and unconstrained nature of the illiberal changes since 2010. Probably not unrelated to these political context features, Viktor Orbán's personal governing style, based on an uncompromising use of power, should also be considered a potentially important factor. These peculiarities make Hungary an extreme case and may explain some of the findings.

We believe this is the case, especially in light of the bureaucracy's responses to the illiberal turn. Remarkably, in the course of the interviews, we have not encountered any evidence of instances of bureaucratic resistance, not even meager ones – nothing that compares to the anecdotes told by Donald Trump's aides, who tried to obstruct or manipulate the President's decisions (Anonymous 2019). We assume that this almost complete absence of bureaucratic resistance is attributable to Hungary's autocratic traditions of, and the government's politically unconstrained implementation of, an illiberal transformation agenda. Tellingly, the administration used its comfortable constitutional majority in Parliament to modify the law regarding public servants immediately after coming to power (and several additional times later). These modifications resulted in a wholesale elimination of civil servants' special labor protections while identifying loyalty as an explicit requirement of employment (and, consequently, its lack as a basis for dismissal). We assume that this is not necessarily an aspect of illiberal tendencies, especially in less fragile democracies.

Notes

1. See www.youtube.com/watch?v=PXP-6n1G8ls (downloaded on March 10, 2020); for a summary in English, see e.g. www.ft.com/cms/s/0/0574f7f2-17f3-11e4-b842-00144feabdc0.html#axzz3ExyGRrtE.
2. To reference briefly some events that have occurred since the field research and that further strengthen our point, in particular, some government reactions to the COVID-19 pandemic deserve mentioning. Internationally, the most visible element of these measures was the adoption of the so-called Authorization Act on March 30, 2020, allowing the government to overrule parliamentary acts without any functional or time limitations, without any debate in Parliament, and without any guarantee for immediate and effective constitutional review.
3. In its 2020 report, the V-Dem Institute described Hungary as an "electoral autocracy," the only one in the EU. See www.v-dem.net/media/filer_public/de/39/de39af54-0bc5-4421-89ae-fb20dcc53dba/democracy_report.pdf (downloaded on March 24, 2020). Two months later, Freedom House classified Hungary, for the first time, as a hybrid regime. See https://freedomhouse.org/sites/default/files/2020-04/05062020_FH_NIT2020_vfinal.pdf (downloaded on May 27, 2020).
4. www.opengovpartnership.org/hungary-withdrawn/ (last accessed September 20, 2020).
5. See the data of Transparency International (https://www.transparency.org/country/HUN# – downloaded on March 28, 2020) and the World Wide Governance Indicators (https://info.worldbank.org/governance/wgi/Home/Reports – downloaded on March 28, 2020).

5 Public Administration in Poland in the Times of Populist Drift

STANISŁAW MAZUR

Introduction

Since 2015, when the so-called United Right[1] came to power in the wake of democratic elections, Polish public administration has been subject to a number of unsettling changes. The theoretical approach applied to the example of democratic backsliding which appears in this chapter is based on the concepts of competition of ideas and ideational disruption. The latter is understood in terms of a reconfiguration of the hierarchy of ideas that triggers institutional change and entails a normative reorientation of key actors toward the prevailing ideas of the day. The source of such a reorientation may be objective reasoning, which emphasizes the disadvantage of retaining certain institutions and the resultant distribution of benefits (e.g. status, material benefits), as well as the emergence of new, competitive, interpretative frameworks which redefine the rules of the social game, including changes in governance and coordination arrangements.

It tends to be assumed that the basic reason for both the rise and fall of institutions is the nature of their relationship with ideas. The litmus test of such a competition of ideas is the strength and durability of their impact on institutions. The latter, in turn, determine the shape and mechanisms of public administration (Mazur 2020).

This chapter begins with an overview of the characteristics of Poland's public administration, with a special emphasis on those features that affect its attitudes toward the dismantling of the liberal-democratic law-governed state. Next, the approach of the PiS (Law and Justice) government to the issues of governance is analyzed using the conceptual framework presented in the introductory chapter of this book, specifically how the PiS government's illiberal policy affects public administration. The impact of external factors on this policy is discussed in the subsequent section. The final section explores further implications of findings from the study, which draws extensively on literature analysis, reports and expert opinions, and data from interviews with civil servants, as well as direct observations made by the authors resulting from their involvement in the process of modernization of public administration in Poland.

The Theoretical Perspective

From Systemic Transformation to Democratic Consolidation

The fast pace at which the principles of the liberal-democratic law-governed state are being dismantled suggests that the process should be studied using the concepts of competition of ideas and ideational disruptions. It appears that without digging into deeper strata of culture, and without adopting a broader historical perspective, reading this process would be superficial and perhaps even misleading. Undoubtedly, in the case of the evolution of the legal and political order in Poland, the impact of path dependence on the process of change is evident, which applies especially to ideas strongly rooted in the sphere of culture.

Ideas

Three great political ideas informed the unique political transformation of Poland initiated at the turn of the 1980s and 1990s: namely, the democratic law-governed state, the market economy, and the civil society. They inspired the collective imagination, triggered social mobilization, and provided a signpost for reformers. They shaped the framework for a liberal-democratic law-governed state and, at the same time, laid the foundations for Poland's full-fledged presence in the Western world thanks to its membership in NATO (the idea of security) and accession to the European Union (the idea of Europeanization) (Mazur 2020).

Institutions

As a result of the political transformation that took place in the first half of the 1990s, authoritarian institutions were replaced by democratic ones – that is, free elections, freedom of speech, transition of power, and the rules for balancing powers superseded the single authority typical of the former system. The system of governance was decentralized through the establishment of local government. In one fell swoop, the economy was radically restructured; as a result of deregulation, liberalization, and privatization the state monopolies collapsed and the private sector became free to develop.

During this political transformation, the basis for the establishment of a modern administrative apparatus was also created, the democratic legal-administrative order was established, local government was instituted, fiscal rules were introduced in the public finance system, and measures were taken to build an efficient public administration (Mazur 2020).

Ideational Disruption

The consequences of the changes that took place in Poland from the fall of the communist regime to EU accession included two instances of ideational disruption. In the first, the ideas of a democratic law-governed state, market economy, and civil society came to dominate the market of ideas, which led to the supremacy of the institutional order rooted in them. The other disruption was associated with Poland's geopolitical about-turn toward the West and meant that the reformed institutional order became, at least formally, comparable to that shared by the EU member states.

Each of these disruptions played a crucial role in changing Poland's development trajectories and in modernizing its administration. The latter quickly became similar to modern administrations in terms of its rules of operation as well as its organizational and functional structures, despite the fact that the process of improving the effectiveness and efficiency of its operation progressed rather slowly (Mazur 2020).

From a Democratic Order to an Illiberal Democracy?

Ideas

Soon after Poland's accession to the EU, new ideas began to emerge in its public space. The ideological reorientation of a part of the political elite was due to a number of interrelated phenomena, including the high socioeconomic costs of political transformation, dissatisfaction with the distribution of economic benefits, disillusionment with democracy and the quality of the political class, as well as the unful-filled expectations of EU membership due to its originally idealized image. They also invoked historical heritage and various mechanisms of governance, including those rejected in the early 1990s, such as illiberal democracy, anti-EU sentiments, and state interventionism.

At its core, the idea of illiberal democracy consists in contesting the liberal order and its attendant institutional arrangement, as reflected in questioning such principles as the rule of law or respect for minority rights and the glorification of majority rule. This is accompanied by attempts to restrict the autonomy of previously independent institutions (e.g. constitutional courts, general courts) and to gain political control over public media.

Anti-EU sentiments manifest themselves as reservations about the values and standards endorsed by European institutions, which allegedly threaten traditional values, leading to a loss of sovereignty of nation states and the transformation of the EU into a federal organization. Poland's ruling coalition stands united by a deep-seated fear that the EU is on the verge of transforming into precisely such a structure. These concerns are rooted in the belief, widely shared by PiS leaders, that Poland's sovereignty will be undermined by deeper European integration, and specifically by the obligation to delegate a range of the government's decision-making powers to EU institutions.

Lastly, the concept of economic interventionism demands broader state involvement and ownership in the economy. Its consequences include, among others, political clientelism and political corruption. The idea of interventionism is also associated with centralization, which weakens the political position of local governments (Mazur 2020).

Institutions

Formal checks and balances still remain in place in Poland; however, what appears to be the main threat to liberal democracy and the rule of law is the violation of the Constitution and its de facto modification by what one may call its creative interpretations by the president, the cabinet, and the parliament. Such interpretations serve to concentrate power in the hands of the ruling party (Dostal et al. 2018, p. 24), as do the radical changes to the judicial system that undermine its independence and European standards in this respect (SGI 2018, p. 184).

Anti-EU sentiments are expressed via the PiS government's criticism of EU institutions and their policies, which allegedly endorse federalist solutions threatening the sovereignty of nation states. A particularly fierce dispute between Poland and the EU concerns issues associated with respect for the rule of law.

In the practice of governance, the idea of nationalization is reflected in the formal strengthening of the central government and increasing state interventionism. This leads to an intensive politicization of the economy, which, among other things, results in its tighter control by those in power. As The Economist's (2018) commentators noted, "'Repolonization' has become a buzzword under PiS, applied to everything from shipbuilding to medicines." As the economy becomes renationalized, numerous positions in state enterprises are filled by members and supporters of the ruling party. Another example of this trend includes limiting the powers of local governments and their revenue sources. As a result, their financial standing is deteriorating, as is the quality of public services they are expected to provide. This is particularly evident in local governments run by politicians who are members of parties in opposition to the ruling coalition.

Changes also affect the institutional sphere of the NGO sector. The PiS government attempts to discredit nongovernmental organizations, especially those financially supported by foreign donors, and to that effect it has enacted measures to control their funding sources. On the other hand, organizations and the media that openly side with PiS receive more support and see their profile raised.

Ideational Disruption

The present events in Poland reveal three kinds of ideational disruptions. The first is associated with the implementation of solutions typical of an illiberal democracy and leads to a reconstitution of the institutional order in the sphere of governance, including the violation of the principle of separation of powers; curbing the autonomy of various independent bodies, including the judiciary; and the subordination of the public media.

The second ideational disruption involves anti-EU sentiments. As its practical consequence, the values and principles espoused by the EU, particularly the rule of law, are violated, and some of its policies, including migration policy, are routinely challenged.

In the normative sphere, the third disruption, nationalization, embodies a longing for an omnipotent state. In the practice of governance, its effects include strengthening the central government's powers, increased state involvement in the economic sphere, state capture, colonization of the administrative apparatus and its politicization, as well as the weakening of local governments (Mazur 2020).

These ideational disruptions, which have found fertile social ground, are catalyzed by political leaders who skillfully communicate with the public using populist rhetoric and national resentment. They constitute a specific group of political entrepreneurs capable of generating new political ideas and of seducing the public with sufficient sway to effect further ideational disruptions (Pakulski 2016).

Equally common and destructive for the institutional order of the democratic system is the instrumentalization of institutions, which involves their subordination to the current objectives of the ruling party. As a result, institutions become weapons in the political struggle that serve to control and capture the state in the name of its radical reconstruction (Mazur, Możdżeń, and Oramus 2018).

The scale and intensity of these phenomena in Poland may lead to institutional regression and the dismantling of the democratic model of governance (Rupnik 2007), resulting in the emergence of an oligarchic administration, in which political loyalty prevails over competence, the public interest is identified with that of the ruling party, and the rule of law is distorted by its instrumentalization. The consolidation of the oligarchic administration model would, in fact, undermine what has been achieved so far in terms of building an efficient and effective public administration based on the principles of a democratic law-governed state.

Characteristics of Public Administration in Poland

Understanding the nature of Poland's public administration requires a brief mention of the legacy of the real socialist era (1945–1989) and the changes which have taken place over the last thirty years. In each of these historical periods, certain processes heavily influenced specific features of the administration deemed important for understanding its attitude toward the erosion of the liberal-democratic law-governed state.

In the times of real socialism (1945–1989), the distinguishing features of the centralized and bureaucratic administrative apparatus subordinated to the party included low competencies of the clerical staff, bureaucratization, nomenklatura, arbitrariness, personalization, corruption, inefficiency and ineffectiveness, domination of informal interdepartmental contacts, and highly constructivistically conceived development planning. Loyalty to the ruling party became the basic criterion for evaluation and promotion (Mazur and Hausner 2010).

After Poland regained its independence in 1989, the malfunctioning administration inherited from the previous system had to be radically reconstructed in terms of both remit and manner of operation. The principles of the democratic rule of law were introduced; the uniform, hierarchical organization of the administrative apparatus in force during the People's Republic of Poland was abolished; and local government was instituted. The mechanism of party administration and its hegemony with respect to the administrative apparatus of the state was, at least formally, eliminated.

The year 2015 saw the resurgence of a strong belief in the importance of political patronage for careers in public administration, especially the power of maintaining personal relations with political leaders, which dates back to real socialism. Under communist rule, these relations were considered crucial for building one's career as an official. This attitude, albeit in a much weaker form, was also discernible after 1989, but has become commonplace since PiS came to power in 2015. In the era of real socialism, the mechanisms of centralized, hierarchical management and the domination of a single political party in the state governance system, including the sphere of public administration, were strongly entrenched. Currently, this mode of managing the state is being revived, as is the instrumentalization of law for political purposes and its inevitable low quality. The latter was an almost universal feature of legislation in the People's Republic of Poland. Even though this trend subsided after 1989, the quality of law-making still remains unsatisfactory. However, since 2015, we have witnessed both a progressive instrumentalization of law as it pertains to public administration and a sharp deterioration in its quality.

The Attitude of the PiS Government Toward Public Administration

The PiS government's attitude toward the Civil Service can be best described as sidelining (i.e. weakening of the Civil Service). It is based on the particular distrust which PiS politicians hold toward high-ranking officials, who are perceived as members of an elite corps which is not working in the best interests of the state. In consequence, any implemented changes put forward by PiS are intended to fully subordinate the institution in question to the ruling party. Examples of such measures include mass replacements of managers, the abolition of competition for recruitment to senior positions, and the general lowering of standards expected to be met by appointees (Kopińska 2018). Vacancies are filled according to the criterion of political loyalty, a practice aggravated by amoral familism (Banfield 1958), which involves employing the relatives of prominent ruling party members in public administration. Nevertheless, the kind of patronage favored by PiS permits fairly effective governance owing to the strong loyalty of the nominees to the ruling elite of the party and its ideology, and, as a result, their determination to achieve the goals set by the government.

Another measure aimed at weakening the position of public administration, especially its segments perceived as too independent of the government, is to create new offices that carry out tasks concurrently or previously performed by well-established institutions (e.g. the National Institute of Freedom – Civil Society Development Centre, the Government Plenipotentiary for Human Rights). PiS also weakens public administration by creating quasi-business agencies entrusted with tasks previously executed, at least to some extent, by public administration (Polish Investment and Trade Agency, Polish Development Fund, National Property Stock). Their management is entrusted to representatives of the private sector, which is a paradox given the government's rhetoric about corrupt elites of which these managers ostensibly are part.

The attitude of PiS leaders toward the staffing of senior positions in the Civil Service stems from the belief that the will of a political leader – which materializes thanks to the avant-garde of the political movement consisting of his most trusted and closest associates – is more important to the process of governance than any formalized rules of operation. The rationale behind this is that the Civil Service in general, and its high-ranking officials in particular, tends not to support populist and illiberal governments. The situation can only be remedied by the concentration of power and the domination of the political factor in formulating and implementing public policies. To that end, key decisions should be made by a narrow group of party activists and political advisers to the Prime Minister. Such an approach reveals the hostility of the PiS leadership toward established governance institutions, which they perceive as undue constraints on their far-reaching plans. Their aversion leads to efforts to discredit the substantive powers that under-lie the special position of the Civil Service, such as the marginalization of evidence-based public policies by the PiS government or a significantly reduced scope of regulatory impact assessment and public consultations (SGI 2018, p. 184; SGI 2019, p. 3).

As a consequence of both social and economic election promises made by PiS, its government is forced to pursue a very active interven-tionist policy, which cannot be achieved without the participation of the Civil Service – a fact of which prominent members of the ruling camp are fully aware. In order to ensure their complete control over the corps, the decision-making mechanisms have been centralized and a staffing policy based on political loyalty and ideological affinity has become widespread.

Strategies for Illiberal Administrative Reforms

Political Declarations

The effects of post-1989 social and political transformation processes, European integration, and membership in the European Union, as well as multilevel governance, have all contributed to the weak state myth. Populists had a field day denouncing the ineffectiveness of state agen-cies, with the palpably low quality of state institutions being an easy and often justified target of their criticism. Populism was fed by the "failure to keep promises" on the part of those in power, the oligarchic ties, the influence of interest groups, the unclear process of public property privatization, the lack of transparency in decision-making processes, egoism, and the particularism of political elites at the expense of the public good (Bobbio 1987; Papadopoulos 2007).

The state and public administration frequently invoke those issues in the political manifestos championed by Poland's United Right. The issues of empowerment of the state and public administration invari-ably constitute important elements of the political raison d'être of this political group and are frequently contrasted with so-called "impossi-bilism," defined in this case as an unwillingness to act, which according to PiS leaders is a common trait of the other political parties. The key element of such empowerment is the administrative apparatus, which is treated as a tool to implement the political plans of the ruling camp.

The 2014 PiS election program reads: "One cannot accept a situation in which the state is unable to mobilize forces and resources for the implementation of large social or economic projects needed for the common good" (PiS 2014, p. 12). The same document contains the following provision: "We shall restore the genuine dimension of the idea of professional, apolitical clerical staff. Members of the Civil Service Corps will enjoy protection and support, but will not go unpunished in the event of poor performance of their duties or violation of applicable standards" (PiS 2014, p. 51).

Promises to enact further changes to public administration appeared in the 2019 PiS election program: "The PiS government has reorganized government administration. It started to build an efficient and at the same time an effective state, in which the citizens play the most important role" (PiS 2019, p. 44).

In the last three years, the logic of backtracking on previous reforms has become increasingly apparent, especially in the light of changes that affect public administration. A number of these changes are intended to strengthen the position of the central government in order to radically alter the rules and mechanisms of economic and social life, without which, in the government's opinion, it is impossible to achieve the strategic objectives of the state. The party in power prefers hierarchical and directive methods of steering and coordinating over the mechanisms typical of multilevel governance.[2]

Directions of Change

The United Right has launched a three-pronged assault on public administration (conceptual reflections on the approaches adopted by illiberal governments are presented in the introduction to this book). First, this attack consists of limiting the autonomy of the Civil Service by centralizing its management mechanisms, creating new offices and agencies entrusted with the implementation of political objectives of particular importance to PiS, and shifting competences between different public administration segments. Second, it involves modifying the budget and human resources allocation principles in order to weaken or strengthen a particular public administration office/agency. As a consequence, although formally speaking the organizational side of

these weakened public institutions remain unaffected, their actual possibilities of operation become substantially reduced. Finally, the third
prong involves mass dismissals of Civil Service managers. The senior
positions thus made vacant are then filled by party nominees who share
PiS's ideology and goals. Apart from dividing up the spoils and building
a group of politically loyal officials, this strategy is also intended to
change the institutional rules and thereby consolidate the newly adopted
solutions (e.g. the liquidation of the Civil Service Council or the abolition of open recruitment for senior Civil Service positions).

The above-mentioned efforts undertaken by PiS exemplify the phenomenon of ideational disruption (discussed in the first part of this
chapter), which consists of questioning the liberal-democratic political
order and, consequently, disavows a number of principles and mechanisms of operation previously deemed typical of public administration. The reason for such an about-face is not that they are considered
ineffective, but a strongly ideologically motivated belief held by populist leaders that it is imperative to reconstruct the mechanisms of state
operation based on different values than those upon which the liberal-
democratic order of governance was originally founded. In their opinion, moving away from the latter model will eliminate the institutional
restrictions that limit the state's development potential and hamper the
realization of the aspirations of its citizens.

Dimensions of Illiberal Public Administration Policies

In an attempt to transform public administration in a manner consistent with illiberal ideology, political leaders resort to a number of
strategies to change the organizational structures, the distribution of
financial and human resources, and the staffing of managerial positions in particular offices and agencies. They also alter their rules of
operation, dismantle accountability provisions, and dilute the established mechanisms of checks and balances (the theoretical aspects of
this issue are discussed more broadly in the introduction to this
book).

(a) Structures
Ostensible Expansion of Prime Minister's Powers
The PiS election program of 2019 reads: "The position of the Prime
Minister has been strengthened, both in administrative and decision-

making terms, as well as in the context of shaping the state ownership policy toward subordinate entities, including companies with Treasury shareholding which have a significant impact on the economic development of the state" (PiS 2019, p. 44).

Specifically, the Chancellery of the Prime Minister was made the key decision-making center for the implementation of the government's policy and was granted extra powers to this end. Additionally, the Centre for Strategic Analysis was established and tasked with the responsibility of developing draft public policy strategies as well as giving opinions on projects submitted to the legislative and programmatic duties of the Council of Ministers. Moreover, a mechanism for coordinating legislative decisions within the Government Legislative Process was introduced (PiS 2019, p. 45).

On the one hand, we are witnessing a process of formal strengthening of the Prime Minister's position, whereas on the other, the government is becoming de-institutionalized owing to the actual concentration of full political authority and real decision-making powers into the hands of PiS leader Jarosław Kaczyński, who formally is only an MP.

Consolidating Management and Control Mechanisms

The central government's powers were expanded by the establishment of new ministries entrusted with the task of implementing PiS's political objectives (i.e. the Ministry of Energy, the Ministry of Investment and Development). Moreover, new instruments intended to help the government more effectively influence the economy were introduced, including the Polish Development Fund, the Start in Poland program, the Polish Agency of Investment and Trade, and the National Real Property Stock. Changes were also made in the area of public property stewardship by reorganizing the General Prosecutor's Office of the Republic of Poland and establishing the National Revenue Administration (KAS) (PiS 2019, p. 46). The expansion of administrative powers in the economy reflected the PiS government's belief in the need for a stronger (i.e. sovereign) state influence on economic matters.

In time, however, the expanding government structures began to be viewed by PiS's upper echelons as less than conducive to the achievement of its original objectives. The announced reduction in the number of ministerial departments from twenty-one to twelve is justified in terms of strengthening the government's coordination capacity. Still, it is worth bearing in mind that the cabinet, including the Prime

Minister, consists of people who were handpicked, or at least approved, by Jarosław Kaczyński, which makes them loyal to him personally. Consequently, they strive to realize his political ambitions fully cognizant of the fact that their careers depend on their personal relations with the leader (SGI 2019).

Limiting the Horizontal Dispersion of Power
According to the experts of the Helsinki Foundation for Human Rights, the years 2015–2019 saw the greatest deterioration in the protection of human rights in Poland since 1989. The ruling majority, despite falling short of the two-thirds majority needed to amend the Constitution, introduced a number of changes to the state governance system, thus undermining the rule of law and the principle of tripartite division of power. By bending legislation to political aims, the rule *of* law was replaced with rule *by* law (Szuleka and Wolny 2019).

Violations of independence, and the changes that were often labelled as "national security," "border protection," and "social order," limited civic rights and liberties and affected the Constitutional Court, the Supreme Court, common courts, and prosecutors' offices. Plans to limit the independence of the Ombudsman were announced, and public media outlets were completely subordinated to the ruling majority. Changes in the distribution of public funds for social organizations and verbal assaults on individual nongovernmental organizations, as well as their representatives, are also a recurrent cause for concern.

From 2015 to 2019, the Polish parliament passed more than twenty acts whose provisions served primarily to expand the political power of the ruling camp at the expense of the judiciary, independent institutions, civil rights, and personal freedoms (Szuleka and Wolny 2019).

PIS's distrust of the principle of dispersal of power and independent institutions that uphold the law is perhaps best illustrated by the party's attitude toward the Ombudsman. The current Ombudsman, Adam Bodnar, actively defends civil and political rights, and for this reason he has been routinely criticized by PiS; simultaneously, his office saw a reduction in funding for statutory activities.

Limiting the Autonomy of Lower-Tier Public Administration
The progressive process of centralization of the state is undercutting the achievements of the last thirty years and the independence of local

authorities. Observers of the Council of Europe noted with concern that:

- The level of autonomy enjoyed by local authorities is being eroded by the re-centralization of several competencies previously transferred to such authorities;
- The widespread interference by state authorities in the local independent functions undermines the assignment to local authorities of full and exclusive powers;
- Although the Joint Committee represents an adequate legal framework for consultation, the recent tendency is to bypass this mechanism, making it ineffective;
- An increasing number of acts of the state impose rigid organizational solutions to local authorities;
- The status of elected representatives, especially their financial compensation, is worsening;
- Supervision of local authorities, carried out by government representatives, is increasingly overused and cannot be considered proportional to the importance of the interests that it is intended to protect;
- The tendency to transfer responsibilities to local authorities without transferring adequate financial resources is increasing;
- Local authorities receive a steadily dwindling share of revenue from local taxes;
- Diminishing autonomy of local authorities to set the rate or fees of local services they are obliged to provide (Report 2019).

(b) Resources
Using Financial Means to Rein in Public Administration Units
The practice of manipulating public administration units by altering the allocation of funds has been extensively applied by the PiS government in several ways. The first method consists of underfunding the tasks delegated to local governments. There is much to suggest that in this case the point is to label individual local governments, many of which remain dominated by opposition parties, in the eyes of their constituencies as inefficient and ineffective. This may result from PiS's ambivalent attitude toward state decentralization and the preference of its leaders for centralized public management mechanisms.

The second way of exerting pressure on public administration is to limit the amount of funds allocated by the parliament, currently dominated by the ruling party, to the activities of administrative agencies which criticize the government's actions, for example the Office of the Ombudsman.[3] Conversely, public institutions that enjoy the sympathy of the ruling political camp, such as the Institute of National Remembrance, are allocated more funds from the central budget.

Yet another practice involves creating alternatives to institutions that disapprove of the government's actions, such as the establishment of the post of Governmental Plenipotentiary for Human Rights (as a Deputy Minister in the Ministry of Justice), even though there is already a constitutional office with the same powers, namely the Ombudsman. The decision was criticized by the latter, who noted that "only the Ombudsman is independent of the authorities. Only one body is independent of the authorities, has the right to deal with complaints from citizens and is mandated by the Constitution and the Parliament, and that is the Ombudsman."[4]

For some time, a disturbing phenomenon has been observed in the distribution of government funds to local authorities. As noted by experts, the political orientation of local authorities became a factor in decisions concerning the allocations from the Local Government Roads Fund. The amount of funding granted to municipalities governed by officials associated with PiS is several times higher than in those run by nonpartisans. Most municipalities where opposition local government officials are in power have received no support from the program.[5]

Additionally, a number of concerns have been raised about the principles of funding allocation under the newly created Local Investment Fund government program, designed as a support measure for local governments in the face of problems caused by the coronavirus pandemic. The main issue is that the underdefined allocation criteria will make it possible to reward PiS-friendly units and foster clientelism among local governments (Drabik 2020).

(c) Personnel
Civil Service Corps
The operation of the Civil Service Corps in Poland is governed by the Constitution. Article 153 states that the Civil Service is established in government administration offices in order to ensure professional,

reliable, impartial, and politically neutral performance of the state's tasks (Konstytucja 1997). The detailed provisions are set out in the Civil Service Act of 21 November 2008, as amended by the Civil Service Act and Selected Other Acts of 30 December 2015 (Civil Service Act 2015). The latter, pushed through parliament by PiS in 2015, introduced fundamental changes to the Civil Service. Among others, it provided that:

1) Senior positions in the Civil Service shall be filled by appointment. In practice, this meant abolishing open and competitive recruitment to higher positions in the Civil Service;
2) Employment contracts with those occupying senior Civil Service positions were terminated as of the date of the Act's entry into force;
3) Modified regulations concerning the status of senior civil servants abolished the obligation to perform preparatory service and to undergo periodic evaluation;
4) Nonmembers of the Civil Service Corps were made eligible for appointment to the position of Head of the Civil Service due to the abolishment of the requirement to have sufficient experience in government administration;
5) The Civil Service Council was abolished.

The above-mentioned changes effectively undermined the foundations of the Civil Service and have resulted in its significant politicization.

On the other hand, 2019 saw the highest increase in the average remuneration of Poland's Civil Service staff in eleven years. Despite this, the average number of candidates for the corps still continues to decline (Sprawozdanie 2020).

Purges

During 2015–2016, the number of bills which, under the guise of reorganization, made it possible to implement far-reaching personnel changes in government administration significantly increased. By the end of 2017, thirty-seven such "human resources acts" were passed by the Polish parliament (Paczocha 2018). The most common tools used for initiating such reshuffles were:

1) Interrupting the term of office of a single- or multiperson authority;
2) Transfer of appointments from local to central level;

3) Abolition of multiperson authorities;
4) Statutory termination of employment contracts (e.g. about one-third of all senior positions in the Civil Service);
5) Abolition of open competitive recruitment for managerial positions in the Civil Service.

The adoption of these acts led to the dismissal of at least 11,368 staff, including approximately 6,773 managers and members of multiperson authorities (February 2018) (Paczocha 2018). However, despite these massive reductions, overall employment figures in the Civil Service are on the rise, especially in managerial positions (Wójcik 2018). Out of 560 people employed by the Prime Minister's office, 290 are heads, advisers, or directors (Radwan 2018).

The so-called "anti-crisis shield" – a package of government actions aimed at stimulating economic development in the face of the consequences of the coronavirus epidemic – contains provisions for summary dismissals of civil servants and salary reductions. Although no executive order to that effect has been issued so far, these threats continue to cause serious concern for officials, which is further exacerbated by staff shortages and the resultant increasing workload per employee due to the pandemic (Kubicka-Żach 2020).

(d) Standards and Principles
Violation of Civil Service Neutrality
Politically motivated appointments to managerial positions in the Civil Service became a generally accepted standard in the wake of the legislative changes introduced by the PiS government in 2015, which was, however, tantamount to breaking with the principle of political neutrality of public administration.

Questioning the importance of political neutrality of the Civil Service stems from the suspicion harbored by PiS circles that the corps as an elite group is neither loyal nor willing to implement the government's ideology or agenda. Thus, in the opinion of PiS ideologues, the politicization of the Civil Service is a necessary step in subordinating public administration and a precondition for the implementation of the reform plans of the ruling coalition. This reasoning clearly reveals the United Right's skepticism about the importance of instructions and formal mechanisms of governance, as well as its unshakable faith in the revolutionary principle of having dedicated staff that subscribe to the agenda of the ruling party. As a consequence, this leads to a reversal of the effects of the previous administrative reforms (Meyer-Sahling 2011).

(e) Quality of Civil Service

Putting party loyalty above the substantive competences of civil servants has had a negative effect on the corps as a whole, with particular detriment to senior positions. The consequences include significantly restricted use of evidence to inform the design and implementation of public policies and limited public consultations of decisions taken by the government. Yet another conspicuous negative outcome of the politicization of the Civil Service is the increasing problem of ensuring effective interdepartmental coordination.

Upon coming to power, the PiS government changed the institutional arrangements of governance. It modified the ministerial portfolios several times, set up new cabinet committees, amended the Civil Service Act, and strengthened the position of central government vis-à-vis subnational governments. However, its successful operation so far has been primarily due to its parliamentary majority, strong party discipline, and the uncontested role of party leader Jarosław Kaczyn´ski. No reforms were introduced to improve the government's strategic capacity, such as openly consulting recognized experts. The main priority of the current government is to implement its ideology and consolidate the executive branch (SGI 2019).

One of the consequences of the unfavorable developments in the Civil Service may be a further decline in young people's interest in training for the jobs available within the sector, which has acutely affected the National School of Public Administration in particular (Radwan 2020).

Institutional Consequences of Populism

(a) "Restoring the State to Its Citizens"

It is worth noting that the criticism of the existing system and its "degenerated" establishment does not lead to design of a new order or new institutions (more on this in the introduction to this book). On the contrary: when populists come to power, they recreate the previous arrangements – they use the already existing institutions in order to gain complete ideological control over them (Müller 2016b). However, this mechanism, which in fact represents a political transformation, becomes obvious only when the populists have obtained sufficient power to enable them to effectively take over the key institutions, as illustrated by the changes introduced in Poland after the 2015 elections. The implementation of changes, which were allegedly aimed at "restoring the state to its citizens," consisted primarily of taking control of the judiciary, namely, the Prosecutor's Office and the Supreme Court, public media, and cultural institutions, as well as key financial institutions and business entities, which were nationalized. Although structural changes do not always provide sufficient pretext for taking control of independent institutions, the instrumentalization of law actually makes it possible. Time and again, the slogan of "regaining control over these institutions" has been touted as an argument for the effectiveness of political action, as well as proof that the party has kept its election promises.

It is worth noting that PiS effectively delivered on what it had pledged during the presidential and parliamentary campaigns of 2014/2015, including 500+ (a monthly benefit of PLN 500 for the second and every subsequent child), lowering the retirement age for women to 60 and for men to 65, improving tax collection, and reducing the preferential CIT rate from 15 percent to 9 percent for small businesses. In the parliamentary election campaign of 2019, PiS pledged to introduce a generous package of social benefits and tax cuts vaunted as the Kaczyński Five. The cost of this program is estimated at PLN 40 billion. In the 2020 presidential campaign, PiS candidate Andrzej Duda made a number of promises, a significant proportion of which fall outside his constitutional powers. His program included, among other things, upholding all the social packages enacted by the United Right government, a solidarity allowance for the duration of the epidemic, and substantial investment in health care.

(b) Accountability
Law-Making
An important aspect of the principle of accountability of those in power toward society is the way in which laws are passed. In the years spanning 2015–2019, under the PiS government, the greatest concern was caused by the tendency to limit parliamentary debate and diminish the importance of public consultations. As a result of the frequent

employment of extraordinary modes of procedure, and in breach of the provisions of the Council of Ministers' Work Regulations, in the last year of its term of office the government held consultations on less than two-thirds of the submitted bills. The consultations lasted on average less than twelve days (XIII Komunikat 2020).

Another serious cause for concern is the so-called concealed bills: bills submitted by the government about which the public is made aware only after they have become part of the parliamentary agenda. These bills make their way into parliament without any prior documents being made available concerning the legislative works in question, either in the List of Legislative and Program Works of the Council of Ministers or on the Government Legislative Process (RPL) platform; nor are they formally discussed as a separate procedure or submitted for consultation or review (XIII Komunikat 2020).

Public consultations are also becoming shorter. In its third year in power, the United Right government devoted only 13.5 days to public consultations. In total, 28 bills (16 percent) received a consultation period shorter than the statutory minimum of fourteen days. The data for the last year of the term of office paint an even more disturbing picture: the average time devoted to public consultations was less than twelve days. Out of the total number of bills subject to consultations (ninety-five), seventeen (17.9 percent) were consulted for a shorter period than the minimum (XIII Komunikat 2020).

On June 1, 2016, the government modified the Work Regulations of the Council of Ministers by, among other things, abolishing the rule that any work on draft legislation must begin with the preparation of relevant framework provisions. This has now become optional (XIII Komunikat 2020).

According to the influential economic organization Employers of Poland (*Pracodawcy Rzeczypospolitej Polskiej*), law-making in Poland is plagued by a number of flaws, the most egregious of which are known as the "seven deadly sins" and include unreliable consultations, secret bills, submitting government draft proposals by individual MPs in a deliberate effort to avoid consultations, rapid pace of work, lack of reflection, overregulation, and instability of legislation (Pracodawcy RP 2019).

The Rule of Law

In the opinion of the Ombudsman, the changes introduced by PiS to the Polish judiciary and the process of taking control of the supreme and central institutions of the democratic law-governed state (i.e. the Constitutional Tribunal, the National Council of the Judiciary, the Supreme Court, common courts, and the Public Prosecutor's Office) significantly constrain their independence.

Despite these major breaches of the democratic rule of law, individual constitutional bodies independent of the executive still have partial powers to control the latter, albeit to an increasingly lesser extent, as the parliament has been "taken over" like the other institutions, and due to the fact that the powers of the Minister of Justice and the Prosecutor General are now vested in a single authority.

On July 16, 2020, the Committee on Civil Liberties, Justice and Home Affairs of the European Parliament (LIBE) officially heard a report on the state of democracy, rule of law, and human rights protection in Poland. According to the report, there is a clear risk of a serious breach by Poland of the EU values listed in Article 2 of the EU Treaty with regard to the following:

• the functioning of the constitutional, legislative, and electoral systems;
• the independence of the judiciary and respect for the rights of judges;
• the protection of fundamental rights, including the rights of minorities.

These disturbing developments were also reflected in the most recent Freedom House democracy ranking, "Nations in Transit," in which Poland recorded its lowest rating since its first inclusion in the survey in 2011. After sharply declining over four consecutive years, further deterioration in the quality of democracy in Poland is reflected by current attacks on the judiciary and local governments as well as hate campaigns targeting the LGBT community and judges themselves. Accordingly, it was reclassified from the category of Consolidated Democracies to Semi-Consolidated Democracies (Freedom House, "Nations in Transit 2020," p. 25).

Response of Officials and Clerical Staff to Change

PiS, by its relentless drive to subordinate the Civil Service, elicits a variety of responses from within the corps itself. These are perhaps best described in the terms proposed by Brehm and Gates (discussed in more detail in the introduction to this book), who categorized the various ways in which bureaucrats may choose to influence policy implementation into working, shirking, or sabotage (Brehm and Gates 1997). Most officials and clerical staff appear to be loyal toward their political superiors based on the assumption that every democratically elected authority is legitimate, and that the role of public administration should be limited to the performance of the tasks entrusted to it. In general, they adopt a strategy known as working – that is, they use their skills and resources to support the government. This is certainly aided by efforts to professionalize and improve the quality of public services (Perry, Hondeghem, and Wise 2010). Naturally, it does not mean that staff who adopt such an attitude remain oblivious to the threats resulting from illiberal and populist policies, but their criticism tends to be expressed in private. Interestingly, about 35 percent of Civil Service staff voted for PiS in the 2015 elections (Wybory 2015).

Among the Civil Service staff who loyally cooperate with their political superiors, there is a group of people appointed to managerial positions thanks to their affiliations with PiS, often by way of political patronage. This is a specific subpopulation, often described as "zealots" (Gailmard and Patty 2007, p. 874), who share the ideologies of their superiors, support their decisions, and, much like politicians, benefit from the new allocation of roles and resources in public administration.

In principle, shirking work or even sabotaging decisions in the Civil Service is rare. Officials who have different political preferences or disagree with certain decisions taken by their superiors hardly ever use their knowledge to undermine the latter's position, as was claimed by Downs (1965). This may reveal not only a strong sense of Civil Service ethos, but also the effects of strict supervision measures instituted by the political superiors, and the attendant fear of losing one's job or having one's career prospects thwarted. Another reason may be that staff members who reject the manner in which the Civil Service is run by the newly appointed management or who disagree with the public policy objectives pursued by the PiS government simply resign from their jobs. If we look at the number of people who have left the Civil Service in recent years, its staff turnover (Sprawozdanie 2019), and the decline in the number of people interested in working for the state administration (Wójcik 2018), the data certainly reveal considerable disagreement with the populist and illiberal moves made by the PiS government.

The Impact of External Factors on the Erosion of the Liberal-Democratic Rule of Law

A number of factors in the political and institutional environment of the present government delay the pace of erosion of the liberal-democratic system of governance. These include: the international-ization of the state, the competencies of officials, the links between the Civil Service and socioeconomic sectors, the model of staffing policy in the Civil Service, the social perception of political-administrative relations, and media activity (more on this subject in the introduction to this book). These factors bolster the capacity of the corps to resist pressure on the part of illiberal governments and to implement public policies with a certain degree of autonomy in relation to the latter's preferences (Evans, Rueschemeyer, and Skocpol 1985; Skocpol 1979).

As an EU member state, Poland belongs to a number of international institutions and supranational networks whose influence can be used to at least partly offset the populist leanings of the present ruling party, especially as regards the judiciary. However, in terms of the Civil Service, and in particular its apoliticality and neutrality, its inter-national links (e.g. professional European networks of public adminis-tration) cannot be said to have sufficiently protected it from extreme politicization. Certain positive impacts resulting from Poland's mem-bership in the EU, especially the pressure exerted by its institutions, failed to prevent the destruction of the rule of law; at best, it may only slow down the process.

The level of professionalism of the Civil Service in Poland still ranks below average amongst EU member states, despite the fact that the quality of its operation has been gradually improving. When PiS came to power in 2015, it started to weaken and politicize the corps, which, combined with the relatively low public opinion of the quality of public administration in Poland, does not serve to enhance its institutional profile or strengthen its capacity to curb the illiberal and populist efforts of those in power.

A factor that mitigates the negative effects of the government's populist measures is the close cooperation between public administration bodies and the business circles with a view to ensuring stable conditions for economic growth (Evans 1995). To some extent, this mechanism is at work in Poland, as evidenced by the condition of the economy and the PiS government's fairly rational policy in this area. It should also be noted that the current government has tried not to harm the economy, although employers' organizations increasingly believe that the Social Dialogue Council has essentially become a smokescreen organization, despite it being mandated to coordinate social and economic policy between the government, the representatives of employers, and employees (Pracodawcy 2018).

In this context, mention should be made of the role of the private media, which often criticizes the current government, including its decisions that affect the Civil Service. As a result, proposed policies are sometimes discredited or the ruling party comes under sufficient pressure to abandon them. At present, however, the propagandist message of the public media prevails, with its mostly negative image of public administration. Moreover, for several years, PiS has been announcing so-called "repolonization" or changes in Poland's media market intended to constrain the influence of foreign-owned opinion sources. This gives rise to understandable fears of violating media pluralism and monopolization of the media space by public television, referred to as "PiS TV" by many.

Conclusions

The events that are currently unfolding in Poland reveal three kinds of ideational disruptions: the dissemination of solutions typical of an illiberal democracy in their populist version, anti-EU sentiments, and nationalization coupled with centralization. They draw on a number of interrelated phenomena, including the high socioeconomic costs of political transformation and the accompanying dissatisfaction with the way economic benefits were distributed, disillusionment with democracy and the quality of the political class, as well as the unmet expectations of EU membership resulting from its idealized image.

This illiberal and populist drift has resulted in a number of changes in the institutional order of governance, including the violation of the principle of separation of powers, the limitation of the autonomy of independent bodies, and the undermining of the rule of law and the independence of the judiciary, as well as the subordination of the public media to the government. Last but not least, the progressive centralization of the state governance system is gradually curbing local government autonomy.

Other effects of this drift include the expansion of central government powers, increased involvement of the state in the economy, state capture, colonization of the administrative apparatus and its politicization, and a weaker position of local governments. The legacy of the real socialist era, as well as the vestiges of the last thirty years – including the precedence of personal ties over institutional mechanisms, loyalty to the ruling party over allegiance to the public interest, and political patronage over substantive competencies – appear to strongly favor these developments.

In pursuing a decidedly populist political agenda, the PiS government reveals its predominant attitude toward the Civil Service, namely sidelining. This is based on the particular distrust which PiS politicians hold toward high-ranking officials, who are perceived as members of an elite corps which is not working in the best interests of the state. In consequence, any implemented changes put forward by PiS are intended to fully subordinate the Civil Service to the ruling party. A central component of this approach is political patronage, including its variant that involves filling senior positions in public administration with pragmatic technocrats who subscribe to PiS's political objectives. This permits the United Right government to operate quite effectively.

Public administration is important for PiS leaders as the capacity to act effectively figures prominently in their political calculations. This ability is contrasted with so-called "impossibilism," which, according to PiS politicians, is a characteristic feature of their political opponents. A way to ensure the full power of this capacity is via a public administration viewed as a tool for the practical implementation of the ruling party's political agenda.

Another key element of this mechanism involves the extreme politicization of the Civil Service. Questioning the significance of political neutrality of the corps is rooted in the belief, highly prevalent throughout the PiS apparatus, that the Civil Service is neither loyal nor willing to implement the government's ideological priorities. However, such criticism of the system and its "degenerated" institutions does not lead to the creation of a new order or to the design of new institutions. On the contrary: when populists come to power, they recreate the previous system based on the already existing institutions in order to gain a dominant position in them and, once completely subordinated, use them to further their political agenda (the theoretical background to this phenomenon is discussed in the introduction to this book).

The policy of the PiS government has drawn a range of responses within the Civil Service Corps. Loyalty toward political superiors still appears to predominate among its officials and clerical staff – after all, every democratically elected authority can legitimately exercise power, whereas the role of public administration should be limited to the performance of the tasks entrusted to it. However, a sizable proportion of the corps rejects the current government's policy, as evidenced by the large number of people resigning from the Civil Service and the declining interest in taking it up as a career.

External factors – such as the internationalization of the state, the competencies of officials, the links between the Civil Service and the economy, the model of personnel policy in the Civil Service, the public perception of political-administrative relations, and the activity of the media – can only partially combat the mechanisms of corruption of both law and the principles of fair governance.

The scale and intensity of the above-described phenomena in Poland may lead to the decline and eventual dismantling of the democratic model of governance, which is likely to result in the emergence of an oligarchic administration wherein political loyalty criteria prevail over competence, the public interest is identified with that of the ruling party, and the rule of law is distorted by its instrumentalization.

The oligarchic administration is essentially a politicized one, with certain distinctive features, including the following:

a) Filling senior positions with those who strongly identify with the ideology of the ruling party;
b) Ideologically motivated loyalty ties between those appointed to senior public administration positions and the leader(s) of the ruling party being a primary criterion of career advancement;
c) Persuading high-ranking public administration officials of the need to radically restructure the social and economic and political order and to oppose the current political and administrative elite;
d) Centralization of governance mechanisms in public administration and concentration of power in the hands of a new administrative elite which shares the ideology and political goals of the ruling party;

e) Using political patronage to fill senior positions in public administration with pragmatic technocrats who enjoy the trust of the
leader(s) of the ruling party;

f) The perception of the "paratroop drop" of party activists into
managerial positions in public administration as a means of making
the latter more democratic;

g) Exemption of senior officials from responsibility for violating the
law if they were forced to act under extraordinary circumstances
(e.g. the parliament is now debating a bill to that effect, citing the
need to combat the coronavirus epidemic).

Notes

1. This term is used as a shorthand for three political parties: Prawo
   i Sprawiedliwość (Law and Justice), Solidarna Polska (Solidarity
   Poland), and Porozumienie (Alliance).
2. From the perspective of liberal democracy, one of the few positive
   examples of reforms carried out in accordance with the principles of
   public policymaking were the changes to higher education pursued in
   the spirit of social dialogue by Minister J. Gowin.
3. www.rpo.gov.pl/pl/raport_1/729
4. https://deon.pl/swiat/wiadomosci-z-polski/bodnar-o-powolaniu-pelno
   mocnika-rzadu-ds-praw-czlowieka-tylko-rpo-jest-niezalezny-od-wladzy,
   669414
5. https://wspolnota.org.pl/news-rankingi/raport-wspolnoty-pieniadze-na-
   drogi-tylko-dla-swoich

6 Technocratic-Populist Mayors and Public Administration in Three European Cities

ELIŠKA DRÁPALOVÁ

Introduction

According to numerous international reports, the state of democracy in the world is declining (Lührmann et al. 2019). This current democratic decline is not caused by coups and sudden moves to autocracy but by the quiet and slow internal erosion of democratic institutions and values (Bermeo 2016; Levitsky and Ziblatt 2018a; Tomini and Wagemann 2018). Associated with such liberal-democratic backsliding is the weakening of traditional political parties and the spectacular rise of antisystemic and populist movements in the USA, Latin America, Asia, and Europe. Whilst the rise of populism and its associated political polarization and instability are acknowledged as important concerns (Albertazzi and McDonnell 2015; Taggart and Kaltwasser 2016), limited attention has been paid to the effect of populists on public administration (Peters and Pierre 2019). Given that a neutral, professionally qualified civil service is one of the pillars of democracy and good governance (Panizza, Peters, and Ramos Larraburu 2019, p. 150), the lack of focus on liberal-democratic backsliding and administration is a critical gap in the literature.

Although subnational government does not figure prominently in either the literature on liberal-democratic backsliding or in the research on populism, local government is a relevant element in both processes (Drápalová and Wegrich 2020). Local governments deliver the majority of public services, distribute resources, and implement public policies. Unequal distribution of resources across territories and local government's low capacity to satisfy citizens' needs are important sources of regime destabilization (Rodríguez-Pose 2017). Cities are often the first level of administration that citizens interact with, and as such their poor performance is likely to shape the trust in and evaluation of the entire system (Weitz-Shapiro 2008) and consequently lead to a higher level of support for populist and antisystem parties (Rodríguez-Pose, Lee, and Lipp 2020).

As with national party systems, European cities have also experienced a rapid decline of traditional parties and the spectacular rise of populist and antisystemic movements. For example, in the Czech Republic, between 2011 and 2019 populist parties grew from having no representation to having a presence in 70 percent of local councils and governing in twelve of the largest cities, including Prague. In Italy, prior to winning the general election in 2018, the Five Star Movement (M5S) won the 2016 local elections in Rome, Turin, and around forty smaller cities. In fact, in many cases populist parties first broke through at the local level and used local resources and experiences as a springboard and testbed for strategies deployed later at the national level (Paxton 2020). Despite the spectacular advance of populist parties in local governments, we know very little about how they behave in government and what their impact on governance is. To what extent does democratic backsliding occur at the municipal level under the rule of local (branches of) populist parties? Do local government characteristics pose specific constraints on the success of populist strategies?

This chapter follows the analytical framework presented in the introduction to this volume and explores the strategies and the impact of populists on public administration in three European cities. It focuses on technocratic populism: a type of populism that blends populism with technocratic discourse and expertise (Bickerton and Invernizzi Accetti 2018). This chapter argues that techno-populists, like all populists, aim at modifying the policy process by rewriting the "operational manual" of the state (Müller 2016a). They do so by shifting the balance of power and concentrating it in the executive government (structure), increasing its grip over the administration (resources, personnel, norms) and limiting societal participation (accountability). Given the technocratic component, this type of populism will use the rhetoric of expertise, efficiency, and results as their mainframes. Moreover, technology and ICT will play a prominent role in their discourse and strategy.

This research contributes to the literature in two ways. First, it adds to the studies of populism by looking at populist strategies vis-à-vis the administration from a local government perspective in three European cities: Prague, Rome, and Barcelona. A subnational focus is still rare in this research even though it offers an excellent vantage point to study the impact of populist governments on administration. This chapter studies three cities with female mayors from the same populist party family in three different administrative systems. Secondly, the chapter complements the literature on liberal-democratic backsliding. It explores the intersection between populist discourse, technocracy, and administrative management. It centers on a technocratic-populist political agenda and its strategies for coping with local government administration and executive governance (Bickerton and Invernizzi Accetti 2017; Drápalová and Wegrich 2020). This particular type of populist party and its appeal to efficiency and effective management through the use of experts might produce a different impact on administration than the more ideologically extreme types of populist parties.

Moreover, the subnational focus employed in this chapter has a significant empirical advantage as many populist parties govern at first at this level and play a crucial role in shaping local politics, public services, and administrative reform. There are many populist mayors who, unlike their national leaders, had the chance to implement their political agenda and use different strategies to reform the public administration. Elected officials are far more operational at the local level than in national politics, and thus are better positioned to attack what they see as rigid and inefficient bureaucratic processes. However, the local level might impose on populists that seek to implement their agendas a unique set of constraining conditions. At the local level, politics and administration are blended, the pressure to deliver is greater, and competence is highly regarded.

The chapter is organized as follows: the next section introduces the concept of technocratic populism and its link with technology. The third section adapts the framework presented in the introductory chapter to the local level. The fourth section deals with the empirical cases of Prague, Barcelona, and Rome to test the proposed framework; it also shows that cases vary concerning the combination of elements deployed in practice. The concluding section points to the potential value and limitations of the framework and to lessons learned for scholars of both public administration and populism.

Technocratic Populism and Technology

Although the definition of populism is still a matter of debate, most authors agree on the dichotomized antiestablishment rhetoric that sets the "people" against the "elite" as the core feature. For example, Mudde (2004, p. 543) defines populism as "an ideology that considers society to be ultimately separated into two homogeneous and antagonistic groups, 'the pure people' versus 'the corrupt' elite, and which argues that politics should be an expression of the 'volonté générale' (general will) of the people." This Manichean division of society makes, however, a weak ideological anchor. Populism thus adapts its content depending on the predominant political cleavage and the establishment against which it is mobilizing (Canovan 1999). This chameleonic nature of populism potentially creates remarkably different types of populist parties on both sides of the ideological spectrum (Stanley 2008).

Hanley and Sikk (2016) have described a distinctive type of centrist antiestablishment party that positions ideology as secondary and instead builds its legitimacy on competence, anticorruption, and efficiency as core features. Within this group, some parties base their discourse on technocratic expertise and the use of ideas and management tools borrowed directly from the private sphere. In the literature, this synergy between technocracy and populist rhetoric is called "technocratic populism" (Bickerton and Invernizzi Accetti 2017; Buštíková and Guasti 2018; Drápalová and Wegrich 2020; Havlík 2019). Bickerton and Invernizzi Accetti (2018, pp. 143–144) define technocratic populists as "anti-pluralist parties with low coalition potential, that contrapose the corrupt elite and honest people and propose a technocratic conception of politics as problem-solving managerial problem orientation." Drápalová and Wegrich (2020, p. 5) add an antibureaucratic element; they define technocratic populism as a "strategy based on combining hostility to (party) politics and the administration, centralization and personalization of executive government and exaltation of seemingly apolitical 'what works' management strategies implemented by experts." For Buštíková and Guasti, technocratic populism consists of the strategic use of "the appeal of technocratic competence and numbers to deliver a populist message. It combines the ideology of expertise with a populist political appeal to ordinary people" (Buštíková and Guasti 2018, p. 334). Some of the most prominent examples of technocratic populism in Europe have been identified in Spain and Italy (Bickerton and Invernizzi Accetti 2018) and in the Czech Republic (Buštíková and Guasti 2018; Císař and Štětka 2016; Havlík 2019).

For some, the combination of populism and technocracy appears contradictory, incompatible, or even counterproductive. Stoker (Chapter 11, this volume), for example, argues that (ill-implemented) technocracy has fueled populism, indicating that bureaucracy has played an active role in providing the context for the emergence of populism by actively pushing for depoliticization, centralization, and technocratic solutions that frequently fed public distrust in governing practices. Hanley and Sikk (2016) find, however, that in political systems with high political corruption and low party consolidation, antiestablishment parties that use the strategy of promoting effective management and expertise are successful. In the context of high corruption and low administrative performance, the technocratic component brings the missing expertise and a promise to provide efficiency and good management (Drápalová and Wegrich 2020). Populists are frequently criticized for their lack of experience, empty rhetoric, and incompetence. Hence, the intersection between populism and technocracy can be understood as a way to compensate for the populist's "competence gap" and to frame the opposition to elites in more pragmatic and less nativistic terms in areas with low government performance (Panizza, Peters, and Ramos Larraburu 2019). Technocratic populists appeal to voters as the competent and clean alternative.

Within the current populist wave, social media and information and communications technology (ICT) have become prominent communication instruments. Populists of all colors rely heavily on the new social media to spread their message, mobilize, and connect with their followers. According to Stoker (Chapter 11, this volume), social media has created echo chambers, fueled distrust among citizens and politicians, and contributed significantly to the rise of populism. In the techno-populist strategy, however, the use of ICT and social media goes beyond mere communication tools and becomes a central component for effective management. For example, M5S, ANO, and Podemos have endorsed the idea of technologically enhanced direct democracy and government. M5S have proposed the use of e-government and ICT-based public sector innovations to tackle chronic problems of the Italian state, such as corruption and the inefficiency of the public sector (Bickerton and Invernizzi Accetti 2018). The attractiveness of ICT tools for technocratic populism lies in the combination of higher policymakers' discretion, control, and its apparent value neutrality (Bloom and Sancino 2019; Cardullo and Kitchin 2019).

Backsliding Strategies from a Local Government Perspective

Despite the limited knowledge about how different populist leaders engage with public administration, the existing literature already provides some clues. According to Nancy Bermeo (2016), populists concentrate power via executive aggrandizement. Margaret Canovan (1999) claims that populists in government, similar to semiauthoritarians, reduce pluralism and undermine the system of checks and balances by weakening the opposition and silencing external pressures. Recent research has associated populists in power with wide-scale patronage, politicization, and decreasing independence and expertise of administration (Borins 2018; Peters and Pierre 2019). The introduction to this book has tried to summarize these disperse propositions in a comprehensive analytical framework in which three possible strategies are identified (sidelining, using, and ignoring of administration) that populists might employ to alter public organizations, programs, and processes. The authors distinguish between different scenarios and provide mechanisms that populists might use: changing administrative structures, personnel, resources, and norms. How these strategies will be employed and whether they will be successful are still open empirical questions.

Local government is an excellent place to search for the impact of technocratic-populist parties on administration because of a combination of theoretical-empirical conundrums unique to the local level. On the one hand, the populist message should fit particularly well at the local level. In municipal politics, the connection between politicians and citizens is by necessity more direct and personalized. Even in more collective forms of local government, the mayor is a prominent political figure and representative. Elected officials are also far more operational and less constrained at this level. Moreover, local government is often perceived as the realm of administration that implements policies mechanically from above and, thus, where technocratic discourses find fertile ground. Technocratic populists should, therefore, be in a better place to answer the performance challenge by evoking managerial expertise that effectively mobilizes the means to deliver (Drápalová and Wegrich 2020). To accomplish this uneasy task of combining responsiveness with responsibility, technocratic populists find in recent ICT innovations handy tools to use for communication, decision-making, and implementation.

On the other hand, this mix of politics and administration, specific to local government, puts additional pressure on the populists' strategies and their political agendas. The municipality has to collect rubbish daily, handle licenses, fix potholes, and organize transport (Burnet and Kogan 2016). Mounting garbage in the streets, lousy performance, and pot-holed roads are immediately observable by citizens. In a city, the gap between radical discourse and actual performance might not be as easy to disguise as it is at the national level. The competence of the mayor is, therefore, a relevant factor that voters pay attention to during elections. Thus, at the local level, populists can barely survive without engaging with the bureaucracy. Indeed, they battle between a radical discourse that wishes to sideline the inefficient administration and the pragmatic need to keep the administrative machine working smoothly to secure re-election. This is even more so in the case of technocratic populists, as they base their legitimacy on output efficiency and the effective delivery of peoples' wishes (Buštíková and Guasti 2018).

This chapter builds on the framework proposed in the introduction, adapts it to government at the local level, and explores empirically the strategies of technocratic populists in city administrations. In particular, it focuses on changes in (1) administrative structure, (2) personnel and resources, and (3) accountability.

Administrative Structure

The most prominent characteristic of populism is the centralization of power in the figure of the leader. Technocratic populists are not different in this respect. According to Daniele Caramani, both populists and technocrats share a "unitary, non-pluralist, unmediated, and unaccountable vision of society's general interest" (Caramani 2017, p. 54). Technocrats and populists alike prefer the unmediated and centralized style of policymaking, wherein "policy outcomes are not based on competition between political factions and interests, or direct intervention by citizens, but are a result of quick and uncontested decisions" (Esmark 2017, p. 502). As a consequence, one can assume that technocratic-populist governance will lead to increases in the concentration of leadership power and decision-making, and, as already mentioned, executive aggrandizement (Bermeo 2016).

In the context of local public administration, this centralization strategy translates into strengthening top-down command and control, accumulation of responsibilities in the figure of the mayor or the executive, and reduction of power dispersion and the autonomy of agencies. Technocratic populists identify the problem as previous low performance in the old-fashioned, inefficient, incompetent, and often corrupt administration. They frequently propose administrative restructuring to streamline the administrative process and techno-logical updates to "bring the administration into the 21st century" through ICT and performance management tools. In the public sector management literature, e-government tools are regarded as effective means to streamline bureaucratic procedures and increase control of administrative performance and actions (Supiot 2017; Yeung 2018).

Personnel and Resources

Populist strategies do not stop at changing the institutional structure but take direct aim at the administrative personnel that might resist or sabotage their actions. The current literature associates the rise of populists in power with the systematic cleansing of staff as well as with the increase of clientelist and patronage practices in recruitment (Borins 2018). As a result, it is expected that populists will have a detrimental effect on the administrative capacity and expertise of policymaking bodies (Pierson 2017). According to the introduction to this volume, populists gain control over the administration through the reallocation of resources and the weakening of control units by cutting agencies' competences as well as their informational resources. Starving the administration is an alternative way to shift the scope of action without touching real competences.

Technocratic populists, in contrast to left- or right-wing populists, do not shy away from expertise. Rather, a focus on professional man-agement is what defines them. Competence and patronage are not conceived of as incompatible; instead, they try to combine them. Technocratic populists prefer to staff the key executive positions with specialists: so-called programmatic technocrats (Panizza, Peters, and Ramos Larraburu 2019). These tend to be from outside of public administration and apply professional, business-like solutions to administration. The expert outsiders are, however, embedded in a network of personal loyalty to the political leader (Drápalová and Wegrich 2020). The pressure to deliver will tend to push technocratic politicians to combine both loyalty and expertise. Therefore, unlike other types of populism, technocratic populists might ultimately increase the capacity of public administration.

Technocratic populists are expected to invest in modernization and information technologies. Although not all investment in technology serves populist goals and strategies per se, in the hands of populists ICT can be an effective smokescreen and a handy tool to control the use of resources. Transparency, online reporting systems, and user ratings can be used to justify the reallocation of resources or termination of agencies. Technology becomes a useful tool to monitor and control the performance of individual bureaucrats. These strategies can also create more control and discipline in the workplace, introducing major uncertainty and new channels for enforcement of compliance.

Accountability

Although populists claim to be in direct connection with the people, embodying their will, paradoxically, when elected, they frequently disregard, limit, or even manipulate citizens' participation (Batory and Svensson 2019; Paxton 2020). Paxton (2020) has shown in the case of three cities that, despite their rhetoric, populist mayors did not implement any participatory mechanisms. Hajnal and Boda (Chapter 4, this volume) mention that the Fidesz government in Hungary uses the participatory process to distort public opinion and manufacture support for Fidesz policies. Moreover, as the introduction suggests, populists will cut back the exchange of information with third parties and restrict media access. While social media is generally presented as a means for allowing an interconnected society and direct and (to a certain extent) unmediated access to information and citizen-oriented services, in the hands of populists technology can become an instrument that reinforces control and the status quo. For example, many technologically enhanced participatory channels promote a reductionist and passive view of the citizens' role and are frequently used as a means of control over participation, channeling it to areas that are less challenging to incumbents (Cardullo and Kitchin 2019).

To sum up, the characteristics of local government (personalization of local politics, direct contact with citizens, policy implementation) may make the success of populism more likely, but at the same time more challenging to sustain in the long term without collaboration with the administration. In line with expectations common to all populist parties, techno-populists will primarily aim at a reconfiguration of the administrative structure that will grant broader authority to the mayor and the executive and limit citizens' input into policies. This concentration might happen through increasing the responsibilities of the mayor or restricting the role of opposition or other relevant actors. Distinctive from other types of populism, technocratic populists base their legitimacy on output efficiency, and thus they will aim at streamlining procedures and cutting costs. They will use efficiency and expertise arguments to limit the independence of bureaucracy and to try to sideline it by hiring external experts (programmatic technocrats) that are, however, loyal to the leader (Panizza, Peters, and Ramos Larraburu 2019). Moreover, technocratic populists will prioritize technological solutions to steer citizens' input and give an illusion of citizens' participation more frequently than other populists and traditional political actors. The next section aims at finding patterns of liberal-democratic backsliding in the three European cities.

Technocratic Populism and Its Strategies in Three European Cities

This chapter draws on a comparative case study of three large European cities – Barcelona (Spain), Prague (the Czech Republic), and Rome (Italy) – governed by populist mayors that deployed a technocratic approach to executive politics. Populist parties frequently first gain representation at the subnational level, and large cities thus might serve as a test case for their performance and capabilities. Therefore, these three cities serve as illustrative examples and also possible indicators of trends in these countries. Although in different countries, large capital cities tend to share many (socioeconomic and cultural) characteristics and challenges (Sassen 2000).

All three cities are governed by mayors from technocratic-populist parties: ANO in Prague (until 2018); Barcelona en Comú in Barcelona (Podemos); and the Five Star Movement (M5S) in Rome. In each case, the local populist government preceded the success of the populist party at the national level. The three local leaders are women with previously limited experience in politics. Moreover, similar factors triggered the success of populist candidates in these three cities, namely the dynamics of party politics, corruption scandals, and inefficiencies in public administration performance (Agerberg 2017). The previous poor management, party system implosion, and corruption scandals in Rome and Prague, and bad management of austerity policies during the economic crisis in Barcelona, certainly played into the hands of populist leaders.

Nonetheless, the cases also differ in several aspects. The three cities represent three different types of local government setting (Mouritzen and Svara 2012): a committee form of government with an indirectly elected mayor (Prague); a strong but indirectly elected mayor (Barcelona); and a strong and directly elected mayor (Rome). This diversity among the cases makes it difficult to test causal claims. Still, at the same time, it provides rich evidence on the mechanisms under consideration and allows us to see how the strategies play out in slightly different contexts (Seawright and Gerring 2008). The empirical part is based on the analysis of local and national newspapers and city government documents in the original language, as well as secondary literature such as academic publications and speeches, as reported in the media. A review of local newspapers was carried out from 2014 to 2019. To analyze the documents, the author focused on populist leaders' claims and proposals and their interaction with the administration.

Five Star Movement, ANO, and Podemos

Between 2014 and 2016, ANO, the Five Star Movement, and Podemos celebrated their first electoral breakthroughs in local elections – victories that foreshadowed what would soon happen at the national level. For the first time ever, Prague, Barcelona, and Rome had not only female mayors but also populist governments. In the 2014 municipal elections, three years ahead of ANO's victory in the Czech general election, ANO won in Prague and sixteen large cities. In Prague, ANO formed a coalition government, and ANO's candidate Adriana Krnáčová, the former manager of the Czech branch of Transparency International, became the mayor of Prague. In Spain, the local election in 2015 represented an earthquake in the political landscape of Barcelona. A brand new party, Barcelona en Comú – a coalition of several political entities, including Podemos – became the primary political force in the city, and its leader, housing activist Ada Colau, became the mayor. In Italy, shortly before the 2016 municipal elections, the government of Rome imploded due to a massive corruption scandal (Pezzi 2019). Virginia Raggi, then a lawyer running for the Five Star Movement (M5S) as the antiestablishment candidate denouncing corruption, won with almost 70 percent at the run-off – the largest margin in the city's history. M5S applauded her landslide victory as a prelude to what would follow at the national level and as a chance to prove that M5S could govern a complex political and administrative system (de la Rosa and Quattromani 2019).

Although they are different parties, all three share a technocratic focus (Bickerton and Invernizzi Accetti 2018; Drápalová and Wegrich 2020; Havlík 2019). The Five Star Movement was founded in 2009 by Italian comedian, activist, and blogger Beppe Grillo (Bordignon and Ceccarini 2013). M5S was generally identified as a populist and antiestablishment party that denounced the widespread corruption and utter incompetence of the Italian political elite (Mosca 2014). More recently, authors have characterized M5S as an example of technocratic populism for its pragmatic and nonideological vision of politics, a strong emphasis on competence, and its enthusiastic support of technology to mediate between the party and citizens (Bickerton and Invernizzi Accetti 2018; Drápalová and Wegrich 2020). In line with the national electoral manifesto, the party's program for the 2016 municipal elections in Rome built on two main points: a sharp critique of the corrupt, incompetent, and self-serving political and administrative elites, and enthusiastic support for e-democracy and e-government.

ANO (Action of Dissatisfied Citizens) was founded in 2011 by Andrej Babiš, a wealthy entrepreneur and the owner of the country's largest food processing company and several media companies. ANO's political discourse has three main components: "the central role of Babiš as the party leader, a discourse that pits an ineffective and corrupt political elite against the hard-working people, and a policymaking style that substitutes politics and deliberation with the rational management of the firm" (Drápalová and Wegrich 2020, p. 11). Adriana Krnáčová followed the party's rhetoric. In her program, she promised a "new style of governance" based on transparency, smart technology, and a team of experts that would reorganize and speed up Prague's public administration. Krnáčová distanced herself from professional politics and highlighted her managerial experience: "I think the mayor is not supposed to be just a ribbon-cutter. The mayor should be a manager," she declared in one of her first public appearances (Krnáčová 2014). ANO's campaign slogans in Prague directly alluded to the need to substitute politicians with competent private sector managers: "Prague is run by idiots! We'll get rid of the godfathers, vote for professionals!" (cited in Drápalová and Wegrich 2020, p. 1).

Whether Podemos and its local confluence with other parties such as Barcelona en Comú should be considered populist is still somewhat controversial. For Bickerton and Invernizzi Accetti (2018), Podemos epitomizes the technocratic-populist party, whereas others see Podemos as a radical left-wing party (Blanco, Salazar, and Bianchi 2019). However, the leadership, discourse, and agenda of Ada Colau show specific aspects of populist and technocratic discourse. In her program and declarations, she describes political elites as a corrupt, dishonest, and self-serving cartel that fails to take into account ordinary peoples' needs. During the electoral campaign, Colau claimed that "what was at stake in the 2015 local elections was a choice between the 'Mafia' or the 'people'" (Colau 2015, cited in Blanco, Salazar, and Bianchi 2019, p. 10). She denounced mainstream parties for their corruption and their complicity with the economic powers. She publicly insisted that her candidacy had arrived "to drive the Mafia out of the city" (Colau 2015, cited in Blanco, Salazar, and Bianchi 2019, p. 10). The party's program also denounces the capture of political parties by economic elites and the limitation and criminalization of citizens' public participation. At the same time, Colau claimed that "her government is committed to common sense, and that she wants to keep what works independent of ideology" (Colau 2015, cited in Blanco, Salazar, and Bianchi 2019, p. 11).

Structure: Centralization of Power and Administrative Reform

From the beginning, newly elected mayor of Rome, Virginia Raggi, faced a great challenge. Previous governments had been investigated over a large corruption scandal (Mafia Capitale), while the staggering debt overburden, the budget, and images of dysfunctional public services (burning buses and mounting garbage in the streets) made it to the international news. Raggi aimed to re-engineer the administrative machine and make it cleaner, faster, and more efficient. A few months after taking office, Raggi announced a large-scale plan for organizational reform of the city hall administration, which aimed to "increase transparency, productivity and innovation and limit opportunities for corruption" (Sina 2016c). Consequently, the new administrative structure should be simpler and aligned according to the competences of expert managers to prevent overlapping and functional fragmentation (Sina 2016b). Among the projects intended to transform and centralize the administration of Rome, those based on technology enjoyed a central place. The mayor announced the creation of a single operations center for the ordinary and emergency management of the city, and the development of a unique communication interface for the public administration (Sina 2016a). Raggi summarizes these points in one of her public declarations:

There is medium-term work to be done to simplify and standardize procedures [in the city]. We must digitalize procedures and eliminate paperwork … and increase the transparency not only of accounts but also of contracts, which must be accessible to everyone. We will make unique, centralized, physical and telematic administrative access points, managed directly by the municipality and not by cooperatives and companies … The bureaucratic machine must be reorganized: there are offices with 800 people and others with four. We will start a staff reallocation, closures and mergers (Metro News 2016, cited in Drápalová and Wegrich 2020, p. 16).

Raggi also repeatedly tried to increase her competences. In 2019 she took over a very visible ICT agenda, and that same year Raggi requested that the central government change the law and increase her competences and executive powers with a governmental decree (D'Albergo 2019).

ANO's leader, Andrej Babiš, is an outspoken advocate for the reduction of the number of parliamentarians, the abolition of the Senate, and cutback of the overgrown and ineffective state administration (Babiš 2016). In Prague, ANO was in a position to implement his vision. In 2015, Krnáčová announced a massive shake-up to the administrative structure. She planned to merge local agencies and transfer core competencies into a single directorate, and to reorganize the city IT department. Under her direction, the new executive team initiated the restructuring of the executive boards of most city companies, merged and redistributed agendas and agencies, abolished one control level, and modified the system of audits (ČTK 2015; Pražský deník 2015). In 2018, Prague initiated the purchase of a majority of the shares of the

Prague Water Company, bringing it back into the city's property portfolio.

Krnáčová tried to reinforce her position by accumulating control over important agendas. She had personal oversight over anticorruption, the legislative agenda, and IT, as well as the commissions controlling public procurement (Oppelt 2017). This accumulation of positions was unusual even in comparison with her predecessors and signaled her intention to gain more direct political control over strategic and politically exposed agendas. Partly due to a complex political situation within the coalition, Krnáčová frequently resorted to hidden and informal bargaining with both the coalition and the opposition. The opposition complained that important decisions were not taken in the council's meetings but in the city hall kitchenette (Otto and Thuong Ly 2018).

The backbone of the program was the technological upgrade of the city governance (Smart Prague Agenda), intended to simplify procedures, increase transparency and connect different agencies and departments. As in Rome, her team has proposed the creation of a unified data platform that would connect the metropolitan government of Prague and different city districts electronically (iDNES.cz 2016). The pilot version of the platform (*Golemio*) was launched in 2018 and was designed to increase control over strategic public service providers.

According to Blanco, Salazar, and Bianchi (2019), Barcelona en Comú set out to disarticulate the previous governance plan, known as "Modelo Barcelona," designed by the predecessors of Xavier Trias. Although Colau and her executive team reorganized several aspects of the administrative structure of the city (the procurement and remunicipalization of the municipal water and energy companies), she has maintained the main organizational elements (city manager structure). The use of technology to connect and organize administration was more prevalent in Barcelona than in the two previous cases, with open source and open license data platforms (Ajuntament de Barcelona 2016). Nonetheless, against theoretical expectations, Colau also promoted political decentralization, transferred responsibilities to city districts, and maintained the administrative autonomy of local agencies.

Changes in the administrative organization are the most radical and long-lasting of populist reforms. The shift in the balance of power has direct consequences for the probability that populist leaders will be able to implement their agenda. In all three cities, populist politicians altered the administrative structure once in office, yet not always in line with this chapter's argument. In Prague and Rome, mayors, with varying degrees of success, have accumulated several relevant agendas (above all the anticorruption, procurement, and ICT agendas) under their direction and made changes to the administrative structure of the city hall. Barcelona, however, has diverged from the two cases. Ada Colau did not pursue an accumulation and centralization of power, but she decentralized some aspects of governance to city neighborhoods. In addition, Barcelona and Prague municipalized strategic services and utility companies, such as water and electricity.

Personnel and Resources: Disciplining the Inefficient Bureaucracy

In Rome, M5S had a strong anticorruption and protransparency rhetoric. Thus, the new executive fiercely set out to prevent the administrative discretion that led, they believed, to nepotism, patronage, and inefficient public service delivery. To prevent corruption, Raggi announced that departmental leaders and employees would be reappointed. This procedure was summarized in an official note: "Each manager will have the opportunity to propose themselves to fill the tasks to be assigned and will, therefore, be chosen based on their curriculum and motivations . . . For the first time, merit will prevail over the old clientelistic logic" (Sina, 2016b). The local government plan to transform the administration was presented in a document entitled "Regulation on the organization of the offices and services of Roma Capitale" (*Regolamento sull'ordinamento degli uffici e dei servizi di Roma Capitale*). This document detailed the new hiring, evaluation, and appointment procedures.

Far from the announced purge of the city bureaucracy, Raggi and her team initiated the process of hiring some 4,800 new city employees. Although a large part of this hiring had been foreseen in the 2020–2022 recruitment plan due to generational replacement, the timing of the "maxi concorsone," in an electoral year, was hardly fortuitous. Raggi proudly announced to the media that "One in four people who now work for Roma Capitale has been hired by this administration" (Perrone 2020). Even more controversial were personnel changes in the executive positions of the public utility companies and agencies (municipal waste, tourism agency, and metropolitan transportation companies), for which Raggi faced harsh criticism, being accused of patronage-based appointments. By 2016 Raggi was already being criticized by the media for filling top posts with collaborators who had been associated with her previous employment in a legal practice. Her head of office had to step down due corruption and nepotism charges. Also, collaboration with the programmatic technocrats was not without problems. Within three years (2016–2019), nineteen of the appointed city advisers (*assessori*) had left or had been replaced (D'Albergo 2019). In a recent scandal, Raggi allegedly threatened and improperly dismissed the manager of the municipal waste collection company after he refused to follow her orders to misreport the budget balance (Fittipaldi 2019; Fiaschetti and Sacchettoni 2019).

In Prague, shortly after taking up the post of mayor, Krnáčová declared that she would bring a team of professional managers to the city hall and announced large-scale personnel restructuring, including a plan to reduce the local administration by 10 percent to limit costs (ČTK 2015; Pražský deník 2015). Despite this public declaration, she did not reduce administrative personnel but continued to hire new employees (Oppelt 2016). The most radical personnel changes targeted the management positions of the municipal utility companies and agencies. During the electoral campaign she promised that municipal companies would be run by professional managers from the private sector, and not by politicians, as had been done previously (Drápalová and Wegrich 2020). Once in office, Krnáčová reorganized the boards of most of the public companies, but used them as a reward system for coalition members (Dolejší and Prchal 2016; iDNES.cz 2018).

Krnáčová also initiated some debatable personnel changes. She dismissed the director of the Prague Institute for Planning and Development (IPR), which is responsible for urban strategy. According to the mayor, the IPR frequently blocked the decisions of the municipal government. She also dismissed the director of the Prague Public Transport Company (ČTK 2016). A city councilor from the Pirate Party complained about politicized hiring in an interview:

"She dismissed the head of the transport company and appointed her own man without a proper open tender, as if Prague was another branch of Babiš's private company" (Oppelt 2016).

In Barcelona, Ada Colau frequently attacked the political establishment, calling it "mafia" and accusing parties of colluding with economic interests. Nevertheless, once in office, she did not target public administration and has repeatedly shown respect for Barcelona's long history of administrative innovation. National austerity measures have paralyzed hiring for all local administrations since the crisis in 2008, and thus Colau had not had any margin for a systemic purge. To the contrary, in 2017 she announced the creation of 2,000 new positions aimed primarily at stabilizing the temporary staff already employed by the city (Blanchar 2017). The new government tried to counterbalance its lack of political experience with expertise. Many of the highest executive positions in the government and the administration have been occupied by professors, experts, and political activists active in the anti-austerity movement, displacing officials appointed by previous governments (Blanco, Salazar, and Bianchi 2019). Perhaps the most internationally renowned appointments were her Smart City manager and critical data scholar, Francesca Bria, and well-known professor, Joan Subirats. The city also hired numerous technology and IT experts and data analysts to increase internal analytical capacity (Ajuntament de Barcelona 2016).

According to the framework in the introduction, the arbitrary distribution of resources, strategic firing, and patronage hiring of administrative personnel are methods used by populists to discipline bureaucracy. In the technocratic version, resources are concentrated mainly in the technological transformation of administration (smart city, digital management tools), and personnel policies are characterized by hiring programmatic technocrats, selected on the basis of their expertise but also their personal loyalty to the party leader. The evidence collected from the three cases under consideration does not point to one unified strategy. All three cities announced and initiated large-scale personnel reorganization, but instead of generalized firing, they opted for increasing the administrative staff. This can be seen as a strategy to colonize public administration with party supporters, but more probably it is a sign of the need to increase the capacity of administrations that have been understaffed as a consequence of previous austerity policies. Where these cities clearly followed the same logic was in the area of higher-level administrative positions. All three cities made personnel shifts at the strategic executive level in municipal companies and agencies. Mayors in Prague, Barcelona, and Rome staffed these positions with experts and managers from academia and the private or public sectors that, despite their expected loyalty to leaders, showed a certain degree of professional independence. However, as the case of Rome shows, those professionals that were too independent were quickly replaced.

Accountability: Omitting Citizens' Participation

The Five Star Movement explicitly linked direct citizen participation with digitalization and ICT. According to its founders, the Internet and new technologies are instruments of "disintermediation" between citizens and institutions and provide opportunities for direct democracy without interruptions (Grillo and Casaleggio 2011). Despite the strong rhetoric, in Rome no significant effort to increase the input of citizens in policymaking was observed (de la Rosa and Quattromani 2019). The party's internal decision-making procedures were frequently criticized for lack of transparency, representativeness, and openness (Mosca 2014). For internal consultations with party members, M5S uses a closed online platform (*Rousseau*), where only registered members and sympathizers are able to vote on party proposals and strategic choices such as the selection of candidates. Although M5S created a specific agenda for digitalization and participation (Roma Semplice), no substantive implementation of e-government and online services took place. As of 2019, only 10,000 citizens had participated in some of the online consultations activated on the Roma Capitale e-government portal, according to the declaration of the mayor.

Prague also shows similar inconsistency between rhetoric and implementation. Although technologically enhanced participatory processes were at the top of ANO's program, the actual implementation was timid at best. Although Krnáčová frequently declared that with the help of technology the city would be more responsive to citizens, there has not been any significant progress in the participative agenda. The only direct consultations took place in Prague districts governed by the opposition. ANO did not organize a single city-wide referendum, nor did it develop online participation projects.

Perhaps the most significant difference between Barcelona and the two other cities is in the centrality of citizens' participation. In contrast to Prague and Rome, Ada Colau radically transformed Barcelona's citizen participation model (Blanco, Salazar, and Bianchi 2019).

Barcelona's participatory agenda is composed of two main axes: a digital platform and agenda-setting engine called *Decidim Barcelona*, and open meetings with the mayor every fifteen days (Cardullo and Kitchin 2019; Drápalová and Wegrich 2020). In her public declarations, Colau emphasizes the role of technology, achieving more participation and effective coproduction of services (Calzada 2018; March and Ribera-Fumaz 2018). In 2016, Barcelona piloted an online participatory platform, *Decidim*, which aims at enhancing citizens' agenda-setting capacity in budgetary and financial matters, environment, and government (Ajuntament de Barcelona 2016). This platform was declared a success due to its high participation rates. The second axis of the participatory agenda was face-to-face open meetings with political representatives in Barcelona districts (Eizaguirre, Pradel-Miquel, and García 2017). Ada Colau also publishes details about her schedule and meetings, and the financial department releases data on the spending and public procurement of all the agencies that depend on the city council.

The findings qualify the proposed theoretical argument. Populist leaders in Prague and Rome did not curtail citizens' participation, they simply ditched any initial plans for inclusion of citizens in policymaking. Technocratic populists claim to bring a new version of technology-enhanced direct democracy that gives a voice to ordinary people, yet the empirical analysis finds a gap between the rhetoric and the policies they enact. Only Barcelona translated the promises of greater citizen participation into concrete policies. Colau implemented participatory budgets, direct meetings with the mayor, and a new participatory online platform, *Decidim*, during her first term. In Barcelona, the latest technologies played an important role as the interface between citizens and the administration.

In summation, the cases under consideration vary concerning the combination of the elements deployed in practice (see Table 6.1). After analyzing the government in the three cities, it is immediately evident that Barcelona en Comú's governmental style differs from that of ANO and M5S. In Prague and Rome we attested clear intentions to centralize the government structures, to substitute executive and managerial positions with programmatic technocrats, and to increase control over administration, as well as a lack of engagement with citizens. Ada Colau's interaction with administration and citizens, however, clashes with the chapter's predictions. Barcelona en Comú

Table 6.1 *Summary of findings*

Dimension	Rome	Prague	Barcelona
Party Structure	M5S Centralization and reorganization of departments.	ANO Centralization of Agendas under the direct supervision of the mayor. Reorganization and merging of departments.	Barcelona en Comú Reorganization and merging of departments. Decentralization of political decision-making.
Personnel/ Resources	Large-scale hiring of civil servants. Changes in the leading managerial positions in public agencies and companies. New managers: experts and connected loyalists.	Large-scale hiring of civil servants. Changes in the leading managerial positions in public agencies and companies. New managers: experts, cronies, and connected loyalists.	Large-scale hiring of civil servants. Changes in the leading managerial positions in public agencies and companies. New managers: experts, academics, and activists.
Accountability	Several direct democracy mechanisms announced. No clear implementation. E-government: limited number of online services. Citizens' input restricted to party sympathizers via platform *Rousseau.*	Several direct democracy mechanisms announced. Few policies were implemented (data platform *Golemio*). Citizens have limited input (approved rules for limited participatory budgeting).	Technologically enhanced participatory mechanisms were implemented: *Decidim* online participatory platform, direct meetings with the mayor, participatory budgeting, public–private cocreation.

decentralized power by increasing the competences of city districts, potentiated cocreation, offered long-term contracts to public employees, and implemented a participatory agenda based on digital tools and open assemblies. Moreover, despite the centrality of technology in populist programs, only Barcelona implemented ICT to organize services and participation.

Conclusion

Democratic backsliding and its effect on state organization and administration are gaining momentum within Public Administration research as populist parties start to implement their political agendas. Despite the increasing relevance of the topic, local government is seldom analyzed. This chapter adopted the framework from the introduction to shed light on the impact of technocratic populism on public administration in three European cities. The findings corroborate the framework presented in the introduction of the book. Technocratic populists tried to sideline and use the administration by means of targeting its organization, personnel composition, and resources. Specifically, ANO in Prague and M5S in Rome made changes to the organization of the city administration and concentrated power in the office of the mayor and her executive team. Both mayors weakened the independence of the administration by strategic replacement of management and executive positions and the subsequent appointment of programmatic technocrats loyal to the party leader, and not by the generalized dismissal of civil servants. In the challenging quest to combine influence over policymaking and maintain the quality of services, technocratic populism increased both the loyalty of administrators and their competence. The direct democracy and participatory agendas quickly faded from their discourse and programs.

There were, however, important differences between the cases in terms of the combination of elements deployed in practice and their impact. Barcelona clearly diverged from Rome and Prague. Ada Colau implemented horizontal power-decentralization, a participatory governance agenda (*Decidim*), and the technologically enhanced (cocreation) of selected policies and services. The success of the new digital participatory platform *Decidim* stands in direct contrast to the lack of action of M5S and ANO. This chapter shows that populist parties are an increasingly heterogeneous family of parties that might have a very different impact on government performance. Barcelona en Comú shows that the populist surge can also give rise to more progressive political forces. Moreover, this sharp difference between Rome and Prague on the one hand, and Barcelona on the other, points to the presence of a variety of populist strategies that do not automatically lead to negative consequences for public administration. The results illustrate that the effect of populist parties in government is contingent on party characteristics, organization, and policy focus. Thus, public administration scholars should pay more attention to the characteristics of parties and their electoral base.

Populist parties thrive across all levels of government. The characteristics of local government – namely, a greater focus on implementation and administration, a closer and direct connection with citizens and a tendency to personalize politics – make cities a suitable springboard and testbed for populist projects, but at the same time a hard testing ground for their success. In municipal politics, the pressure to deliver is greater, and competence is highly regarded. Populists in cities are forced to combine their anti-elite discourse that wants to sideline bureaucracy and the need to engage with the administration to effectively deliver services. Technocratic populists seemed to find the key to this conundrum by combining populist strategy with technocracy. However, this mix creates tensions that are visible in the medium to long terms and poses a significant threat to the sustainability of this political project (Drápalová and Wegrich 2020). ANO in Prague did not stand for re-election in 2019. In Barcelona, Ada Colau lost the election but maintained her position only because Socialist's Party of Catalonia (PSC) feared her less than they feared the Catalan separatists. Virginia Raggi, once the mayor with the highest level of support, stands little chance of re-election. The electoral support of the populist parties was broken due to their lack of tangible results and conflicts between the programmatic technocrats and the populist politicians. Political scientists dealing with the impact of populist parties should take into consideration such conflicts with public administration, especially in situations where the administration poses significant challenges to the implementation of the populist agenda.

As argued in the introduction, the institutional context influences both the populists' strategies and public administration's resilience. This concern is especially relevant for subnational politics, where the different organization of local government, the multilevel relations with the central government, and local autonomy will shrink or expand the governance space for populists to implement their agenda. In this chapter the organization of local government varies across cases, the three cities being examples of the three most diffuse types of local government organization. Despite the institutional variation, we observed remarkable similarities in technocratic-populist strategies across the three cases. This finding strengthens the generalizability of the framework and points to a new exciting research agenda combining public administration and populism.

New challenges will undoubtedly arise with emergencies such as the current COVID-19 pandemic and ensuing economic downturn that will put the viability of the technocratic-populist project to the test. Will technocratic populists be more responsible than other populist types? Effective cooperation with the administration and multilevel coordination are going to be crucial in implementing policies that aim to combat the unprecedented health emergency. During this emergency, local governments should become effective coordinators between citizens and the central government. Will populists limit themselves to this role, or will they be tempted to exploit the crisis to attack the elites and show off their leadership skills. Will the COVID-19 pandemic further compel the populists to government and territorial centralization or, on the contrary, allow for more subnational experimentation? These are all open empirical questions. The findings of this chapter and the theoretical framework provide a possible starting point.

7 Populism and the Deep State: The Attack on Public Service Under Trump

DONALD MOYNIHAN

Introduction

This chapter addresses how the Trump administration exemplified and accelerated a long-term trend toward democratic backsliding in the United States by undermining public sector institutions, with particular focus on the federal career public service. As noted in the introduction to this volume, populist leaders can employ a mixture of strategies, from ignoring to sidelining or using the bureaucracy. While previous presidents sought to take more direct control of the parts of government they are ideologically at odds with, the Trump administration went further. It sidelined administrative expertise and scientists in many areas. Trump chose public leaders whose lack of qualification was frequently matched only by their disdain for their organizational mission. To exert bureaucratic control, the Trump administration pushed the boundaries of the law beyond its breaking point. While avoiding a direct legislative attack on the civil service via a governmentwide reform, it claimed it could eliminate civil service protections via executive order, weakened the ability of public sector unions to negotiate for benefits, punished individuals and units deemed not to be politically loyal, and weakened oversight bodies such as Inspectors General. All of this was accompanied by a rhetoric of delegitimization, whereby the president and his supporters frequently invoked conspiratorial theories of "deep state" plots that have become embedded in the Republican Party. Trump may be an outlier, but he is not an anomaly in terms of US democratic backsliding. And while the 2020 election may have handed Trump a loss, it did little to persuade the Republican Party to abandon the authoritarian elements of Trumpism.

There can be little doubt that the Trump administration counts as a populist movement. What Mudde and Rovira Kaltwasser (2017, p. 6) define as populism surely fits: "a thin-centered ideology that considers society to be ultimately separated into two homogeneous and antagonistic camps, 'the pure people' versus 'the corrupt elite,' and which argues that politics should be an expression of the volonté générale (general will) of the people." Trumpism has few fixed ideological points of reference. Its marriage to traditional Republican policies has resulted not in more redistributive policies via a more generous welfare state, but in greater tax cuts tilted toward higher earners, largely unsuccessful attacks on health and welfare programs, and economic nationalism characterized by trade wars and reduced immigration (both legal and illegal). The rhetorical marriage of Trumpism and the paranoid style that resided largely in the Republican Party since the 1960s has been a more natural union, built on shared assumptions that "(1) a small number of people is (2) secretly plotting to (3) do significant harm" (Hart 2020, p. 363), where the members of the career civil service are cast among the usual suspects (Hofstadter 2012).

Trump's portrayal of the public service reflects a tendency to present the world in Manichean terms: as a battle between the forces of evil and good. He began his official campaign by characterizing Mexican immigrants as rapists, continued to portray immigrants and shadowy "globalists" as invaders threatening America, and blamed his loss on massive electoral fraud. Even before he became a candidate, he built a base within the Republican Party by joining the birther movement that questioned whether President Obama was actually born in America, and thus, by extension, whether his Presidency was legitimate. Opposition Democrats were routinely portrayed as corrupt. This populist rhetorical style was extended to the public sector. While previous presidents engaged in some form of bureaucracy-bashing, Trump went dramatically further, portraying the broader administrative system as a "deep state" or "swamp" that only he could fix.

The difficulty in any evaluation of Trump's populism is making sense of the sheer volume of material: separating a grandiose tweet from meaningful administrative change. What would be extraordinary in any other administration – a senior career official making allegations of serious wrongdoing against the president, for example – became routine under Trump. The other challenge is separating broader patterns of democratic backsliding from those specific to Trump. As we shall see, the erosion of public sector institutions did not start with Trump; many were already in place, though were not previously exploited by a leader with such clear authoritarian tendencies. The Trump administration pursued democratic backsliding with greatest effects in the politicization of personnel and norms, and an evasion of traditional mechanisms of traditional accountability.

These tendencies, and their consequent costs, are illustrated in two brief case studies: Trump's impeachment process, and a botched response to COVID-19. The chapter concludes by discussing how the intense polarization of the US electorate provided a protective shield for the Trump administration. This raises perhaps the most worrying aspect of the US case: democratic backsliding is largely understood through a partisan perspective, with one party largely the author of such backsliding, and with its backers largely indifferent to or supportive of the process. It becomes hard to see how a polarized electorate can permanently break this cycle.

Patterns of Backsliding

How do we recognize backsliding in liberal democracies in the context of public administration? Bauer and Becker (2020) identify centralization of structure and resources, politicization of personnel or norms, and evasion of accountability as key indicators (see also the Introduction to this volume). As I explain in the coming sections, and in the case studies, documenting how Trump stacks up against these criteria means recognizing that such tendencies have been long part of the US federal government. Indeed, one aspect of US exceptionalism is populist suspicion of the federal bureaucracy, evident even in the origins of the state. A chief criticism of Alexander Hamilton by his Republican rivals was that he was creating an army of federal bureaucrats. President Andrew Jackson heralded the spoils system as a way to prevent a permanent class of bureaucrats. The introduction of the civil service system at the end of the nineteenth century tempered this pattern, and for much of the twentieth century good government advocates succeeded in expanding investments in expertise and neutrality by giving federal employees more protections (Gailmard and Patty 2013).

Whatever consensus existed about the role of the administrative state in supporting democracy, political influence remained. The civil service grew partly by presidents expanding career status protections to their appointees, while still retaining a small army of political appointees to help them run the government (Ingraham 1995). The "paranoid style" of American politics framed federal bureaucrats as part of the ruling elite, as evidenced by McCarthyite attacks on career civil servants as Communists during the 1950s (Hofstadter 2012).

In the decades that followed, the parties moved further apart in their evaluation of the career public service. The Nixon administration undertook a campaign of political control of career bureaucrats, aspects of which would be repeated by future presidents, but used most aggressively by Republicans and taken to a new level by Trump. Nixon and his successors saw federal bureaucrats as self-interested, intent on protecting their programs, and unresponsive to any leader seeking change – and, in particular, to conservative presidents seeking to reshape and reduce the administrative state (Moynihan and Roberts 2010).

Scholarly trends followed suit to some degree. The applications of principal–agent theory that emerged in the same time period began with assumptions of agent misbehavior, but offered little concern about the motives of the principal (Moe 1985; Niskanen 1971). Some research documented the tensions between bureaucrats and their political masters during the Reagan (Durant 1992; O'Leary 2020) and Bush administrations (Lewis 2008; Moynihan and Roberts 2010; Resh 2015). But attention to how a more politicized presidency weakened agency effectiveness, articulations of the American state that emphasized the role of bureaucracy as a democratic safeguard (e.g. Rohr 1986) fell out of fashion in both public administration and political science.

As we shall see, the setting therefore allowed Trump to employ a mixture of strategies. The habit of political patronage and politicized control facilitated a sidelining of the bureaucracy and a reliance on political appointees. Trump pushed these traditions further than normal. Appointees with little competence were selected due to their political loyalty. The Trump administration overturned expert and science-based advice from career bureaucrats. In pockets of the administration, most notably in restricting immigration, Trump used the bureaucracy to successfully implement populist policies that he had no legislative support for. In the next sections we further review how the specific strategies presented in the introduction worked during the Trump administration.

Centralizing Control

The Nixonian model of presidential control took two main forms (Moynihan and Roberts 2010). One was centralization of policy-making; the other was control of personnel. The first approach fits well with Bauer and Becker's (2020) strategy of centralizing structures. The White House, rather than individual agencies where career staff held sway, became the heart of policymaking from the Nixon administration on. In this, the Trump administration was similar to past administrations, but with one obvious difference. Members of the White House inner circle included the president's own family and others with little experience in, and much skepticism of, government. At various times, the president's son-in-law was tasked with leading initiatives addressing the opioid epidemic, diplomatic relations with Mexico and China, criminal justice reform, Middle East peace, a shadow COVID-19 task force, and overall government reforms, where he promised to make the federal government "run like a great American company" (Parker and Rucker 2017)

While past presidents had drawn on "kitchen cabinets" of informal advisers, the quality of those advisers and their roles were different under Trump. Three members of Trump's private Mar-A-Lago club were given extraordinary influence over the Department of Veteran's Affairs, the largest federal agency in terms of employees, to the point that they helped to push out its Secretary (Arnsdorf 2018). The president directed his private lawyer, Rudy Giuliani, to represent him to foreign governments, which partly precipitated his first impeachment. Trump avidly watched and consulted with conservative television commentators, with a revolving door between the White House and its most vocal media defender, Fox News, that sometimes resembled a state-controlled propaganda outlet (Mayer 2019).

The centralization of resource allocation that Bauer and Becker (2020) identify fits less well with the US context than with parliamentary systems, given the separation of powers in the budget process. As many presidents have learned, Congress jealously guards the power of the purse. Trump called for large cuts in his proposed budget, leading to the unusual sight of agency heads explaining to Congressional appropriation committees that they needed less money. But the president's budget proposal is just that: a proposal, with limited influence on actual budget decisions. The president does have some powers in budget execution. As detailed below (see Case 1: Impeachment), Trump's abused those powers, resisting Congressional controls. In the context of the impeachment process, efforts to centralize resources backfired by moving the White House into the realm of illegality. But, again, this is not new. The standard of a powerful president exerting tight policy and resource control dates back at least to Nixon, with similar skirting of the law.

Politicization of Personnel

The second form of control pursued by prior presidents was closer political control of the bureaucracy. Here, the Trump administration again repeated prior patterns, while moving well beyond the norms of past presidents.

The United States is unusual in terms of the prevalence and power of noncareer political appointees. The reliance on about 4,000 appointees is partly a historical echo of the spoils system, wherein government positions were effectively treated as the property of political parties, and partly reflects a conservative suspicion of bureaucrats, and with it an abiding belief that the president needs his own people. This philosophy reached an apotheosis under Trump, who sees the career civil service as "the deep state" permanently plotting his demise. A Trumpian worldview that divides public servants into either loyalists or deep state leaves little room for neutral competence.

It is easy to think of politicization of personnel as occurring on one dimension: the neutral expert is replaced with someone selected on the basis of political loyalty. The degree to which that loyalty matters in selection, the greater the politicization. If political appointees offer responsiveness to elected officials through their loyalty, this responsiveness comes at a cost. The best evidence we have is that appointees generate poorer organizational performance relative to career officials (Lewis 2007). On this dimension, the Trump administration became more politicized. Many experienced Republicans were reluctant to work for him given his volatility and character (Rein and Philip 2017). The administration relied heavily on political loyalists who often had little interest in or knowledge about their job, or lobbyists looking out for clients (Lewis 2018). To an unprecedented degree, senior leaders appointed to agencies expressed suspicion or outright hostility to elements of their agency's mission in a vast array of policy areas, including environmental, energy, and federal land regulation; public education; housing; and health and social programs.

There are two other criteria relevant to politicization that affect the quality of government and seem especially pertinent under populist regimes. The first is what we might call depth. The Trump administration simply did not have enough qualified players to field a full team. The second criterion is stability. The expert is generally assumed to be a career official, with job security that allows them to last from one administration to the next. The appointee is less secure, serving at the pleasure of the president. US political appointees typically last 18–24 months. In the Trump administration, turnover was higher. Trump removed key officials, and stated a preference for temporary appointees rather than submitting them to the Senate for formal approval. Four out of five senior White House positions turned over during the Trump presidency, and one-third of senior leadership positions were still vacant even by 2020 (Steinhauer and Kanno-Youngs 2020).

Such temporary leaders cannot establish medium-term goals, make credible commitments or offer a vision for the direction of their agency. They have all of the credibility of a substitute teacher. By one calculation, the most senior Cabinet-level jobs were filled by "acting" officials for one-ninth of Trump's administration, about three times the rate of the prior Obama administration (Blake 2020).

One implication of the lack of depth is tied to the lack of stability, which is the role of career officials in filling out leadership positions. Presidents tend to concentrate their most qualified appointees in high-profile agencies, policy settings where they want to make an impact, or agencies they distrust (Lewis 2008). In agencies lacking these characteristics, it is more likely that career officials are left in senior positions of leadership. This may seem to provide a protection against democratic backsliding, and perhaps is better than the counterfactual. But the US system is designed to work with political appointees in place. For example, the Federal Vacancies Act of 1998 allows career officials to step into political appointee leadership roles normally subject to confirmation of the Senate, but limits the number of days that an official can hold a senior position as "acting" leader to less than a year. Thus, the instability of the system continues even when career officials are designated as leaders.

These aspects of politicization – expertise, depth, and stability – combined to produce a shambolic outcome, in terms of a more politicized personnel and performance. Trump's effectiveness at side-lining or ignoring the bureaucracy was hampered by an inability to build and maintain a parallel structure of competent political appointees.

In other areas Trump undermined federal employee protections. In terms of legislation, Congress passed the Department of Veterans Affairs Accountability and Whistleblower Protection Act in 2017, which weakened employee protections in the largest federal agency, making it easier to fire them and harder for employees to appeal disciplinary actions. At the same time, Trump has offered no serious attempt to legislate governmentwide civil service reform. A proposal to eliminate the governmentwide human resource agency, the Office of Personnel Management, was rebuffed by Congress. In part, this is because the White House generally lacked policy entrepreneurs that could turn such ideas into legislation, as is reflected in Trump's thin legislative record.

Trump waited until shortly before the 2020 election to push his most ambitious change to the civil service system: "Executive Order on Creating Schedule F in the Excepted Service." This order established a new class of political appointees. Any career employee with a policy advisory role could be swept into the category, meaning that tens of thousands (or even more) career civil servants would lose their job protections. The sheer scale of the order was breathtaking, indicating a view by Trump officials that the constitution provides the president near-absolute control over the bureaucracy, and that the president has a right to demand absolute loyalty from federal employees (Rein, Dawsey, and Olorunnipa 2020).

The irony of Trump's assault on the bureaucracy is that he turned to the very administrative state that he had denounced when his legislative initiatives failed. A huge proportion of his more significant policy goals – in immigration, regulatory, and welfare policy areas, for example – have been pursued via executive orders and the rulemaking process.

Such administrative tools have also been used for public administration policy changes. Trump signed Executive Order 13839 in 2018: Promoting Accountability and Streamlining Removal Procedures Consistent with Merit System Principles, which set up a broader governmentwide framework to make it easier to fire and discipline career employees. He has pursued a broad battle against public sector unions. One rule allowed federal employees to opt out of paying their union dues, a strategy which had elsewhere been used by Republican governors to significantly weaken public unions in their states. As far back as 2017, White House officials mapped out the goal of decertifying such unions as a way of undercutting the "left-wing ideologues" who run them (Kullgren 2019). In January of 2020, President Trump proposed eliminating collective bargaining in the Department of Defense, creating the potential to remove bargaining rights from 500,000 federal employees. This pattern again echoed the past. The Bush administration had similarly sought to remove collective bargaining rights from Department of Homeland Security employees when the Department was created (Moynihan 2005).

For federal employees, there are obvious concerns about how weakening bargaining rights will hurt their pocketbook. In his proposed budgets, Trump sought to make employees pay more toward their benefits and limit pay raises. There are broader concerns not just about whether such cuts undermine the ability of the federal government to recruit and retain talent, but also about the potential for a less-protected federal workforce to be more subject to politicization. Unions are not perfect, but they offer one organized form of resistance against politicization. Stripped of their bargaining powers, unions become less relevant, and less able to defend their members from politicization.

Politicization of Norms

The line between the politicization of personnel selection processes and weakening of protections, and the politicization of norms, is blurry. With Trump, it is fair to say that such strategies are intertwined. One aspect of the politicization of norms is Trump's enthusiastic embrace, and creation, of norms of public sector delegitimization. Trump seems to believe the deep state conspiracy theories he gives frequent voice to. It is impossible to find a president since the civil service was constructed who was so taken with the idea that career officials are a force of evil that he needs to control. Within the space of forty years, Republican messaging went from "government is not the solution to our problem; government is the problem" in Reagan's inaugural speech to a more conspiratorial-minded evocation of public officials as not just dysfunctional but determined to undermine the president. The change in tone is mirrored in one senior White House official, Steve Bannon, promising the "deconstruction of the administrative state" (Rucker and Costa 2017), reflecting a philosophy that government officials had little to offer in terms of expertise, and the rules and regulations they had designed should be removed where possible. In a speech in Poland, Trump warned of "the steady creep of government bureaucracy that drains the vitality and wealth of the people" (Clark 2017).

When Trump engineered the longest shutdown of services in federal government history, he tweeted (incorrectly) "that most of the people not getting paid are Democrats," indicating a belief that the furloughed federal employees were his partisan opponents. The cumulative effect of this mix of cynicism and conspiracy-mongering is not just to weaken the motivation of current employees, but to also make it harder to recruit the next generation of public servants. The deep state conspiracies also provided a useful excuse for Trump's failures and scandals. In various tweets, Trump proposed that the "deep state" was the reason why his political rivals were being protected from prosecution, while he was being victimized by unjustified smears by a government akin to Nazi Germany.

The president was not alone. His Chief of Staff, Mick Mulvaney, former head of the Office of Management and Budget (OMB), expressed frustration that it was not easier to fire career officials he viewed as being liberal (Dawsey 2020). Elsewhere, Mulvaney applauded a forced relocation of a unit of federal scientists as "a wonderful way to sort of streamline government" because so many quit (Katz 2019). The researchers had offered evidence that Trump's trade policies were hurting farmers, resulting in what appeared to be a retaliatory move to force them to move to Kansas City or exit their federal jobs. One of the informal methods the Nixon administration had developed to sideline troublesome federal bureaucrats was such forced relocations, with the hope they would quit, or at least become less influential (Ingraham 1995). But the Nixon administration had never attempted anything on such a scale. Of the 224 employees scheduled to move, three-quarters quit (Guarino 2019). Trump's executive order to remove job protections from civil servants with policy advisory roles sought to eliminate the need for such laborious efforts; instead, he could just fire civil servants who delivered evidence he disagreed with (Rein, Dawsey, and Olorunnipa 2020).

Another option to ignore the bureaucracy involves simply replacing career positions. While Congress resisted the proposed cuts, the Trump administration dragged its feet in hiring in some areas in particular. The Environmental Protection Agency lost 700 scientists, only half of whom were replaced, indicative of a broader trend of a 1.5 percent drop in scientists hired during the first two years of the administration, compared to an 8 percent increase during the equivalent period of the Obama administration (Gowen et al. 2020). Trump also ordered the elimination of one-third of outside advisory committees – that is, outside scientists who give free expertise to government – on the grounds that such committees are wasteful (Gowen et al. 2020). Within scientific agencies, Trump appointees looked for ways to minimize scientific expertise by shutting down studies, ignoring scientific advice on decisions, discouraging scientists from providing public information, and ruling certain areas of research or terminology as off-limits (Plumer and Davenport 2019). This environment, more extreme than before, caused many scientists to exit the administration.

Avoiding Accountability

The US system is designed to check power and provide transparency. Trump's moves into democratic backsliding depended upon an unwinding of many of those traditional mechanisms of accountability. Republicans in Congress were skeptical of critics of Trump, and Trump's Department of Justice was led by political appointees seemingly intent on protecting the president.

The Office of Inspector General was created as a post-Nixon good government reform intended to provide a form of internal accountability by placing corruption watchdogs in each agency. A flaw in the design of the position is that it is technically a presidential appointment, although the norm has been that presidents rarely remove Inspectors General and only for cause, unlike other political appointees. To an unprecedented degree, Trump replaced Inspectors General he judged as being disloyal (Ward 2020). This gives employees little reason to report, or to cooperate with Inspectors General who could be replaced with a loyalist. Congressional investigators into wrongdoing found some whistleblowers willing to testify, but little cooperation from the Trump administration, which has tended to resist legislative investigations.

If an employee alleged unfair treatment by a political appointee, they could theoretically appeal to the Merit Systems Protection Board, the body charged with monitoring and preventing politicization of the career workforce. However, due to a slow appointment process, the Board lack a quorum during the Trump administration, meaning that cases could not be heard. Central government agencies such as the Office of Personnel Management have shown little willingness to speak out against abuses such as reassignment of career officials for political reasons (US Government Accountability Office 2020).

Trump fired the heads of both the FBI and Department of Justice for perceived lack of loyalty, a crucial quality given Trump's legal troubles. Historically, the Department of Justice sought to maintain some measure of independence from the president in order to be able to investigate his actions. This distance was largely erased with the appointment of William Barr as Attorney General. Barr was an enthusiastic advocate of the unitary executive theory, proposing in a Department of Justice memo that "Constitutionally, it is wrong to conceive of the President as simply the highest officer within the Executive branch hierarchy. He alone *is* the Executive branch. As such, he is the sole repository of *all Executive powers* conferred by the Constitution" (emphases in original) (Barr 2018). On this basis, Barr actively limited investigations into the president's actions. He also directly intervened and overruled career federal prosecutors in cases where they were investigating the president's associates, most notably withdrawing a prosecution of the president's former National Security Adviser, Michael Flynn, *after* Flynn pleaded guilty. Almost 2,000 former Department of Justice alumni wrote an open letter calling for Barr to resign.

Table 7.1 summarizes the evidence on how Trump lines up against the categories of potential backsliding outlined in the introduction. As we shall see, these strategies set the stage for bureaucratic responses, which are examined in the next section.

Reactions of the Bureaucracy

It is impossible to separate the politicization of government from the response of public officials. Do civil servants engage in exit, voice, loyalty, as Hirschman proposed, or engage in acts of sabotage or neglect (Golden 1992; Hirschman 1970; Guedo-Neto and

Table 7.1 *Continuity or change? Patterns of backsliding under Trump*

	Continuity or change	Examples
Centralizing structures	Largely continuity, but with high degree of informality in decision-makers	Members of the president's private club controlling the VA, the president's son-in-law given extraordinary responsibilities
Centralizing resource allocation	Largely continuity, failed efforts at cuts, more overt control of funds	Trump illegally withheld appropriated funds from Ukraine, triggering impeachment
Politicizing staff	Similar tactics to the past, but used more aggressively	Moving staff seen as disloyal, assigning them to unpleasant tasks, weakening labor protections, executive order stripping civil service protections
Politicizing norms	Unprecedented in attacks on public servants, retribution for disloyalty	Characterization of the "deep state," public attacks and efforts to punish public servants seen as disloyal
Reducing external accountability	Unprecedented effort to limit legal oversight of his actions	Firing Inspectors General, refusal to cooperate with Congressional oversight

Source: own compilation.

Peters, Chapter 10, this volume)? We saw a mixture of responses under Trump, though with relatively weak evidence of sabotage. As noted earlier, exits increased in certain areas, such as the scientific community. In 2017 there was a marked increase in exits overall, with a 16 percent increase over the prior year, but such exits leveled off soon after (Heckman 2018). Even that statistic needs context, since a very large proportion of federal employees are eligible for retirement, meaning an exit does not necessarily mean quitting mid-career.

Some career officials combined voice with exits, making public statements critical of Trump as they resigned, including an Ambassador to
Panama, an acting Ambassador to China, a State Department
employee who protested against the treatment of immigrants, a CIA
official motivated by Trump's denigration of his agency, and
researchers who detailed hostility to science and abuse of personnel
powers at the Department of Agriculture, the Environmental
Protection Agency, and the Department of the Interior. Some officials
chose to engage in whistleblowing, which involved formal channels for
raising concerns of inappropriate behavior, and most notably triggered
the first impeachment investigation. For example, one whistleblower
described Department of Homeland Security appointees downplaying
both the risk of Russian interference in US democracy and the growing
threat of white nationalism to fit with Trump's populist agenda (Cohen
2020).

The use of such voice has provided firsthand, on-the-record accounts
of politicization that were highlighted by American media, which has
generally provided compelling investigative accounts of the inner
workings of the Trump administration. But such exercise of voice
was discouraged by a weakening of employee protections and limited
effect. Beyond creating embarrassment for administrations, the chief
power of voice is to encourage other politicians to act. Within the
Trump administration, being hard on bureaucrats was closer to
a badge of honor than a scarlet letter. An administration largely indifferent to the bad press that came from whistleblowers – which generally
pales in comparison to whatever other scandal was happening that
week – was immunized against the power of voice.

Bureaucrats who combined voice with loyalty ran the risk of being
sidelined. For example, career employees who raised concerns about
ethics violations that would ultimately cause the head of the EPA to
resign were put into less influential positions or told to find a new job
(Lipton, Vogel, and Friedman 2018). Senior State Department officials,
including former ambassadors, alleged they were punished by being
assigned to clerical work. In the Department of the Interior, dozens of
senior career officials were reassigned by a Secretary who complained
his staff included "30 percent of the crew that's not loyal to the flag"
(Fears 2017). While there is no way of knowing the degree to which
bureaucrats used the voice option via anonymous leaks to the media, it
seemed par for the course for a famously leaky administration.

Beyond examples of voice, bureaucratic sabotage has been hard to observe, partly because such actions generally happen below the radar (O'Leary 2020), partly because Trump has vastly overstated the degree of actual sabotage on the parts of bureaucrats, and partly because any visible acts of resistance face an unmerciful backlash. Senior FBI agents who were involved in efforts to investigate potential corruption and connections with Russia by the Trump campaign were subject to extraordinarily hostile personal attacks by the president, followed by firings and the threat of criminal investigation for offenses such as writing text messages critical of the president, or simply supervising such investigations (Bertrand 2019).

In areas where the Trump administration maintained consistent policy goals and capable appointees, the bureaucracy has been responsive. On some of the most controversial policies – scrapping the Iran treaty and Paris accord, withdrawing from the Transatlantic Pacific Partnership – the president's goals were implemented. The area of immigration is instructive. The Trump White House immediately produced a travel ban on predominantly Muslim countries. Poorly crafted, the policy failed to hold up to legal scrutiny. But political appointees ultimately found a bureaucracy that was quite responsive to political direction, albeit working slowly and requiring formal administrative steering. Trump's travel ban was revised in a way that survived legal scrutiny, and legal processes of immigration largely ground to a halt through a variety of administrative mechanisms and absent any significant policy change from Congress. In this policy area, the administrative state proved itself remarkably loyal to the wishes of an anti-immigrant president.

Case 1: Impeachment

It is instructive to examine, even if briefly, two cases that illustrate the consequences of the Trump administration's approach to governance. In both cases, patterns of democratic backsliding resulted in overreach and failure. The first put the Trump presidency in peril; the second worsened the response to the pandemic and may have cost him a second term.

President Trump was impeached on Thursday, January 16, 2020, by a Democratic-controlled House of Representatives. A Republican-

controlled Senate voted not to convict him on February 5. At the root of
the case against Trump was an accusation that he had misused his office
for political purposes. He had delayed the release of much-needed
military funds to Ukraine, and appeared to make the release of those
funds conditional on Ukraine providing information that would hurt
Joe Biden, his presidential rival.

The problem was that this money was not Trump's to bargain with.
Both Congress and the Supreme Court have been clear on this point,
responding to abuses by President Nixon. The Supreme Court reasoned
(*Train* v. *City of New York* 1975) that a president could not impound
(selectively choose not to spend allocated funds) as it effectively gave
him budget-making powers to advance his own priorities. Congress
passed the Congressional Budget and Impoundment Control Act of
1974 to also limit executive abuse of budget power, requiring that any
future president explicitly request from Congress if he did not want to
spend funds. The White House did not follow the procedures of the
Act; indeed, it sought to ensure Congress did not discover the failure to
spend for as long as possible, and it was only when Congress started
asking about the spending that was the money released. The
Government Accountability Office, a congressional watchdog agency,
would ultimately determine that the Trump administration had violated the Act by withholding the funds.

Within the administration, political appointees brushed aside legal
concerns raised by career staff about the withholding of funds. Two
career lawyers at OMB objected and resigned. The career official at
OMB who oversaw military spending was removed from overseeing
the process when he questioned how the aid could be withheld while
still complying with the Impoundment Act. The same aide would be the
only one of a number of OMB officials subpoenaed who actually
testified to the House of Representatives as part of its impeachment
inquiry (Lipton, Haberman, and Mazetti 2019). A senior financial
official at the Department of Defense also flagged concerns, asking if
the decision to hold money had been approved by legal counsel. She
explained for months that the delay would make it impossible to release
funds in a way consistent with the law. Once the news of the funding
hold broke, OMB appointees drafted a letter that tried to shift blame
to career staff at the Department of Defense, to which the Defense
official responded "You can't be serious. I am speechless" (Brannen
2020).

The Trump administration made no effort to justify these actions publicly as they undertook them. Political appointees at the White House and the Department of Justice did offer a secret legal formulation that Trump could effectively ignore the law. The claim drew on the unitary executive theory, which holds that the president can violate the law in cases when national security is at risk (Cook 2020). The Bush administration drew extensively on this theory – again with secret legal memos – to justify surveillance of its citizens and acts of torture of detainees as part of the war on terror, and elements of this approach continued under the Obama administration (Edelson 2016). It is the same theory that justified Trump's executive order allowing him to fire civil servants.

While the delay of funding became public via the media, the president's alleged quid pro quo did not emerge until a whistleblower approached the Intelligence Inspector General. News of the whistleblower's complaint leaked. Trump appointees initially declined to share the complaint, even as Trump defended his actions publicly and released a transcript of a phone call with the Ukrainian leader, which only seemed to confirm a quid pro quo. Eventually, the whistleblower's complaint was provided after the House announced an impeachment inquiry on September 24, 2019.

A series of current and former career officials and political appointees testified first in private, and then in public, to the House investigation, providing additional evidence of a quid pro quo. Evidence also emerged that Trump had withdrawn a career official who was serving as Ambassador to Ukraine, Marie Yovanovitch, based on inaccurate rumors that she was not loyal to him – rumors perpetuated partly by the president's private lawyer, who was in Ukraine trying to find evidence to damage the president's opponent. The president publicly attacked Yovanovitch, who retired, causing some State Department officials to also resign when their department leader failed to defend their staff.

The Trump administration refused to provide any requested documents as part of the impeachment inquiry, and forbade executive branch officials or even former officials from testifying. Such outright blockading of Congressional oversight is extraordinary, and an extreme example of Trump's evasion of accountability. This lack of cooperation with standard accountability processes would itself form the basis for an article of impeachment. Nevertheless, there was little doubt about the outcome. The Senate Majority Leader signaled he would work in "total coordination" with the White House, and, breaking with all previous impeachment trials, refused to call additional witnesses or seek documents.

The manner in which Trump's evasion of accountability processes were closely tied to politicization of norms was clear. Throughout the impeachment process, Trump and fellow Republicans attacked the whistleblower. Whistleblowers have historically been offered anonymity, but one Republican Senator named the alleged whistleblower on the Senate floor. Career public servants who agreed to testify were also subject to public attack, not just from Trump but from other high-profile Republicans too. Such a break with traditional norms guaranteed that future career officials would be reluctant to come forward.

When the impeachment concluded, the White House swiftly delivered on a promise of payback to those who had testified, retaliating against career civil servants who had not yet resigned by removing them from their positions, blocking promotions, or demoting them to the degree allowed by law. The Department of Defense finance official who had raised concerns about the legality of withholding the Ukraine funds saw her nomination to a senior position pulled. A White House military official who testified was removed from his position. The Inspector General who had informed Congress of the whistleblower complaint was removed, as was the Director of National Intelligence who eventually provided it (Cheney, Betrand, and McGraw 2020). Such officials were characterized by the president and his supporters as part of a deep state conspiracy to remove him. The atmosphere could hardly have been more hostile to any official wishing to share evidence of wrongdoing through legal accountability processes.

Case 2: COVID-19 Response

Trump remained fortunate in his first three years to avoid a crisis that exposed the costs of his leadership style. He faced no Great Recession, no 9/11. The economy continued on the same positive trajectory that held for most of the Obama administration.

As Trump emerged from his impeachment largely intact, another test loomed on the horizon, one where the shortcomings of his management of the administrative state would become impossible to ignore: the COVID-19 pandemic. The administration missed warning signs about the seriousness of the disease, including a series of intelligence reports. Lack of preparation led to a flat-footed response, insufficient medical supplies, and no coherent plan to provide them. Long after most peer countries had flattened the spread of the disease, it continued to grow in the United States. By election day, 230,000 were dead as a result of COVID-19. Trump failed in basic aspects of communication. Rather than provide consistent messaging about public health risks, he varied the messaging, at first downplaying risks and promising the virus would quickly disappear, then emphasizing the need to reopen the economy, while mixing in bizarre and untested medical theories. Daily press events often devolved into heated attacks on reporters who dared to ask uncomfortable questions.

Preliminary evidence suggests that the disdain for science of the Trump administration contributed to the poor response. Before the pandemic, scientists at the Centers for Disease Control (CDC) had seen the president seek to cut their funding and divert their funds to anti-immigration programs, and had been told to avoid the use of the terms "evidence-based" and "science-based." Trump had also cut funding for global health programs that could have improved preparation for the response, and public health positions based in China intended to offer early detection of disease outbreaks (Goodman and Schulkin 2020).

Political interference with CDC career officials increased dramatically as the pandemic response faltered. Political appointees expressed mistrust toward agency scientists, categorizing them as "deep state" (Lipton et al. 2020) and speculating that they were trying to damage the president (Diamond 2020a). They also blocked CDC public guidance on travel and social distancing that conflicted with the desire to reopen the economy, posted less stringent testing guidance that CDC scientists had not approved (Mandavilli 2020), and demanded the right to review and change CDC scientific reports (Diamond 2020a). A senior CDC official was sidelined after her acknowledgment in late February that they were preparing for a pandemic was judged by Trump to lead to a drop in the stock market (Lipton et al. 2020). Trump's personnel office gave inexperienced White House liaisons, some of whom had not completed their college degree, power over his own appointees and career officials, with a license to police for any perceived disloyalty in CDC or its parent department, Health and Human Services (Diamond 2020b). One whistleblower scientist said he was ignored and excluded from meetings when he raised concerns about severe shortages of medical supplies, and was ultimately moved to another position when he resisted pressure to make untested drugs promoted by the president widely available (Abutaleb and McGinley 2020). Four former CDC Directors wrote an open letter headlined "We ran the CDC. No president ever politicized its science the way Trump has" (Frieden et al. 2020). The long-term credibility of the agency was badly damaged.

The failure of the Trump administration's COVID-19 response is best understood as a failure of political leadership. The responsibilities of political appointees loom larger in times of crisis (Boin, Stern, and Sundelius 2016). Bureaucracies do well with routine tasks where they can develop standard operating procedures. But for novel tasks or the types of ambiguous decisions situations created by a crisis, the career civil service needs political leaders who can provide urgency, resources, and strategic decisions under rapidly changing and complex conditions. Populists who fail to direct the administrative state find themselves at sea when asked to respond to crises that necessarily require administrative skills.

In a crisis, good bureaucracy cannot fix bad political leadership. The political appointments made by a president become much more crucial. Even amongst those with relevant experience, pandemic planning was low on their priority list. For example, Trump's National Security Adviser, John Bolton, shuttered the National Security Council Directorate for Global Health Security and Biodefense, and jettisoned National Security Council members with expertise in global health security and emergency preparedness. The head of the CDC was a medical scientist, but lacked experience of running a federal agency.

The instability of personnel became a significant problem. The Obama administration had laid out a pandemic preparedness plan for Trump officials, and even ran a transition event on pandemic training. Of the thirty senior officials who participated in the training, only eight Trump officials were still in place when COVID-19 arrived, none of whom had a public health or crisis response background (Goodman and Schulkin 2020). Two-thirds of senior positions in the Department of Homeland Security were either vacant or filled with acting appointees when COVID-19 hit (Pettypiece 2020).

In the aftermath of the impeachment, which coincided with the start of the pandemic, Trump doubled down on prioritizing loyalty over expertise. He empowered a former personal aide to search for and remove disloyal appointees while tweeting that "we want bad people out of our government" (Diamond 2020b). At this time the Director of National Intelligence, whose office had warned about the risks of a pandemic, was replaced by a Trump loyalist with no discernible intelligence experience. Trump also removed an Inspector General from the Department of Health and Human Services who had provided reports that documented a severe shortage of medical supplies. Other senior officials in agencies found that their staff were replaced with Trump loyalists by the White House, and without their approval. In an apt reflection of where the power lay in these fights, the head of the Office of Personnel Management, who has oversight of the entire federal personnel system, resigned when she objected to a reporting structure created by the head of the Presidential Personnel Office (Swan 2020).

It is hard to defeat a pandemic with a temp agency where the staff are terrified to tell the truth. When the Secretary of the Department of Health and Human Services initially tried to brief the president about the problem, Trump dismissed the reports as alarmist and wanted instead to talk about vaping products (Goodman and Schulkin 2020). Under such conditions, when Trump promised that "one day, like a miracle, it will disappear" (Rogers 2020), who would challenge him?

Trump's responses to the pandemic demonstrated other elements of democratic backsliding. At various times he appeared to suggest that access to federal resources would depend on hearing praise from state officials, or support for his goal of quickly restarting the economy. When Congress passed a relief bill it included $500 billion in funds for economic spending overseen by the White House. Signing the bill, Trump rejected the accompanying oversight requirements that Congress had established, applying unitary executive theory to con-clude that it infringed on executive branch rights – a stark contrast to the intense oversight of the stimulus spending during the Great Recession under his predecessor. Congress appointed a federal panel to provide oversight run by Inspectors General, and a special Inspector General to oversee the spending. The president removed the chair of the panel from his Inspector General post, making him ineligible to serve, and nominated as the special Inspector General a White House lawyer closely aligned with Trump. Thus, Trump's ability to control resources and personnel, and avoid accountability, combined to give him greater leverage in doling out funding while minimizing the risk of blame. A basic expectation for bureaucracy in a liberal democracy is public accountability for where tax resources go. In this case, the president unceremoniously erased this expectation, turning the bureaucracy into an instrument that dispersed funds but without the accompanying accountability, and inviting speculation of favoritism toward the president's supporters and donors. It is difficult to maintain public trust under such conditions.

A Changing Environment

As the introduction to this volume makes clear, the environment matters to the potential for democratic backsliding, and to understand Trump it is therefore important to understand the broader environment in which he operates and how it has changed in recent decades. It is true both that the system of US government has shown resilience and constrained his authoritarian impulses, but also that Trump went beyond his predecessors, even as he also exploited the rhetoric and tools of previous presidents.

In many respects, the US state is designed to withstand democratic backsliding. The institutional constraints that make change difficult – federalism, a separation of powers, and multiple levels of accountability – were made with the intent of constraining the would-be authoritarian. Trump cannot centralize administrative authority in the way that, for example, Orbán has in Hungary (see Hajnal and Boda, Chapter 4, this volume). Most Americans also lived in a state with a Democratic governor, after Democrats picked up seven governorships in the 2018 election. Several of Trump's signature policy initiatives, most notably in the areas of immigration and social policy, were blocked or at least slowed by the judiciary. His most significant legislative achievement – a large tax cut that favored higher earners – is standard Republican policy and not terribly populist. In short, the institutional context made Trump a weak strongman.

It would, however, be a mistake to assume these institutions forcefully rejected Trump. Republican members of Congress energetically defended him, echoing his attacks on career civil servants. Between the House and the Senate, only one Republican member voted in favor of impeachment. The Court's constraint of President Trump has also been partial. The Supreme Court allowed, for example, a modified version of

Trump's travel ban from majority-Muslim countries, and fast-tracked more decisions in favor of the president than has previously been the case (Vladeck 2019). Even apparent defeats, such as the use of the census to solicit citizenship information or efforts to end the Deferred Action on Childhood Arrivals program, were made on procedural grounds, signaling the courts would allow Trump's more extreme positions if the administration properly followed procedures for rulemaking.

Of course, the Court is not fully independent of Trump. The president nominates federal judicial appointees, and Trump did so at an impressive pace. By the end of 2019, one in every four circuit court judges (the level directly below the Supreme Court) were Trump appointees. In one term, Trump appointed three of the nine Supreme Court justices, giving conservatives a 6–3 majority. Indeed, Trump's most lasting impact may be handing lifetime appointments to a generation of judges who share to some degree his worldview.

Some powers of the presidency are constrained less by institutions and more by the character of the person holding the office. An example is the use of unitary executive theory referenced throughout this chapter. In its modern form, Reagan was the first president to employ signing statements that drew on the unitary executive theory, and it became a staple of the George W. Bush administration, gaining wide acceptance in conservative legal circles and, by extension, among the judicial branch. The elements of this approach – secret legal reasoning to ignore existing laws – are deeply problematic to democratic values of transparency, separation of powers, and the rule of law. The risks of such legal theories become exponentially more distinctly dangerous in the hands of a president with an authoritarian mien, willing to use it to fire public servants he suspects of disloyalty.

As documented in this chapter, many of the tools of democratic backsliding embraced by Trump were ready and at hand when he arrived to the presidency. It would be incorrect to say that both political parties have been equal offenders. While Democrats have centralized policymaking and used political appointees, the key elements of democratic backsliding are more centrally established in the Republican Party, which has incorporated, encouraged, and deified the paranoid style of conspiratorial thinking. It is in this political party that suspicion toward bureaucrats, the elite, and science has curdled into something darker. While some version of populism exists on the left, it is not one centered on the premise of deconstructing the administrative state. Based on a study of policy positions by Republicans and Democrats over time, Lührmann, Medzihorsky, Hindle, and Lindberg (2020, p. 1) conclude that "the Republican party in the US has retreated from upholding democratic norms in recent years. Its rhetoric is closer to authoritarian parties, such as AKP in Turkey and Fidesz in Hungary. Conversely, the Democratic Party has retained a commitment to long-standing democratic standards." Their data shows that Republican support of democracy, demonization of opponents, and willingness to incite violence were already displaying patterns of illiberalism before Trump emerged as a political figure, but dramatically accelerated with his arrival.

Trump amplified conspiracy theories that are frequently anti-institutional and antistatist in nature. A study of his political statements found he utilized the paranoid style more than any presidential candidate since 1948 (Hart 2020). Good governance ultimately demands some basic rationality, but Trump succeeded in delegitimating many fact-based institutions that democracies depend on – the media, or government expertise, for example. While trust in government is important in its own right, deep distrust brings with it the risk of violence. In 1995, 168 federal employees were murdered by a domestic terrorist with antigovernment beliefs. In recent years, such beliefs appear to be on the rise again (Graff 2020). In the aftermath of his election defeat, Trump promoted conspiracy theories of massive fraud that undermined public faith in democratic processes, and insisted that millions of legal votes were illegitimate, further cementing antidemocratic positions within the Republican Party.

Perhaps the most worrying aspect of the Trump era is that it has reinforced partisan differences in competing philosophies of governing. If Trump's chaotic approach is one outcome of Reagan's dictum that government is the problem, it depends on a degree of intense polarization that hides the actual costs of this philosophy for many. Processes of motivated reasoning blind partisans to the performance effects of poor administration (Jilke and Baekgaard 2020). Partisan alignment has not just ensured party unity for Trump; it has also ensured that a large fraction of the public continues to retain confidence in him, dismiss as fake news evidence to the contrary, and become more committed to the idea that the federal government failed Trump, since Trump himself can never fail.

One other environmental factor bears mention. The United States features a highly professionalized bureaucracy, where entry has largely been based on merit, albeit with a large side-door of appointees selected for other reasons. At the same time, more and more of the business of government is undertaken not by public actors, but by private or nonprofit contractors. By one estimate, in 2015 there were 2.6 contract employees or people paid by federal grants for every civilian federal employee (Light 2017). The degree of transparency of such actors – especially those operating in the homeland security field – is lower than for their public peers. While procurement rules seek to limit corruption, the potential for political influence is higher in a setting where contractors are focused only on the terms of their contract and winning the next one. We know relatively little about potential abuses in this domain during the Trump administration.

Conclusion

Trump approached the US system using a mixture of strategies identified in the introduction to this volume. In some pockets of the administration, Trump was able to use the bureaucracy, most notably when he had skillful political appointees overseeing functions where Congress has delegated much power to the executive. Trump also ignored the bureaucracy. A small army of political appointees, many very junior and with little expertise, sought to impose their will on career staff. The outcome has been far from successful. Some bureaucrats left, and many used their voice to point to abuses of power. Apart from the true believers, there is no real constituency that believes Trump improved the quality of governance. Morale declined among public employees, due in no small part to Trump's relentless attacks, suggesting that rhetorical delegitimization deserves to be considered as a democratic backsliding strategy alongside using, ignoring, and sidelining the bureaucracy.

Crises reveal government capacity, but they especially reveal the limits of political leadership. Incompetence and instability among political appointees did more to undermine Trump's goals than bureaucratic resistance ever could have. COVID-19 brought to the fore many elements of democratic backsliding under Trump, while revealing the limits of his philosophy of governing. Career officials were sidelined. Trump repeated unproven theories about medical solutions while promising a crisis response that he proved unable to deliver. Despite warnings, his political appointees had not prepared for the pandemic, and seemed asleep at the switch when the threat turned into reality.

The impeachment process also revealed much: a president who propagated conspiratorial theories about the actions of his political opponent and career officials. A set of political appointees apparently unable to stop the process, but willing to provide a legal theory to enable law-breaking, while silencing and sidelining career officials who ultimately could have prevented the president from violating the law had they been listened to. Attacks on the whistleblower, and stonewalling of crucial documents from Congress. Punishment meted out to career officials who responded to Congressional requests to testify. Perhaps the sharpest contrast the case offered was between the career public officials who found themselves thrust into the spotlight and spoke persuasively of the importance of integrity in public service, and the shabby way in which they were cast aside by the White House.

One solution to these problems is to simply reduce the role of political appointees. Good government reformers in the United States have argued for decades that restricting the number of appointees offers a straightforward way to improve the quality of government. Doing so would also blunt a primary weapon in attacks on the bureaucracy, limiting the degree to which unqualified outsiders can politicize processes.

Providing, and enforcing, other protections for bureaucrats would also serve to protect bureaucracy: stronger legislative protections for whistleblowers and Inspectors General, and Congressional enforcement of penalties for failing to cooperate with basic accountability processes, would make it more likely that bureaucrats could use their voice to provide an early warning against democratic backsliding in administrative processes. If the Trump administration has demonstrated anything, it is that the goals of political principals may need to be checked by principled agents.

Such solutions depend upon a commitment from both of the main parties in the United States toward good government. That commitment has been largely absent, driven primarily by the Republican Party incorporating, and cultivating, waves of conspiratorial antigovernment sentiment. With few resources, Trump took control of the oldest American political party with remarkable ease by recognizing and appealing to the paranoid style of thinking among its members. His governing style reflected this approach, and remains.

While Trump was defeated in 2020, Trumpism was not repudiated. The election was close, and many new voters flocked to the Republican Party. Republicans who stayed close to Trump faced no electoral penalty. In the immediate aftermath of the election, potential party leaders competed to capture Trump's populist base with a more polished approach. A leader who succeeds in doing so and can govern more competently could vastly expand the patterns of democratic backsliding that Trump pursued. Trump's loss should therefore not be read as a return to normality.

As long as one party in a two-party system is no longer invested in good government, the quality of government will erode. Career officials value the opportunity to develop and use their expertise (Gailmard and Patty 2013). If every election risks throwing up a president whose goal is to frustrate such opportunities, it will be increasingly difficult to attract a talented workforce motivated by public service.

8 | "Doublespeak Populism" and Public Administration: The Case of Mexico

MAURICIO I. DUSSAUGE-LAGUNA

Introduction

Democratic backsliding has become an international concern, but, as the editors of this book note, its implications for public administration have so far received only limited attention (Batory and Svensson 2019; Bauer and Becker 2020; Bauer et al., Introduction, this volume; Borins 2018; Goodsell 2019; Peters and Pierre 2019; Stoker 2019a). Understood as a "deterioration of qualities associated with democratic governance, within any regime" (Waldner and Lust 2018, p. 95; see also Bermeo 2016), the concept has gained visibility with populist leaders such as Viktor Orbán, Hugo Chávez, Evo Morales, and Donald Trump. However, while "[d]emocratic backsliding today begins at the ballot box," as stated by Levitsky and Ziblatt (2018a, p. 5), some of its most significant consequences are only felt by citizens at a later stage, through changes in public programs, services, and organizational arrangements. Therefore, studying how democratic backsliding impacts public policies and bureaucratic structures is a relevant and much-needed endeavor.

Taking current international debates on the subject as a point of departure, particularly as presented in the analytical framework provided by the editors of this volume, this chapter discusses how the Mexican public administration is being affected as a result of the

I thank participants in the "Democratic Backsliding and Public Administration" workshop, sponsored by the European University Institute, the editors of this volume, and professors María del Carmen Pardo, Cas Mudde, David Arellano-Gault, José Olivas, Rodrigo Velázquez, and Maira T. Vaca-Baqueiro for their kind comments and relevant suggestions. Also, Patricia Guzmán, Nahely Ortiz, Antonio Villalpando, Luis Estrada, and Pedro Canales offered very valuable insights on this chapter during our doctoral seminar. Last but not least, Marcela Aguilar provided excellent research assistance and relevant ideas for the completion of this chapter. Funding from CIDE's FAI scheme is gratefully acknowledged.

backsliding process triggered by the current government of Andrés Manuel López Obrador (2018–2024). The Mexican case is particularly interesting because this country is usually perceived as an unconsolidated democracy (Bruhn 2013). Indeed, until the late 1990s, elections in Mexico were not competitive. López Obrador's electoral victory with the support of his political party *MORENA* (or *Movimiento de Regeneración Nacional*) is only the third political party change in government since the democratic transition began in 2000, following seventy years of uninterrupted dominance by the so-called "party of the revolution" established in the late 1920s. Moreover, some of the practices that are currently associated with backsliding, such as increased patronage and politicization of public programs, have historically been a feature of the Mexican administrative tradition (Cejudo 2017; Dussauge-Laguna 2011; Méndez 1997; Méndez and Dussauge-Laguna 2017; Merino 2013). A significant challenge is thus to assess what is new and what is just "business as usual" in Mexico's governance dynamics. Also, despite the growth of studies on backsliding and populist trends internationally, including in the Latin American region (De la Torre 2017), contemporary political and administrative developments in Mexico are yet to be fully explored.

This chapter argues that Mexico is experiencing a case of what could be labelled "doublespeak populism," which is transforming the country's public administration in profound ways. Doublespeak populism refers, first, to a situation in which political leaders use the traditional populist rhetoric (mainly based on the idea of a conflict between "corrupt elites" and "good people"; see Mudde and Rovira 2017; Müller 2016b) to disguise their true policy intentions. Phrases and terms that supposedly advance the long-forgotten needs of the people actually hide a rather different (even opposite) intention. Second, doublespeak populism allows politicians to present their political strategies in a positive light, thus deflecting political contention over their real meaning and consequences. In the end, doublespeak populism matters because the rhetoric used by politicians to package their proposed policy and administrative changes, allegedly "wanted by the people," in fact brings with it measures that hurt the basic needs of the population they are supposed to benefit.

In the Mexican experience, López Obrador's agenda has been embedded in terms and phrases traditionally associated with the political left (e.g. equality, "helping the poor"), despite including policy measures closer to the right (e.g. reducing the state, austerity policies). Moreover, these measures have been introduced with deliberate concealment of their ultimate intentions and potential effects. For instance, cuts have been labelled "savings," yet resource scarcity has not been a problem when providing new direct cash transfers to social groups by the president. The centralization of decision-making procedures and the use of new controls have been described as efforts to fight inefficiency, waste, and corruption, yet they have been used to undermine the independence of institutions and regulators. The portrayal of a so-called "golden" (e.g. privileged and rich) bureaucracy has served to advance budgetary and salary reductions, only to provide funding for dubious presidential projects. As a result, López Obrador's reforms have further deteriorated Mexico's bureaucratic institutions and public services, thus affecting the overall welfare and basic rights of the people they are supposed to help.

The remainder of the chapter is structured into three main sections. The first section introduces the Mexican case by looking at President López Obrador's main political features, including his past political behavior, to better understand where he is coming from and why he can be considered a populist leader. The second section follows the analytical dimensions identified by the editors in the introduction to this volume to explain how the current government initiatives are affecting Mexico's administrative institutions and public policies. The chapter closes with some concluding thoughts and comments about the broader consequences of López Obrador's doublespeak populism on Mexico's democratic governance.

The chapter draws on three main sources of information: policy proposals and other government-related information as reported in the media; speeches, commentaries, and statements by the president; and expert analyses and commentaries from academics and policy specialists (Casar 2019a; 2019b; Cejudo and Gómez-Álvarez 2018; Chaguaceda 2019; Monroy 2019; Pardo 2020; Puente 2020).

Doublespeak Populism in Contemporary Mexico: The Case of López Obrador

To understand the process of democratic backsliding in Mexico and how it affects the country's public administration structures and procedures, one needs to first ask some questions about López Obrador's political reasoning and doublespeak-populist style. His political features are best understood when compared to traits commonly associated with populist leaders around the world. In particular, the continuous references to "the (good) people" as a group opposed to the "corrupt" or "perverse" elites; the disregard for established legal norms and practices that are perceived as "unfair"; and the assumption that the leader is the only actor who really understands what political and administrative changes "the people" are demanding (Mudde and Rovira 2017; Müller 2016b; Stoker 2019a). When seen in this light, the historical performance of López Obrador as a politician and government official certainly fits the populist description (Bruhn 2013; Puente 2020). Many of López Obrador's recent public statements have not only repeated his earlier political messages and patterns of political action, they have also echoed contemporary populist trends. Furthermore, they have inspired his overall approach toward public policy and administration reforms, including his disdain for bureaucrats and government structures he thinks are obstructing his political agenda.

The political and personal characteristics of López Obrador have long attracted attention from political analysts. At least since the early 2000s, when he became Mexico City's mayor, López Obrador has frequently appeared in the media, and his actions have been widely reported. In 2006, right before the presidential elections, Enrique Krauze (2006) noted that López Obrador "used a rhetoric of social polarization ... His political vocabulary became impregnated with class conflicts. His enemies were the enemies of the people: 'those at the top', the rich ... the 'posh', the 'exquisite'." During his recent political campaign (2017–2018), López Obrador often stated that "there cannot be a poor people with a rich government," and he vowed to "cut all the privileges" of former presidents and high-level public servants.[1] In his public appearances, he would often speak about the so-called "power mafia," allegedly formed by the two biggest political parties (the *Partido Revolucionario Institucional* [PRI] and the *Partido Acción Nacional* [PAN]), rich businessmen, and other members of the establishment that were plotting "against him" (Aguilar-Camín 2018, p. 36). The same words and phrases were included in his inaugural speech in December 2018 (López Obrador 2018). Similarly, his daily press briefings as a president have been peppered with direct attacks against public servants (*chapulines fifí*), scientists (*mafia científica*), and the media (*hampa del periodismo*); Bravo 2019; López 2019; Redacción Animal Político 2019b; Rosagel 2019).

López Obrador has long sustained an ambivalent relationship with regard to the rule of law. Since his early days as a state-level politician, whenever he lost a political battle, he privileged political mobilizations over legal disputes (Aguilar-Camín 2018; Krauze 2006). For instance, back in 2003, when his government lost a legal case regarding some land appropriation, he declared that: "a law that is not fair is useless. The law is for the man, not the man for the law. A law that does not provide justice has no sense . . . The court cannot be above the sovereign people" (Krauze 2006). An even clearer illustration of López Obrador's attitude toward the rule of law was his behavior after losing the 2006 presidential election (Aguilar-Camín 2018). Instead of accepting the results once all legal channels were followed, López Obrador called upon his followers to block one of Mexico City's central avenues (*Reforma*) for more than a month and a half. Later, at a political meeting, he called himself the "legitimate president," appointed a cabinet, and proposed a governing manifesto (El País 2006). Nowadays, as president, this ambivalent attitude toward the rule of law has resurfaced. He has publicly stated that, "if one has to opt between the law and justice, you do not have to think too much about it: decide in favor of justice" (Redacción 2019).

A third aspect that merits attention is López Obrador's own understanding of his role as a political leader. According to Jesús Silva-Herzog (2018), he is "convinced that the solution for Mexico is him. He believes that, to finish with corruption, his presence suffices. If the president is honest, then everyone will be honest, as he has said." Many other commentators have noted that López Obrador sees himself as a historical figure leading a "transformation" (like previous Mexican presidents, such as Benito Juárez or Lázaro Cárdenas; see Aguilar-Camín 2018; Fonseca 2018; Woldenberg 2019). Recently, he stated he will "purify" Mexico's public institutions and political life, even if people call him a "messianic" person (Morales 2019).

What kind of populist strand does López Obrador represent? According to Kathleen Bruhn (2013), back in the 2000s López Obrador presented himself as a left-of-center politician, strongly concerned about poverty and inequality issues. Indeed, some of his policies as Mexico City's mayor were focused on providing cash transfers to underprivileged social groups (single mothers, old people, the poor). However, when Bruhn assessed his platform and actions, López Obrador's policies appeared to be even more conservative than his own party's agenda (at the time, the leftist *Partido de la Revolución Democrática, PRD,* or Democratic Revolution Party). Bruhn suggests he governed more as a "moderate" than as a leftist mayor. Recently, as the leader of *MORENA,* López Obrador has been portrayed again as a leftist politician (The Economist 2019), and as the first-ever leftist president of Mexico (Ahmed and Villegas 2018).

Yet things become more complex when looking into many of López Obrador's decisions and actions. First, during the 2018 election he established a political alliance with the Evangelist Party (Pantoja 2017). Since in government, his meetings with evangelic groups and the religious undertone of his political messages and press briefings have been widely reported (and criticized). Second, he has been ambivalent with regard to certain subjects traditionally associated with the left, such as abortion, gay rights, and drugs (e.g. cannabis) legalization. Similarly, he has ignored the public outcry and scientific evidence regarding the environmental risks and negative impacts of some of his pet projects (e.g. the Dos Bocas oil refinery in his home state of Tabasco, and the Maya Railway in the Yucatán Peninsula). Third, instead of expanding public benefits and services through stronger welfare state structures, López Obrador has advanced a "minimal state" approach, heavily reliant on direct cash transfers. Indeed, in contrast to previous Mexican populist leaders who made extensive use of public funds, López Obrador has introduced a strong "austerity policy" agenda which seems closer to the neoliberal policies of the 1990s. The recent COVID-19 pandemic has been used to reinforce the need for government cuts and budgetary redistributions. However, it is not clear whether the resources have been transferred to the health and social policy sectors, where they are much needed, or to the president's political projects instead.

Therefore, while López Obrador has employed a populist rhetoric using phrases and references traditionally associated with the left, in many respects his agenda is closer to the right of the political spectrum. More importantly, his understanding of the role the public sector should play in state–citizen interactions is having profound practical implications. His rhetorical defense of the needs of the people, particularly the poor, has served him to package a series of reforms that advance a smaller government and centralize power and bureaucratic decision-making. These measures are portrayed as beneficial for "the people" (e.g. cuts are presented as "savings"), and some may actually provide much-needed help for certain social groups (e.g. cash transfers). However, in the longer term most of them will affect the Mexican state's administrative capacity to provide public goods and services in an impartial, nonpoliticized fashion. Indeed, some beneficiaries (e.g. working parents, cancer patients, and recipients of conditional transfers) are already facing the consequences of budgetary cuts and program termination. Thus, the doublespeak-populist rhetoric is not putting "the poor first," as López Obrador claims. The following section will describe in more detail how this doublespeak-populist governing style is being translated into changes in Mexico's public administration institutions, programs, and principles.

Doublespeak Populism and the Transformation of Mexico's Public Administration

The following paragraphs present López Obrador's public administration reform initiatives based on the analytical framework provided by the editors of this volume. As the section shows, the depth and breadth of his doublespeak-populist style is overhauling Mexico's federal public administration. In systematically sidelining the bureaucratic apparatus (even if sometimes using certain public offices for clearly political purposes), López Obrador has pursued a series of strategies that have simultaneously increased his control over the bureaucratic apparatus and reduced the administrative capacities of the Mexican state. Behind a rhetorical façade which reflects a profound mistrust of bureaucrats and disguises administrative changes as alleged responses to "the people's needs," López Obrador is transforming governance patterns and structures in ways that are hurtful to beneficiaries and public service users.

Sidelining (But Sometimes Using) a Mistrusted Bureaucratic Infrastructure

During the 2018 electoral campaign, López Obrador proposed a set of public administration reforms to be pursued once he entered office.

These were included in his manifesto "50 general guidelines to fight against corruption and apply a policy of republican austerity" (AMLO 2018;[2] Cejudo and Gómez-Álvarez 2018). The guidelines stated, for example, that: a) he would earn half the salary of the previous incumbent; b) bonuses, private health insurance, and retirement savings accounts of all federal public servants would be terminated; c) the number of "positions of trust" (*puestos de confianza*, which include a mixture of policy analysts, mid-level and senior officials, and political appointees) would be reduced by 70 percent; and d) pension payments to former presidents would be abolished.

Most of these measures had an obvious symbolic objective in mind, but others were clearly aimed at changing the structure and functioning of the federal bureaucracy to suit his political agenda. Indeed, they reflect López Obrador's doublespeak populism, as the reasons for advancing some changes "in the name of the people" have lacked any reasonable justification, other than his mistrust of public officials. As the reform strategies described will show, he has expressed profound disdain toward federal bureaucrats and public programs established in previous administrations. He has thus tried to substitute existing structures and procedures with new centralized and personalistic channels of control, even if these sometimes sideline the members of his own cabinet.

While his overall approach has been that of sidelining bureaucratic actors and structures, López Obrador has also used some government areas for political purposes, with the help of personal loyalists he has appointed. For instance, the heads of the Ministry of Public Administration (*Secretaría de la Función Pública*) and the Financial Intelligence Unit (*Unidad de Inteligencia Financiera*) have publicly denounced alleged illegalities and corrupt acts in public institutions in which the president has faced resistance to his reform agenda. Similarly, the head of the National Council for Science and Technology (*Consejo Nacional de Ciencia y Tecnología*) has cut funding to long-existing research programs and has conditioned the renewal of financial incentives to scientists, purportedly "to generate savings," though this has been mainly done to punish a policy community (scientists) that the president thinks is unfairly privileged. Lastly, the Mexican state's information agency (*Notimex*) has been used both to attack individuals perceived to be political enemies, and to spread propaganda and untruthful messages that support the presidential agenda (Cultura Colectiva 2019).

Extending Control and Undermining the Autonomy of Existing Organizations

One of the main strategies López Obrador has pursued is to increase his personal control over public institutions while at the same time seeking to undermine the legitimacy and autonomy of institutions established in previous governments either to perform specialized regulatory functions or to serve as "check and balances" on the executive power (Rubio 2019).

Presidential control has been sought through various means. The most notorious one is the use of daily press briefings, a practice he formerly used when he was mayor of Mexico City. During these briefings, which last about 1.5 hours, López Obrador presents public programs, discusses recent events, and introduces newly appointed high-level officials; but, above all, he mainly seeks to stir and control the national political agenda. This communication strategy has been complemented by two measures. First, a very active participation in social networks (Twitter and Facebook) by López Obrador's head of communications, as well as the use of all institutional accounts from federal institutions to reinforce key political messages from the president. Second, the dismantling of ministerial communication offices to concentrate their resources in the office of the president (A. López 2018). As a result, the president has become the main selling point of his government to the public. Also, he has sent the message (both externally and within his own cabinet) that it is only he who calls the shots with respect to government decisions.

The second way in which the president has tried to personalize decision-making is by creating administrative structures that are directly accountable to him. One is that of the so-called *superdelegados*, a group of thirty-two officials that represent the federal government in each one of the states (Pardo 2020). While in the past federal ministries had their own delegations to deal with state governments (which are constitutionally autonomous because Mexico is a federal system), the *superdelegados* are now in charge of dealing with all federal business. Moreover, they report their activities to the *Coordinación General de Delegados*, whose head is a close adviser to the president (Morales and

Zavala 2019). This new intergovernmental arrangement has been heavily criticized because it gives too much power to the presidential representatives, but also because some of the *superdelegados* are clearly being positioned for an eventual candidacy for state governorships. Another administrative structure outside the executive branch's personnel system is that of the *siervos de la nación*, an ad hoc group of newly hired public servants directly managed from the presidential office. This group of public servants has been given the task of building a census of potential beneficiaries for López Obrador's new social programs. However, there have been many criticisms regarding the way they were recruited, the robustness and transparency of the survey methodologies they have used, and the overt politicization of their activities (e.g. they used promote López Obrador's image while doing their visits; see Rosas 2019).

In his effort to extend presidential control over the bureaucratic apparatus, López Obrador's actions have also affected public institutions that are outside the executive power. Budgetary adjustments, for instance, have applied to the set of nonmajoritarian institutions established during the past two decades. These are called "constitutional autonomous agencies" and include the central bank (Banco de México), the National Council for Social Policy Evaluation (CONEVAL), the National Geography and Statistics Institute (INEGI), the Federal Telecommunications Institute (IFT), the National Electoral Institute (INE), the National Institute for Transparency and Data Protection (INAI), the General Attorney's Office (FGR), the National Human Rights Commission (CNDH), and the Federal Economic Competition Commission (COFECE) (Dussauge-Laguna 2015).

López Obrador has often criticized these institutions, which according to him "had grown like mushrooms after the rain" (Rodríguez 2018). Hence, he has sought to undermine their reputation and autonomy through a variety of means. For instance, he has unfairly blamed the central bank for some of the economic difficulties that have taken (or could take) place during his administration, even if these are due to poor decisions from his own government (Maldonado 2018). He has also criticized the INAI (the transparency institute) for the lack of results in the fight against corruption, an area which is not under the remit of that institution (SDPnoticias 2018). In terms of appointments, López Obrador has nominated people who have been politically close to him for several years for a seat on the board of the central bank (González 2018), and for the position of founding head of the new attorney's office that should be formally independent from the executive power (Arellano and Mercado 2019). Similarly, the head of CONEVAL was removed from office after criticizing the president's social policies and budgetary cuts to his institution (Expansión Política 2019). Even more significantly, López Obrador introduced a constitutional reform to reverse the "education reform" of the previous administration. This legal change included the termination of the National Institute for Education Evaluation (INEE), a nonmajoritarian agency established in the early 2000s to evaluate the government's education policy (Cortés and Soto 2019).

With these and other measures, the president is aiming to personally centralize political and bureaucratic decision-making. Furthermore, his actions are undermining the legal, institutional, and budgetary features of the Mexican state established during the past thirty years (Méndez and Dussauge-Laguna 2017). These include the constitutional autonomous agencies created to depoliticize and specialize certain state functions, such as the management of elections, the measurement of national statistics, the regulation of economic competition, and the evaluation of education and social policies.

Redistributing Resources and Reshuffling Administrative Areas

López Obrador has also followed a strategy of discretionally redistributing resources across government policy areas. This has sometimes implied the dismantling of organizations and programs. The implementation of "austerity policies" and the fight against corruption (and, more recently, the COVID-19 pandemic) have been commonly flagged as the reasons behind these measures. However, his administration has not provided convincing cost–benefit analyses or strong evidence of previous wrongdoing. Ultimately, resource redistribution would seem to be motivated merely by the need to divest funds to finance López Obrador's political priorities and pet projects.

For instance, there have been systematic efforts to reduce the size of the federal government. Some agencies including the Council for Promoting Tourism (*Consejo de Promoción Turística*; Paredes 2018), the Agency for Promoting Foreign Investment in Mexico (*ProMéxico*), and the National Institute for Entrepreneurship (*Instituto Nacional del*

Emprendedor [INADEM]) have been terminated (La Razón 2018). In other cases, the Ministry of Finance (*Secretaría de Hacienda y Crédito Público*) instructed the firing of thousands of public servants in several federal institutions, including the tax agency (*Servicio de Administración Tributaria*; Ureste 2018), the Ministry of Education (*Secretaría de Educación Pública*; El Heraldo de México 2019a), and the Energy Regulatory Commission (*Comisión Reguladora de Energía*; El Financiero 2018). Similarly, without providing clear explanations, the president has ordered the elimination of senior bureaucratic positions labelled "deputy director general" (*directores generales adjuntos*; El Heraldo de México 2019b). More recently, López Obrador decreed the termination of a dozen ministerial undersecretary structures (Miranda and Guerrero 2020). At the time of writing, some reports had stated that more than 500,000 public positions (including temporary and permanent positions) had been eliminated from the federal bureaucracy (Muédano 2019).

Budgetary cuts have also affected the institutions that form the so-called National Anti-Corruption System (*Sistema Nacional Anticorrupción* [SNA]). This includes seven agencies from the various federal powers, including the Ministry of Public Administration (MPA), the INAI, the FGR, the Supreme Audit Institution (*Auditoría Superior de la Federación*, ASF), the Council of the Federal Judiciary, and the Federal Tribunal for Administrative Justice, all of which are coordinated by an Executive Secretariat. Except for the ASF and the MPA, all other agencies have faced budgetary cuts. Indeed, the system was subject to a budgetary reduction of MX\$ 5,000 million in FY2019 (García 2018), a measure directly at odds with the president's alleged commitment to fighting corruption.

Furthermore, the federal budget was rearranged on a clearly discretionary basis during the first years of the López Obrador administration. While "austerity" has been flagged to justify cuts in several policy areas, a few institutions and programs have seen considerable budget increases. This has been the case, for example, for the energy sector, particularly the national oil company *Petróleos Mexicanos* (PEMEX), which is a top priority for the president. Similarly, newly created public programs, such as *Jóvenes Construyendo el Futuro* and *Sembrando Vidas*, have received significant amounts of money despite lacking clear policy designs or monitoring and evaluation plans. Extra funding for these programs is supposed to come from governmentwide "savings";

in practice, it comes from cuts applied to other policy areas, such as science, technology, and health (Miranda 2019; Redacción/LP 2019).

Finally, López Obrador has terminated important social programs inherited from previous administrations. Three cases have gained significant public attention: the *Programa de Estancias Infantiles*, *Prospera*, and the *Seguro Popular*. The first provided subsidies to private daycare centers to aid working parents. According to the president, private providers charged for services they were not actually delivering. However, his government has not been able to prove any cases of wrongdoing (Villegas 2019). In the case of *Prospera* (a conditional cash transfer program established in the 1990s that provided benefits to poor people, subject to school attendance and medical checkups), López Obrador argued (again without showing evidence) that bureaucrats were stealing funds from these families and thus decided to change the program to unconditional direct transfers (Ramírez 2020). Similar accusations were raised against the *Seguro Popular*, a mechanism for providing health support to poor people who did not have social or private insurance. However, most social policy experts have said that (despite their limitations) *Prospera* and the *Seguro Popular* were effective programs, and that the proposed changes will not help reduce poverty levels or increase health services among vulnerable groups (Frenk and Gómez 2019; Gómez-Hermosillo 2019a, 2019b; Villalpando 2019).

Therefore, public finances have been managed and redistributed without any clear justification other than the president's wishes. Alleged corruption and inefficiencies have been flagged publicly, but the president has not provided supporting evidence. Budgetary cuts have been applied governmentwide in the name of austerity, but resources for presidential pet projects and preferred institutions (PEMEX) have been plentiful. Another problem is that newly created programs lack basic principles of good policy design and program-evaluation criteria. There is thus a high risk that public spending will serve short-term political objectives, but it will also represent a huge waste of public resources in the longer term.

Exerting Influence over Public Personnel Management

A third strategy pursued by López Obrador is that related to public personnel management. On top of the large-scale dismissals already mentioned, civil service structures have been under attack mainly on two fronts: salary levels and patronage pressures. The politicization of public sector appointments has long been a feature of Mexico's public administration (Dussauge-Laguna and Casas, in press). Yet current patronage practices have been different in two senses: they have been carried out in open defiance of established meritocratic procedures (previously respected at least formally); and they have privileged appointees' loyalty to the president and his political movement, disregarding their professional skills.

With the support of *MORENA*'s political majority in both legislative chambers, López Obrador promoted a new federal remunerations law in early November 2018, a month before his inauguration (Arias et al. 2018; DOF 2018). This affected the payment levels of thousands of public servants across all public policy sectors. Originally, salary reductions were supposed to apply only to higher public servants (e.g. secretary of state, undersecretary of state, head of unit, director general, and deputy director general), as well as to anyone with a higher salary than the president (about US$5,000 per month, after taxes). However, lower-level officials and other public servants in nongovernmental positions (e.g. public university workers and researchers) were also affected. The law prohibited payments through vouchers, bonuses, incentives, and other salary items historically used to compensate for low public salary levels. The private health insurance premium that thousands of public servants had received since the administration of Ernesto Zedillo (1994–2000) was terminated as well (Hernández 2019). These payment cuts also had impacts beyond the executive power, such as among the constitutional autonomous agencies and the judiciary power. These changes were justified by López Obrador as a measure to end the "privileges" of what he called the "golden bureaucracy" – something no longer acceptable in a poverty-ridden country such as Mexico. However, important factors such as salary variations across labor market prices, or the experience, skills, and acquired rights of public employees, were not taken into account.

Federal bureaucratic structures have also been affected by an extensive use of patronage-based appointments. Naturally, the president has taken advantage of his political prerogative to appoint cabinet members and many other high-level officials. This has traditionally been the norm in Mexico, even though the introduction of a civil service law back in the early 2000s did introduce some constraints on patronage-based appointments (Dussauge-Laguna and Casas, in press; Merino 2013). However, anecdotal information and media scandals suggest that incoming appointees have asked subordinates (including some in the civil service structure) to hand in their letters of resignation, regardless of their experience or political affiliation. A rather extreme case of patronage took place when the incoming minister for energy unlawfully asked for the resignation of the heads of the semiautonomous National Hydrocarbons Commission and Energy Regulatory Commission (Camarena 2018). The president thus managed to appoint a group of loyalists after a highly politicized and contentious process, in which the expertise and independence of the new regulators was severely questioned by both legislators and energy sector experts. More recently, the president publicly stated he expected "blind loyalty" toward his political project from public servants (Morales 2020).

These measures have extended López Obrador's control over the bureaucracy, but they have also damaged the quantity and quality of human capital inside the federal government (Maldonado 2019). Working conditions have deteriorated and the ability of public organizations to recruit experts has been curtailed. The politicization of the civil service structure has increased, while the already limited analytical and implementation capacities of the federal administration are being further stretched.

Overhauling Administrative Principles and Bureaucratic Norms

López Obrador has explicitly stated his wish to transform the values that govern Mexico's public administration (López Obrador 2018). However, the actions his administration has advanced often go against widely accepted good governance principles, such as the need for evidence in policymaking or the separation between the state and the church. Furthermore, sometimes his attitude regarding the use and diffusion of fake news clearly resembles that of other populist leaders.

All reform initiatives implemented by the López Obrador administration have shared one key feature: a lack of solid background studies, diagnoses, data, or evidence showing their adequacy or potential usefulness. Neither the president nor his cabinet members have explained how or why civil service cuts, salary reductions, or budgetary redistributions will improve government performance. The call for "republican austerity" (*austeridad republicana*) has been the mantra under which every policy proposal fits. When he is confronted by journalists about data on subjects such as public safety, economic growth, or employment levels, López Obrador usually calls into question the quality and validity of information sources, and asserts that he has "alternative data" (El Sol de México 2019; Impacto redacción 2019). Recently, during the COVID-19 crisis, López Obrador has tried to minimize the relevance and truthfulness of international data and comparisons which clearly show the serious mistakes his government has made in response to the pandemic (Peci, González, and Dussauge-Laguna 2020[3]). Because of all this, a leading journalist has suggested that "[t]he morning press briefings are not in line with a strategy that favors transparency. It is a strategy – a very effective one, according to the polls – of communication and propaganda. Useful to elude inter-mediaries. Of little use in terms of accountability" (Moreno 2019).

The president has caused public uproar on several occasions for using biblical references or religious terms during his speeches and press briefings (González 2019). This runs in stark contrast to his alleged admiration for former president Benito Juárez (who decreed the separation between the church and the state in the nineteenth century). A clear example of how López Obrador deliberately blurs the lines between the public sphere and individual religious beliefs is when he publicly asked the leader of the Evangelic church to distribute the *Cartilla moral* (Juárez 2019). Originally written by a public intel-lectual (Alfonso Reyes) in the mid-twentieth century, López Obrador considers the *Cartilla Moral* to be a useful document to advance his objective of building a new public morality in Mexico. However, in choosing a religious group as the main channel of distribution, instead of the ministry of education or a nongovernmental organization, the president has raised concerns about the extent to which his religious views have an influence on his policy decisions.

Thus, López Obrador has undermined the quality of public debates, while at the same time he has contributed to the spread of fake news and misinformation, even for very important issues such as the COVID-19 pandemic. This goes against the evidence-informed move-ment that had slowly gained strength in the federal public administra-tion during recent decades (Méndez and Dussauge-Laguna 2017). Similarly, despite the secular tradition of the Mexican bureaucracy, the language used by the president in public events is introducing a perilous quasi-religious tone in government actions and decisions.

In the end, López Obrador's alleged understanding of the people's will and of relevant moral standards has become a valid substitute for any technical explanation or policy justification.

Bypassing Established Deliberative, Procedural, and Legal Channels

A final strategy López Obrador has pursued through some of his actions is to either go against basic administrative principles such as the rule of law or deliberately bypass established bureaucratic norms. While previous governments regularly tried to disguise dubious legal actions, and often reversed decisions once they were publicly criticized for lacking proper legal or administrative justification, López Obrador has shown an openly ambiguous attitude toward legal principles and procedures.

Some of the administration's most publicized decisions have shown a clear disregard for basic bureaucratic standards. For instance, when announcing the monthly cash transfers to high school students and adults aged over 68 years, López Obrador declared the funds would be directly transferred through bank accounts managed by *Banco Azteca* (Reporte índigo 2019). However, he did not explain the reason for using this bank (which is owned by a member of the presidential economic advisory committee) without first going through an open tendering process. In the face of criticisms from the Head of the Federal Economic Competition Commission and several political commentators, López Obrador stated that the law did not require him to use a competitive process for buying financial services (which is not entirely true). Similarly, during an unprecedented gasoline shortage crisis in December 2018–January 2019, the president decreed the acquisition of 571 tank trucks (at a cost of US$ 85 million) to facilitate gasoline distribution (Animal Político 2019). Once again, the decision was not fully explained and López Obrador simply argued he was dealing with a national emergency. He then added that "because we have not got any problems of conscience, because we are not corrupt, that is why we proceeded in this way" (etcétera 2019). This lack of interest in applying competitive tendering processes, which runs against his public commitment to fighting corruption, has remained a feature of his administration: at least three-quarters of all public contracts have been awarded directly (Redacción Animal Político 2019a).

Another example of López Obrador's uneasy relationship with the rule of law is the discretional (and even illegal) use of public consultations. Back in October 2018, months before he entered office, he asked "the people" to decide whether construction for Mexico City's new international airport should continue in the same location, or whether a new building process should start in a different location he had publicly favored (políticomx 2018). After a highly criticized public consultation exercise, the US$ 13,000 million project (which had kicked off in 2015 and was expected to finish in 2024) was cancelled. A few weeks later, in another public consultation, López Obrador "asked the people" whether the government should implement a list of ten "top priority projects" (the Maya railway, free internet for all, social programs, etc.). Both exercises were severely questioned by analysts and experts, who criticized the lack of statistical representation of the results, the bias in the wording of questions, the overtly political location of voting sites, and the absence of antifraud mechanisms (Cruz 2018; Garrido 2018; I. López 2018; Woldenberg 2018).

Finally, despite having the support of political majorities in both legislative chambers, López Obrador has decreed a series of executive memoranda on subjects such as the cancellation of the previous administration's education policy reform and the implementation of government austerity policies. According to several legal experts, these measures lack a proper legal basis (La redacción Proceso 2019b; López-Ayllón 2019; Pérez de Acha 2019; Vivanco 2019). They also put public officials in the middle of bureaucratic and ethical conundrums.

Overall, these actions show López Obrador's disrespect for basic administrative and legal principles. He has used his democratic legitimacy and popular support to avoid procedural and bureaucratic routines. In doing so, the president is damaging the country's already fragile respect for the rule of law. At the same time, the biased implementation of consultation procedures, such as those described here, is eroding both the usefulness of this tool for policy design and its longer-term value for policy legitimation.

Conclusions

The study of how democratic backsliding trends may affect public administration is highly relevant, for both practical and theoretical reasons. As the number of populist politicians in government increases around the world, it has become necessary to describe and analyze the potential consequences that illiberal policies have on bureaucratic structures and procedures. This allows us to better understand whether and how backsliding is a temporary issue, or something that will have long-standing consequences on the administrative infrastructure of the state. This knowledge may also provide us with ideas about how to better fight against the erosion of democratic governance principles.

To add to our comparative conversation, this chapter has investigated the recent experience of Mexico under Andrés Manuel López Obrador's government. In line with contemporary populists, López Obrador's political rhetoric is filled with images of "corrupt elites" and "good people." At the same time, in a clearly illiberal fashion, he has expressed a deep mistrust of institutional checks and balances. With the support of a strong electoral win in the presidential election of 2018, López Obrador has been able to pursue an ambitious institutional reform agenda which he says reflects the "will of the people." He has thus decreed the termination of certain public organizations and social programs; reallocated budgetary resources in a highly discretionary fashion; increased the personalization of decision-making powers; and attacked already fragile principles and practices related to evidence-based policymaking, the rule of law, and civil service professionalization. These measures fall in line with the categories and variables introduced by the editors of this volume, which shows both the wider applicability of this analytical framework and the profound relevance that the research questions discussed in this book have for our time (see Roberts 2019).

While some of the features of the Mexican experience are similar to those taking place elsewhere, a particularity of this case is that the administrative changes advanced by López Obrador have been embedded in a doublespeak populist style of governing. He has allegedly furthered a leftist government program to favor poor people, but in practice his agenda has been closer to the right in many respects. For instance, he has sidelined bureaucratic actors and institutions, sought to reduce the size of the state, and promoted a governmentwide "austerity" agenda. The latter has received added emphasis since the onset of the COVID-19 pandemic. Instead of investing in public service infrastructure, which may provide higher-quality public services in the longer term, López Obrador has preferred the use of direct transfers to some social groups (young unemployed and old people), which may become political clienteles and thus provide him with short-term political dividends. Along the way, he has terminated social programs that were widely recognized for their effective policy design and positive impacts on working parents, poor people, and uninsured social groups. Similarly, while significant cuts have been applied in autonomous institutions, civil service salaries, and policy sectors such as science and health, resources have been made plentiful for the president's pet projects. Therefore, a profound contradiction exists between López Obrador's leftist rhetoric and his reform measures, which are clearly directed to curtail the administrative apparatus of the Mexican state.

Second, López Obrador's doublespeak-populist style has become manifest in the way he wraps his strategies in phrases that simultaneously express concern about the "people's will" while disguising his true political intentions. For instance, the centralization of decision-making is said to be about eliminating political abuse, but is never presented as a measure to personalize control; austerity is about savings, not about cuts; the introduction of direct transfers is about streamlining bureaucratic procedures, not about linking benefits to the presidential image; public consultations are about hearing the people's will, not about manipulating public decisions; and the use of executive decrees or noncompetitive tendering processes, which go against established legal principles, is said to be merely a measure to accelerate the so-called "transformation" the people asked for. Furthermore, because his electoral triumph was partly a popular reaction to many years of government corruption, López Obrador has assumed he can employ corruption control tools as he sees fit, even if that requires using confidential information to publicly attack his political adversaries. Last but not least, his administration's ill-conceived policy projects (such as investing in risky and environmentally dangerous mega-projects, or social programs that lack basic elements of good policy design or monitoring and evaluation criteria) are defended by arguing they will bring much-needed resources to long-forgotten communities.

Ultimately, López Obrador's doublespeak populism is quickly eroding Mexico's administrative infrastructure. Public agencies, bureaucratic procedures, personnel structures, budgetary allocations, and administrative principles are all being challenged "in the name of the people." As a result, public organizations are facing capacity shortages and public service provision channels are being undermined. Indeed, not a day passes by without news of beneficiaries (working parents, cancer patients, public sector employees, scientists) being affected either by the so-called "republican austerity" or by presidential initiatives aimed at terminating previous policies. Thus, an administration that is supposedly focused on providing for the "needs of the people" is actually curtailing the Mexican state's bureaucratic capacity to face both the country's biggest social challenges (e.g. poverty, inequality, and corruption) and its basic day-to-day services at the frontlines.

It is undeniable that Mexico's bureaucratic institutions already struggled with important administrative deficits which developed nations are only now facing because of democratic backsliding processes. Widespread patronage, an ambivalent attitude toward the rule of law, and a highly discretionary use of budgetary and other public resources have long been features of the Mexican state (Méndez 1997; Merino 2013). However, several institutional reforms were implemented in the past thirty years to increase government transparency, the use of evidence in policymaking, merit-based personnel management, and policy coherence in social programs. At the same time, new nonmajoritarian institutions were established to advance bureaucratic specialization and reduce the politicization of policy decisions (Méndez and Dussauge-Laguna 2017). In implementing his reform agenda, López Obrador is allegedly following "the will of the people." In practice, he is promoting changes that reflect a profound disdain for democratic governance principles. Beyond his doublespeak-populist rhetoric, López Obrador's actions are already leaving behind a smaller and weaker state – one more responsive to the presidential wishes but less capable of responding to Mexico's social needs, including those of its poorest and weakest people.

Notes

1. https://lopezobrador.org.mx/temas/privilegios/
2. AMLO (2018). 50 lineamientos generales para el combate a la corrupción y la aplicación de una política de austeridad republicana.

3. Peci, A., González, C. & Dussauge-Laguna, M. I. (2020). Presidential narratives and the (mis)use of scientific expertise: Comparing Covid-19 policy making responses in Brazil, Colombia, and Mexico. Unpublished manuscript.

9 Venezuela: Sidelining Public Administration Under a Revolutionary-Populist Regime

WOLFGANG MUNO AND HÉCTOR BRICEÑO

Introduction

According to various democracy measures, such as Freedom House or V-Dem, there has been a global net decline of democracy for fourteen consecutive years. V-Dem discusses a "third wave of autocratization" (Lührmann and Lindberg 2019). The most prevalent form of democratic decline has become the erosion of democracy by incumbents, which sparked a debate on democratic backsliding. While comparative democracy research has recently addressed various aspects of democratic backsliding, the administrative dimension is still a desideratum, as the editors of this volume have shown in the introduction. What happens to state bureaucracies when authoritarianism emerges? How do autocrats seek to use the administration to their ends, and how does it react? These questions are addressed in this volume.

We will analyze Venezuela as an example for a decline of democracy, although it is somewhat special because its democratic decline has led not only to an erosion of democracy but also to the establishment of an autocratic regime. The country has been a (more or less) functioning democracy since 1958. Within the system of the so-called "Puntofijismo," major parties agreed to a consensual model of democracy, sharing offices and distributing revenues from the oil rent. The public administration supported and managed the distribution. This led to stability and wealth in regional comparison, at least for parts of the population. Due to several inherent problems, the political-economic model crumbled in the 1980s and 1990s. In 1998, Hugo Chávez, a former military officer and failed putschist, assumed the presidency in Venezuela. He installed a revolutionary-populist regime: the Venezuelan "Socialism of the 21st century." In the following years, Venezuela experienced a severe decline of democracy and is today, under President Maduro, an autocratic regime. Freedom House categorizes Venezuela as "not free"; VDem classifies it as "electoral autocracy" (FH 2020; Lührmann et al. 2020b). Under Chavismo–Madurismo, the general objective of the regime was to expand and co-opt all the state institutions, including public administration, to subordinate it to the "revolution" and to gain control over oil revenues.

As the central aspect of the chapter, we will analyze the strategies of the Chavista governments vis-à-vis the administration to achieve its goals. More concretely, after discussing the concept of "democratic backsliding" and the role of public administration, we will show, first, how democratic backsliding in Venezuela happened. Second, based on the analytical framework developed by the editors in the introduction to this volume, we analyze how the Venezuelan governments of Chávez and Maduro treated public administration in the process of democratic backsliding. We identify three main strategies to sideline the bureaucracy: repression and firing, circumventing and neglecting, and militarization. With these strategies, Chavismo–Madurismo dismantled the former existing public administration and installed a new administration, loyal to the regime, as part of the process of democratic backsliding, which ultimately led to autocratization.

Democratic Backsliding and Public Administration

Scholars have recently started to conceptualize democratic regression or backsliding in more detail (Bermeo 2016; Levitsky and Ziblatt 2018a; Svolik 2018; Waldner and Lust 2018). Democratic backsliding does not necessarily lead to democratic breakdown. This may be the worst-case outcome. On the other side, backsliding may entail "only" a more fine-grained deterioration of democratic quality (see also Lührmann and Lindberg 2019). On one hand, Venezuela is a typical case for democratic backsliding, where democracy eroded slowly and incrementally over time (for more detail, see Corrales 2020a). On the other hand, Venezuela is special, because its democratic backsliding led to the breakdown of democracy. As Javier Corrales notes, "It is hard to find recent cases of democratic decline anywhere in the world that can match Venezuela's fall" (Corrales 2020b, p. 39).

Comparative research on democratization or democratic backsliding has thus far left out the administrative dimension to a considerable degree, as the editors of this volume discuss (Bauer et al., Introduction, this volume). If at all, bureaucracy is mentioned in the context of an effective state which requires a state apparatus (Merkel et al. 2003, pp. 55*ff.*). Juan Linz and Alfred Stepan note the necessity of "a state bureaucracy that is usable by a new democratic government," albeit without analyzing this in detail (Linz and Stepan 1996, p. 7). The term "usable" alludes to the fact that bureaucracy is not seen as an independent actor or unit of analysis; the debate is more concerned with the question of "stateness" in general. The concept of bureaucratic authoritarianism, as developed by Guillermo O'Donnell, explicitly mentions "bureaucracy," but is rather a state theory, too (Collier 1979; O'Donnell 1979). A partial exception is the concept of neopatrimonialism, which is used in the analysis of African transitions (Bratton and van de Walle 1997; Erdmann 2013). In this, perspective, explicitly referring to Max Weber, neopatrimonialism is conceptualized as a hybrid regime in which traditional and legal-rational authority is mixed, there is no distinction between private and public, the state is the private property of the ruler, and the bureaucracy is solely responsible to the ruler, usually bound by clientelism.

The idea of a "usable" or "neutral bureaucracy" relies on Weber's ideal-type concept of bureaucracy as part of the rational-legal authority (Weber 2005; see Cornell, Knutsen, and Teorell 2020 as a recent example for the relevance of Weber's concept). A "Weberian" bureaucracy might not object to democratic backsliding because changes often are, at least on the surface, based on formal-legal decisions. Additionally, a "Weberian" bureaucracy is subordinated to authority, and hence tends to accept new authorities. The basis for Weber's ideal type, the Prussian-German bureaucracy, shows just that. Starting under an absolutist monarchy, working for a constitutional monarchy, the Weimar democracy, Nazi Germany, and later either communist or democratic Germany, German bureaucracy has been quite flexible. In particular, the democratic backsliding under Weimar and the takeover of the NSDAP, where there has been no big resistance, seems to be an example of subordination to authority (see Strobel and Veit, Chapter 2, this volume). To sum up, a neutral, "Weberian" bureaucracy might not be an obstacle to democratic backsliding and, more importantly, might not be seen as an obstacle by the backsliders.

A second perspective on bureaucracy emphasizes the political role – that is, the bureaucracy is conceptualized as a political actor. In a moderate, liberal-pluralist version, the bureaucracy is one political actor among many, with private interests and political preferences. This idea is attributed to pluralist theories, as developed by Robert Dahl and Ernst Fraenkel (Dahl 1961; Fraenkel 2011; see also, with special reference to Fraenkel, Bauer, and Becker 2020). Other approaches, linked to Rational Choice theory, emphasize bureaucrats' private interests or interests in increasing budgets and aggrandizing their organization (Downs 1965; Niskanen 1971). If bureaucracy is democratic, it is an obstacle for democratic backsliding, but if private interests dominate, bargaining between politicians and bureaucrats might redefine the relationship between politicians and bureaucrats, as conceptualized by Hood and Lodge (Hood and Lodge 2006; see Bauer et al., Introduction, this volume). Guarantees of privileges and positions, salaries and promotions – the exchange of rewards for competency and loyalty might reconcile bureaucrats with backsliders.

The perspectives on bureaucracies mentioned here are discussed in more detail in the introduction to this volume, but for the Venezuelan case an additional third perspective has to be introduced: a more radical variant, which can be found in Marxist perspectives of a politicized administration (see Farazmand 2010). The bureaucracy is seen as an instrument of the ruling class, helping to maintain the status quo and resist change, especially revolutionary change. Hence, the bureaucracy has to be abolished completely (see Farazmand 2010). This perspective is especially relevant for the Venezuelan case because the regime has understands itself as a socialist-revolutionary regime: the so-called "Socialism of the 21st Century."

As shown, bureaucracy is not necessarily an obstacle to democratic backsliding, but it may be. If so, backsliders will try to neutralize or eliminate bureaucrats. From an analysis of empirical historical and actual cases, Bauer et al. delineate five strategies for administrative sidelining in the context of democratic backsliding (Introduction, this volume): the centralization of administrative structure, the disciplining of the bureaucracy through the redistribution of resources, the cleansing of administrative staff and the recruitment of loyalists, the devalorization of the norm of neutrality, and the cutting back of accountability mechanisms. Another central aspect of the analytical frame as developed in the introduction refers to the reaction of the bureaucracy, offering three possible paths: working, shirking, or sabotage. Bauer et al. expect that a strong bureaucracy which is staffed with highly professional and expertise-based bureaucrats will have a high level of autonomy that ultimately can function as a brake on an authoritarian regime's attempts to dominate society (Introduction, this volume).

In the next section, we will apply the above-mentioned concepts to the Venezuelan case, showing that the regime has applied all tactics of sideling the bureaucracy. Additionally, we will show that the resistance efforts of the bureaucrats were futile, although there has been a high level of autonomy and a strong bureaucracy in Venezuela, simply because the Venezuelan governments crushed all resistance.

Democracy, Public Administration, and Backsliding in Venezuela

In December 1998, former failed putschist leader and former military officer Hugo Chávez won the presidential election with 56 percent of the votes.[1] After his election, Hugo Chávez immediately started reshaping Venezuela's political landscape. A forty-year democracy started backsliding. In the following paragraphs, we describe, first, the old political system, and second, the process of democratic backsliding, with a special focus on the role of public administration.

After decades of authoritarian rule, Venezuela was democratized on January 23, 1958. The military dictator Marcos Pérez Jiménez fled after massive opposition, public protests, a general strike, and a military mutiny (see Levine 1978; Levine 1989). On October 31, 1958, the main existing parties agreed to forge the so-called *Pacto de Punto Fijo*, in which they accepted democratic elections, a joint government, and a new democratic constitution, which was ratified in 1961. Additionally, pacts were made with unions, entrepreneurs, and the military. These pacts founded an elitist-corporatist, but relatively stable, democracy (see Rey 1976). Oil income played the central role, both in the elite consensus-building process and in meeting popular demands, and the public administration organized the distribution of the oil rent to all sectors of society, leading to an extensive bureaucracy. During this period, the public administration was centralized; the central coordination office of the presidency (Cordiplan) was responsible for planning and organizing the public administration from the capital. The public expenditure quota represented more than 60 percent of GDP, and Venezuela was called a "bureaucratic developmental state" (Sonntag 1988). The bureaucracy was not neutral: positions were distributed between parties, which critics called "partidocracia."

A quarter of the population was part of the public administration somehow, in a highly clientelistic manner. Selecting governing teams commonly involved five criteria: political circumstances, personal relationships, partisan ties, external commitments, and professional competencies (Iturbe 2017, p. 201).

Initially, Venezuelan democracy kept its development promises. During the 1960s and '70s, important economic and social advances were registered: the GPD per capita increased from US$ 955 in 1960 to US$ 3,893 in 1980, and life expectancy at birth improved from 59.83 in to 68.54 in the same period. Illiteracy rates decreased from 44.8 percent in 1961 to 14 percent in 1981. The political system gained high levels of support from both the elites and the population: democracy consolidated. After two consecutive electoral victories by the Social Democratic Party (AD) in 1958 and in 1963, Rafael Caldera, the leader of the opposition Social Christian Party (COPEI), won the election in 1968. His victory was particularly significant: for the first time in Venezuelan history, the leader of the main opposition party came to power by peaceful means. Democracy was massively supported. Electoral turnout was more than 90 percent. In 1973, by the end of the third democratic government, surveys showed that 64 percent of the population identified with a political party, while 75 percent considered that the parties were important (Rey 2009, p. 183).

Despite the initial success, in the 1980s the political-economic model started to crumble. The first alarm went off on February 18, 1983 (known as *Viernes negro* – Black Friday), when the exchange pattern of the national currency Bolívar, which had enjoyed great stability for a long period of time, suffered a significant devaluation, showing the clear weakness of the economic model. Aware of the social and political deterioration that the country was experiencing, in 1984 President Jaime Lusinchi appointed a broad committee to reform the state (COPRE – Presidential Commission for State Reform) with the aim of evaluating and proposing a modernization plan for the national public administration, which had developed over the preceding decades as "an uncoordinated, ineffective sector without effective controls, which had grown by simple aggregation of parts, without a coherent development plan" (Cordiplan 1990), leading to the expansion of administrative corruption and the inefficient provision of public services.

In reality, reforms were limited, and, just five years later, in 1989 a massive social outbreak evidenced the exhaustion of the sociopolitical model. In December 1988, the leader of the social democratic party Carlos Andrés Pérez was elected for a second presidential term, after having governed during the oil boom years of the mid-1970s. However, this time his government had the completely opposite ideological orientation. If in his first term he promoted the expansion of the state and economic intervention, now he took the flags of the neoliberal "Washington Consensus" as a government plan, which, just a month after the beginning of his mandate, led to a violent social outbreak known as "El Caracazo," showing the social dissatisfaction toward a development model that had accumulated at least a decade in political and economic decline, in which poverty went from 10 percent at the beginning of 1979 to 63 percent at the beginning of 1989.

In the coming years, three consecutive events occurred, indicating the deepening of the crisis and its political manifestation. In 1992, there were two coups attempts (February and November), showing that discontent had reached the militaries, and also that the formerly professionalized military did not want to remain subordinate to the civil power but, rather, to become active protagonists of politics and national development. The 1992 coup attempt had been led by a formerly unknown army officer, Hugo Chávez, who used his televised arrest to become the most popular politician in Venezuela. In May 1993, President Carlos Andrés Pérez, who had become the target for all criticism, lost the support of his party in Congress and was impeached and prosecuted for corruption. At the end of the same year, Rafael Caldera won the presidential election for a second term – this time, however, as leader of an alliance of small parties and against his former party COPEI, proclaiming with his victory the beginning of the collapse of the bipartisan system that had governed the first thirty-five years of democracy, in a clear prelude to what would happen. Caldera was not able to solve the political, social, and economic crises, but pardoned Hugo Chávez.

To sum up, the democratic developmental state in Venezuela, relying on a public administration distributing the oil rent, started as a success story in regional comparison, but soon crumbled. The erosion of the political-economic developmental state model led to the rise of Hugo Chávez. Running for the presidency,[2] Hugo Chávez mainly presented an anticorruption agenda, heavily criticizing the ineffective and corrupt bureaucracy. After winning the election, he started reforming Venezuela (Corrales and Penfold 2011; Ellner and Tinker Salas 2007). A new constitution expanded presidential rights (including the possibility of re-election), established many social rights in the constitution, and further expanded rights of participation, especially through plebiscites. The "re-legitimization" of the public powers continued with the so-called mega-election of 2000. On July 30, the President of the Republic, the members of the National Assembly, the governors of the State, the Mayors, and the Councils to legislative bodies were elected simultaneously. Six months later, Venezuelans went back to the polls to choose the members of the Municipal Councils and the Parish Councils. In both events, Chávez succeeded in imposing, to differing degrees, his electoral majority over an opposition that acted uncoordinated. This way, ironically, Chávez used the new Magna Carta to advance his control of the political system. Democratic backsliding happened and, increasingly, elements of a revolutionary, left-wing politics of "Socialism of the 21st Century," the Bolivarian Republic, was installed in Venezuela. The ideology of a "Socialism of the 21st Century" remains unclear: Chávez mixed Marxism, participative democracy, populism, and even elements of liberation theology with a strong orientation toward Cuba and the Socialist one-party system of Castro. This included the ambition of controlling the complete state apparatus, from the judiciary, education system, and electoral authorities to the public administration in general.

A central element of the regime was the use of economic resources to legitimize its revolutionary political project. In order to do so, the regime needed to control the bureaucracy. During the governments of Hugo Chávez and Nicolás Maduro, 49.8 percent of all Venezuelan real oil exports between 1958 and 2016 took place, including, in the first years of the Chávez presidency, the highest prices for oil in history, resulting in the largest oil boom in Venezuelan history. With the huge amount of money amassed due to oil revenues, the regime expanded public spending through various mechanisms, including public policies known as social missions. The expansion of public spending helped reduce poverty from 48 percent to 27.5 percent between 1999 and 2007, which was intended to legitimize both the new regime and its undisputed leader. But the sustainability of the model was unfeasible, and it began to reverse from 2013 onwards.

In 2013, Hugo Chávez died of cancer. Despite the democratic back-sliding, he enjoyed widespread support, especially among the poor, throughout his terms. His successor, Nicolás Maduro, vice-president and interim-president after Chávez' death, and chosen by Chávez himself as his political heir, was elected on April 14, 2013, with just 50.66 percent of the votes, although the election was far from free and fair. Maduro made extensive use of the advantage of being the incumbent, the opposition was intimidated, and there were many irregularities. The narrow victory of Nicolás Maduro in the presidential election of 2013 showed the electoral weakness of the new government. In the December 2015 parliamentary election, the opposition received, for the first time, a clear majority, with 56 percent of the vote share, thereby achieving total control of the National Assembly. To counter this, Maduro, leveraging the subordination of the public powers system inherited from Chávez, completely deprived the legislative body of powers with the help of the loyal Supreme Court. In May 2017, Maduro called for a National Constituent Assembly, a clear violation of the constitution, with the objective of building a parallel legislative power loyal to his project. The first notion of the National Constituent Assembly was the dismissal of the National General Attorney, a former ally of Chávez and critic of Maduro's actions. This move allowed the regime to deepen control over all public powers. Chavismo–Madurismo also systematically destroyed electoral conditions, based on decisions of the Supreme Court of Justice and the National Electoral Council (CNE). The main strategies applied were the political disabling of the most popular leaders, the illegalization of the most important political opposition parties, the manipulation of the vote through change and redistribution of the electorate in polling stations, the annulment of the election of the Deputies of the state of Amazonas, the advance convocation of the presidential election, and the development of a clientelist control mechanism based on the issuance of the so-called "Carnet de la Patria," which had been introduced to administer the distribution of food and medicine and was used to intimidate voters. The deterioration of the electoral conditions was combined with the harassment, persecution, and dismantling of the opposition (see Briceño and Bautista de Alemán 2019,[3] Corrales 2020).

The continuing expansion of control over the public and institutional powers of the state, persecution and dismantling of the opposition, and the increase in repression and social controls systematically undermined democracy and continued the process of democratic backsliding. More recently, the elimination of the elected National Assembly marks the turning point toward an authoritarian regime. Freedom House ratings support this categorization: political and civil rights deteriorated slowly but steadily, and, since 2017, Venezuela is rated as "Not Free" (FH 2020).

To summarize, the rise of Hugo Chávez to power in 1998 realized the breakdown of democracy that was born forty years earlier and ushered in the rise of a new revolutionary political system, "Socialism of the 21st Century" or Chavismo–Madurismo, that was based on three pillars: (i) the manipulation of the constitutional norms, (ii) the populist (mis)-use of elections, and (iii) the use of oil revenue as a source of political legitimacy. In order to secure the oil revenues and the distribution of the oil rent, the regime had to control the state apparatus and bureaucracy, which is described in detail in the following section.

Public Administration and Democratic Backsliding in Venezuela

Public administration had been a central element of the oil-rent democracy in Venezuela, and despite the economic, social, and political crises of the 1980s and '90s, bureaucracy was still functioning. As mentioned, under Chavismo–Madurismo, the objective was to expand and co-opt all the state institutions, including public administration, to subordinate them to the revolution. The regime perceived the bureaucracy as an enemy rather than neutral, as an obstacle to revolutionary changes rather than usable and useful, and as part of the old regime, as described in the aforementioned radical perspective. Hence, in the context of democratic backsliding, the Venezuelan backsliders tried to neutralize, sideline, or eliminate bureaucrats. We identified three main strategies to sideline the established bureaucracy: first, repression and firing; second, circumventing and neglecting, which means creating a "parallel state"; and third, militarization of the "civil" service.

Repression and Firing

A crucial moment was a failed coup d'état in 2002 and massive strikes organized by unions affiliated with the old parties in 2002 and 2003. Chávez was "fighting for survival" (Corrales and Penfold 2011, p. 78). Many public servants participated in this strike, trying to resist the new

government. A central role was played by the state corporation
Petróleos de Venezuela SA (PDVSA), a stronghold of the opposition.
The oil industry in Venezuela had been in the hands of foreign companies since the beginning of the twentieth century. But in 1975, during
the government of Carlos Andrés Pérez, from the Social Democratic
Party Democratic Action (Acción Democrática AD), oil was nationalized. In 1976, the state oil company PDVSA had been created as a state-
owned, but somewhat independent oil company: a holding company in
charge of coordinating the operation of the various nationalized companies that from then on functioned as subsidiary companies. Among
them, two stand out: Lagoven SA, a company that had acquired all the
assets and concessions of the North American Creole Petroleum
Corporation; and Maraven SA Dutch subsidiary, Shell de Venezuela.
An important key to the period that began in 1975 is that both PDVSA
and its subsidiaries were conceived as public companies under private
law (corporations), with the Venezuelan State as the sole shareholder,
represented by the government. They also maintained their independent operating structures as they had operated until 1975, and, thanks to
their status as a corporation, enjoyed great operational and managerial
autonomy with respect to the government, simultaneously guarantee-
ing high income to the State through three channels: collection of
royalties, collection of income tax, and participation in the profits of
the company through dividends (Espinasa 2006). Oil companies,
unlike the rest of the public administration, were constantly evaluated
on their own business and commercial merits (Espinasa 2006). Hence,
this part of state bureaucracy, staffed with highly professional experts,
traditionally enjoyed a very high level of state autonomy in the sense
mentioned in the introduction to this volume, working almost as a state
within the state. In order to secure the oil funds, Chávez fired the
management of PDVSA and took direct control of the company and,
through this, the very important oil revenues. Chávez fired around
18,000 employees, among them most of the top and middle management. The new presidents of PDVSA were no longer independent, but
members of the presidential cabinet, and hence controlled directly by
the president. In various divisions of PDVSA, between 40 and 100 percent of all PDVSA-employees were removed, almost all in the financial
and human resources departments, and four out of five engineers were
fired. The positions were filled with loyal Chavistas, very often regardless of qualification. Today, there are around 150,000 people working

Table 9.1 *Growth of public administration, 1998–2016*

Entity	1998	2007	2012	2016
Vice-presidencies	0	1	7	7
Ministries	16	27	28	32
Missions	0	?	?	29
Decentralized bodies	313	-	812	1.287
Autonomous bodies	6	9	9	9
Employees National Public Administration	740.125	1.202.316	1.590.065	1.686.580[a]
Employees PDVSA	50.821	78.739[**]	132.086	150.032[*]
Public Employees, total	1.395.326	1.966.413	2.579.113	2.713.324[*]

Own compilation, sources: Iturbe 2017, Instituto Nacional de Estadística, Notes: *Data 2015. **2008.
[a]: Estimates.

for PDVSA (three times as many as before Chavismo), and the former autonomy has been abolished completely (see Table 9.1).

In the process of recruiting new bureaucrats loyal to the political project, the Chávez government implemented as a selection filter the so-called "Lista Tascón":[4] a database listing the names of the 3.2 million voters who requested the realization of the presidential recall referendum of the year 2004. Obviously, these voters were thereby ineligible for a job in public administration. The new loyal employees were also recipients, promoters, and bearers of a new political and institutional culture characterized by its exclusionary futures and alignment with the revolutionary political project. Referring to the colors that identify the United Socialist Party of Venezuela (PSUV), and the Chavista–Madurista political project in general, in October 2006 the oil minister and president of the Venezuelan state oil company between 2004 and 2013, Rafael Ramírez, coined the slogan "PDVSA es roja rojita" (PDVSA is red, very red) with the aim of reaffirming that only those who shared the ideology and objectives of the Chavista political project could work in the most important Venezuelan public company.

After securing control over PDVSA, Chávez ordered the creation of a new fund for social expenditure: FONDESPA. Paid immediately by the oil rent, the fund was not controlled by any entity but Chávez himself. Through this, PDVSA became the "spending arm of the central government" (Corrales and Penfold 2011, p. 81). In 2006, PDVSA had a transaction volume of US$ 102 billion and made a profit of about US$ 25 billion. Chávez used this immense amount of money for social expenditure – in 2006 alone, this amounted to more than US$ 13 billion. Between 1999 and 2014, the world witnessed an impressive process of oil price expansion, which in the Venezuelan case combined with the largest exports of the commodity. This allowed President Chávez to undertake any project he wanted to.

The case of PDVSA clearly illustrates several aspects of administrative sideling in the context of democratic backsliding as mentioned by Bauer et al. (Introduction, this volume): centralization of administrative structures, cleansing of administrative staff and recruitment of loyalists, and the devalorization of the norm of neutrality. But Venezuela contradicts the assumption mentioned in the introduction that a strong bureaucracy, staffed with highly professional and expertise-based bureaucrats, will enjoy a high level of autonomy that ultimately can function as a brake on any backsliding aspirations of a regime. The Venezuelan case shows that this is not necessarily so. Although PDVSA was an example of a strong, highly professional, expertise-based bureaucracy, resistance was crushed simply by firing the leading oppositional staff and intimidating others. If a backslider regime is using its powers to change the rules of the game, then a professional public administration is no protection at a systemic political level; it would only be able to resist if left intact. The case of Venezuela clarifies the scope conditions for such a situation as mentioned in the introduction.

Circumventing and Neglecting

The oil money was used to start new social programs: the so-called "missions" (Burchardt 2005). The missions constituted the hard core of social initiatives, which are meant to reach the poor without bureaucratic hurdles. Institutionalized bureaucracy was completely bypassed: on the one hand, because it was regarded as inefficient and not qualified; on the other hand, it was suspected to be on the opposition's side, not supporting the new social measures targeting the poor. The Chávez government's constant fear of sabotage explains the "extra-institutional character" of the missions. The conception, planning and implementation of the missions were exclusively in the hands of the presidency, and their financial aspects were not regulated by official budgets. Special funds from the presidency and PDVSA (controlled by the presidency) financed the missions. The missions were executed by a new parallel bureaucracy, independent from the established national public administration, responding exclusively to the president (D'Elia and Cabezas 2008).

According to the PDVSA annual report for 2016, between 2001 and 2016, its contributions to FONDEN and FONDESA reached US$ 265 billion. The missions are still the dominant means of social policy in Venezuela today, as Chávez's successor, Maduro, has continued the missions.

The website of the Venezuelan government currently lists thirty-five missions: the most important ones cover virtually every social aspect, such as health, education, poverty, housing, land reform, etc. (see Venezuela 2020). To illustrate the measures, some are listed in Table 9.2. Ostensibly, the missions are universal, not conditional, which means they provide service to everyone. In reality, they are located and implemented particularly in poor neighborhoods, thus mainly benefiting supporters of Chavismo–Madurismo.

Table 9.2 *Selected Missions in Venezuela*

Name	start	Aim
Zamora	2001	Poverty: land reform
Robinson	2003	Education: alphabetization of adults
Ribas	2003	Education: graduates of Misión Robinson can achieve higher education
Sucre	2003	Education: free academic studies
Barrio Adentro	2003	Health: free health care for everyone
Habitat	2004	Social housing
Milagro	2004	Health: eye operations for blind
Sonrisa	2006	Health: free dental prostheses
Negra Hipólita	2006	Poverty: support for street children, elderly, and indigenous
José Gregorio Hernández	2008	Health: support for handicapped

Own compilation; data source: Venezuela 2020

It is impossible to give exact information on how many people work for the missions, or on how they are financed, as no precise data is published on these issues, only estimates. A notable fact is that several missions are executed with Cuban help. Cuban teachers help in the education missions, and Cuban nurses and doctors in the health missions, especially Barrio Adentro, which installed free health posts in shanty-towns run by Cuban medical staff. An estimated 10,000–20,000 Cubans work in the Venezuelan health missions; in return, until recently, Venezuela has sent about 90,000 barrels of oil per day to Cuba (Muno 2015).[5] The new social programs had participatory components that allowed the beneficiaries to directly participate in the design of public policies, although in most cases citizen participation was ineffective and limited, since the spaces were controlled from above, which allowed the government to fulfill two political objectives. First, it kept all the beneficiaries of the Missions and other social programs active and mobilized in favor of the political project. Second, these participatory spaces operationalized a direct relationship between the people (beneficiary from public policies) and the charismatic leader. The image that the Missions were public policies of the exclusive and direct responsibility of Hugo Chávez was promoted by the government and shared by the beneficiaries, and the participatory components represented spaces in which citizens could communicate with the president and convey their opinions on the function of the institutions.

The case of the Missions illustrates other aspects of administrative sideling in the context of democratic backsliding as mentioned by Bauer et al. (Introduction, this volume): we can identify the cutting back of accountability mechanisms, but, most notably, we see the disciplining of the bureaucracy through the redistribution of resources. The established bureaucracy lost access to the population and, through this, lost possibilities to function as a clientelist broker. Instead, the missions could establish new clientelist links between the Chavista–Madurista regime and the poor population (see Penfold-Becerra 2007).

Militarization

Another central strategy of sidelining the established bureaucracy was the militarization of public administration, which means the military has increasingly taken over the function of public administration in various areas. Corrales recently spoke of "function fusion" to describe what happened in Venezuela (Corrales 2020, p. 40). He used that label to describe, among other features, the enhanced role of the military in the economy and public administration.

From the transition to democracy until the failed coup d'états of 1992, the Venezuelan military had cultivated a professional autonomy, respecting the Pact of Punto Fijo and refraining from exerting political influence. No military officers were members of the cabinet or held high-ranked political positions. In the wake of the crisis of Venezuelan democracy, the military re-awakened as a political actor, becoming involved in the fight against riots and, ultimately, in the failed coup d'états (see Trinkunas 2002). Chávez, as a former military officer, managed to integrate the military into his regime as a revolutionary partner, taking over many nonmilitary tasks that had formerly been the duty of the public administration (Norden 2008). The first initiative started immediately after the election of Hugo Chávez in February 1999: "Plan Bolívar 2000." A total of 40,000 soldiers were deployed to distribute food and organize educational programs. Through this, Chávez showed the military his personal trust, the military started engaging in nonmilitary affairs (unlike previously, whereby the military engaged only in purely military affairs), and the image of the military in Venezuelan society improved substantially. With this initiative, the military gained firsthand experience in substituting the established bureaucracy. And, of course, the military gained access to additional resources. One year after the start of "Plan Bolívar 2000," the program was suspended due to allegations of widespread corruption among the military officers responsible for the implementation. Nevertheless, the military continued carrying out state affairs, as a substitute for public administration.

Over the years, Chávez expanded government influence and the role of the state in the Venezuelan economy (Arenas 2010). Not only PDVSA but also other companies, such as the telecommunication company CANTV, cement companies, airports, and harbors, were nationalized. Many of these companies were handed over to the military or retired military officers. The influence of the military in the government, the state, and the state economy steadily increased. In 2012, nine out of twenty governors elected from the Chavista party PSUV were former generals. In 2018, eleven out of twenty governors were former military officers (Hetland 2017; Polga-Hecimovich 2019).

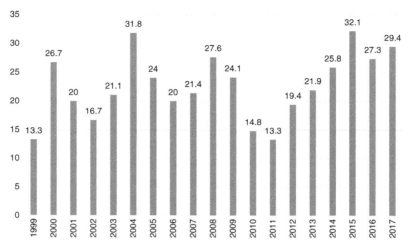

Figure 9.1 Number of military members in the cabinet 1999–2017, percentage of cabinet
Source: Own compilation; data sources: Maingon 2017,[6] Diario El Nacional 2015, own calculations

Military representation in the cabinet has fluctuated between 13 percent and 32 percent (see Figure 9.1).

Since 2015, the military not only participates in the cabinets, but also heads the state oil company PDVSA and many other state companies. In 2020, active or retired military officers play an essential role in Venezuela: eight out of thirty-three ministries and seven out of nineteen governorships are in their hands, and at least sixty state-owned companies are managed by them. Additionally, since 2013, President Maduro has founded fourteen companies which are directly owned by the military, and several Venezuelan generals have founded and/or own forty-one private companies which have received 220 state contracts (Corrales 2020). The revolutionary-socialist strategy of nationalization of the economy was combined with militarization of the state, state enterprises, and public administration, which is a special feature of Chavismo–Madurismo and partially explains the stability of the autocracy.

To secure the loyalty of the military, Chavismo–Madurismo promoted many officers to higher ranks. The number of generals in Venezuela rose from 50 in 1993 to 4,000 in 2016, according to Bloomberg estimates (Bloomberg 2016). As a comparison, the US military currently employs 653 generals, while the German Bundeswehr had in total 49 since its creation in 1955. Military officers acquired a number of privileges, power, and access to resources. In addition to formal benefits, their offices and mandates enabled them to gain informal benefits from corruption and illegal activities, such as smuggling and drug trafficking (Corrales 2020). This made them loyal supporters of Chavismo–Madurismo and a pillar of the regime. The regime, on the other hand, secured the support of the most important actor group in Venezuelan politics, and could use the assumed efficiency and organizational capacities of the military for administrative purposes.

The partisan attachment and bureaucratic politicization of the Venezuelan military at the established bureaucracy's expense reveals several of the aforementioned strategies of administrative sidelining, especially the disciplining of the bureaucracy through the redistribution of resources, the recruitment of loyalists, the devalorization of the norm of neutrality and the cutting back of accountability mechanisms (Bauer et al., Introduction, this volume). This can be seen as a special form of sidelining the bureaucracy. The militarization of public administration, as described here, ultimately led to a parallel military-evolutionary public management agency: on one hand, a stable pillar of the regime; on the other hand, a "deep state" or a "state within a state."

Conclusion

Venezuela has been analyzed as a typical or representative case for the decline of democracy, ultimately leading to democratic breakdown. Focusing on the administrative dimension has helped in understanding the process of democratic backsliding and breakdown.

Venezuelan democracy has deteriorated substantially under Chavismo–Madurismo, the regimes of presidents Hugo Chávez and Nicolás Maduro, who established a populist regime with a revolutionary ideology: the "Socialism of the 21st Century." Under Chavismo–Madurismo, the general objective was to expand and co-opt all the state institutions, including public administration, to subordinate them to the revolution and to gain control over oil revenues and the distribution of oil rents. The established bureaucracy, linked with the former old regime of an elitist democracy, was seen as an enemy and an obstacle to revolutionary changes, and therefore had to be sidelined. We identified three main strategies for sidelining the bureaucracy. First, repression and firing: critique or resistance of public employees led to firing and the exchange of staff – the state-owned oil company PDVSA is an example of this strategy. After a strike, thousands of employees, even management, were fired, and loyal supporters were installed. Second, circumventing and neglecting, which means creating a "parallel state": The Chávez government started with a new public policy – the so-called Missions – which were carried out by new organs, circumventing the established administration. Third, militarization of the "civil" service: the army took over more and more tasks of the public administration, and ministries and public bodies were led by officers loyal to the regime.

These strategies dismantled the existing public administration and installed a new administration, loyal to the regime, as part of the process of autocratization. Hence, the case of Venezuela fits with the strategies outlined in the introduction: the centralization of adminis-tration, redistribution of resources and the sidelining of the established bureaucracy through new organizations, the cleansing of personnel and recruitment of loyalists, the devalorization of the norm of neutral-ity, and the cutting back of accountability mechanisms. Additionally, we identified the militarization of bureaucracy as a new element. The military helps carrying out the strategies and serves as loyal supporter of the regime. The Venezuelan military has become a central pillar of the Venezuelan Chavismo–Madurismo regime.

In this respect, the Venezuelan case supports the assumptions out-lined in the introduction about sidelining bureaucracy in the context of democratic backsliding. But in an important aspect, Venezuela modi-fies the assumption that a strong bureaucracy, staffed with highly professional and expertise-based bureaucrats, will enjoy a high level of autonomy and may function as a brake on backsliding aspirations of a regime. The Venezuelan case shows that this is not necessarily so. Although PDVSA was an example of a strong, highly professional, expertise-based bureaucracy, resistance was crushed, as the opposing staff was simply fired. If the backslider regime is strong enough to change the rules and abolish the autonomous bureaucracy, its profes-sionalism is no obstacle anymore.

The (new) positions in the public administration were heavily used for clientelist distribution and filled with loyalists of Chavismo–

Madurismo, often regardless of qualification. Between 1998 and 2016, the number of public employees more than doubled, the number of ministries duplicated, and the number of employees in the state-owned oil company PDVSA tripled.

Venezuela is not only an example of democratic backsliding which resulted in a corrupt and clientelist autocracy, but also an interesting and special case of administrative sideling in a populist-revolutionary regime. The new public administration, filled with loyalists, and especially the military, has become a pillar of the new regime and essentially contributes to the stability of the autocracy.

While this strategy helped stabilize the autocracy, it had severe socioeconomic side effects. When Chávez assumed office, daily oil production surpassed 3 million barrels per day; in 2018, only 1.38 million barrels were produced per day. Lack of investment, mismanagement, and corruption destroyed oil production, the PDVSA, and the country as a whole. The government crushed and sidelined the established bureaucracy for political and ideological reasons, but it ultimately undermined the base of the state. Bureaucracies, as mentioned by Bauer et al. in the introduction, are "crucial in preparing and implementing policies." The result of a politicized, loyalist, but largely unqualified bureaucracy is obvious: today, more than 80 percent of Venezuelans live below the poverty line, every seventh child is severely undernourished, and more than 5 million Venezuelans have fled the country, according to UN information. Inflation is exploding: by more than 1 million percent in 2018, and with the IMF estimating 10 million percent in 2019. Venezuela is highly indebted, with at least US$ 17 billion in Russia, more than US$ 60 billion in China, and a total of about US$ 170 billion worldwide. In ordinary times, this would be no problem: the country has more than 300 billion barrels of proven oil reserves, the highest in the world. But Venezuela is not only an example of democratic backsliding and sidelining public administration: the economic consequences of the regime policies have ruined the country.

Notes

1. Parts of the following paragraphs are based on Muno (2005) and Briceño, H. and Bautista de Alemán, P. (2019). From democracy to authoritarianism. Venezuela 2018. Prospects for regime change. Rostock University, mimeo.

2. "Relegitimation" was the name given to the process of election of new authorities of the five public powers to adapt them to the requirements of the new Constitution. This was carried out through elections (executive and legislative at the national, state, municipal, and parochial levels) and appointment by the parliament (TSJ, CNE, General Comptroller's Office, Public Defender's Office, and General Prosecutor's Office).
3. Briceño and Bautista de Alemán (2019).
4. Named for Deputy Luis Tascón of the government party Movimiento Quinta República [MVR], the Tascón list is a database that contains the names of all Venezuelan voters registered in the Electoral Registry, identified by political identity according to their participation or not in electoral processes, if they voted in elections, and if they signed to request the realization of the 2004 presidential recall referendum. This information was placed on a public access website by the deputy.
5. No actual data is available, but experts estimate that the number has been decreased due to the ongoing production crisis in the oil sector in Venezuela.
6. Maingon, T. (2017). Database of ministers, 1998–2017, CENDES-UCV, mimeo.

10 Working, Shirking, and Sabotage in Times of Democratic Backsliding: An Experimental Study in Brazil

JOÃO VICTOR GUEDES-NETO AND B. GUY
PETERS

Introduction

A Grande Família (in English, the Great Family) was a popular sitcom that aired from 2001 to 2014 on Globo, Brazil's most popular TV channel. The show focused on a stereotypical middle-class family headed by Lineu Silva, a 50-year-old veterinarian working as health inspector at a local public bureaucracy. Lineu represented the Weberian ideal type of civil servant: methodical, law-abiding, honest, and politically correct at all times. However, his boss and friend, Mendonça, was far from sharing this profile. This manager was a prankster and an opportunist who did not like work. Whenever possible, he used the local bureaucracy for his own benefit. Whereas this dichotomy is not representative of the entire public service, similar satires have frequently been presented in global popular culture (e.g. *Spin City* and *Parks and Recreation*, to name a couple of others in the American context).

Shirking and sabotage are usually portrayed on TV and, to a great extent, in the academic literature, as negative behaviors. However, these potential reactions also place bureaucrats in a strategic gatekeeping position. In fact, the ability to refuse to implement the will of policymakers may in some circumstances contribute to the stability of democratic institutions. Take, for instance, the case of elected officials who promote illiberal reforms, as are discussed in other chapters of this book. In these scenarios, shirking and sabotage become normatively desirable because they may avoid democratic backsliding. However, they come at the expense of personal risk, such as retaliation from the ruling party or their superiors in the organization. In this sense, one must verify empirically the willingness of bureaucrats to act as gatekeepers of democracy.

Do bureaucrats work, shirk, or sabotage when assigned to implement undemocratic projects? This chapter proposes to answer that question based on an experimental study conducted in two Brazilian cities. It aims at capturing bureaucrats' intention to shirk or sabotage when faced with projects that restrict democratic rights, such as the freedoms of press and expression. Furthermore, it considers a series of heterogeneous treatment effects, including type of government job, leadership position, political appointment, discretion, and expected gains in a different job in the private sector.

Brazil is an ideal case to assess the bureaucratic response to democratic backsliding. In October 2018, the country elected the right-wing populist Jair Bolsonaro. A former army officer and long-term legislator, the current president has spent his political career expressing admiration for the military regime that controlled the country from 1964 to 1985 (Duque and Smith 2019). In power since January 2019, Bolsonaro formed a cabinet with a high proportion of military officers and has constantly attacked the press and the Supreme Court (Amorim Neto and Pimenta 2020). This led several authors to suggest that Brazil is on the path toward autocratization (Lührmann and Lindberg 2019; Skaaning 2020).

Amorim Neto and Pimenta (2020) identify pertinent similarities between Bolsonaro and Jânio Quadros – the last president elected before the military coup in 1964. Yet, as Bermeo (2016) explains, the nature of democratic backsliding is somewhat different now than in previous decades. While Linz's (1990) main fear was that of new military interventions, the modern form of movement toward autocracy is more subtle. Nowadays, illiberal politicians engage in reforms that allow executive aggrandizement and strategic electoral manipulation, rather than following classic interventions such as coups d'état and election-day frauds (Bermeo 2016).

Schmitter (1971, 1972) argues that many bureaucrats were co-opted by the military dictatorship that ended in 1985. One explanation for this was the brutality of the regime. Refusing to cooperate could mean not only loss of employment, but also imprisonment. Now, these types of extreme punishment are unlikely to exist. Yet, bureaucrats are still tasked to implement the policies enacted by the presidency. Following the propositions of this book for system transformation research, this responsibility for implementation positions public employees as central players in the prevention of democratic backsliding.

Consider the recent appointment of the chief of the Public Prosecutor's Office in September 2019. Appointments for this position often follow the recommendation of the Associação Nacional dos Procuradores da República (the prosecutors' national association). However, Bolsonaro decided to choose a political ally, Augusto Aras, who was not on the list of names suggested by the association. Since his appointment, Aras has engaged in a number of confrontations with other prosecutors (Teófilo and Souza 2020) and has lobbied against Operação Lava Jato (Shalders 2020), the national effort to punish money laundering that has seen several politicians jailed, including former president Luiz Inácio Lula da Silva.

The reactions of the bureaucracy against Bolsonaro's chief prosecutor range from shirking to sabotage. The list of confrontations includes, among others, a public petition signed by prosecutors objecting to the appointment of Aras (Oliveira 2020) and an open letter criticizing his recent policies and discourses read by subprosecutors during a meeting of the Conselho Superior do Ministério Público (the bureaucracy's main council) (Camarotti 2020). Evidence of shirking is identified in the attempt of Aras to appoint new prosecutors to Operação Lava Jato as a means of weakening the autonomy of those civil servants who have been working in this investigation since 2014 (O Antagonista 2020). Whereas this would be seen as a dream job to many prosecutors, only twelve careerists applied for the position.

In the following sections of this chapter, we develop a theory of bureaucratic response to democratic backsliding and test whether this anecdotal illustration is representative of the Brazilian bureaucracy. This chapter is divided as follows. First, we develop our theory based on Brehm and Gates' (2002) working, shirking, and sabotage triad. Second, we hypothesize that bureaucrats should be willing to shirk or sabotage if faced with a project that undermines political rights. We further discuss how personal and professional characteristics may influence these results. Then, we present our research design, which includes two list experiments and one vignette experiment. Finally, we present our results. We demonstrate significant findings that confirm six out of our nine theoretical expectations.

Working, Shirking, or Sabotage

The notion that politics and administration should be treated as separate spheres is not new. Wilson (1887, p. 212) portrays the latter as the "detailed and systematic execution of public law," and therefore apolitical. However, as argued by Peters (2018a, p. 164), "this presumed separation of administration and politics allows them [public administrators] to engage in politics." This means that once bureaucrats are not directly accountable to the public, they use their technical and legal knowledge to affect policymaking. In this sense, their criteria may replace the ones expected by political leaders.

Brehm and Gates (2002) offer three broad paths which bureaucrats may use to influence the policy process: working, shirking, and sabotage. The authors affirm that government employees are moved by functional preferences – that is, the feeling that they are accomplishing something important. Therefore, they may be interested in taking part in the policies they are supposed to implement. Take, for instance, Lipsky's (1980) suggestion that teachers are the street-level ministers of education. These civil servants have at least two strong motivations to work: they are educating cocitizens, and they directly represent the State to the population. Nonetheless, what happens when they do not believe that their efforts are being directed toward something desirable?

The literature offers some insights. Gailmard and Patty (2007, p. 874) divided bureaucrats into two types: "policy-motivated ('zealots') or policy indifferent ('slackers')." Consider the case of zealots. If they hold the same ideological preferences as the principal and invest in professional expertise, the bureaucracy's output should be greater (Gailmard and Patty 2007). However, if they hold different policy preferences than the principal, zealots' expertise may be superior to that of the principal. This accumulated information and experience would allow the administration to guide the policy process along a different path than the one expected by the political class (Downs 1965).

Some insights are provided by the literature on public service motivation as well (see Perry, Hondeghem, and Wise 2010). This includes, for instance, the "desire to do the job" (Wilson 1989, p. 159). Whilst several studies point out a positive correlation between bureaucrats' motivation and work performance (Andersen, Heinesen, and Pedersen 2014; Bellé 2012; Vandenabeele 2009), the results are mixed. A recent study found that public service motivation could not predict measures of job attendance, and in-role and extra-role performance (Wright, Hassan, and Christensen 2017). Still, public sector motivation is not the main variable of interest when dealing with the interactions between politics and the administration. Demotivation may indeed be related to political conflicts, but the variables should not be treated as synonymous. The core interest of the present chapter is political compliance (or not) with the principal.

Naturally, we acknowledge that shirking and sabotage are not the only outputs of political disagreement. The administration of Ronald Reagan in the United States functions as a good example. The Public Choice School predicts that bureaucrats' policy preferences are related to self-interest. This should lead government employees to fight for a larger public sector that grants themselves greater power and budgets (Niskanen 1971; Tullock 2004). If this assumption is correct, Reagan worked against the self-interest of bureaucrats. He implemented reforms that aimed at reducing the size of the government. Thus, bureaucrats' rational behavior should have been to either shirk or sabotage. Whereas Aberbach and Rockman (2000) confirm that serious conflicts indeed took place during this administration, Golden (2000, p. 163) says that "compliance was the predominant [bureaucratic] response."

Peters and Pierre are critics of the Public Choice approach to the shirking hypothesis (see Peters and Pierre 2017; Pierre and Peters 2017). According to them, the "Brehm and Gates' study has become somewhat of a standard reference for those who argue in support of the shirking thesis" (Pierre and Peters 2017, p. 13). However, as they highlight, Brehm and Gates themselves have rejected it: "the assumption that subordinates necessarily prefer shirking over working is unnecessarily simplistic … Workers will prefer producing some outputs over other outputs; they don't necessarily shirk at every opportunity" (Brehm and Gates 2002, p. 43). But does this hold true if they believe some fundamental values of democracy are being threatened?

Public Administration in Times of Democratic Backsliding

In the present work, we test whether political disagreement between politicians and bureaucrats leads to working, shirking, or sabotage. However, we take into consideration Peters and Pierre's critiques of the Public Choice literature in public administration. We also accept three suggestions from recent contributions to the study of the policy process: a greater interaction between comparative public administration and comparative politics (Peters 2018b), the consideration of democracy as an important element of policy studies (Ingram, deLeon, and Schneider 2016), and the use of experiments to assure greater causal relationships (Peters 2018b).

First, Peters (2018b) suggests that students of the policy process could benefit from a greater integration with the field of comparative politics. He cites, for instance, the work of Tsebelis (2002) on veto players – that is, actors that have the power to block a political agenda. In this sense, Peters (2018b) highlights the importance of institutional design, but also creates an avenue for further explorations of the role of bureaucrats as veto players in the policy process. If they are indeed capable of shirking or sabotaging, decision-makers should pay particular attention to government employees when passing a law. Civil servants may individually function as veto players, for instance at the street level, when they refuse to comply with the rules or use their own criteria to implement a policy (Zacka 2017). Furthermore, scholars should consider not only the self-interest of individual bureaucrats, but also their collective interests. For instance, government employees tend to respond to organizational influences such as loyalty, professional norms, and peer-pressures (Pierre and Peters 2017).

Second, Ingram, deLeon, and Schneider (2016, p. 175) refer to democracy in the field of policy studies as "the elephant in the corner." It is relevant, visible, and, in many instances, wounded, but still not discussed directly by many scholars. As the authors argue, there are several policies that directly affect democracy, such as in matters of redistribution, participation, and civil liberties. Indeed, this topic should be approached particularly in times of democratic backsliding (Levitsky and Ziblatt 2018b; Mainwaring and Pérez-Liñán 2014). Yesilkagit (2018) cites the emergence of populist parties and politicians in countries such as Italy, Hungary, Poland, and the United States, as well as the cases of Venezuela's socialist regime and the recent Brexit vote, as examples of democratic backsliding. This context is ideal for studies relating public bureaucracies to the sustainability of democracy.

So far, we have presented at least four elements of interest: shirking and sabotage, collective interests, veto players, and democratic backsliding. They lead to the core question of this research: *Do bureaucrats work, shirk, or sabotage when assigned to implement undemocratic projects?* Here, civil servants are faced with a task that does not necessarily go against their rational self-interest. Their reaction is a matter of collective interest. By supporting an undemocratic agenda, the government employee may be acting against the collective interest of the population of which she is a part. Alternately, if she shirks or sabotages, she could be functioning as a veto player in defense of democratic institutions. Whereas shirking and sabotage are normatively undesirable in the narrative of most policy scholars, here they could be considered positive behaviors.

We answer this research question in relation to a third suggestion. Peters (2018b, p. 97) proposes that experiments "offer potentially greater understanding of causal relationships." Many scholars of the social sciences have engaged in this method because it assures stronger internal validity, thus allowing more precision in the causal inference (McDermott 2002). However, as Peters (2018b) highlights, there is the risk of compromising external validity. To constrain this, we consider heterogeneous treatment effects – that is, pretreatment observational data "to describe how treatments differ across categories" (Kam and Trussler 2017, p. 729). This allows us to point out how the treatment interacts with institutional and individual characteristics of interest.

As summarized in the next section, we propose that bureaucrats will be more prone to shirk or sabotage if assigned to work on a project that undermines democracy than when faced with other tasks. However, given the risks involved in sabotaging an initiative, we expect the shirking hypothesis to deliver stronger results. Overall, we are assuming that bureaucrats should perceive undemocratic projects as undesirable, thereby providing incentives to work against their principal – that is, the elected maker.

We also expect that these treatment effects will be mediated by preexisting characteristics.[1] First, we hypothesize that tenured civil servants should be more affected by an undemocratic task than untenured employees. As noted by Pierre and Peters (2017, p. 167), "shirking is more likely in traditional career civil service systems in which civil servants have tenure and may have less motivation to perform." The fact that there is a lesser risk of losing their job may afford greater flexibility to deny compliance with principals. However, the contrary should be true for civil servants who are political appointees or responsible for supervising peers. Whereas promotion and appointment are not always granted to the principal's ideological clones (Bertelli and

Feldmann 2007), peer pressure and loyalty should make these individuals more prone to comply with the principal.

Finally, we expect that an undemocratic project should increase the propensity of shirking more among bureaucrats that enjoy greater levels of discretion and think that they could earn a higher salary in the private sector. The latter hypothesis follows a similar argument to the one regarding tenured employees. Once the bureaucrat believes she could enjoy similar or greater benefits in a different job, she should be more willing to risk her current employment. However, this variable may also demonstrate that the civil servant is in the public service due to self-selection, and therefore potentially more influenced by functional preferences (i.e. the willingness to contribute to desirable, democratic, goals). Discretion, on the other hand, could simply function as the basic means to allow shirking.

Summary of Hypotheses

We developed a series of hypotheses about the attitudes and behaviors of civil servants when faced with undemocratic policies. We are interested in two possible motivations for citizens to shirk or sabotage. One is that a policy is illiberal or undemocratic; the second is that the project may be bad for the country in other policy terms. In this experimental setting we do not, of course, observe actual behaviors, but consider the willingness of civil servants to shirk or sabotage.

Hypothesis 1: Bureaucrats are more prone to shirk than to work when assigned to work on a project that restricts political liberties such as freedom of expression or freedom of the press.

Hypothesis 2: Bureaucrats are more prone to sabotage than to work when assigned to work on a project that restricts political liberties such as freedom of expression or freedom of the press.

Hypothesis 3: Bureaucrats are more prone to shirk than to sabotage when assigned to work on a project that restricts political liberties such as freedom of expression or freedom of the press.

Hypothesis 4: Bureaucrats are more prone to shirk if assigned to work on a project that is perceived as bad for the country and harmful to citizens' political rights than if assigned to a project that is bad for the country but not harmful to citizens' political rights.

Hypothesis 5: Bureaucrats have a higher propensity to shirk in the face of projects that restrict political rights in comparison to projects that do not when they are tenured (*servidor público de carreira* in Brazil) than when they are not tenured.

Hypothesis 6: Bureaucrats have a lower propensity to shirk in the face of projects that restrict political rights in comparison to projects that do not when they are responsible for supervising other civil servants than when they are not responsible for supervising others.

Hypothesis 7: Bureaucrats have a lower propensity to shirk in the face of projects that restrict political rights in comparison to projects that do not when they are political appointees (*cargo de confiança*) than when they are not political appointees.

Hypothesis 8: Bureaucrats have a higher propensity to shirk in the face of projects that restrict political rights in comparison to projects that do not when they have high discretion than when they do not have it.

Hypothesis 9: Bureaucrats have a higher propensity to shirk in the face of projects that restrict political rights in comparison to projects that do not when they think they could earn a higher salary in the private sector than when they do not think that.

Experimental Design

Case Selection

The experiments were conducted with convenience samples of Brazilian bureaucrats from two medium-sized cities: one in the southern Brazilian state of Santa Catarina (hereafter, SC), and another in the southeastern state of Minas Gerais (hereafter, MG). In cooperation with the local administration, the municipal government sent out an e-mail inviting every bureaucrat to answer an online questionnaire. The response rate was notably low: 68 full responses in SC and 60 in MG out of roughly 2,500 bureaucrats in each city. However, this does not impact the results: first, because we did not intend to make these samples nationally (or locally) representative, thus proper randomization across groups should eliminate issues of systematic bias; second, as will be further explained, because the tests resulted in satisfactory statistical results.

Brazil represents an ideal case for several reasons. In recent years, a left-wing president was impeached, and her predecessor from the same political party arrested. Santos and Guarnieri (2016) label the former as a parliamentary coup and consider many of its procedures as fascist (see Avelar 2017 for a different perspective). Pérez-Liñán (2018) and Nunes and Melo (2017) argue that whereas democracy has not been put at risk during these events, there was certainly a stark political crisis. This possible democratic backsliding was exacerbated by the 2018 election. In October 2018, the right-wing candidate Jair Bolsonaro was elected president. Classified as authoritarian and populist in recent papers (Hunter and Power 2019; Levitsky 2018), the new president has repeatedly praised the military dictatorship (1964–1985) and spoken against human rights.

Whilst Brazilian democracy had enjoyed relatively high levels of stability in the years before the political crisis (Nunes and Melo 2017), the narrative of democratic backsliding was often present in the public sphere. In 2004, only 63 percent of the population considered the left-wing President Lula to be democratic (Folha de São Paulo 2004b). In the same year, Folha de São Paulo (2004a), one of Brazil's most popular newspapers, asked sectoral leaders whether Lula's government was undemocratic. Back then, the secretary general of the Confederação Nacional dos Trabalhadores do Serviço Público Federal (a major union of federal civil servants) and the president of the Brazilian bar association argued that the country was heading along an authoritarian path. Some examples presented in the national media included the trials to regulate the press (Nery, Seabra, and Franco 2011) and to reduce the powers of the legislative (Senado Federal 2014).

This information led to the assumption that the debate on the erosion of democratic institutions has been salient for a reasonably long time on both sides of the political spectrum, and has been intensified by the recent election of Jair Bolsonaro. Therefore, it is adequate to study the potential reactions of Brazilian bureaucrats if assigned to implement a project that is perceived as undemocratic.

It must be highlighted that the interaction between the Brazilian public service and authoritarian governments has already been the focus of previous studies. Schmitter demonstrated a strong relationship between high-level bureaucrats' corporatist organizations and political elites from 1930 to 1965 (Schmitter 1971), and the public service and the military dictatorship after the coup in 1964 (Schmitter 1972). In both cases, the public sector and their organizations were either co-opted or threatened into compliance with the government. Here, as discussed earlier, we propose a "change of heart" in the bureaucratic reaction to undemocratic policy change: first, because the level of authoritarianism in earlier periods was starkly higher than since the redemocratization of the 1980s; second, because our measurement of the intention to shirk or sabotage is different than actually engaging in such behaviors. For instance, as we shall discuss later, we do not consider the costs of dissent.

The Experiments

List Experiments

As subjects enter the online questionnaire, right after two eligibility questions, they are presented with a list experiment. They are told that:

The following four scenarios are common in public departments around the world. There is evidence that some of these scenarios demotivate civil servants, leading them to dedicate fewer efforts than they would dedicate to other activities. For instance, they may try to assign another colleague to do these tasks, they may do them partially, miss deadlines, or do not do them.

The control group reads four baseline situations that potentially demotivate civil servants when carrying out regular tasks:

A civil servant was assigned to work on a project that . . .

. . . is very similar to every other project that she/he has always worked on.
. . . favors only her/his own political group.
. . . is entirely new to her/him, requiring training and additional efforts.
. . . creates a political advantage to groups that she/he is against.

They are required to answer how many of these tasks would make an average bureaucrat "dedicate fewer efforts to the project in comparison to other activities" (i.e. to shirk). The treatment group, on the other hand, will have access to five situations: the same four as the control group, plus "a project that restricts citizen's political rights, for instance, freedom of expression or press." They should also state how many projects should make an average bureaucrat shirk (**list_shirk**[2]). The difference between the outcome of each group is the percentage of subjects affected by the treatment. This strategy is helpful to reduce the impact of social desirability bias, given that respondents are not required to say which specific tasks would make them shirk.

In addition, we use the same design to ask about the possibility of sabotage (**list_sabotage**). Subjects are presented with the same situations after reading the following introduction:

Now, consider the possibility of sabotage. A common reaction in different public departments is that some civil servants decide to work against a project which they were assigned to work on. In other words, instead of implementing it, they decide to do whatever they can so that the project does not move forward.

The question is worded as follows:

In your opinion, how many of the previous scenarios would lead a standard civil servant to work against the project instead of implementing it? **Please, answer only the number of scenarios.**

It should be acknowledged that expected behavior and actual behavior may starkly differ. The costs to say that one would shirk or sabotage in the face of an undemocratic project is lower than to actually shirk or sabotage. However, this design captures the intention to engage in such behaviors in the face of undemocratic projects in comparison to other situations. In this sense, this measurement is still valid for the purposes of this research.

Vignette Experiments

At the end of the questionnaire, the same subjects participate in a vignette experiment. This is designed as follows:

Paulo is a civil servant in Brazil. Recently, he was assigned to work on a project which he disagrees with. According to Paulo, "*[this project does not reduce the freedom of expression and of the press of the population, but / this project reduces the freedom of expression and of the press of the population, and]* it is still terrible for the country."

Using his own autonomy, Paulo decided to **not carry out** his tasks related to this project.

If you were in Paulo's shoes, what is the probability that you would have **not carried out** your tasks related to this project as well? Please, use the 0–10 scale, where 0 means "very improbable" and 10 "very probable."

After reading about Paulo, a fictional civil servant, subjects receive a vignette affirming that the project he was assigned to work on is not perceived to be harmful to the freedoms of expression and of the press. The treatment group, on the other hand, is told that Paulo considers the project harmful to these freedoms. To provide justification for a potentially socially undesirable situation, we affirm that Paulo decided to shirk. Finally, we ask how probable it is that subjects would also be willing to shirk (**vign_shirk**). As in the case of the list experiment, the difference between the outcome of the treatment and the control groups is the effect of interest. Again, the reader should bear in mind that intended and actual behavior may differ. Thus, this design only captures differences in the intention to shirk in face of different scenarios.

Covariates and Heterogeneous Treatment Effects

Before the list experiment, subjects are asked about their age range[3] (**age**) and whether they work for the public sector. Subjects below 18 years old or not working for the public sector are then excluded from further participation. In between the list and the vignette experiments, we ask questions related to individual and institutional characteristics. They regard discretion[4] (**discretion**), administrative level (**admin_level**), administrative power (**power**), years of experience[5] (**experience**), level of education (**education**), expected salary difference if working for the private sector[6] (**salary**), gender (**male**), her location (**state**), and whether the subject supervises other people (**boss**), is a tenured civil servant (**tenure**), and a political appointee (**appointee**). These questions will appear in a randomized order.

Methods of Analysis

We analyze the results using a two-tailed t-test between the outcomes of different groups (i.e. difference of means) and OLS regression analyses. Following Table 10.1, we are interested in the effect of each treatment – that is, A-B (H_1), C-D (H_2), and E-F (H_4), which we expect to be positive, as well as in the difference between (A-B)-(C-D) (H_3), which

Table 10.1 *Average treatment effects*

	Treatment	Control	Hypothesis
List (shirk)	A	B	1: A>B
List (sabotage)	C	D	2: C>D
Vignette (shirk)	E	F	4: E>F

Source: designed by the authors.

Table 10.2 *Heterogeneous treatment effects*

	Hypothesis
tenure	5: (E-F) is greater if tenure=1 than if tenure=0
boss	6: (E-F) is lower if boss=1 than if boss=0
appointee	7: (E-F) is lower if appointee=1 than if appointee=0
discretion	8: the higher discretion is, the higher is (E-F)
salary	9: the lower salary is, the higher is (E-F)

Source: designed by the authors.

we also expect to be positive. The heterogeneous treatment effects will be analyzed using two-tailed t-tests taking into consideration the shirking list experiment.[7] The expected results are described in Table 10.2. In the final work, the results will be presented per public department and pooled.

Each regression will have the outcome of interest as the dependent variable – that is, responses for the shirking list experiment, sabotage list experiment, and vignette experiment. The independent variable of interest is a dichotomous variable for the treatment, where 1 means treated and 0 is the control group. The remaining data shall be used as control variables only if balance across groups is not achieved through the randomization process.

Results

On average, the convenience sample so far is primarily composed of females who are not political appointees and do not supervise other bureaucrats. They tend to be between 32 and 45 years old and have between 6 and 15 years in the public sector. Mostly, they believe that their level of discretion is medium to high and that they would earn more or a similar salary if they were working in the private sector. Even though these characteristics may not be representative of the general population of their fellow bureaucrats, balance across groups was achieved in all categories (Table 10.3). Thus, this validates the randomization strategy.

As subjects entered the online questionnaire, they were presented with the list experiment that assesses their willingness to shirk in the face of a number of situations. Whereas the control group only sees four options, the treatment group is presented with an additional alternative. As explained in the previous section, subjects are asked to state how many items in the list would make an average public sector employee shirk. According to the responses of the 128 subjects who were randomly distributed across the two groups, 84 percent of the bureaucrats in this convenience sample believe that an average civil servant would shirk if assigned to work on a project that is perceived to undermine rights such as the freedoms of press and expression (Figure 10.1). This confirms H_1.

Whereas this result is already considerably strong, the sabotage treatment yields even stronger effects. The difference of means across groups is 1.04 (Figure 10.1). This supports H_2. First, it means that subjects expect bureaucrats to sabotage more than to shirk in the face of undemocratic projects. Second, undemocratic projects have a triggering effect which leads respondents to consider sabotaging a normal behavior in the face of other projects as well. In other words, making both sabotage and democratic backsliding salient creates an additional incentive to fight against other undesirable projects.

The results from the pooled sample reject H_3 – that is, the proposition that the treatment effects would be greater for shirking than for sabotage. However, when the same tests are conducted considering each of the cities, the findings vary (Figure 10.2). In both cases, the first two hypotheses are confirmed. However, the stark increase in post-treatment sabotage is driven by SC. In MG, responses follow the hypothesized expectation that post-treatment shirking should be greater than sabotage. This suggests that bureaucrats may hold different preferences in each of these cities.

Table 10.3 *Balance table*

	List			Vignette		
	Control	Treatment	Difference	Control	Treatment	Difference
Age	3.43	3.37	0.06	3.00	3.47	0.47
Male	0.21	0.25	0.04	0.29	0.19	0.10
University	3.34	3.48	0.14	3.42	3.33	0.09
Tenure	0.81	0.78	0.02	0.81	0.81	0.01
Boss	0.35	0.35	0.00	0.29	0.35	0.06
Appointee	0.29	0.28	0.02	0.24	0.30	0.06
Experience	2.51	2.33	0.18	2.18	2.46	0.27
Discretion	6.15	6.53	0.39	6.42	6.19	0.23
Salary	1.82	1.90	0.08	1.92	1.86	0.06
N	68	60	-	38	57	-

Data for the vignette groups only considers subjects that passed the manipulation check. None of the differences of means is significant at conventional levels.

Source: calculated based on own data.

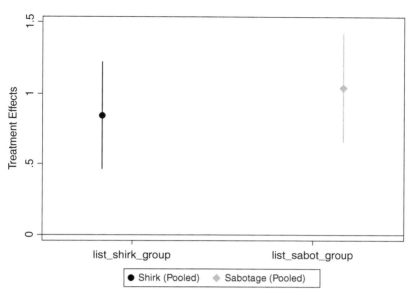

Figure 10.1 List experiments (shirk and sabotage)
The vertical line on the left represents the treatment effects of the shirking list experiment. The vertical line on the right represents the treatment effects of the sabotage list experiment.
Source: calculated based on own data.

We present the results for the vignette experiment in Figure 10.3. Here, subjects read the fictional story of Paulo, a civil servant who decided to shirk when assigned to work on a project that he considered to be terrible for the country. Respondents in the control group were told that the project did not harm the freedoms of press and expression, while treated subjects were told that this project did harm such rights. First, our manipulation seems to have caused confusion in some subjects in the control group. Out of 64 subjects assigned to this control vignette, only 38 remembered (or noticed) that the project did not pose a threat to the rights of press and expression. It is possible that some of them did not read the vignette carefully enough to perceive the negative phrase. In the treatment group, 57 out of 64 subjects passed the manipulation check. Second, in both cases – that is, considering the full sample and only subjects who passed the manipulation check – differences across groups are not significant at conventional levels. We present these outcomes in Table 10.5.

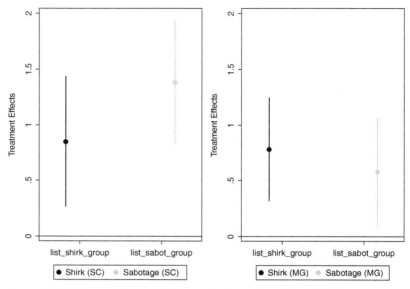

Figure 10.2 List experiments (shirk and sabotage) in SC and MG
The graph on the left represents the treatment effects for both experiments in
SC. On the right, the treatment effects for both experiments in MG.
Source: calculated based on own data.

Finally, if nonsignificant differences are to be considered, they
present mixed results. The pooled and the MG sample confirm H_4.
However, the SC sample presents the opposite result. That is, in the
southern city, when subjects were told that Paulo considered this
project terrible because it went against democratic rights, their understanding of "terrible" was softened, thus reducing their intention to
shirk. Whereas the nonsignificance indicates that it should be understood merely as noise, it may also suggest that some bureaucrats may
consider threats to democratic rights not as "terrible" as other
threats.

Furthermore, the stark difference in the results obtained from the
list and the vignette experiments suggests evidence of social desirability bias. While the former allowed a higher sense of anonymity
and asked about an "average civil servant," the latter asked for the
specific reaction of the subject. Put differently, bureaucrats were
more willing to present preferences for shirking and sabotage when

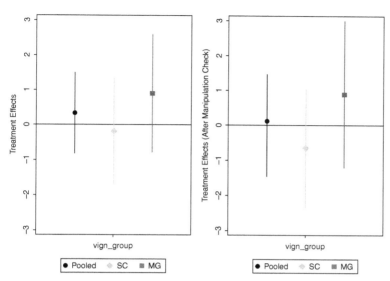

Figure 10.3 Vignette experiment (pre- and postmanipulation check)
The graph on the left presents the treatment effects for the full sample. The graph on the right presents the treatment effects of the sample after excluding subjects who did not pass the manipulation check.
Source: calculated based on own data.

talking about an "unknown peer" than about themselves. A recent study conducted by Gonzales-Ocantos et al. (2012) on vote-buying in Nicaragua presents similar results and reinforces the validity of list experiments to study attitudes that may be affected by social desirability bias.

We present the heterogeneous treatment effects of the shirking and sabotage list experiments in Table 10.4. We must highlight that this is a deviation from our original analysis plan, which was pre-registered on the Evidence in Governance and Politics (EGAP) platform. Originally, we proposed studying the heterogeneous treatment effects of the vignette experiment. However, once differences of means were found to be insignificant given our unexpected treatment effects, it made more sense to focus on the experiment that yielded results more relevant to the shirking hypotheses. We added the results of the heterogeneous treatment effects of the sabotage list experiment, even though our hypotheses were only valid for the shirking alternative (Table 10.6).

Table 10.4 *Difference-of-means of list experiments*

	Control	Treatment	Difference	Power
Shirk (pooled)	1.95 (1.03) [68]	2.80 (1.13) [60]	0.84***	1.00
Sabotage (pooled)	1.68 (0.87) [68]	2.72 (1.30) [60]	1.04***	1.00
Shirk (SC)	2.12 (1.12) [34]	2.97 (1.29) [34]	0.85**	1.00
Sabotage (SC)	1.70 (0.90) [34]	3.09 (1.36) [34]	1.38***	1.00
Shirk (MG)	1.79 (0.91) [34]	2.58 (0.86) [26]	0.78**	1.00
Sabotage (MG)	1.65 (0.85) [34]	2.23 (1.07) [26]	0.58*	0.99

In the "Difference" column, *** p-value<0.001; ** p-value<0.01; * p-value<0.05.
Standard deviation between parentheses and sample size between brackets.
Source: calculated based on own data.

Table 10.5 *Difference-of-means of vignette experiments (after manipulation check)*

	Control	Treatment	Difference	Power
Pooled	5.24 (3.32) [38]	5.35 (3.42) [57]	0.11	0.06
SC	6.67 (3.10) [21]	6.03 (3.11) [33]	−0.64	0.32
MG	3.47 (2.72) [17]	4.42 (3.68) [24]	0.95	0.43

Note: None of the results are statistically significant at conventional levels. Standard deviation between parentheses and sample size between brackets.
Source: calculated based on own data.

First, subjects who have a tenured position are more likely to concur that civil servants would shirk in face of an undemocratic project. This characteristic, which confirms H_6, represents the second largest difference across groups. However, the opposite is true for the sabotage experiment, since treatment effects were considerably higher among nontenured subjects.

H_6 and H_7 are rejected. Both follow a similar rationale. It was expected that the closer subjects were to their principals, the less prone they would be to affirm that average civil servants shirk in the face of undemocratic projects. However, this is not true for respondents who hold a supervision position or a political appointment.

Table 10.6 *Heterogenous treatment effects of the list experiments*

Groups	TE (Shirking)	TE (Sabotage)
Tenured	0.96 (0.000) [55]	0.93 (0.000) [47]
Not tenured	0.38 (0.311) [13]	1.46 (0.001) [13]
Boss	0.99 (0.004) [24]	1.00 (0.005) [21]
Not boss	0.77 (0.002) [44]	1.06 (0.000) [39]
Appointee	1.12 (0.005) [20]	1.31 (0.000) [17]
Not appointee	0.74 (0.001) [48]	0.93 (0.000) [43]
Low discretion	0.74 (0.065) [22]	1.58 (0.000) [16]
High discretion	0.90 (0.000) [46]	0.85 (0.000) [44]
Low-to-medium salary	1.06 (0.000) [47]	1.07 (0.000) [39]
High salary	0.38 (0.217) [21]	0.95 (0.007) [21]

Treatment effects (TE) are calculated as the difference of means across groups. They represent the percentage of subjects who potentially chose the fifth element. P-values are presented in parentheses and sample size in brackets.
Source: calculated based on own data.

Heterogeneous treatment effects for the sabotage experiment are mixed. Whereas difference-of-means among bosses is slightly lower than among others, political appointees are considerably more influenced by the treatment effects than others.

H_9 – that is, the prediction that subjects with higher discretion will be more prone to shirk – is also confirmed. Still, the opposite is true in the sabotage experiment. Finally, H_{10} is also validated. It proposed that subjects who perceive their current salary as being the same or lower in the public sector than it could be in the private sector are more willing to shirk than subjects who believe they are better paid now. Similar results are found after the sabotage experiment.

Discussion

This chapter expects to contribute to the literature of comparative public administration and comparative politics – and, more specifically, the debates on public sector motivation and democratic backsliding. It does so by proposing three experimental designs to answer whether bureaucrats work, shirk, or sabotage when assigned to undertake undemocratic projects. The results confirm six hypotheses and reject three. Although these findings are about Brazil only, they are relevant for the other cases of democratic backsliding found in this book. For example, do bureaucrats in Hungary or Venezuela have similar attitudes about continuing to work in the public sector?

The general finding, therefore, is that civil servants are willing to take democratic norms into account when making decisions. Going against the usual Weberian model of the bureaucrat being apolitical and following the formal rules, these respondents reported that they would consider the extent to which government proposals undermined democracy when making decisions. The decision to work, shirk, or sabotage therefore requires the individual to choose between implementing the policies of a democratically elected government or following their own values about what is substantively democratic. The willingness to shirk or sabotage may be an important barrier to the excesses of populist regimes such as that recently elected in Brazil.

However, this intention to act is shaped by professional characteristics. First, tenured civil servants are more likely to expose a preference for shirking in cases of undemocratic policy reforms than untenured ones. This reinforces the relevance of job stability as a determinant of action against the principal. Additionally, it could also reflect, to a certain extent, a public sector motivation. In other words, tenured civil servants may see the public service differently than temporary untenured employees. Thus, they may try to defend the democratic institutions more than others. The assumption of public sector motivation is enhanced as we confirm that subjects who believe that their salary is low or medium (compared to salaries in the private sector) are more prone to shirk. Thus, their loyalty to the public sector is more related to desire than to necessity.

Contrary to our hypothesized expectations, closeness to the principal enhances the propensity to shirk in the face of policies that restrict the rights of expression and the press. It was theorized that loyalty, professional norms, and peer pressure would make bosses and political appointees more likely to adhere to the wishes of their principals. However, the opposite seems to be true. It may be the case that they are willing to use their position to defend desirable political goals. This would align with the discretion hypothesis – that is, the validated proposition that civil servants with higher degrees of discretion tend to be more prone to shirk in these cases than other civil servants. Further studies should assess this causal mechanism.

There are two additional findings that should be further explored in future research. First, the vignette and the list experiments led to starkly different results. There are at least two explanations for this. The first, as mentioned earlier, is social desirability bias. Subjects may have felt more comfortable talking about shirking and sabotage when they were not the "focus of the conversation." That is, when talking about "an average civil servant," it was easier to say that shirking or sabotage would take place than when talking about themselves. As noted in the introduction to the volume, shirking and sabotage are often portrayed in popular culture and in the literature as negative behaviors. This peer pressure generates a social desirability bias that influences civil servants even when such behaviors are normatively desirable. Following this rationale, the list experiment allowed them to talk about themselves while avoiding any potential costs that that may have. Alternatively, it may be the case that, during the list experiment, they were actually talking about someone else.

In any case, this opens doors for further studies that consider the costs of deviance. Lab-in-the-field experiments could add costs to shirking – for instance, punishment from the principal or peers (e.g. when a civil servant shirks, she may leave the task, or the problem, to a colleague who may not be happy to be assigned to it). Furthermore, whereas shirking may be an individual decision, it may also depend on collective action. Such experiments should consider willingness to shirk in the face of different settings or players.

Second, treatment effects varied across cities and, most importantly, across groups when comparing the shirking and sabotage alternatives. The first issue should be further addressed through comparative studies that also consider macrolevel variables. In essence, which characteristics of the public department, city, region, or country, among others, lead to different intentions to act? Additionally, why do intentions to shirk and to sabotage vary, sometimes in opposite directions, across groups of professional characteristics? While this work restricted itself to hypothesizing the former, looking into both cases may advance our understanding of bureaucratic behavior.

Finally, democratic backsliding and discussion of democratic backsliding are different elements. The actual costs and the environment faced by bureaucrats during authoritarian regimes are considerably higher and may lead to different reactions (Schmitter 1972). Furthermore, the perception of subjects with respect to what an undemocratic policy change is varies. This chapter considers it from a broad perspective: a policy that restricts the freedoms of expression and press. It allows comparability and fits the current reality of Brazil, where a new government has recently taken office. However, further studies could consider specific policies, so as to understand how concrete examples affect intention to shirk.

One further piece of ongoing research to help verify these results is a survey experiment of the same sort in the United States, involving civil servants faced with the policies of the Trump administration. Another set of further studies, which is already planned and being implemented, is to use laboratory experiments that will enable us to manipulate the extent of deviation of policies from liberal-democratic norms, as well as possible costs to the respondents, and thus gauge their probable behavior. We cannot, of course, be sure if the results in other systems will be similar, but we can be sure that the challenges to maintaining liberal democracy are similar and significant. Finally, we could attempt interviews with civil servants to assess how they conceptualize the choice to follow policies with which they disagree. We believe our initial research has demonstrated the willingness of civil servants to consider alternatives to implementing some policies, and we will continue to work to explore the external validity of these findings.

Notes

1. Here, we deviate from our preregistered analysis plan. In the original research design, we hypothesized that the higher the administrative level, the higher the treatment effects would be (e.g. federal vs. local level). However, we have been unable to conduct this experiment at an administrative level other than municipalities.
2. Variable names are presented in bold.
3. Instead of asking for age as a continuous number, the questionnaire offers age ranges. This strategy is adopted to assure that subjects will remain anonymous. Once the populations of interest are reasonably large, it is unlikely that this information will be sufficient to identify the respondents.
4. "Some civil servants have great autonomy to make decisions. In other words, they can decide how to implement their tasks, what should be prioritized, which answers should be given in each scenario, etc.

However, other civil servants have to follow strict rules and have no autonomy to make decisions in their day-to-day work. In general, how much autonomy do you have in your daily work? Please answer following the 0–10 scale, where 0 means 'no autonomy' and 10 means 'a lot of autonomy'."

5. The question regarding years of experience follows the same strategy as the one for age – that is, ranges of years.

6. "Imagine that a civil servant, who has the same experience and contacts as you have, decided to leave his current job and look for a job in the private sector. When he finds a new job, what do you think the salary of this ex-civil servant will be? The salary in the private sector will be higher; The salary in the private sector will be the same; The salary in the private sector will be lower."

7. Here, we deviate from the preregistered analysis plan. Whereas we proposed testing for heterogeneous treatment effects based solely on the vignette experiment, we decided to run these tests considering the shirking list experiment. Our reasoning is discussed after the results are presented.

11 Public Administration: How to Respond to Populism and Democratic Backsliding

GERRY STOKER

Introduction

Three statements sum up the message of this chapter. When considering how to respond to populism, public administration needs to recognize that some of its practices may have created an opening for the populist charge. Effectively challenging populism means understanding more clearly what it is and what it is not. The threat of democratic backsliding, driven by populism, should stimulate public administration not to hunker down but to search for better ways of operating.

The two worlds of public administration and politics have become interlinked in a symbiotic relationship. In most liberal democracies, for much of the twentieth century politics and administration developed their "dance" around two broad camps: professionalized mainstream parties seeking the power to govern, served by a neutral, expert public service. This partnership between politics and public administration required careful management and a delicate balancing of roles and influence, a point recognized by both partners. But the dance partners increasingly became deeply intertwined, reacting off one another. Established or mainstream politics sought to bend public administration to fit its purposes and objectives, which were primarily about demonstrating achievement in order to sustain electoral success. Public administration boasted of its delivery capacity and presented new procedures, management schemes, and reforms to demonstrate its worth. As politicians became more concerned with delivery and the politics of competence (Green and Jennings 2017), they inevitably stepped into a closer relationship with public administration, thereby creating opportunities for ambitious public servants to offer solutions.

One of the most prominent of those solutions was the idea of New Public Management, a style of public administration aping business practices to a degree and offering effective delivery against preset goals.

Its origins can be traced back to the 1970s, but as a paradigm it achieved global fame in the 1990s. Another solution offered was the movement toward evidence-based policymaking, which also has a long and troubled history (Lindblom 1990) but came to prominence in the 1980s and '90s as politicians demanded to know "what works" in terms of policy interventions (Cairney 2016; Davies, Nutley, and Smith 2000). Finally, more developed official participation and consultation schemes were seen by many in public administration and beyond as part of the answer to the challenge of improving citizens' experience of public services and programs (Cornwall 2008; Lowndes, Pratchett, and Stoker 2006; OECD 2001).

Mainstream politics looked for a managerial or technical response to relieve pressures created by a new governing context. Populism came up with a different, more blatantly political response: let's get some better politicians into power, more in tune with citizens. A public service that claims the capacity to serve past governments, current ones, and future holders of power is not likely to be viewed by populists as a reliable partner, since that stand indicates a lack of appreciation of the populist's signature claim to have discovered the authentic voice of the people. Populism therefore poses a potential danger to the conventional practices of public administration, as part of a more general democratic backsliding. As the introduction to this volume argues, if your claim is to serve the people against the elite, then it is inevitable that public bureaucracies are going to be a potential focus of attention. From the perspective of all populists, public service providers will need to be bent to serve the will of the people more effectively. Within extreme versions of populism, driven by fear of a deep state conspiracy against the people among its new populist representatives, public servants may become more direct targets for attack.

Public administration, however, cannot simply be designated as a potential victim of a changed politics. The favored public administration reforms helped to create the conditions for populism. Performance management, citizen consultation, and evidence-based policymaking were popular managerial tools, but the evidence presented in this chapter suggests they may have encouraged a loss of public trust due to the way they were put into practice. By developing New Public Management reforms that stimulated cynicism about mainstream governing practices, public administration helped fertilized the ground for an emerging populism to grow more vigorously. Public administration has, in turn, developed misguided responses to the rise of populism that indicates that many of its leaders still fail to grasp the nature of the populist challenge. New thinking and new practices are required for public administration as part of its response to populism.

Before proceeding, there is an important caveat to note. This chapter is primarily focused on public administration in established liberal democracies, and even then the practices that are explored are more prominent in Anglo-Saxon countries than others – although, given the power of those nations, their ideas on public administration and management have tended to have global influence. Populism takes different forms outside liberal democracies and again, following the theme of the book on democratic backsliding, this chapter is focused on the emergence of populism within liberal-democratic countries. The chapter may lose out on comparative breadth, but it does focus attention, helpfully, on how widespread practices in public administration have played their part in facilitating the rise of populism and in failing to address its underlying causes.

The Changed Governing Context

The focus on the competence of politicians and the matching responses by the public administration were driven by a changed governing context. Three stark developments – reduced national political space, the rise of challenging or critical citizens driven in part by higher levels of education, and a more pluralistic information environment – contributed to a setting wherein mainstream politics could not rely as much on established loyalties of class and identity to sustain support. Politicians needed to show that they were competent and could deliver better performance in the economy, public services, and the environment. The pertinent question for voters became: what can you do for me?

The forces driving change in governance encouraged mainstream adaption but also the populist onslaught (Stoker 2019a; b). The first change reflects shrinking nation-state capacity under the impact of globalization. Democracy emerged primarily in nation states that were powerful and autonomous actors, to a substantial degree in charge of their own destiny. But nation states for the last few decades have found themselves considerably more constrained. The combined impact of the increased forces of social and economic globalization, matched by the movement of powers and decision-making to international or supranational bodies, has not removed but has reduced the capacity for national politics. Key matters – human rights, trade rules, environmental responsibilities – have been shifted to the legal (often international) arena away from politics. The "taking out" of politics from decisions about setting interest rates, control of money supply, and so on limits the capacity of national politicians, although in this and other cases some of the restrictions are self-imposed. The implications are spelled out by Cas Mudde (2017, pp. 3–4): "This has depleted the political debate and created a gap between public expectations and political powers at the national level – often worsened by the fact that national politicians still pretend to be all powerful in election campaigns, but claim powerlessness when the public criticizes certain developments (from economic crisis to refugees crisis)." Beyond a politics of over-promising and blame avoidance, there has also been a sense for many citizens that mainstream politics offers only marginally different versions of the same agenda. Slick, professional, driven by sound bites and controlled media access, mainstream politics became a massive turn-off for large sections of the population (Clarke et al. 2018).

Alongside a reduced national political space, there is another development that indicates a major change in the governing environment: the rise of critical citizens. The developments of easier access to education and wider social change have led to "cognitive mobilization" (Dalton 1984), a process by which education levels and political skills drive both lower trust in government and the emergence of new, less elite-directed forms of political action. Norris (1999) argues that citizens across much of the world – and especially younger citizens – continue to support regime principles (democracy as an ideal form of government) but have withdrawn support from regime institutions (the performance of parties, parliaments, governments). These processes are combined with the impact of partisan dealignment (Dalton 1984), so citizens are less tied to a mainstream party and more likely to display volatility in their voting preferences. These forces create a political landscape wherein parties can rely less on loyalty and must attract voters by claims of competence or, as in the case of populists, by exploiting resentment (Stoker 2019b). The irony is, as Mudde (2017, p. 4) comments: "In many ways, only now the population is what democratic theorists have long prescribed: a collection of critical and independent citizens. This means that they have to be convinced of political programs and only give their support conditionally and temporarily. They hold politicians accountable, punishing them if they don't do (everything) they promised."

A final shift in the governing context, however, means that critical citizens struggle to take on their democratic role in a transformed information and communication environment. Clarke et al. (2018) argue that in the middle decades of the twentieth century, citizens encountered politicians and formal politics most prominently via long radio speeches and rowdy political meetings. These contexts afforded certain modes of political interaction (listening, hearing, challenging), which enabled citizens to adopt a strategy viable in the low-trust environments inherent to democratic politics (Hardin 2006): trust, but verify. Long speeches and face-to-face encounters supported a capacity for judgment. In the early twenty-first century, citizens encountered politicians most prominently in media coverage of "stage-managed" debates, photo opportunities, and through sound bites, plus associated opinion polls and expert analysis. In these contexts, citizens have found it harder to judge or verify the actions of politicians, and thus have drifted in large numbers toward a default "no trust" or cynical position. The changing structure of the media has also made a difference. In the early decades of the twentieth century many media outlets had party affiliations or connections, but in more recent decades "most media are privately-owned and inspired not by ideology or organizational loyalty, but by profit. Media need listeners/readers/viewers to sell advertisements and the best way to get those, is offer things that 'sell': conflict, rarities, and scandals" (Mudde 2017, p. 5).

It is necessary to add to these developments the arrival of social media over the last decade, which both challenges mainstream media – encouraging perhaps even more focus on the extreme and on crisis – and at the same time has become a focal point for bubbles and echo chambers (wherein like-minded people endlessly repeat the same political outlooks to one another) or fake news (erroneous or false new stories created either by political opponents within a system or international adversaries beyond it). The other side of the social media revolution is of course the free flow of information and knowledge. Expertise has become a more pluralistic claim. Within social media, material self-generated by users and citizens – reviews of products and services, commentaries on news and events, crowd sourcing of ideas –

has transformed the trust environment to the extent that top-down information and expertise is quite often matched by trust in user- or peer-produced insights.

These three stark developments in governing context – reduced national political space, challenging citizens, and a more pluralistic information environment – have necessitated change. Mainstream politics and public administration began to shift their practices in the light of new governing conditions, with a different response later emerging with force from populists.

Responses from Public Administration: Performance Management, Consultation, and Evidence

The reaction from mainstream politics to a changed context of governing dragged public administration center stage. In political science, the term "valence politics" (Clarke et al. 2004; 2009) has been used to capture some of the features of this political practice – in fairness, the model stretches beyond the narrower focus on competence, but it does have that at its heart. The argument is that voters are primarily focused on the ability of governments to perform in those policy areas that people care about most, especially the economy. Citizens, it is argued, can engage in quite complex judgments. Green and Jennings (2017) show how political parties come to gain or lose "ownership" of issues, how they are judged on their performance in government across policy issues, and how they develop a reputation for competence (or incompetence) over a period in office. Their analysis tracks the major events causing people to re-evaluate party reputations and the costs of governing which cause electorates to punish parties in power. A public administration that gives the appearance or hope of effective delivery moved to the heart of politics in response to these pressures.

The last four decades have seen a major drive toward public service reform, and although the direction of travel has varied between countries, with greater emphasis on contracting-out and privatization in Anglo-Saxon countries and more emphasis on efficiency and effectiveness improvements in continental European countries (Pollitt and Bouckaert 2004), there are some widely shared programs of change. The focus of attention here is on three reform themes: performance targets, consultation, and the use of evidence. These reforms share a claim to be about supporting and extending the legitimacy of public services and programs in the context of a challenging governing environment, but each has been developed within public administration in a manner that in turn can invite public distrust or even cynicism, and a positive climate for populist exploitation.

Performance Measurement

As Boswell (2018, p. 1) notes, "The use of performance measurement as a tool of governance is now ubiquitous across economically developed countries." An idea that was originally developed in the private sector started to spread to large sections of the public services from the 1980s onwards. Targets, rankings, and league tables are commonplace instruments of public service management. In different ways, these measures were about getting public servants to focus on delivery. Incentives were not just financial (performance bonuses and higher pay for higher-level managers), but also reputational (making performance league tables available in the public domain to effectively "name and shame" poorly performing managers and service units). Poorly performing service managers were pressurized to quickly improve inadequate performance. The ultimate sanction for poor managerial performance was dismissal of individual managers and/or sending so-called "hit squads" of new management teams to take over management of failing public service units. As Lewis (2015) notes, performance measurement is governed by a rational-technical logic, but also by a political-realist logic. The former is focused on measuring to improve outcomes, but the latter is about the exercise of control, the manipulation of information, and ambiguous rhetoric.

The political logic behind the expansion of performance measurement was to demonstrate a firm grip by governors on achieving better outcomes in order to appease a critical public. The aim was to increase trust in the capacity of public services to deliver: "Traditional resources for establishing relations of trust between politicians and voters – in the form of familiarity or symbolic sources of authority – have been eroded. Instead, political leaders need to fall back on alternative modes of producing trust. One important device is to create new mechanisms of accountability, by establishing forms of performance measurement" (Boswell 2018, p. 3).

However, performance measures do not automatically build trust. One example will have to suffice. In the UK, in the 2000s targets were agreed by the Home Office (the responsible department) with respect to asylum seekers (see Boswell 2018, pp. 84–89). The first related to processing 75 percent of applicants within two months, and the second involved removing a greater proportion of failed asylum seekers. Special units were set up and new procedures established. But targets were consistently missed, in part because core aspects of the process of managing asylum seekers were outside the control of the Home Office and were in the hands of others, such as the courts; "sloppy administration" created further delays. There was also gaming, with a focus on the easier-to-handle cases in order to hit targets. Another tactic was the reshaping of goals, so the target was redefined as the initial handling of cases, leaving the subsequent time-consuming phases of the process (such as appeals and removals) out of consideration. Eventually, after a political scandal and a rejigging of targets, a large-scale commitment of further resources was made. But, by then, both public and ministerial (political) trust in the system was lost.

There are wider grounds for doubting the full veracity of the performance information that lies behind government claims about improvements in public services. Hood (2006) describes how standard gaming strategies in the context of target-setting regimes were practiced by players and identified by those supervising the systems in higher levels of government. These included:

rachet effects – underperforming in order to avoid being set too high a target next time around;

threshold effects – targets that reward average performance and give no incentive to high performers to go further; and

output distortion practices – by, for example, temporarily shifting extra resources into an area of practice in order to hit a target.

As Hood (2006) argues, various attempts were made to tackle the worst abuses and to deter outright lying about performance data, but many within public administration tolerated some elements of gaming, in part because they wanted to report success to citizens and their political masters. On occasion, targets that were missed, and that could have been politically embarrassing, were quietly buried and abandoned.

If anything, the impact of performance measurement has been to increase distrust and cynicism. Boswell (2018, p. 8) demonstrates, in her careful analysis, "that targets have not succeeded in producing

24Gerry Stoker

political trust, either on the part of voters or between political leaders and their bureaucracies." The obsession with performance measurement and auditing in management culture over recent decades cannot escape criticism. Of course, there is nothing wrong with evaluating programs or services. But in practice they are too often exercises by which government officials tried to manipulate the way that citizens judged their performance. Positive data was given prominence; less helpful data was sometimes hidden. Messages about achievements were honed, lists of achieved targets were broadcast. Meanwhile, frontline public servants and many citizens found that the claims of success contrasted with their own, more negative experiences. Far from promoting trust, paradoxically the packaging of performance may have contributed to the distrust of governance later exploited by populism.

Consultation

Consultation joins performance measurement as one the most widespread of public administration practices to have developed from the 1970s and '80s onwards. The public service had long-established relationships through iron triangles or networks with key stakeholders in most areas of policy interest, but the pressures of a changing governing context, more critical citizens, wider media scrutiny, and a fear on the part of national political actors that they no longer had the resources to achieve positive outcomes opened the way to the practice of public participation or consultation. The OECD (2001, p.18) review makes clear the thinking behind this extension of engagement between government and citizens.

Information, consultation, and active participation give citizens the chance to learn about government's policy plans, to make their opinions heard, and to provide input into decision-making. This involvement creates greater acceptance for political outcomes. Government shows openness, which makes it more trustworthy for the citizen – the sovereign in any democracy. By building trust in government and better public policies, strengthening government–citizen relations enhances the legitimacy of government.

There is considerable evidence to suggest that consultation as practiced by governments has not always strengthened relationships with the public. Two examples will have to suffice. Wang (2001, p. 334), reporting from the United States on participation schemes in cities, discovered that "participation in administrative decision making may not lead to public trust toward administrations." Concerns about a democratic deficit within the decision-making of the European Union (EU) encouraged consultation and participation schemes, but when it comes to being effectively and sustainably responsive few could disagree with the judgment of Follesdal and Hix (2006, p. 548) that the EU "track record so far is not sufficient ... to ensure acceptable outcomes in ways that provide crucial trustworthiness."

The issue is not so much a lack of effort in undertaking consultation, but rather a lack of capacity to deliver effective participation opportunities. Just as in the case of performance measurement, there is a gap between idea and delivery. Research shows that one of the biggest deterrents to participation is citizens' perception of a lack of response from official consultation schemes, often described as "consultation fatigue" (Lowndes, Pratchett, and Stoker 2006). Officially sponsored consultation has too often been blighted by asking for public engagement when decisions have already been made, or where there is no commitment to respond to the ideas that are generated (Cornwall 2008). Pressures from the changed context and political leaders can lead to the promotion of the idea of participation, but the edifice of the way that decisions are made in public administration is altered only marginally. The number of practitioner guides on how to do participation better are an indication that the path of public consultation has been strewn with limitations and failures, broken with occasional successes.[1] Consultation practices are as likely to have led to greater public distrust as to heal the divide between government and citizens.

Evidence-Based Strategies

The evidence-based policy movement and "it's what works that matters" is another response from within public administration to pressures to support and justify policy decisions in a more demanding environment. Like performance data and consultation, the mantra that "we are driven by evidence" could provide public administrators with an additional legitimacy tool. There is much of value in using evidence to drive policy decisions. In general terms, it would win public support, and it would seem a matter of good governance to deliver it. Yet again, the gap between idea and delivery has opened the approach to attack. That political leaders tend to select evidence to support their policy preferences (and were often aided in that process by public administrators), rather than the other way around, has contributed to a climate wherein expertise could be trashed by populists.

Within the EU, and at national levels of government, many experts driving policy and regulation debates appear to be closely connected to various business or other sectional interests. This situation has helped to bring the idea of expert-based policy into disrepute. Practice is about generating policy legitimacy as much as learning from evidence (Boswell 2008). These doubts about the claims of evidence-based policy are commonplace within the public administration literature (going back to Weiss 1979). Evidence collecting is widely regarded as a cynical exercise by public servants. A series of executive workshops with senior policy officials held in Australia, the United Kingdom, and New Zealand during 2012–2014 (reported in Stoker and Evans 2016, p. 17) indicated that most viewed evidence as window dressing rather than as the decisive factor in decision-making. There was an overwhelming acceptance that good evidence was an important condition for better policymaking, but in practice roughly eight in ten officials suggested they spent more time retro-fitting evidence to policy, rather than the other way around, and that short-term policy imperatives precluded any prospect of using evidence. Six in ten agreed that an issue was that their political masters were "indifferent to facts." A strategy to let evidence drive policy as a mechanism to bolster legitimacy has too regularly become a practice of fitting evidence to policy preferences. Policy-based evidence-making is the appropriately pejorative term to describe this practice of using evidence in order to support a policy which has already been decided.

Playing into the Hands of Populism

For populism, the delivery dilemma was not essentially about the capacity to manage; rather, it was about getting into power politicians better connected to the popular will. Distrust in mainstream governance provides the fuel to its rise. As the introduction to the book notes, the relationship between liberal democracy and populism is complex. Populism today finds its most common expression inside democracies, and in most cases it has forged a relationship with democratic institutions (Albertazzi and McDonnell 2008; Chwalisz 2015; Elchardus and Spruyk 2016). These modern forms of populism do not propose to abolish free elections or install dictatorship; on the contrary, their demand is for a democracy that "delivers what the people want." Populism finds its modern voice as a critic of the perceived failings of governing in contemporary democracies.

That challenge is defined by three elements of political practice of negativism that feed off a distrust of mainstream politics and public administration: anti-elitism, antipluralism, and direct representation (Mudde and Kaltwasser 2017; Müller 2017; Stoker 2019a; Urbinati 2014). Populists are critical of elites for usurping the people's democratic control. Populism relies on the distinction between a pure and sovereign people, on the one hand, and a corrupt and unresponsive political elite on the other, as well as the moral primacy of the former over the latter. When the "Us" triumph over the "Them," politics finds its true function as expressing the moral right of the people to rule. Populism glorifies "the people" but offers a singular take on who "the people" are; as such, a second crucial feature is that it is opposed to a pluralistic understanding of society. Populists deny diversity among citizens and rely on the myth that there is an authentic, homogeneous "people" whose values and interests they understand. Finally, populists give a special role to the leader who can express the viewpoint of the "people." Populists have a "noninstitutionalized notion of the people" (Müller 2017, p. 31). The leader discerns what the people know and want, and intermediary institutions such as parliament, the civil service, nongovernmental organizations, and the media that threaten this direct representation are a focus for criticism or control (Urbinati, 2014).

Modern populism stands apart from conventional political forces because of the extent to which it combines democratic and authoritarian elements. Populists aim to win power through elections, but make claims that deny legitimacy to voices other than their own and privilege the power of the populist leadership to push forward change without constraint. Populism, as the introduction to the book notes, threatens core practices in public administration, including appointment on merit, openness to alternative governing partners, and the stance of neutrality. Public administration, through the prism of populism, could be viewed negatively, as part of the establishment, a defender of pluralism, and a doubtful aid in delivering its agenda. Populism can pose a danger to the conventional practices of public administration in contemporary democracies. It can also use the bureaucracy as tool to achieve its goals, as the introduction to this book points out.

But, as this chapter argues, populism has also fed from the failings of public administration reforms: performance measurement, consultation, and evidence collecting. Each in principle could have contributed to a better government–citizen relationship, but the twisted practice of each opened the possibility of increasing public distrust and ultimately of a populist response. Whether that response emerged in particular countries, and the form it took, depends on a complex of variables.

Researchers can identify both demand and supply factors driving the emergence of populism and argue that since populism is about a different political relationship between elites and citizens, both factors are likely to be in play (Kaltwasser 2015; Mudde and Kaltwasser 2017, pp. 98–108). On the demand side is a sense among citizens of social discontent reflecting forces that can include economic loss, policy failures, corruption scandals, or threats to cultural values, which in turn is accompanied by a broad sense that the political system is unresponsive. The failed public administration reform projects that offered to measure performance objectively but failed to do so, that proposed to listen to the people but often did not, and that advocated policy driven by evidence but often failed to deliver, added and contributed to these demand-side drivers of populism. On the supply side, populists found their niche by pointing to a perceived convergence among mainstream parties in outlook and policy, and by identifying certain groups that had been left behind in the drive to modernize and meet the challenges of globalization. The public administration reforms played to these narratives as well, given that their preferred reforms could be presented as connected to global demands and trends for a shift to public service delivery transformation and modernization. The flawed practices of public administration contributed to sense of citizen discontent and perceived governmental failure that populism could exploit.

Responses from Public Administration to Populism: Flawed and Mistaken

The responses to the threat of populism adopted by public administrators indicate a continued failure to grasp the driving forces and trajectory of populism. Public administration played a part in enabling populism and appears to misunderstand how best to respond.

Keeping a Low Profile: Double-Down on Competence

One comeback of public administrators to populism has been to double-down on the argument that their role is a technocratic one: Let the populists run the frontstage of governing but let public administration keep a grip on the backstage of implementation, and so steer policy development away from the razzmatazz of populism. Administrators can manage the backstage practices themselves to develop and implement practical policies to solve societal problems and steer clear of the frontstage of media-focused and media-oriented politics – that arena loved by populists (Klijn 2016). The message is that while politicians may move on to the populist terrain, officials can still use administrative control techniques to get things done.

Yet there is no reason to assume that, when in government, populists will leave the backstage processes of governance alone. Moreover, as Müller (2017, pp. 44–49) notes, when in power populists want to intervene rather than leave the delivery of government services alone. They are keen to colonize government positions, seeing this as an opportunity to exercise more personal control over the bureaucracy. They engage in mass clientelism, offering material or symbolic benefits in return for votes (e.g. by offering free bus passes for the young or trade sanctions to protect core, favored industries), which means they want to direct policy for political purposes, not leave it to officials.

Kettl (2017) suggests that government officials could earn back public respect and trust by getting better at doing what he calls the retail level functions of delivering, operationally, policies that are fair and effective, and that are connected to what people want. In a turbulent environment, the argument is to stick to the basics of implementation governance and do it well.

But taking to the backstage misses out vital elements in rebuilding trust. As the OECD (2017) argues, performing with greater technical competence and operational capacity is one platform around which to build trust, but the heart of the matter goes to values that reflect whether citizens see themselves as treated with respect, fairness, and integrity. Processes matter as well as performance. These value dimensions in responding to lack of trust are perhaps less comfortable terrain for public administration. Many large-scale private sector organizations have an explicit and sustained trust-building strategy – appealing for customer loyalty through reason but also emotion – that more traditional understandings of public administration might argue is inappropriate. But given that populism works in part through its appeal to emotion, can public administration afford to leave it out of its armory?

Tell a Better Emotional Story

Another common response is to argue that populists win arguments with the public because they appeal to emotions and irrational feelings. One suggestion, therefore, from those advising officialdom, is to develop a stronger human-interest or emotional dimension in the way that that official information is presented. This argument runs the risk of failing to understand that populism is not irrational but rather antitechnical; it wants values, moral prejudices, and self-actualized truths to rule the day. The saving of public administration cannot be achieved by developing a few human-interest stories, but rather by a reorientation that responds to "why" questions as much as to "how" questions. Populists and their supports fear that current governing practices lead to rule by special interests, corruption, putting profits before people, and so on. What is needed is a recognition of the partial truth of that accusation, and a greater willingness to reform and challenge what has become a comfortable form of governing for political and administrative elites.

More Civic Education

Those looking for a response to populism sometimes call for more for citizenship education. But that is unlikely to make a difference. Populism does not see the need for the people to be educated; rather, it is assumed that the people already have those skills, and the good sense to make wise decisions. Debates around the rise of measles in Italy and other European countries pitted experts arguing that what was needed was a recommitment to full vaccination programs against populists pointing out that their whole point was that they trusted people more than experts. As one defender of populism argued:

"Those who continue to traduce populism as a rejection of experts, even a rejection of the truth itself, are refusing to recognize it for what it really is: a rejection of the political exploitation of expertise. We are not rejecting the truth; we are rejecting *their* self-styled truth" (Black 2018, p.2).

More "Real" Participation

A similar level of doubt could be expressed about another proffered response to populism: a call for better citizen participation, more democratic innovations, or even more referendums. By better forms of engagement with citizens, the hierarchical and alienating features of formal representative democracy can be softened. There are many examples of this kind of claim. Claudia Chwalisz (2017) presents a clear commentary and calls for more innovative democratic responses to the charge of populism, claiming willingness on the part of citizens in general and those that support populist parties to engage with these innovations. New forms of political engagement should be presented not as a threat to formal systems of government, but as much-needed enrichment. But a laudable concern to further democratize networks of governance is unlikely to convince those who sign up to the populist perspective that views the problem as networks, and the other governing mechanisms, because they stand in the way of the direct popular will. The populist argument is for a simple connection between the people and a responsive leader, not for a push to make new demands on citizens or add layers of complexity to decision-making (Canovan 1999).

Reconnecting Public Administration to Democratic Politics: A Strategy for Responding to Populism

It is no surprise to any administrator to hear an argument that the making of a policy choice is the start of the journey not the end. Complex processes of service delivery and programs dealing with wicked problems do not run smoothly without continuous and careful oversight. Steering and rowing cannot be separated. Both require continual engagement, reconnecting them to claims about achieving public value (Stoker 2006). Politics and public admission are not separate worlds; rather, they are deeply intertwined. Public administration needs to develop a culture of justifying decisions that expresses its arguments in nontechnical terms. Populism needs to be challenged by moral, emotional, and human arguments. It's not only what works that matters, but also what can be justified as good, right, fair, and legitimate. Public administration, if it is going to survive the populist assault, needs to change its overarching mantra "to do less steering and more validating." It needs to reconnect with rather than cut itself off from the frontstage of politics by encouraging political leadership that is willing and able to make the moral case (as well as the practical case) for what is being done in terms of governing, policy, and service delivery (Stoker 2019a).

Public administration needs also to find a way to address the various elements of the changed context for governance. The first issue is how to frame governance in a world where national sovereignty is inevitably constrained by the impact of globalization and the influence international organizations and systems. Given that "take back control" was a theme in the Brexit campaign in the UK and is a mantra shared by many populist movements, some might argue that measures that give control to citizens should be the leitmotif of reform. Populists demand a democracy that "delivers what the people want." Democracy has been premised to a large degree on this understanding, but in practice delivering control for citizens has proved to be illusive. In a world that has become more globalized, interconnected, and subject to rapid technological change, control is no longer a tenable option. Many politicians still make promises of control, but in doing so they ultimately stoke the sense of disappointment with democratic politics. Another objection is that who "the people" are is not so clear-cut in societies that have become more fragmented by geographical mobility, patterns of immigration, and greater respect and support for diversity. Finally, in most democracies the sense of belonging to a successful "national" project is being questioned as income inequality widens. There are increasing numbers of people who are either completely economically marginalized or feel economically insecure, fearful for their jobs in an age of continual restructuring, cost containment, and casualization.

If democracy cannot deliver control, what can it offer its citizens? The answer is influence and an offer of engagement in a creative process. Citizens are looking for opportunities to get things done, to find their own solutions, individually and collectively. Public administration needs to be part of a framework driven by greater connectivity and enabling activity, and characterized by open sharing and conditional affiliation. A growing practice that expresses this style of working is citizen-centered design (Bason 2018; Evans and Terrey 2016). Citizens and service providers work together, using design techniques, to develop better practices of service provision. Codesign breaks with the idea that public servants have a monopoly of expertise about services and recognizes that users' experiences and reflections can help also in redesign. The creative dynamics of the design process add to the sense that there is a joint journey of discovery to be traveled, with a shared shaping of the problems, joint exercises to stimulate solutions, and a commitment to trialling options with rapid feedback, followed by further adaptions if appropriate. As Bason (2018, p. 33) argues, "managers and staff must display *the courage to lead innovation* at all levels, against the odds and in spite of the daily constraints and pressures ... the overall challenge to public leaders is to give up some of their power and control by involving people – thereby achieving power to achieve the desired outcomes."

There is an expanding group of international public servants that are pushing the idea of *One Team* government.[2] The core starting point is to break down barriers between policy making and delivery and instead work in creative partnerships that join public servants at all levels with citizens and civil society. Many of the seven principles of these public service reformers are familiar: cross-boundary working, testing and trialling ideas, working in an open and inclusive way. In addition, one driver is to

work for users and other citizens affected by our work; everything we do will be guided by our impact on them. We will talk to them, early and often; we will use the best research methods to understand them better. We will be distinguished by our empathy – for users and for each other. The policy that we develop will be tested with real people as early as possible and refined with their needs in mind.[3]

The second governing challenge is set by the rise of critical citizens. Established mechanisms of public participation and consultation (even if they avoid being tokenistic), as we have argued, have not proved adequate to meeting the challenge of better educated, less deferential, and more skeptical citizens. But there are other options. The prime lesson is that politicians and public administrators need to take a great deal more care about building legitimacy. The Centre for Public Impact argues that governments need to better understand what legitimacy looks like in today's conditions).[4] Echoing some of the thinking of the *One Team* pioneers, The Centre for Public Impact identifies five behavior patterns that can support the search for legitimacy: work together with people toward a shared vision, bring empathy into government, build an authentic connection, enable the public to scrutinize government, and value citizens' voices and respond to them. These ideas are of course not novel, but there is a more consistent emphasis on developing a human-centered approach to designing public services and practices. Public administration will achieve legitimacy in the new context of governing not through boastful and implausible target-setting, fake public consultation, or claims to be always driven by evidence, but instead by displaying authenticity, engagement with people's lives, and an openness to ideas and criticism.

The third big governance challenge is set by the rise of a media environment that is more fragmented, more prone to sensationalism, and more generally a rejection of top-down information provision. The importance of user-generated material in that environment, and the way that information from such sources is considered more authentic and therefore more trustworthy, does not sit easily with the standard governmental approach of sending out information messages, promotions, and marketing to its citizens and users of public services. Public administration needs to offer a different type of approach to the use of expertise. The core argument comes from Lindblom (1990), but it finds reflection in other debates about public policy. Public administration has too often been framed by science-led models where experts on how humans think and behave offer practical ideas that draw on their knowledge to improve public policy. As Lindblom argues, such a science-led model has a long but not always honorable history. Given societal complexity and the limits to knowledge, a more pluralistic approach might be more appropriate. The alternative framing which Lindblom refers to could be labeled as problem-solving for self-guiding societies. It calls for policy to mix insights from experts and public officials with those of citizens and other actors. It is a process whereby experts are not in the lead, but they are supporters to a process of change driven by citizens and others. It calls for a policy process that is open and dynamic. It looks to a competition of ideas in a never-ending search for solutions to social problems.

Conclusions

Public administration needs to recognize how its practices have played into the hands of the populist surge. It needs to rethink some of its central premises, as well as defend core principles such as appointment on merit, a commitment to pluralism, and the rule of law. Diminishing national political space, emerging critical citizens, and a shifting media environment have transformed the conditions for governing in established democracies. The opportunities for populism, and even practices of stepping back from democratic practices, reflect the impact of changed governing conditions. But many of the initial responses from public administration – tilting toward technocracy, the explosion of disingenuous performance measurement and cynical public consultation strategies – have fed public distrust and thereby also aided the rise of populism and created space for democratic backsliding. Public administration has met populism with misguided responses based on strategies that seek to deny or bypass the forces of change. Only by developing different practices that embrace the new governing conditions can public administration respond to populism and deliver on its public service ethos in a new era.

Public administration, if it is going to survive the populist assault, needs to drop its defense of the politics–administration dichotomy. This mantra, which was reinforced in the 1980s by the commitment to "less rowing, more steering," argued that political leaders could set the direction, and others, either as in-house public servants or as external contractors, get on with the delivery. That perspective was always problematic, but now it is bankrupt. The mantra left the door open for populists to argue that only a strong leader can steer and ensure that the rowing stays on track. The simplification of the model – a naïve principal–agent frame – provided the pathway to a simplistic populist solution. We need to develop a public administration that can work across political and administrative boundaries, partner with critical citizens, and exploit new technology as the best defense against populism and democratic backsliding.

Notes

1. Two examples can be found at https://participedia.net/ and www
   .involve.org.uk/resources/publications.
2. www.oneteamgov.uk/principles
3. www.oneteamgov.uk/principles
4. www.centreforpublicimpact.org/assets/documents/Finding-a-more-
   Human-Government.pdf

12 Conclusions: Public Administration Under the Rule of Democratic Backsliders

JON PIERRE, B. GUY PETERS, MICHAEL
W. BAUER, STEFAN BECKER, AND KUTSAL
YESILKAGIT

Populists in government are not inevitably condemned to fail. There is no automatic populist exhaustion from wielding executive power, nor are liberal parties destined to eventually return to control government (Albertazzi and McDonnell 2015). Populism can be defeated in democratic elections. It can, however, also become entrenched and transform the political system toward illiberalism or outright autocracy (Pappas 2019). Moreover, comparative research on populism finds little support for the thesis that populists in government act most often as mere democratic correctives. Rather, "populist rule leads to liberalism's decay and sometimes even to democratic breakdown" (Pappas 2019, p. 82). Populists achieve such ends by assaulting the formal and informal institutions of liberal democracy, such as the rule of law, minority rights, parliaments, the judiciary, and the media, not to mention violating the informal conventions of the political game (Levitsky and Ziblatt 2018a; Manow 2020; Rovira, Kaltwasser, and Taggart 2016; Weyland and Madrid 2019).

While the impact of populist rule on the political system and society has received increasing attention, the role of the central instrument to prepare and implement public policies – namely, the state bureaucracy – has remained outside the focus. It is against this background that the complex relationship between populist governments and their bureaucratic apparatus constituted the center of the theoretical and empirical analyses of this book. In eight case studies covering Europe (East and West) and America (North and South) the fate of public administration systems after populists came to power has been examined. Two additional chapters delve deeper into patterns of bureaucratic reactions and the complex relationship between populism and public administration.

This final chapter discusses the most important findings. It starts with the drivers behind the populist surge as indicated in the case studies, before outlining the main lessons on the populist approach toward the bureaucracy, including their reform strategies, and the reaction of the bureaucracy. It concludes by advancing recommendations on how to foster administrative resilience in times of populist threats.

Drivers of Populism

Scholarship has identified numerous drivers behind the recent surge of populism (Albertazzi and McDonnell 2008; Eatwell and Goodwin 2018; Germani 1978; Levitsky and Ziblatt 2018a; Manow 2020; Rovira Kaltwasser et al. 2017). The chapters in this volume echo this mix of different dynamics. They suggest that populism – or, more generally, antiliberal sentiment – has been fueled by decreasing trust in public institutions and political actors (Mexico, the United States, Germany in the 1930s, and technocratic populism at the local level); military-socialist radicalization (Venezuela); "doublespeak populism" (Mexico); a backlash against globalization and a resurgence of nationalism and xenophobia (Hungary, Poland, the United States); a response to continuing failures of governance and corruption (Italy); a revolt against pluralism and the mainstreaming of liberal values and human rights (Poland, Hungary); and a negative reaction to neoliberalism (again Mexico).

Despite some commonalities, however, the case studies in this volume caution that populist movements do not lend themselves to a simple, one-dimensional classification. They may, in fact, contradict themselves regularly. Di Mascio, Natalini, and Ongaro (Chapter 3, this volume) ascribe a marked difference between rhetoric and practice to both the right-wing Lega Nord and the more left-leaning Five Star Movement. Dussauge-Laguna states the same for the populist resurgence in Mexico. Leaders of conventional political parties would probably be asked to explain such inconsistencies, but that seems to be much less common for populist parties. Part of the reason why populist leaders are rarely challenged for this "doublespeak" (Dussauge-Laguna, Chapter 8, this volume) might be that such accountability is emblematic of liberal democracy which the populists – leaders and followers – do not appear to appreciate (Mény and Surel 2002;

Müller 2017; Pappas 2019, p. 73). Populist leaders also tend to enjoy a revered status within their parties that protects them from uncomfortable questions, and they denigrate or suppress the press that may raise questions about their inconsistencies, or even overt falsehoods.[1]

While the issue of what explains the emergence of populism is not the main focus of the present analysis, we suggest that understanding the social and political forces that brought populist leaders to power may help us understand how those leaders have perceived the bureaucracy and how they have chosen to relate to the public service. As the empirical chapters in this volume substantiate, the specific political projects pursued by populists in government, and the degree to which they express either a positive, collaborative relationship or an adversarial engagement with the bureaucracy, provide a key piece of the jigsaw of contemporary populism.

The main features of populism in government are a reliance on charismatic leadership; the strategic pursuit of political polarization; a drive to seize control of the state, emasculate liberal institutions, and impose an illiberal constitution; and, last but not least, the systematic use of patronage to reward supporters and crowd out the opposition (Pappas 2019, p. 74). From those elements, it is the seizure of state control, as well as the colonization of the state institutions via patronage, that directly affect the public administration systems. However, the extent to which populists in government treat the bureaucracy as one of those ruling elite institutions they want to unify "the people" against depends on the particular mixture of their ideological claims. There seems to be an affinity of right-wing nativist branches of populism with procapitalist agendas toward bureaucracy bashing. All things considered, we recognize, however, an uncomfortable ambiguity in populists' relationship to the bureaucracy. Whether this relationship is coined by more inimical or rather indifferent stances depends on the ideological elements of populists' political manifests, to which we now turn.

Populism and the Public Bureaucracy

The analyses presented in the empirical chapters highlight the diverse nature of populism (see Maerz et al. 2020; Müller 2017; Peters and Pierre 2020; Rovira Kaltwasser et al. 2017). Under the umbrella concept of populism we can see political projects that differ in terms of their political objectives and targets, and also in terms of the social constituencies they seek to mobilize to pursue those goals. This means that different strands of populism will look differently at the state, and particularly at the public administration. Thus, leftist populists such as Andrés Manuel López Obrador in Mexico have adopted a different strategy to engage the public bureaucracy than the more right-wing and nationalist Donald Trump in the United States.

The approaches toward the public bureaucracy by the populist governments studied in this volume differ as much as their ideologies. The introduction presented three general scenarios for populists in government: they can *sideline*, *ignore*, or *use* the established bureaucracy. All three scenarios have real-world equivalents, as the case studies show, with sidelining and using the bureaucracy being the routes most taken. The majority of cases, however, do not fall neatly into one of those categories. The Venezuelan case comes closest to representing one single scenario, with Chavismo showing a strong tendency to sideline the established bureaucracy and recreating a new one as a branch of the military. Apart from that, populists have differentiated approaches toward the public bureaucracy. They sideline one agency, while ignoring another and using yet another to implement their favored policies (see the cases of Brazil and Hungary).

The differentiated approaches may, on the one hand, stem from topical priorities. As a stark example, the National Socialist approach combined using or ignoring the established bureaucracy in more technical fields such as post and transport, while it was sidelined in the highly salient "racial policy" areas (Strobel and Veit, Chapter 2, this volume). On the other hand, the differentiated approach may be task based. The Hungarian and, to a certain extent, the Polish cases show that populist governments may strip ministerial bureaucracies of any policy formulation duties while sustaining or even strengthening their implementation role – seeking, in effect, to establish a new politics–administration dichotomy that has featured so prominently in Public Administration scholarship since its inception (Overeem 2005; Rosenbloom 2008).

While some populists have a unified or a differentiated approach, others seem to have no clear stance toward the public bureaucracy. Chapter 3, on the Italian case, shows that after the last Berlusconi government, which was influenced by New Public Management, the subsequent populist governments have adopted a rather pragmatic approach. This may have benefits, since sidelining and using the bureaucracy at the same time does have its costs. As Eliška Drápalová exemplarily shows in her chapter on technocratic populism in three European cities (Chapter 6), this mixed strategy creates tensions and poses a significant threat to the sustainability of populist projects.

As argued earlier, the approaches populists adopt toward the established bureaucracy depend on their specific brand of populism. The bureaucracy itself poses a complex challenge to populist regimes, for a number of reasons. The first reason concerns the bureaucracy's considerable regulatory leverage to exercise formal authority; as Max Weber (1978, p. 220) argued, "the exercise of authority consists precisely in public administration." Put simply, complete ignorance of the established bureaucracy is hardly a choice for populists coming into government – especially if they want to deliver on their election promises or increase their chances of re-election. Again, at the risk of being repetitive, if populists seek to implement change, substantive or institutional, they need to take a stand vis-à-vis the bureaucracy.

Secondly, public bureaucracies are inherently legalistic organizations. As such, their scope of action and the type of tasks they can be asked to carry out (or not carry out) are detailed in legislation and regulations. A populist leader ordering political and administrative action that falls outside that framework will immediately encounter opposition from the bureaucracy, and the populist leader may or may not accept that argument from the bureaucracy.[2]

To some extent, the nature of populism is *not* to acknowledge legal constraints on political action. Indeed, some populists specifically attack the legal framework of the bureaucracy, which they tend to portray as the epitome of red tape and bureaucratic rigidity. Seeking to portray themselves as outsiders to the political system and its elite, populists sometimes make a point of challenging the rules of political and administrative processes on the grounds that they are "unfair," as Dussauge-Laguna argues in Chapter 8 on populism in Mexico. Law and rules are often argued to be instruments by which the "Deep State" protects itself from accountability and imposes its wishes on the rest of society.

Third, the public service is characterized by strong normative frameworks of integrity, impartiality, accountability, and professionalism. As is the case with the legalistic nature of the bureaucracy, this framework presents obstacles to the populist project in terms of ensuring responsiveness and loyalty to the populist regime. Unlike legislation and regulation, however, these normative dimensions of public administration cannot be abolished overnight. Instead, some populist regimes seek to ensure administrative loyalty by replacing career bureaucrats with loyal followers. The comparative evidence suggests that increasing the politicization of the bureaucracy – or increasing the number of politically appointed loyalists in strategic posts in the public service – is a common populist strategy to take control of the bureaucracy.

Thus, given the centrality of the bureaucracy in governance and the formal–legal authority it harbors, populist regimes must relate in one way or another to the public bureaucracy. The empirical chapters have shown different patterns of populist behavior vis-à-vis public administration. Apart from general approaches, the introduction has outlined five specific strategies that populist leaders can pursue: centralization of structure, centralization of resources, politicization of personnel, politicization of norms, and reduction of accountability. It has argued that, generally, none of these strategies are necessarily problematic. Indeed, as research on comparative public administration shows, attempts to politicize personnel, for instance, can have legitimate reasons and plentiful historical precedents.

However, taken to their extreme, both individually and combined, the strategies bear the potential to dismantle democratic public administration and contribute to what Guillermo O'Donnell calls "the slow death of democracy" (O'Donnell 2011, p. 30; see also de la Torre and Ortiz Lemos 2016; Bauer and Becker 2020). To take this discussion further, we need to differentiate between different types of populism and the strategies they tend to apply as they engage the public bureaucracy. Here, Peters and Pierre (2020) have outlined a typology of populist movements based on two dimensions: whether they are "inclusionary democratic" (rather left-wing, internationalist) or "exclusionary authoritarian" (rather right-wing, nativist) in their overall political goals; and whether they are a mass- or elite-based political movement (see also Norris and Inglehart 2019; Mudde and Rovira Kaltwasser 2013). Also, we need to distinguish between populism as a social and political movement on the one hand, and populist leaders in executive positions on the other, as it is in the latter role that populism's relationship with the public administration becomes a salient issue.

The strategies presented here seem to relate primarily to authoritarian populists, as covered in this volume, while democratic populists are more likely to open up new avenues for citizens and clients into the public sector and to remove public sector employee privileges. Thus, both the democratic and the authoritarian populists pose a major challenge to the public service, albeit in different ways. Authoritarian populists, as mentioned earlier, are reluctant to submit to the formal–legal authority of the public administration. They are therefore likely to consider using any or all of the strategic options outlined by Bauer and Becker (2020) – namely, to capture, dismantle, sabotage, or reform the bureaucracy so as to turn it into a loyal and responsive instrument controlled by the regime. Populists seeking to enhance democracy, by contrast, tend to mobilize their movements to challenge the public administration by attempting to enhance participation and crowd intelligence.

They also justify increasing politicization of the bureaucracy as a strategy to attack the purportedly self-serving "Deep State" and to give political leaders more control over the public service. In the minds of the populist political leaders, at least, reducing the role of the career public service in governing is democratic, following the will of the voters, even though in doing so they may violate legal or even constitutional principles.

Thus, different types of populists prefer different approaches to the bureaucracy owing to factors such as their overall ideological orientation, where leftist-inclusionary populists would take a more positive view of the public administration and the state more broadly while right-wing exclusionary populists would seek to either tighten the political control of the bureaucracy, change its modus operandi, or simply obstruct or sabotage its work (Bauer and Becker 2020). Likewise, populist governments based on the appeal of a leader or leaders may be more dismissive of the public administration than are those representing an organizational basis in the society, and representing citizens who want services delivered.

Bureaucratic Structures Conditioning Populists Transformation Strategies

In addition to the ideological dimension of the populist government, there are also several aspects of the public bureaucracy itself which logically will shape the populist strategy of engagement for both political leaders and for the bureaucracy. A populist leader of government may wish to make the public bureaucracy conform to his or her wishes, but the nature of that bureaucracy can make the task confronting that political leader more or less difficult. Given that most populists coming into office have relatively little experience with the public sector, they may not understand the likely reactions of their civil servants to the changes in governance styles and purposes.

Administrative autonomy, formal, and real. The first characteristic of public administration that may affect its ability to resist pressures from political leaders is its autonomy. In some cases that autonomy may be formal, with statutes or even constitutions describing the role of the bureaucracy and its place within governance. This factor is similar to Knill's (1999) distinction between autonomous and instrumental bureaucracies, with the former having some independent organic status within the state while the latter is merely an instrument to be wielded by the government of the day.

Although the formal position of public administration in governance is certainly important, the perceived role and autonomy may be important also. Although legally vulnerable to political pressures, a highly respected civil service may be able to maintain its autonomy when confronted with populist governments. There are no examples in our collection of cases where a functioning and reasonably well-performing public service is confronted with populist political leadership, but if that were to occur there is the possibility for major confrontation over control of government programs. We will come back to the theme of bureaucratic autonomy when we consider administrative potentials for resilience.

Professionalism and intrinsic motivation. The professionalism of the civil service and its commitment to public service (Vandenabeele, Brewer, and Ritz 2014) will also influence the manner in which the institution as a whole, as well as individual public servants, respond to populist governments. The professionalism of the public service is related to the extent to which the service is merit-based and constitutes a career. Professional civil services will resent any attempts to undermine their involvement in, or control, over, policy and management within the public sector. This professionalism and commitment may lead those populist politicians to characterize them as the "Deep State," while the civil servants may see themselves as only doing their job.

High levels of intrinsic motivation of public servants, and the associated belief that they are in their positions to serve the public interest, are also likely to engender more conflict with populist political leaders. As well as serving the law, civil servants consider themselves to be serving the public. This commitment to public service may be especially important at the lower levels of the bureaucracy – the street level bureaucrats (Hupe 2019). If populists with a right-wing ideology take power, then street-level bureaucrats with commitments to their clients may be motivated to resist the actions of that government, and to continue to support their clients.

Management system and sensitivity to political level. What a bureaucracy does may also be important for its relationship with populist leaders. All bureaucracies are responsible for implementing law and managing public programs, but those that focus on those basic administrative functions and do not involve themselves heavily in policy-making may be less influenced by the advent of populist politics. Even within a single administrative system, agencies or other more or less autonomous organizations may be able to insulate themselves from political pressures. Administrative organizations with effective insulation from politics are likely to resist populist pressures and to maintain something approaching "business as usual." Other segments of the bureaucracy, especially those in close – even daily – contact with political leaders, will develop other forms of interaction ('t Hart and Wille 2006). What is to be stressed here is that the relationship between the populist leadership and the bureaucracy is to a large extent a function of individual political-administrative relationships.

The trend in public management reform over the past couple of decades has been toward increasing focus on results and performance while giving managers more autonomy in relation to the political level of government. The main role of elected officials in this management system is setting long-term objectives for the public service; politicians in this system of management are removed from any operational role, and several of their traditional levers to control the bureaucracy have been weakened or even abolished (see Pollitt and Bouckaert 2017). While this reform has triggered extensive debate about the loss of political control and accountability, it may help protect the public service from populist regimes ascending to power.

History of politicization and patronage. Finally, some administrative systems have a history of being more influenced by political control and by patronage appointments than others. Although it appears that politicization is becoming more common in all political systems (Neuhold, Vanhoonacker, and Verhey 2013), patronage appointments are the norm rather than the exception in some countries. Many of the countries of Latin America, for example (see Dussauge-Laguna, Chapter 8; and Muno and Briceño, Chapter 9, this volume; see also Peters, Ramos, and Alba, forthcoming). And in Europe, several CEE countries already had high levels of patronage appointments in public administration prior to the surge in populist politics (see Hajnal and Boda, Chapter 4; and Mazur, Chapter 5, this volume; see also Kopecký, Mair, and Spirova 2012).

Countries with a significant history of patronage appointments will find it more difficult to resist efforts on the part of populist leaders to take over administration using their own supporters in public service positions (Kenny 2017). These systems will already have numerous positions designated as being open to appointment. Further, having extensive patronage appointments in these administrative systems will not be seen as violating the canons of good government, as they might be in systems with more autonomous and professional civil services. Patronage will simply be business as usual, albeit with a rather different type of appointee.

That difference in the type of appointees may be important for both governance and for the interaction of career public servants and those appointees. As already noted, most populists coming into office have limited experience in government – Donald Trump is a prime example. Therefore, many of the appointments made by populist politicians are likely to be people with limited experience. Indeed, in the ideology of the populists, having little or no experience in government may be a virtue and not a vice.

Administrative Responses to Populism

The foregoing sections discuss some of the structural and institutional factors associated with differing responses of bureaucracies to populist governments. In addition to those factors, we also need to consider the individual responses of bureaucrats and the ways in which they can cooperate with, or resist, populist governments that may in their view be undermining proper governance and administration. The tendency among citizens, and even scholars, has been to assume that public bureaucrats have few ideas of their own, or that the only values they have are based on self-interest. That assumption tends to be incorrect, and individuals within government are often committed very strongly to policies and programs (Brehm and Gates 2002).

When confronted with challenges to their preferred policies, or their way of administering them, bureaucrats have several options (see Brehm and Gates 2002; Guedes-Neto and Peters, Chapter 10, this volume). The simplest option is that they accept the directives of the government of the day and implement changes to their ways of doing things – *working*. They can also choose to work as slowly as possible, following all the procedural rules and attempting to slow down the implementation of programs – *shirking*.

The third option available to bureaucrats – *sabotage* – is the most interesting and the most unusual. If bureaucrats believe that fundamental legal or moral values are being violated by the policies of their government, they may choose to find ways to prevent that from happening (see O'Leary 2006, 2017). Choosing sabotage as a response represents choosing their own legal and perhaps constitutional commitments over their usual responsibilities of serving the government of the day and faithfully working in their jobs. When faced with what they may consider illegal commands from their superiors, this is for some civil servants the only acceptable alternative other than resignation.[3]

That said, however, there are also circumstances wherein public servants do not necessarily disagree with the ideas and objectives of the populist regime. Thus, in their analysis of the bureaucrats' reaction to the consolidation of Nazi power in Germany in the early 1930s, Strobel and Veit (Chapter 2) note that "while the majority of civil servants were loyal to the democratic governments at first, many of them eventually welcomed Hitler's rise to power in 1933 ... there was no *structural* resistance in the civil service, that is, most civil servants worked loyally for the Hitler regime" (italics in original). Whether this was because of a sense of duty to assist the government of the day, regardless of its ideology, or loyalty to the office of a public servant, or sympathy with the populist regime, or simply wanting to keep their positions in government, the observation is important as it dispels the myth that public servants, by definition, disagree with populists.

The empirical chapters display a pattern in contemporary populist rule of anticipating adverse bureaucratic reactions and therefore taking recourse to centralizing control over the bureaucracy, sidelining potential resistance (often via appointments of followers to strategic positions but also as rank-and-file), or outright creating from anew loyal structures (the latter, for example in Venezuela). Our empirical accounts, however, find little evidence of collective, let alone systematic resistance to populist transformations in any substantial way. After all, populists in government tend to bend the rules, rather than blatantly break them. That helps explain why "no overt reaction of the higher civil service" (Di Mascio, Natalini, and Ongaro, Chapter 3, this volume) can be detected, and why the more common reaction to growing demands of centralized control of the bureaucracy "is obedience, instead of either shirking or sabotage" (Hajnal and Boda, Chapter 4, this volume). Bureaucrats who are trained in loyalty and due process suffer from the ambiguity of the populist leaders and become insecure if they find themselves in disagreement with the line of their government. They often appear to "internalize" their disagreement and the emerging incongruence with the effect of ever-lower moral, growing turnover, and increasing lack of initiative (Hajnal and Boda, Chapter 4, this volume). There is no culture of resistance within the machineries of governments; "bureaucracy has always known its place. It's been extremely rare that someone from the administration would have opposed the intentions of the government" (Hajnal and Boda, Chapter 4, this volume).

As a consequence, many civil servants flee into a passive role and focus on literally fulfilling their assignments. The exception of such "risk averse" behavior becomes more likely when bureaucrats see the danger of bringing individual culpability upon themselves by following orders which are apparently unlawful (and thereby risking their jobs). Then, the signs of shirking become clearer (Hajnal and Boda, Chapter 4, and Guedes-Neto and Peters, Chapter 10, this volume). However, only small groups of bureaucrats sabotage the orders of the populist rulers – even in countries like Poland and Hungary, where the populist trespassing arguably went furthest (see Mazur, Chapter 5, as well as Hajnal and Boda, Chapter 4, this volume).

What is more, parts of the New Public Management reform wave reinforced the yes-men trend as it produced a complying technocracy focused on top-down efficiency and effectiveness – thereby downsizing other public administration values (Stoker, Chapter 11, this volume). In that sense, the majority of the chapters speak a clear language: "Weberian" bureaucracy does not seem to be much of an obstacle to democratic backsliders (Muno and Briceño, Chapter 9, this volume). But it is values beyond efficiency and effectiveness, such as participation, fairness, and due process, which are prerequisites of a democratic bureaucracy. Such values, however, do not emerge by themselves but rather need to be nurtured deliberately within the public sector and beyond.

The chapters in this volume highlight how the administrative responses to populism for the most part display conflict between norms and values at both the institutional and individual levels. Democratic government is contingent on the loyalty of public servants in government and agencies, but that commitment becomes seemingly untenable when an elected government does not subscribe to fundamental ideas about democracy. At the institutional level, bureaucracies and the norms they represent and reproduce can sustain a populist leader over the short term, but are less likely to do so over an extended period of time.

In the long run, if populist governments pursue their illiberal project, democratic bureaucrats will be squeezed out of service (by their own choice or by structural gaming of populist governments; see Muno and Briceño, Chapter as well as Hajnal and Boda, Chapter 4, this volume). The key point here is that state bureaucracies per se are no hotbeds of resistance against illiberal rule – an observation which triggers questions about how to structurally and professionally protect the public service against populist takeovers.

Administrative Resilience

It would be to overtax bureaucrats' role to portray them as guardians of liberal democracy. But we can ask what kind of institutional, structural, procedural, or normative bureaucratic features might be more resilient against populist transformations than others. The chapters testify that contexts and traditions do matter, so general recommendations must always be adapted to local conditions. However, measures in three areas may help prevent democratically elected governments from reneging on the terms of the institutionalized relationship with the bureaucracy.

One suggestion is to revisit the question of bureaucratic autonomy (Bauer and Ege 2016; Carpenter 2001; Huber and Shipan 2002; Yesilkagit and van Thiel 2008). Bureaucratic autonomy is necessarily relative and acceptable to the extent that it is necessary for the administration to do an efficient job. Populist takeovers bring to the fore advantages if the access – and thus capacity for reversal – of the central executive is cushioned by some safety measures. Fiduciary relationships that insulate against political volatility might here be seen in a different, more positive light (Majone 2001). While recommending insulating the bureaucracy from political provisions would be throwing the baby out with the bathwater, a solution could be to bring in the parliaments as arbiters. Instead of centralizing power in a single executive institution or even in an individual ruler, broadening the range of political institutions involved in bureaucratic oversight and control might be a precaution in view of the risk of populist takeovers.

The second suggestion concerns the social embeddedness – broadly understood – of the bureaucracy. Multilateral treaties and ties to civil society, business, or trade unions can – in substance – counterbalance transformative intentions of populists in government. In more corporatist public administration systems, such collaboration with organized interests has led to the establishment of strong institutions and forms of collaborative autosteering of those interests under the guidance of the bureaucracy. While such arrangements may stand in the way of populists, they are not unsurmountable for them, although political effort and time are needed to change them. The same applies to multilateral commitments. Populist governments – and especially if they run on a nativist, antiglobalization ideology – may pull out of international treaties which in their view are but constraining deals. However, the leaving of international regimes and organizations probably needs time and sequencing to keep the domestic repercussions at bay. So, arrangements of bureaucratic embeddedness can slow down, even if only temporarily, the administrative submission toward populist agendas.

Finally, capacity for resilience also lies in the professional standards and ethics of individual bureaucrats. It would be unfair to rely upon individual bureaucrats – under the risk of their professional existence – to stand up against elected populist governments. However, that does not preclude keeping civil servant ethical standards in high esteem and investing further in professional as well as ethical education of (future) civil servants, if only to boost awareness that the individual bureaucrat eventually serves the citizens and has pledged to protect the democratic constitution. This might sound overly heroic, but it can be seen as pragmatic advice nevertheless.

Perspectives for Public Administration Research on Democratic Backsliders

The current crisis in many political systems, stemming from the power of populist politics, represents the clash of two equally important political principles. The first is the principle of democracy. Populist leaders come to power through a democratic process, although some attempt to maintain their power through less than democratic means. The second principle is liberalism, with an emphasis on freedom, the rule of law, and the protection of individual rights. This principle appears a threat in many contemporary populist governments.

The message of this book is that the conflict between liberalism and illiberalism is not only fought at the ballot box or in debate forums. Given the centrality of the public bureaucracy to any government, liberal or otherwise, ensuring control over the public service one way or the other is a crucial element of that conflict between liberal democracy and its temporary enemies (Popper 1962). Somewhat paradoxically, perhaps, one of the key lessons we can draw from the current analysis is that the role of the bureaucracy may be to uphold democratic governance and the rule of law in the face of threats to both democracy and liberalism. Most people tend to think of bureaucracy and democracy as antithetical to one another, but they are closely linked, and an independent and effective bureaucracy may be essential for liberal democracy (Meier and O'Toole 2006).

The populists under scrutiny in this volume have, with differing choices and intensities, pursued all bureaucratic transformation strategies, from centralization of structure, over-centralization of resources, politicization of personnel, politicization of norms, and reduction of accountability. Some cases, such as Venezuela and, to a lesser extent, Mexico and Hungary, have witnessed all five dynamics, while others have seen combinations or one rather dominant strategy (e.g. politicization of personnel and norms under Trump, or seeking to eschew traditional accountability measures in the case of technocratic populism at the local level). Across all cases, politicization of personnel and centralization of structure have been the most frequent strategies. Needless to say, they are also the easiest to detect. Politicization of bureaucratic norms, if done more silently than in Trump's case, and the reduction of accountability, if accomplished in less obvious fashion than in Orbán's case, are harder to observe. Now that we have enough "probable cause" for further inquiry, future research should delve deeper into these strategies by conducting more fine-grained and systematically comparative case studies.

Regarding the reform strategies, future research should also seek to develop measurement scales – qualitative or, where possible, quantitative – to allow for a more comparable outlook. Methodologically rigorous designs will enable scholars of political science and public administration to move beyond descriptive or even normative case studies of backsliding. The studies in this volume showcase the variety of methodological approaches that can be employed for the systematic study of the changing bargains between politicians and bureaucrats. Showing the way for future studies of bureaucratic backsliding, the chapters should therefore also be seen as demonstrations of the merits (and caveats) of research designs that vary from qualitative single-country and comparative designs to quantitative, longitudinal, and even historical analysis (as in Strobel and Veit, Chapter 2, this volume).

Since democratic backsliding exposes civil servants to moral dilemmas and difficult choices, this field will also, we expect, drive up the demand for more experimental and behavioral approaches (as in Guedes-Neto and Peters, Chapter 10, this volume). As an exploratory exercise, the cases in this book have refrained from starting from too-rigid analytical categories. Again, as first suspicions have been confirmed, more data should be gathered. However, the case studies also show that each populist government operates in a very specific environment. This may not only complicate data gathering; it must also be kept in mind when interpreting the data. What is deemed unusual in one political system may not be so unusual in another.

Future research also needs to look for – at first glance – paradoxical trends in these strategies. While, for instance, technocratic populism seeks to circumvent traditional channels of political accountability, it uses referenda or online participation tools to further its causes. It is, therefore, a rather selective insulation of the bureaucracy. Another seemingly paradoxical development is found in the Polish case. While recent reforms have strengthened the Prime Minister's office and thus, as expected, centralizing formal structures, it has at the same time been de-institutionalized, with PiS party leader Kaczyński effectively pulling the strings. Both developments make sense at close range. As for the differentiated approaches toward the bureaucracy in general, however, such intricacies should be acknowledged when generalizing about populists in government.

Finally, as in many other areas, the COVID-19 pandemic deals new cards to liberal and illiberal political leaders. On a general level, the economic hardship of the pandemic will be much worse than that of the last recession – which, by and large, could be kept within the financial markets. The economic hardship this time will be global and will hit the poorer states, with fiscally less potential to counteract, harder than the richer world. And it will also hit the poorer layers of society in rich countries harder than any recession has done for decades – as the rising numbers of business insolvencies and unemployment rates herald. Economic depression in general, and unemployment in particular, are easily exploitable for populists of any sort – especially if they are in the opposition. It is no coincidence that the current wave of populists rose to government after – and mostly as a consequence of – the economic downturn after 2008. This darkens the outlook for the coming years. In the middle term, the unavoidable worsening of economic conditions around the globe might feed into radicalization at the ballots, and thus into greater electoral opportunities for populists to get into power. Unfortunately, research on the impact populists in government have on bureaucratic systems will stay relevant for the foreseeable future.

While the pandemic is likely to help populists to conquer political power, its impact on populists governing through the crisis is a different matter, and one that appears worthy of more systematic exploration. While Orbán in Hungary appears to be doing fine, the ability of strongmen populists such as Bolsonaro or Trump to effectively cope with the COVID-19 crisis is, by all standards, poor. One part of their failure to limit the impact of the pandemic has to do with their refusal to listen to experts, and in particular in refuting advice from their health bureaucrats. In other words, the situation is ambivalent. While populists in government may be able to exploit the extreme situation created by the health emergency to further dismantle liberal-democratic arrangements – also within the administrative systems – it is an open question whether populist rule in general will benefit from the current health crisis. The jury is still out on whether COVID-19 will boost or dampen populist aspirations. What can be said, however, is that the challenge of populists in government will remain with us for some time to come (Albertazzi and McDonnel 2015; Pappas 2019, p. 82; Taggart and Rovira Kaltwasser 2016). This book has shown how populist transformations of the public administration affect institutions and, eventually, the lives of citizens. The analytical concepts developed herein, as well as the empirical cases studied, will hopefully help to promote the necessary debate about populism and democratic bureaucracy, both inside and outside the discipline of Public Administration.

Notes

1. By the count of the Washington Post, Donald Trump passed the landmark of 18,000 falsehoods on April 17, 2020; see *Washington Post Fact Checke*r, April 17, 2020. www.washingtonpost.com/politics/2020/04/14/president-trump-made-18000-false-or-misleading-claims-1170-days/
2. Thus, for example, when Kirstjen Nielsen, then the Director of Homeland Security in the United States, told President Trump that federal law enforcement was prevented by law from executing some specific tasks he requested, Trump responded "then we'll pardon them" (Rucker and Leonnig 2020, p. 307).
3. The other trichotomy available to civil servants may be "exit, voice or loyalty" (see Hirschman 1970).

References

Abelshauser, W., Fisch, S. & Hoffmann, D. (2016). *Wirtschaftspolitik in Deutschland 1917–1990*. Oldenburg: de Gruyter.

Aberbach, J. D., Putnam, R. D. & Rockman, B. A. (1981). *Bureaucrats and Politicians in Western Europe*. Cambridge, MA: Harvard University Press.

Aberbach, J. & Rockman, B. (2000). *In the Web of Politics: Three Decades of the US Federal Executive*. Washington, DC: Brookings.

Abutaleb, Y. & McGinley, L. (2020). Ousted Vaccine Official Alleges he was Demoted for Prioritizing "Science and Safety," *Washington Post*, May 5.

Agerberg, M. (2017). Failed Expectations: Quality of Government and Support for Populist Parties in Europe. *European Journal of Political Research*, 56(3), 578–600. https://doi.org/10.1111/1475-6765.12203

Aguilar Camín, H. (2018). A las puertas de AMLO, *Nexos*, June, 31–39.

Aguilar Camín, H. (2019). La destrucción transformadora, *Milenio*, July 8.

Ahmed, A. & Villegas, P. (2018). López Obrador, an Atypical Leftist, Wins Mexico Presidency in Landslide, *The New York Times*, July 1.

Ajuntament de Barcelona. (2016). *Open & Agile Digital Transformation Toolkit*. Available from https://ajuntament.barcelona.cat/digital/en/digital-transformation/technology-for-a-better-government/transformation-with-agile-methodology

Albertazzi, D. & McDonnell, D. (2005). The Lega Nord in the Second Berlusconi Government: In a League of its Own. *West European Politics*, 28(5), 952–72.

Albertazzi, D. & McDonnell, D. (2008). *Twenty-First Century Populism: The Spectre of Western European Democracy*. Basingstoke: Macmillan.

Albertazzi, D. & McDonnell, D. (2015). *Populists in Power*. Abingdon: Routledge.

Alford, J., Hartley, J., Yates, S. & Hughes, O. (2017). Into the Purple Zone. Deconstructing the Politics/Administration Distinction. *The American Review of Public Administration*, 47(7), 752–63.

Amorim Neto, O. & Pimenta, G. A. (2020). The First Year of Bolsonaro in Office: Same Old Story, Same Old Song? *Revista de Ciencia Política*, 40(2), 187–213.

Andersen, L. B., Heinesen, E. & Pedersen, L. H. (2014). How Does Public Service Motivation Among Teachers Affect Student Performance in Schools? *Journal of Public Administration Research and Theory*, 24(3), 651–71.

Animal Político. (2018). Equipo de AMLO presume que programas obtuvieron más del 90% de aceptación; Tren Maya, el menos votado. *Animal Político*, 26 November.

Animal Político. (2019). Gobierno compra 571 pipas por 85 mdd; AMLO garantiza que se estabilizará abasto de gasolina. *Animal Político*, January 21.

Anonymous. (2019). *A Warning*. New York, NY: Twelve Books.

Arellano, S. & Mercado, A. (2019). Gertz Manero, fiscal general por 9 años. *Milenio*, January 19.

Arena Pública. (2019). Advierte Cofece "potencial daño permanente" por adjudicación directa a Banco Azteca. *Arena Pública*, January 24.

Arenas, N. (2010). La Venezuela de Hugo Chávez: rentismo, populismo y democracia. *Nueva Sociedad*, 229, 76–93.

Arias, L., Barrientos, E., Fócil, M., et al. (2018). Análisis de los Lineamientos de Combate a la Corrupción y Aplicación de una Política de Austeridad Republicana en materia de recorte de plazas, reducción de salarios, cancelación de prestaciones y aumento de la jornada laboral al personal de confianza. *Nexos*, September.

Arnsdorf, I. (2018). The Shadow Rulers of the VA. *ProPublica*, August 7. Available from www.propublica.org/article/ike-perlmutter-bruce-moskowitz-marc-sherman-shadow-rulers-of-the-va

Atkinson, M. M. & Coleman, W. D. (1989). Strong States and Weak States: Sectoral Policy Networks in Advanced Capitalist Economies. *British Journal of Political Science*, 19(1), 47–67.

Avelar, I. (2017). A Response to Fabian Santos and Fernando Guarnieri. *Journal of Latin American Cultural Studies*, 26(2), 341–50.

Babiš, A. (2016). *O Čem Sním Když Náhodou Spím*. Prague. Available from www.anobudelip.cz/file/edee/2017/o-cem-snim-kdyz-nahodou-spim.pdf

Bach, M. (1990). *Die charismatischen Führerdiktaturen. Drittes Reich und italienischer Faschismus im Vergleich ihrer Herrschaftsstrukturen*. Baden-Baden: Nomos.

Bach, M. & Breuer, S. (2010). *Faschismus als Bewegung und Regime. Italien und Deutschland im Vergleich*. Wiesbaden: Springer Fachmedien.

Badell, D., Di Mascio, F., Natalini, A., Ongaro, E., Stolfi, F. & Ysa, T. (2019). Too Big to Fail? The Dynamics of EU Influence and Fiscal

Consolidation in Italy and Spain (2008–2016). *Public Management Review*, 21(9), 1307–29.

Baker, R. (2002). *Transitions from Authoritarianism. The Role of the Bureaucracy*. Westport, CA: Greenwood Publishing Group.

Banfield, E. (1958). *The Moral Basis of a Backward Society*. New York, NY: Free Press.

Barr, W. (2018). Mueller's "Obstruction" Theory. *Internal Department of Justice memo*, June 8. Available from https://int.nyt.com/data/document helper/549-june-2018-barr-memo-to-doj-mue/b4c05e39318dd2d136b3/ optimized/full.pdf

Bartha, A., Boda, Z. & Szikra, D. (2020). *When Populist Leaders Govern: Conceptualizing Politics and Governance*. Politics and Governance, 8(3), 71–81.

Bason, C. (2018). *Leading Public Sector Innovation. Co-SCreating for a Better Society*, 2nd ed., Bristol: Policy Press

Batory, A. (2016). Populists in Government? Hungary's "System of National Cooperation." *Democratization*, 23(2), 283–303.

Batory, A. & Svensson, S. (2019). The Use and Abuse of Participatory Governance by Populist Governments. *Policy & Politics*, 47(2), 227–44.

Bauer, M. W. & Becker, S. (2020). Democratic Backsliding, Populism and Public Administration. *Perspectives on Public Management and Governance*, 3(1), 19–31.

Bauer, M. W. & Ege, J. (2016). Bureaucratic Autonomy of International Organizations' Secretariats. *Journal of European Public Policy*, 23(7), 1019–37.

Becker, A. (2017). The Circulation of Oligarchs. In B. Magyar & J. Vásárhelyi, eds., *Twenty-Five Sides of a Post-Communist Mafia State*. Budapest: Central European University Press, pp. 111–27.

Bekke, H. A. G. M., Perry, J. L. & Toonen, T. A. J. (eds.) (1996). *Civil Service Systems in Comparative Perspective*. Bloomington & Indianapolis, IN: Indiana University Press.

Bellé, N. (2012). Experimental Evidence on the Relationship between Public Service Motivation and Job Performance. *Public Administration Review*, 73(1), 143–53.

Bermeo, N. (2016). On Democratic Backsliding. *Journal of Democracy*, 27(1), 5–19.

Bertelli, A. & Feldmann, S. (2007). Strategic Appointments. *Journal of Public Administration Research and Theory*, 17(1), 19–38.

Bertrand, N. (2019). Peter Strzok Accuses the Federal Government of Violating his Rights. *Politico*, December 30. Available from: www.politico .com/news/2019/12/30/peter-strzok-accuses-government-violating-his-rights-091156

Bickerton, C. & Invernizzi Accetti, C. (2017). Populism and Technocracy: Opposites or Complements? *Critical Review of International Social and Political Philosophy*, 20(2), 186–206. https://doi.org/10.1080/ 13698230.2014.995504

Bickerton, C. & Invernizzi Accetti, C. (2018). Techno-Populism as a New Party Family: The Case of the Five Star Movement and Podemos. *Contemporary Italian Politics*, 10(2), 132–50.

Black, T. (2018). Now They are Blaming Populists for Measles. *Spiked*, August 27. Available from www.spiked-online.com/2018/08/27/now-the yre-blaming-populism-for-measles/#.W5E05LgnaUk

Blake, A. (2020). Trump's Government Full of Temps. *Washington Post*, February 21.

Blanchar, C. (2017). Colau crea 2.000 plazas de funcionario para reducir un 70% los interinos. *El País*, December 14. Available from https://elpais.com/ ccaa/2017/12/14/catalunya/1513254236_344383.html

Blanco, I., Salazar, Y. & Bianchi, I. (2019). Urban Governance and Political Change under a Radical Left Government: The Case of Barcelona. *Journal of Urban Affairs*, 42(1), 18–38.

Bloom, P. & Sancino, A. (2019). *Disruptive Democracy: The Clash Between Techno-Populism and Techno-Democracy*. London: SAGE Publications Ltd.

Bloomberg. (2016). Venezuela's Military Needs to Get Out of Business. Generals and Soldiers are Profiting from a Dysfunctional Economy. *Bloomberg*, May 6. Available from www.bloomberg.com/opinion/articles/ 2016-05-06/venezuela-s-military-needs-to-get-out-of-business

Bobbio, N. (1987). *The Future of Democracy: A Defence of the Rules of the Game*. Minneapolis, MN: University of Minnesota Press.

Boin, A., Stern, E. & Sundelius, B. (2016). *The Politics of Crisis Management: Public Leadership Under Pressure*. Cambridge: Cambridge University Press.

Boräng, F., Cornell, A., Grimes, M. & Schuster, C. (2018). Cooking the Books: Bureaucratic Politicization and Policy Knowledge. *Governance*, 31(1), 7–26. https://doi.org/10.1111/gove.12283

Bordignon, F. & Ceccarini, L. (2013). Five Stars and a Cricket. Beppe Grillo Shakes Italian Politics. *South European Society and Politics*, 18(4), 427–49. https://doi.org/10.1080/13608746.2013.775720

Borgonovi, E. & Ongaro, E. (2011). The Civil Service in Italy. In A. Massey, ed., *The International Handbook of Civil Service Systems*. Cheltenham: Edward Elgar, pp. 103–24.

Borins, S. (2018). Public Sector Innovation in a Context of Radical Populism. *Public Management Review*, 20(12), 1858–71. https://doi.org/10.1080/ 14719037.2018.1441430

Boswell, C. (2008). The Political Functions of Expert Knowledge: Knowledge and Legitimation in European Union Immigration Policy. *Journal of European Public Policy*, 15(4), 471–88.

Boswell, C. (2018). *Manufacturing Political Trust*. Cambridge: Cambridge University Press.

Bovaird, T. (2007). Beyond Engagement and Participation: User and Community Coproduction of Public Services. *Public Administration Review*, 67(5), 846–60.

Bozóki, A. (2011). Occupy the State: The Orbán Regime in Hungary. *Debate: Journal of Contemporary Central and Eastern Europe*, 19(3), 649–63.

Bozóki, A. (2015). Broken Democracy, Predatory State, and Nationalist Populism. In P. Krastev & J. van Till, eds., *The Hungarian Patient: Social Opposition to an Illiberal Democracy*. Budapest: Central European University Press, pp. 3–36.

Bracher, K. D. (1983). *Nationalsozialistische Diktatur 1933–1945. Eine Bilanz*. Düsseldorf: Droste (Bonner Schriften zur Politik und Zeitgeschichte, 21).

Bracher, K. D., Sauer, W. & Schulz, G. (1962). *Die nationalsozialistische Machtergreifung. Studien zur Errichtung des totalitären Herrschaftssystems in Deutschland 1933/34*, 2nd ed. Cologne: Westdeutscher Verlag.

Brannen, K. (2020). Unredacted Ukraine Documents Reveal Extent of Pentagon's Legal Concerns. *Just Security*, January 2. Available from www .justsecurity.org/67863/exclusive-unredacted-ukraine-documents-reveal-extent-of-pentagons-legal-concerns/

Bratton, M. & van de Walle, N. (1997). *Democratic Experiments in Africa. Regime Transitions in Comparative Perspective*. Cambridge: Cambridge University Press.

Bravo, C. (2019). El hampa del periodismo. *Letras Libres*, September.

Brehm, J. & Gates, S. (1997). *Working, Shirking, and Sabotage: Bureaucratic Response to a Democratic Public*. Ann Arbor, MI: University of Michigan Press.

Brehm, J. & Gates, S. (2002). *Working, Shirking, and Sabotage. Bureaucratic Response to a Democratic Public*, 4th ed. Ann Arbor, MI: University of Michigan.

Briceño, H. (2017). La diversidad ideológica en la formación de las políticas públicas durante el chavismo. In F. Spiritto, ed., *Decisiones de gobierno en Venezuela. Apuntes para su comprensión histórica y de políticas públicas*. Caracas: Publicaciones Universidad Católica Andrés Bello, pp. 115–36.

Bruhn, K. (2013). To Hell with your Corrupt institutions! AMLO and Populism in Mexico. In C. Mudde & C. Rovira, eds., *Populism in Europe and the Americas: Threat Or Corrective for Democracy?* Cambridge: Cambridge University Press, pp. 88–112.

Brunsson, N. (1989). *The Organization of Hypocrisy: Talks, Decisions, and Actions in Organizations.* Chichester: Wiley.

Buchheim, C. (2008). Das NS-Regime und die Überwindung der Weltwirtschaftskrise in Deutschland. *Vierteljahrshefte für Zeitgeschichte*, 56 (3), 381–414.

Burchardt, H.-J. (2005). Das soziale Elend des Hugo Chávez: Die Wirtschafts- und Sozialpolitik der Fünften Republik. In O. Diehl & W. Muno, eds., *Venezuela unter Chávez – Aufbruch oder Niedergang?* Frankfurt: Vervuert, pp. 99–126.

Burnett, C. M. & Kogan V. (2016). The Politics of Potholes: Service Quality and Retrospective Voting in Local Elections. *The Journal of Politics*, 79(1), 203–14.

Buštíková, L. & Guasti, P. (2018). The State as a Firm: Understanding the Autocratic Roots of Technocratic Populism. *East European Politics and Societies*, 33(2), 302–30. https://doi.org/10.1177/0888325418791723.

Cairney, P. (2016). *The Politics of Evidence-Based Policymaking.* London: Palgrave Macmillan.

Calzada, I. (2018). (Smart) Citizens from Data Providers to Decision-Makers? The Case Study of Barcelona. *Sustainability*, 10(9), 32–52. https://doi.org/10.3390/su10093252

Camarena, S. (2018). Rocío Nahle vs. la CNH y la CRE. *El Financiero*, November 14.

Camarotti, G. (2020). Carta aberta com crítica a Aras é lida em reunião de conselho do MP; procurador-geral reage. *G1*. Available from https://g1 .globo.com/politica/blog/gerson-camarotti/post/2020/07/31/carta-aberta-de-procuradores-com-criticas-a-aras-e-lida-em-reuniao-do-conselho-superior-do-mp.ghtml

Canova, A., Herrera Orellana, L., Rodríguez Ortega, R. & Graterol Stefanelli, G. (2014). *El TSJ al servicio de la Revolución. La toma, los números y los criterios del TSJ venezolano (2004–2013).* Caracas: Editorial Galipán.

Canovan, M. (1999). Trust the People! Populism and the Two Faces of Democracy. *Political Studies*, 47(1), 2–16. https://doi.org/10.1111/1467-9248.00184

Capano, G. (2003). Administrative Traditions and Policy Change: When Policy Paradigms Matter. The Case of Italian Administrative Reform During the 1990s. *Public Administration*, 81(4), 781–801.

Caplan, J. (1988). *Government Without Administration. State and Civil Service in Weimar and Nazi Germany.* Oxford: Clarendon Press of Oxford University Press.

Caramani, D. (2017). Will vs. Reason: The Populist and Technocratic Forms of Political Representation and Their Critique to Party Government. *American Political Science Review*, 111(1), 54–67. https://doi.org/10.10 17/S0003055416000538

Cardullo, P. & Kitchin, R. (2019). Being a "Citizen" in the Smart City: Up and Down the Scaffold of Smart Citizen Particition. *GeoJournal*, 84, 1–13.

Carpenter, D. P. (2001). *The Forging of Bureaucratic Autonomy: Reputations, Networks, and Policy Innovation in Executive Agencies, 1862–1928.* Princeton, NJ: Princeton University Press.

Casal, J. (2001). El constitucionalismo venezolano y la Constitución de 1999. *Revista de la Facultad de Derecho UCAB*, 56, 137–80.

Casar, M. A. (2019a). El gran benefactor. *Nexos*, March.

Casar, M. A. (2019b). Estado y gobierno: ¿la disminución? *Nexos*, September.

Cassese, S. (1993). Hypotheses on the Italian Administrative System. *West European Politics*, 16(3), 316–28.

Cassese, S. (1999). Italy's Senior Civil Service: An Ossified World. In E. C. Page & V. Wright, eds., *Bureaucratic Elites in Western European States*. Oxford: Oxford University Press, pp. 55–64.

Cejudo, G. M. (2017). Policy Analysis in the Mexican Federal Government. In J. L. Méndez & M. I. Dussauge-Laguna, eds., *Policy Analysis in Mexico*, Bristol: Policy Press, pp. 31–44.

Cejudo, G. M. & Gómez-Álvarez, D. (2018). La austeridad y la podadora. *Nexos*, September 1.

Chaguaceda, A. (2019). México: contexto y antecedentes de la cuarta transformación. *Diálogo Político*, June 21.

Chandler, R. C. (1983). The Problem of Moral Reasoning in American Public Administration: The Case for a Code of Ethics. *Public Administration Review*, 43(1), 32–9.

Cheney, K., Betrand, N. & McGraw, M. (2020). Impeachment Witnesses Ousted Amid Fears of Trump Revenge Campaign. *Politico*, February 7. Available from www.politico.com/news/2020/02/07/donald-trump-pressure-impeachment-witness-alexander-vindman-111997

Christensen, J. (2017). *The Power of Economists within the State*. Stanford, CA: Stanford University Press.

Chwalisz, C. (2015). *The Populist Signal*. London: Policy Network.

Chwalisz, C. (2017). *The People's Verdict*. London: Rowan & Littlefield.

Císař, O. & Štětka, V. (2016). Czech Republic. The Rise of Populism from the Fringes to the Mainstream. In T. Aalberg, C. Reinemann, F. Esser,

J. Stromback, & C. De Vreese, eds., *Populist Political Communication in Europe*. Abingdon: Routledge, pp. 285–99.

Civil Service Act. (2015). Ustawa z dnia 30 grudnia 2015 r. o zmianie ustawy o służbie cywilnej oraz niektórych innych ustaw (Dz.U. 2016, poz. 34).

Clark, Charles. (2017). Deconstructing the Deep State. *Government Executive*, September 17. Available www.govexec.com/feature/gov-exec-deconstructing-deep-state/

Clarke, H. D., Sanders, D., Stewart, M. C. & Whiteley, P. (2004). *Political Choice in Britain*. Oxford: Oxford University Press.

Clarke, H. D., Sanders, D., Stewart, M. C. & Whiteley, P. (2009). *Performance Politics and the British Voter*. Cambridge: Cambridge University Press.

Clarke, N., Jennings, W., Moss, J. & Stoker, G. (2018). *The Good Politician. Folk Theories, Political Interaction, and the Rise of Anti-Politics*. Cambridge: Cambridge University Press.

Cohen, Zachary. (2020). Whistleblower accuses Trump Appointees of Downplaying Russian Interference and White Supremacist Threat. *CNN*, September 9. Available from: www.cnn.com/2020/09/09/politics/dhs-whistleblower-white-supremacist-threat/index.html

Collier, D. (1979). Overview of the Bureaucratic-Authoritarian Model. In D. Collier, ed., *The new authoritarianism in Latin America*. Princeton, NJ: Princeton University Press, pp. 19–32.

Conze, E., Frei, N., Hayes, P., Zimmermann, M. & Weinke, A. (2010). *Das Amt und die Vergangenheit: Deutsche Diplomaten im Dritten Reich und in der Bundesrepublik*, 4th ed. Munich: Blessing.

Cook, B. (2020). Restraining the Unitary Executive: A Regime Ethics Basis for Administrator Defiance of Presidential Directives. *Public Integrity*, 22(4), 305–15.

Coppedge, M., Gerring, J., Knutsen, C. H., et al. (2018). *V-Dem Codebook v8. Varieties of Democracy (V-Dem) Project*. University of Gothenburg.

Corbin, J. M. & Strauss, A. L. (2015). *Basics of Qualitative Research: Techniques and Procedures for Developing Grounded Theory*, 4th ed. Los Angeles, CA: SAGE.

Cordiplan. (1990). *El Gran Viraje: Lineamientos generales del VIII Plan de la Nación, Presentación al Congreso Nacional*. Caracas.

Cornell, A., Knutsen. C. & Teorell, J. (2020). Bureaucracy and Growth. *Comparative Political Studies*, online first. Available from https://doi.org/10.1177/0010414020912262

Cornwall, A. (2008). Unpacking "Participation" Models, Meanings and Practices. *Community Development Journal*, 43(3), 269–83. http://dx.doi.org/10.1093/cdj/bsn010

Corrales, J. (2020a). Democratic Backsliding through Electoral Irregularities: The Case of Venezuela. *European Review of Latin American and Caribbean Studies*, 109, 41–65.

Corrales, J. (2020b). Authoritarian Survival: Why Maduro Hasn't Fallen. *Journal of Democracy*, 31(3), 39–53.

Corrales, J. & Penfold, M. (2011). *Dragon in the Tropics. Hugo Chávez and the Political Economy of Revolution in Venezuela.* Washington, DC: Brookings.

Cortés, N. & Soto, E. (2019). Eliminan al primer órgano autónomo. *El Heraldo de México.* March 15.

Costa Pinto, A. (2004). Fascist Era Elites (3). Salazar's Ministerial Elite, 1933–44. *Portuguese Journal of Social Science*, 3(2), 103–14.

Cruz, J. (2018). El "error de Texcoco" puede marcar a AMLO. *Proceso*, November 5.

ČTK. (2015). Radní schválili změny na magistrátu. Bude se i propouštět. *Pražský deník*, March 17. Available from https://prazsky.denik.cz/zpravy_region/radni-schvalili-zmeny-na-magistratu-bude-se-i-propoustet-20150317.html

ČTK. (2016). Krnáčová je v čele Prahy dva roky, nyní řeší metropolitní plán. *Pražský deník*, November 25. Available from https://prazsky.denik.cz/zpravy_region/krnacova-je-v-cele-prahy-dva-roky-nyni-resi-metropolitni-plan-20161125.html

Cultura Colectiva (2019). Think Tanks y las otras polémicas de Notimex, la agencia oficial del gobierno de AMLO. *CC News*, May 20.

D'Albergo, L. (2019). Campidoglio, la giunta Raggi vara il rimpasto: fuori Baldassarre, Marzano, Castiglione e Gatta. E apre al Pd. *Repubblica.It*, September 23. https://roma.repubblica.it/cronaca/2019/09/23/news/campidoglio_la_giunta_raggi_vara_il_rimpasto_fuori_baldassarre_marzano_castiglione_e_gatta-236729404/

D'Elia, Y. & Cabezas, L. (2008). *Las Misiones Sociales en Venezuela.* Caracas: ILDIS.

Dahl, R. (1961). *Who Governs? Democracy and Power in an American City.* New Haven, CT: Yale University Press.

Dahlström, C., Lapuente, V., & Teorell, J. (2012). The Merit of Meritocratization: Politics, Bureaucracy, and the Institutional Deterrents of Corruption. *Political Research Quarterly*, 65(3), 656–68.

Dalton, R. J. (1984). Cognitive Mobilisation and Partisan Dealignment in Advanced Industrial Democracies, *Journal of Politics*, 46(1), 264–84.

Davies, H., Nutley, S. & Smith, P. (eds.) (2000). *What Works? Evidence-based Policy and Practice in Public Services.* Bristol: Policy Press.

Dawsey, J. (2020). In Speech, Mulvaney Says Republicans Are Hypocritical on Deficits. *Washington Post*, February 19.

De la Torre, C. (2017). Populism in Latin America. In C. Rovira-Kaltwasser, P. A. Taggart, P. Ochoa, & P. Ostiguy, eds., *The Oxford Handbook of Populism*. Oxford: Oxford University Press, pp. 195–213.

De la Torre, C. & Ortiz Lemos, A. (2016). Populist Polarization and the Slow Death of Democracy in Ecuador. *Democratization*, 23(2), 221–41.

De la Rosa, R. & Quattromani, D. (2019). Ruling Rome with Five Stars. *Contemporary Italian Politics*, 11(1), 43–62.

Della Porta, D. & Vannucci, A. (2007). Corruption and Anti-corruption: The Political Defeat of "Clean Hands" in Italy. *West European Politics*, 30(4), 830–53.

Denhardt, R. B. & Denhardt, J. V. (2002). The New Public Service: Serving Rather than Steering. *Public Administration Review*, 60(6), 549–59.

Denhardt, R. B. & Perkins, J. (1976). The Coming of Death of Administrative Man. *Public Administration Review*, 36(4), 379–84.

Diamant, A. (1968). Tradition and Innovation in French Administration. *Comparative Political Studies*, 1(2), 251–74.

Diamond, D. (2020a). Trump Officials Interfered with CDC Reports on COVID-19. *Politico*, September 11. Available from www.politico.com/news/2020/09/11/exclusive-trump-officials-interfered-with-cdc-reports-on-covid-19-412809

Diamond, D. (2020b). Trump Administration Shakes up HHS Personnel Office after Tumultuous Hires. *Politico*, September 21. www.politico.com/news/2020/09/21/trump-administration-hhs-personnel-shake-up-419519

Diamond, L. (2016). Democracy in Decline: How Washington Can Reverse the Tide. *Foreign Affairs*, 95(4), 151.

Di Mascio, F. (2014). Exploring the Link Between Patronage and Party Institutionalization: An Historical-Institutional Analysis of the Italian Transition. *Democratization*, 21(4), 678–98.

Di Mascio, F., Feltrin, P. & Natalini, A. (2019). I sindacati del settore pubblico e la riforma Madia della pubblica amministrazione. *Rivista Italiana di Politiche Pubbliche*, 14(2), 213–46.

Di Mascio, F., Galli, D., Natalini, A., Ongaro, E. & Stolfi, F. (2017). Learning-shaping Crises: A Longitudinal Comparison of Public Personnel Reforms in Italy, 1992–2014. *Journal of Comparative Policy Analysis*, 19(2), 119–38.

Di Mascio, F., Maggetti, M. & Natalini, A. (2018). Exploring the Dynamics of Delegation Over Time: Insights from Italian Anticorruption Agencies (2003–2016). *Policy Studies Journal*, 48(2), 367–400. https://doi.org/10.1111/psj.12253

Di Mascio, F. & Natalini, A. (2014). Austerity and Public Administration: Italy between Modernization and Spending Cuts. *American Behavioral Scientist*, 58(12), 1634–56.

Di Mascio, F. & Natalini, A. (2015). Fiscal Retrenchment in Southern Europe: Changing Patterns of Public Management in Greece, Italy, Portugal, and Spain. *Public Management Review*, 17(1), 129–48.

Di Mascio, F. & Natalini, A. (2016). Ministerial Advisers Between Political Change and Institutional Legacy: The Case of Italy. *Acta Politica*, 51(4), 517–38.

Di Mascio, F., Natalini, A. & Cacciatore, F. (2019). The Political Origins of Transparency Reforms: Insights from the Italian Case. *Italian Political Science Review*, 49(3), 211–27.

Di Mascio, F., Natalini, A., Ongaro, E. & Stolfi, F. (2019). Influence of the European Semester on National Public Sector Reforms under Conditions of Fiscal Consolidation: The Policy of Conditionality in Italy 2011–2015. *Public Policy and Administration*, 35(2), 201–23. https://doi.org/10.1177/0952076718814892

Di Mascio, F., Natalini, A. & Stolfi, F. (2013). The Ghost of Crises Past: Analyzing Reform Sequences to Understand Italy's Response to the Global Crisis. *Public Administration*, 91(1), 17–31.

Di Palma, G. (1979). The Available State: Problems of Reform. *West European Politics*, 2(3), 149–65.

DOF (2018). Decreto por el que se expide la Ley Federal de Remuneraciones de los Servidores Públicos, Reglamentos de los artículos 75 y 127 de la Constitución Política de los Estados Unidos Mexicanos y se adiciona el Código Penal Federal. *Diario Oficial de la Federación*, November 5.

Dolejší, V. & Prchal, L. (2016). Zrušte Trafiky, Volte Profíky, Hlásala Krnáčová Před Volbami. Dnes Rozdává Funkce Za Loajalitu. *Hospodářské Noviny*, May 18. Available from https://archiv.ihned.cz/c1-65295940-zruste-trafiky-volte-profiky-krnacova-porusuje-slib-ano-aby-ziskala-loajalitu

Dostal, V., Győri, L., Meseznikov, G., Przybylski, W. & Zgut, E. (eds.) (2018). *Illiberalism in the V4: Pressure Points and Bright Spots.* Budapest: Political Capital and Friedrich Naumann Stiftung.

Downs, A. (1965). A Theory of Bureaucracy. *American Economic Review*, 55(1/2), 439–46.

Drabik, P. (2020). Fundusz Inwestycji Lokalnych. Miliardy tylko dla stronników PiS? Available from https://biznes.radiozet.pl/News/Fundusz-Inwestycji-Lokalnych.-Start-naboru-wnioskow

Drápalová, E. & Wegrich, K. (2020). Technocratic Populism and Subnational Governance. *Government and Opposition: An International Journal of Comparative Politics*, 1–21.

Duque, D. & Smith, A. E. (2019). The Establishment Upside Down: A Year of Change in Brazil. *Revista de Ciencia Política*, 39(2), 165–89.

Durant, R. F. (1992). *The Administrative Presidency Revisited: Public Lands, the BLM, and the Reagan Revolution*, New York, NY: State University of New York Press.

Durant, R. F. & Ali, S. B. (2012). Repositioning American Public Administration? Citizen Estrangement, Administrative Reform, and the Disarticulated State. *Public Administration Review*, 73(2), 278–89.

Dussauge-Laguna, M. I. (2011). The Challenges of Implementing Merit Based Personnel Policies in Latin America: Mexico's Civil Service Reform Experience. *Journal of Comparative Policy Analysis*, 13(1), 51–73.

Dussauge-Laguna, M. I. (2015). Mitos y realidades de los Organismos Constitucionales Autónomos. *Revista de Administración Pública*, 50 (138), 225–45.

Dussauge-Laguna, M. I. & Casas, A. (in press). Patronage in the Mexican Public Sector. In F. Panizza, B. G. Peters, & C. Ramos, eds., *Patronage in Transition Across Latin America*. Pittsburgh: Pittsburgh University Press.

Eatwell, R. & Goodwin, M. (2018). *National Populism: The Revolt Against Liberal Democracy*. London: Pelican.

Ebinger, F., Veit, S. & Fromm, N. (2019). The Partisan–Professional Dichotomy Revisited: Politicization and Decision-making of Senior Civil Servants. *Public Administration*, 97(4), 861–76. https://doi.org/10.1111/padm.12613

Edelson, C. (2016). *Power Without Constraint: The Post 9/11 Presidency and National Security*. Madison, WI: The University of Wisconsin Press.

EIU – The Economist Intelligence Unit. (2017). Democracy Index 2017: Free Speech Under Attack. Available from www.eiu.com/public/topical_report.aspx?campaignid=DemocracyIndex2017

Eizaguirre, S., Pradel-Miquel, M. & García, M. (2017). Citizenship Practices and Democratic Governance: "Barcelona En Comú" as an Urban Citizenship Confluence Promoting a New Policy Agenda. *Citizenship Studies*, 21(4), 425–39. https://doi.org/10.1080/13621025.2017.1307609

El Financiero (2018). Regulador de energía recorta a 367 empleados, el 60% de su personal. *El Financiero*, December 17.

El Heraldo de México (2019a). Nadie puede ganar más que el presidente, asegura López Obrador. *El Heraldo de México*, May 6.

El Heraldo de México (2019b). SEP anuncia el despido del 30% de empleados de confianza. *El Heraldo de México*, January 17.

El Nacional (2015). Siete días, *El Nacional*, October 25. Retrieved from www.el-nacional.com/siete_dias/Militares-controlan-ministerios-Maduro-Chavez_0_725927455.html [link defunct at publication].

El País (2006). López Obrador se proclama "presidente legítimo" de México. *El País*, November 20.

El Sol de México (2019). Yo tengo otros datos. AMLO desestima reporte de Bank of America. *El Sol de México*, January 16.

Elchardus, M. & Spruyt, B. (2016). Populism, Persistent Republicanism and Declinism: An Empirical Analysis of Populism as a Thin Ideology. *Government and Opposition*, 51(1), 111–33.

Ellner, S. & Tinker Salas, M. (eds.) (2007). *Venezuela: Hugo Chávez and the Decline of an "Exceptional Democracy."* Lanham, MD: Rowman & Littlefield.

ENCOVI (2020). *Proyecto Encuesta Nacional de Condiciones de Vida de la Población Venezolana), Presentación de resultados 2014–2018.* Retrieved from https://encovi.ucab.edu.ve/divulgacion/indicadores/ [link defunct at publication].

Erdmann, G. (2013). Neopatrimonialism and Political Regimes. In N. Cheeseman, D. Anderson, & A. Scheibler, eds., *Routledge Handbook of African Politics*. London: Routledge, pp. 59–69.

Esmark, A. (2017). Maybe It Is Time to Rediscover Technocracy? An Old Framework for a New Analysis of Administrative Reforms in the Governance Era. *Journal of Public Administration Research and Theory*, 27(3), 501–16. https://doi.org/10.1093/jopart/muw059

Espinasa, R. (2006). El auge y el colapso de Pdvsa a los treinta años de la nacionalización. *Revista Venezolana de Economía y Ciencias Sociales*, 112(1), 147–82.

etcétera (2019). Justifica AMLO compra de pipas sin licitación; no tenemos problemas de conciencia, asegura. *Etcétera*, January 21.

Evans, P. (1995). *Embedded Autonomy: States and Industrial Transformation*. Princeton, NJ: Princeton University Press.

Evans, M. & Terrey, N. (2016). Co-design with Citizens and Stakeholders. In G. Stoker & M. Evans, eds., *Evidence-based Policymaking in the Social Sciences*. Bristol: Policy Press, pp. 243–62.

Evans, P., Rueschemeyer, D. & Skocpol, T. (eds.) (1985). *Bringing the State Back In*. Cambridge: Cambridge University Press.

Expansión Política (2019). Gonzalo Hernández Licona es relevado de Coneval. *Expansión Política*, July 22.

Farazmand, A. (2010). Bureaucracy and Democracy: A Theoretical Analysis, *Public Organization Review*, 10(3), 245–258.

Fears, D. (2017). Zinke says his Workers are Disloyal. They say his Personnel Moves Break the Law. *The Washington Post*, September 27.

FH. (2020). *Freedom House: Freedom in the World Report*. Available from https://freedomhouse.org/report/freedom-world

Fiaschetti, M. E. & Sacchettoni, I. (2019). Roma, esposto dell'ex ad di Ama «Devi cambiare il bilancio». Le parole che imbarazzano la sindaca Raggi. *Corriere della Sera*. April 18. https://roma.corriere.it/notizie/politica/19_aprile_18/devi-cambiare-bilancio-dell-amale-parole-che-imbarazzano-sindaca-5b7156f0-6217-11e9-83f5-ccf392377deb.shtml

Fischer, E. & Wittmann, R. (eds.) (2015). *Geschichte des deutschen Buchhandels im 19. und 20. Jahrhundert*. Berlin: de Gruyter.

Fittipaldi, E. (2019). Rifiuti, Virginia Raggi: «Modifica Il Bilancio». Ma Il Manager Dice Di No e Viene Licenziato. *L'Espresso*, April 18. Available from http://espresso.repubblica.it/plus/articoli/2019/04/18/news/virginia-raggi-ama-lorenzo-bagnacani-esclusivo-1.333936

Folha de São Paulo (2004a). 54% Acreditam Que Lula Trabalha Muito. *Folha de São Paulo*. Available from www1.folha.uol.com.br/folha/brasil/ult96u66437.shtml

Folha de São Paulo (2004b). Há Um Viés Autoritário No Governo Lula? *Folha de São Paulo*. Available from www1.folha.uol.com.br/fsp/brasil/fc1508200417.htm

Follesdal, A. & Hix, S. (2006). Why There Is a Democratic Deficit in the EU: A Response to Majone and Moravcsik. *Journal of Common Market Studies*, 44(3), 533–62.

Föllmer, M. (2001). Der "kranke Volkskörper." Industrielle, hohe Beamte und der Diskurs der nationalen Regeneration in der Weimarer Republik. *Geschichte und Gesellschaft*, 27(1), 41–67.

Fonseca, D. (2018). AMLO: Yo o el diluvio. *The New York Times*, December 2.

Fraenkel, E. (2011). *Deutschland und die westlichen Demokratien*. Baden-Baden: Nomos.

Freedom House. (2020). *Report: "Nations in Transit 2020,"* p. 25. Available from https://freedomhouse.org/sites/default/files/2020-04/05062020_FH_NIT2020_vfinal.pdf

Frenk, J. & Gómez, O. (2019). Salud: manual de una contrarreforma reaccionaria. *Nexos*, December.

Frieden, T., Koplan, J., Satcher, D. & Besser, R. (2020). We Ran the CDC. No President Ever Politicized Its Science the Way Trump Has. *The Washington Post*, July 14.

Fukuyama, F. (1989). The End of History? *The National Interest*, 16, 3–18.

Fukuyama, F. (2006). *The End of History and The Last Man*. New York, NY: Free Press.

Gailmard, S. & Patty, J. W. (2007). Slackers and Zealots: Civil Service, Policy Discretion, and Bureaucratic Expertise. *American Journal of Political Science*, 51(4), 873–89.

Gailmard, S. & Patty, J. (2013). *Learning While Governing*. Chicago, IL: University of Chicago Press.

Galston, W. A. (2018). *Anti-pluralism: The Populist Threat to Liberal Democracy*. New Haven, CT: Yale University Press.

García, I. (2018). ¿Y el presupuesto anticorrupción? *Reporte índigo*, December 19.

Garrido, S. (2018). Los municipios de la consulta del aeropuerto. *Nexos*, October.

Germani, G. (1978). *Authoritarianism, Fascism and National Populism*. New Brunswick, NJ: Transaction.

Golden, M. M. (1992). Exit, Voice, Loyalty, and Neglect: Bureaucratic Responses to Presidential Control During the Reagan Administration. *Journal of Public Administration Research and Theory*, 2(1), 29–62.

Golden, M. M. (2000). *What Motivates Bureaucrats? Politics and Administration During the Reagan Years*. New York, NY: Columbia University Press.

Gómez-Hermosillo, R. (2019a). Réquiem por Progresa-Oportunidades-Prospera. *El Universal*, June 11.

Gómez-Hermosillo, R. (2019b). Secuela de la desaparición de Prospera. *El Universal*, June 25.

Gonzales-Ocantos, E., De Jonge, C. K., Meléndez, C., Osorio, J. & Nickerson, D. W. (2012). Vote Buying and Social Desirability Bias: Experimental Evidence from Nicaragua. *American Journal of Political Science*, 56(1), 202–17.

González, L. (2018). ¿Esquivel, el próximo gobernador del Banxico? *El Economista*, November 26.

González, S. (2019). Conferencias matutinas de AMLO no deben ser una homilía: Coparmex. *La Jornada*, April 14.

Goodman, R. & Schulkin, D. (2020). Timeline of the Coronavirus Pandemic and US Response. *Just Security*, April 13. Available from www.justsecurity.org/69650/timeline-of-the-coronavirus-pandemic-and-u-s-response/

Goodsell, C. T. (2019). The Anti-Public Administration Presidency: The Damage Trump Has Wrought. *The American Review of Public Administration*, 49(8), 871–83.

Görtemaker, M. & Safferling, C. (eds.) (2014). *Die Rosenburg. Das Bundesministerium der Justiz und die NS-Vergangenheit – eine Bestandsaufnahme*, 2nd ed. Göttingen: Vandenhoeck & Ruprecht.

Gössel, K.-D. (2002). Beamtentum im Nationalsozialismus. In M. Friedensberger, K.-D. Gössel, & E. Schönknecht, eds., *Die Reichsfinanzverwaltung im Nationalsozialismus. Darstellung und Dokumente*. Bremen: Ed. Temmen, pp. 95–142.

Gotto, B. (2006). Polykratische Selbststabilisierung. Mittel- und Unterinstanzen in der NS-Diktatur. In R. Hachtmann, ed., *Hitlers Kommissare. Sondergewalten in der nationalsozialistischen Diktatur.* Göttingen: Wallstein (Beiträge zur Geschichte des Nationalsozialismus, 22), pp. 28–50.

Gottwaldt, A. B. & Bartelsheim, U. (2009). *Eisenbahner gegen Hitler. Widerstand und Verfolgung bei der Reichsbahn 1933–1945.* Wiesbaden: Marix Verlag.

Gowen, A., Eilperin, J., Guarino, B. & Ba Tran, A. (2020). Science Ranks Grow Thin in Trump Administration. *The Washington Post*, January 23.

Graff, G. (2020). 25 years after Oklahoma City, domestic terrorism is on the rise. *Wired*, April 19. Available from www.wired.com/story/oklahoma-city-bombing-christopher-wray/

Green, J. & Jennings, W. (2017). *The Politics of Competence. Parties, Public Opinion and Voters.* Cambridge: Cambridge University Press.

Grillo, B. & Casaleggio, G. (2011). *Siamo in Guerra per Una Nuova Politica.* Milan: Chiarelettere.

Gualmini, E. (2002). The Case of Italy. In B.G. Peters and M. Braans, eds., *Rewards for High Public Office in Europe and Northern America.* London: Routledge, pp. 96–110.

Guarino, B. (2019). USDA relocation has delayed key studies and millions in funding, employees say. *Washington Post*, October 2.

Hachtmann, R. (2011). Elastisch, dynamisch und von katastrophaler Effizienz – zur Struktur der Neuen Staatlichkeit des Nationalsozialismus. In S. Reichardt & W. Seibel, eds., *Der prekäre Staat. Herrschen und Verwalten im Nationalsozialismus.* Frankfurt: Campus Verlag, pp. 29–74.

Hajnal, G. (2016). Illiberal or Simply Unorthodox? Public Administration Education in Hungary and Europe: A Comparative Perspective. *Teaching Public Administration*, 34(2), 206–25.

Hajnal, G., & Csengődi, S. (2014). When Crisis Hits Superman: Change and Stability of Political Control and Politicization in Hungary. *Administrative Culture*, 15(1), 39–57.

Hajnal, G. & Rosta, M. (2016). A New Doctrine in the Making? Doctrinal Foundations of Sub-National Governance Reforms in Hungary (2010–2014). *Administration & Society*, Online first.

Hanley, S. & Sikk, A. (2016). Economy, Corruption or Floating Voters? Explaining the Breakthroughs of Anti-Establishment Reform Parties in Eastern Europe. *Party Politics*, 22(4), 522–33. https://doi.org/10.1177/1354068814550438.

Hardin, R. (2006). *Trust*, Oxford: Polity.

Hart, D. K. (1984). The Virtuous Citizen, the "Honorable bureaucrat," and Public Administration. *Public Administration Review*, 44(1), 111–20.

Hart, R. P. (2020). Donald Trump and the Return of the Paranoid Style. *Presidential Studies Quarterly*, 50(2), 348–65.

Havlík, V. (2019). Technocratic Populism and Political Illiberalism in Central Europe. *Problems of Post-Communism*, 69(6), 369–84.

Heady, F. (1996). Configurations of Civil Service Systems. In H. A. G. M. Bekke, J. L. Perry, & T. A. J. Toonen, eds., *Civil Service Systems in Comparative Perspective*. Bloomington & Indiana, IN: Indiana University Press, pp. 207–26.

Heckman, J. (2018). Are More Federal Employees Leaving under a Trump Administration? *Federal News Network*, March 26. Available from https://federalnewsnetwork.com/workforce/2018/03/federal-employee-turnover-increases-in-trump-administrations-first-year/

Heclo, H. (1974). *Modern Social Politics in Britain and Sweden*. New Haven, CT: Yale University Press.

Hehl, U. V. (2001). *Nationalsozialistische Herrschaft*, 2nd ed. Munich: Oldenbourg Wissenschaftsverlag.

Heinze, A. S. (2018). Strategies of Mainstream Parties Towards their Right-wing Populist Challengers. *West European Politics*, 41(2), 287–309.

Hernández, A. (2019). Gobierno notifica a Metlife cancelación de seguro de gastos médicos. *El Universal*, January 2.

Hetland, G. (2017). From System Collapse to Chavista Hegemony. The Party Question in Bolivarian Venezuela. *Latin American Perspectives*, 44(1), 117–36.

Hirschman, A. O. (1970). *Exit, Voice, and Loyalty: Responses to Decline in Firms, Organizations, and States*. Cambridge, MA: Harvard University Press.

Hoffmann-Lange, U. (2018). Methods of Elite Identification. In H. Best & J. Higley, eds., *The Palgrave Handbook of Political Elites*. London: Palgrave Macmillan UK, pp. 79–92.

Hofstadter, R. (2012). *The Paranoid Style in American Politics*. New York, NY: Vintage.

Hood, C. (2006). Gaming in Target World. *Public Administration Review*, 66(4), 515–21.

Hood, C. & Lodge, M. (2006). *The Politics of Public Service Bargains: Reward, Competency, Loyalty – and Blame*. Oxford: Oxford University Press.

Huber, J. D., & Shipan, C. R. (2002). *Deliberate Discretion? The Institutional Foundations of Bureaucratic Autonomy*. Cambridge: Cambridge University Press.

Hunter, W. & Power, T. J. (2019). Bolsonaro and Brazil's Illiberal Backlash. *Journal of Democracy*, 30(1), 68–82.

Hupe, P. (2019). *Research Handbook on Street-Level Bureaucracy.* Cheltenham: Edward Elgar.

Hustedt, T. & Salomonsen, H. H. (2014). Ensuring Political Responsiveness: Politicization Mechanisms in Ministerial Bureaucracies. *International Review of Administrative Sciences*, 80(4), 1–20.

Hüttenberger, P. (1976). Nationalsozialistische Polykratie. *Geschichte und Gesellschaft*, 2(4), 417–42. Available from www.jstor.org/stable/40185021

Ichino, P. (2006). *I nullafacenti.* Milan: Mondadori.

iDNES.cz. (2018). ANO Dělá Veletoče v Dozorčích Radách. Rozdávají Se Trafiky, Tvrdí Opozice. *iDNES.Cz*, April 9. Available from www.idnes.cz/praha/zpravy/ano-dozorci-rady-mestske-firmy-praha-kompetence-zkusenosti.A180409_084258_praha-zpravy_rsr

Illés, G., Körösényi, A. & Metz, R. (2018). Broadening the Limits of Reconstructive Leadership: Constructivist Elements of Viktor Orbán's Regime-Building Politics. *The British Journal of Politics and International Relations*, 20(4), 790–808.

Impacto redacción (2019). Yo tengo otros datos, el desempleo a disminuido: AMLO, *Impacto*, May 17.

INE (2020). (Instituto Nacional de Estadística), *Poverty indicators Database 1998–2013.* Available from www.ine.gob.ve

Ingraham, P. W. (1995). *The Foundation of Merit: Public Service in American Democracy.* Baltimore, MD: Johns Hopkins University Press.

Ingram, H., de Leon, P. & Schneider, A. (2016). Conclusion: Public Policy Theory and Democracy: The Elephant in the Corner. In B. G. Peters & P. Zittoun, eds., *Contemporary Approaches to Public Policy: Theories, Controversies and Perspectives.* London: Palgrave Macmillan, pp. 175–200.

Iturbe, E. (2017). La institucionalidad administrativa de la revolución bolivariana y las políticas públicas. In D. Urbaneja, ed., *Desarmando el modelo. Las transformaciones del sistema político venezolano desde 1999.* Caracas: ABCEdiciones, pp. 195–224.

Jilke, S. & Baekgaard, M. (2020). The Political Psychology of Citizen Satisfaction: Does Functional Responsibility Matter? *Journal of Public Administration Research and Theory*, 30(1), 130–43.

Juárez, M. (2019). Masones reclaman que evangélicos hagan reparto de la Cartilla Moral. *La Razón*, July 8.

Kaltwasser, C. (2015). Explaining the Emergence of Populism in Europe and the Americas. In C. de La Torre, ed., *The Promise and Perils of Populism: Global Perspectives.* Lexington, KY: University Press, pp. 189–227.

Kam, C. & Trussler, M. (2017). At the Nexus of Observational and Experimental Research, Specification, and Analysis of Experiments with Heterogeneous Treatment Effects. *Political Behavior*, 39(4), 789–815.

Katz, Eric. (2019). Mulvaney: Relocating Offices is a "Wonderful Way" to Shed Federal Employees. *Government Executive*, August 15. Available from www.govexec.com/workforce/2019/08/mulvaney-relocating-offices-wonderful-way-shed-federal-employees/158932/

Kenny, P. D. (2017). *Populist and Patronage: Why Populists Win Elections in India, Asia and Beyond*. Oxford: Oxford University Press.

Kettl, D. (2017). *Can Governments Earn Our Trust?* Cambridge: Polity.

Kickert, W. & Ongaro, E. (2019). Influence of EU (and IMF) on Domestic Consolidation and Reform: Introduction. *Public Management Review*, 21(9), 1261–64.

Klijn, E.H. (2016). Managing Commercialised Media Attention in Complex Governance Networks: Positive and Negative Effects on Network Performance, *Policy and Politics*, 44(1), 115–33.

Knill, C. (1999). Explaining Cross-national Variance in Administrative Reform: Autonomous versus Instrumental Bureaucracies. *Journal of Public Policy*, 19(1), 113–39.

Konstytucja (1997). *Konstytucja Rzeczypospolitej Polskiej z dnia 2 kwietnia 1997 r.* (Dz.U. 1997, nr 78, poz. 483).

Kopecký, P., Mair, P., & Spirova, M. (eds.) (2012). *Party Patronage and Party Government in European Democracies*. Oxford: Oxford University Press.

Kopińska, G. (2018). *Stanowiska publiczne jako łup polityczny. Polityka personalna w okresie od 16 listopada 2015 do 31 października 2017 roku*. Warsaw: Fundacja im. Stefana Batorego.

Kordt, E. (1938). The Public Servant in Germany. *Public Administration*, 16(2), 173–84.

Korkut, U. (2012). *Liberalization Challenges in Hungary*. New York, NY: Palgrave Macmillan.

Kornai, J. (2015). Hungary's U-Turn. *Capitalism and Society*, 10(1), 1–24.

Körösényi, A. & Patkós, V. (2017). Liberal and Illiberal Populism. The Leadership of Berlusconi and Orbán. *Corvinus Journal of Sociology and Social Policy*, 8(38), 315–37.

Kovács, É. & Hajnal, G. (2017). Hungary's Central State Administration 1990–2014. In J. Nemec & D. Spacek, eds., *25 Years of Public Administration Developments and Reforms in the V4 Region*. Brno: Masarik University, pp. 48–83.

Krastev, I. (2017). *After Europe*. Philadelphia, PA: University of Pennsylvania Press.

Krauze, E. (2006). El mesías tropical. *Letras Libres*, June.

Krnáčová, A. (2014). Adriana Krnáčová: Žvanit Neumím. Já to Prostě Udělám. *ANO Bude Líp (blog)*. July 10. Available from www.anobude lip.cz/cs/makame/archiv/z-medii/adriana-krnacova-zvanit-neumim.-ja-to-proste-udelam-18708.shtml

Kubicka-Żach, K. (2020). *Urzędnicy: Państwo też powinno chronić miejsca pracy*. Available from www.prawo.pl/samorzad/redukcja-etatow-i-zmnie jszenie-wynagrodzen-w-administracji-maja, 500386.html

Kulcsár, K. (2001). Deviant Bureaucracies. Public Administration in Eastern Europe and in the Developing Countries. In A. Farazmand, ed., *Handbook of Comparative and Development Public Administration*. Public Administration and Public Policy 94, New York, NY: Marcel Dekker, pp. 941–52.

Kuller, C. (2013). *Bürokratie und Verbrechen: Antisemitische Finanzpolitik und Verwaltungspraxis im nationalsozialistischen Deutschland*. Munich: Oldenbourg.

Kullgren, I. (2019). White House Memo Details Divide-and-Conquer Labor Strategy. *Politico*. September 4. Available from www.politico.com/news/2019/10/04/federal-employees-white-house-memo-028954

La Razón (2018). Confirmado: Economía desaparece ProMéxico e Inadem. *La Razón*, December 20.

La redacción Proceso (2019a). Inai ordena a la SEP informar el costo de las 100 universidades "Benito Juárez." *Proceso*, June 17.

La redacción Proceso (2019b). Memorándum contra reforma educativa, fácilmente impugnable: José Ramón Cossío. *Proceso*, April 17.

Lehmbruch, G. (1991). The Organization of Society, Administrative Strategies, and Policy Networks. In R. M. Czada & A. Windhoff-Héritier, eds., *Political Choice: Institutions, Rules, and the Limits of Rationality*. Boulder, CO: Westview Press, pp. 121–55.

Levine, D. (1978). Venezuela since 1958: The Consolidation of Democratic Politics. In J. Linz & A. Stepan, eds., *The Breakdown of Democratic Regimes*. Baltimore, MD: Johns Hopkins University Press, pp. 82–109.

Levine, D. (1989). Venezuela: The Nature, Sources, and Prospects of Democracy. In L. Diamond, J. Linz, & S. Lipset, eds., *Democracy in Developing Countries, Volume 4: Latin America*. Boulder, CO: Westview, pp. 247–89.

Levitsky, S. (2018). Latin America's Shifting Politics: Democratic Survival and Weakness. *Journal of Democracy*, 29(4), 102–13.

Levitsky, S. & Ziblatt, D. (2018a). *How Democracies Die*. New York, NY: Crown Publishing.

Levitsky, S. & Ziblatt, D. (2018b). *How Democracies Die: What History Reveals About Our Future.* London: Viking.

Lewis, D. E. (2007). Testing Pendleton's Premise: Do Political Appointees Make Worse Bureaucrats? *The Journal of Politics,* 69(4), 1073–88.

Lewis, D. E. (2008). *The Politics of Presidential Appointments: Political Control and Bureaucratic Performance.* Princeton, NJ: Princeton University Press.

Lewis, J. (2015). The Politics and Consequences of Performance Measurement. *Policy and Society,* 34(1), 1–12. https://doi.org/10.1016/j.polsoc.2015.03.001

Lewis, M. (2018). *The Fifth Risk.* New York, NY: W.W. Norton & Company.

Light, P. (2017). The True Size of Government: Tracking Washington's Blended Workforce 1984–2015. *Volcker Alliance Issue Paper.* Available from www.volckeralliance.org/publications/true-size-government

Lindblom, C. (1990). *Inquiry and Change.* New Haven, CT: Yale University Press.

Linz, J. (1990). The Perils of Presidentialism. *Journal of Democracy,* 1(1), 51–90.

Linz, J. & Stepan, A. (1996). *Problems of Democratic Transition and Consolidation. Southern Europe, South America, and Post-Communist Europe.* Baltimore, MD: Johns Hopkins University Press.

Lipset, S. M. (1959). Some Social Requisites of Democracy. Economic Development and Political Legitimacy. *American Political Science Review,* 53(1), 69–105.

Lipsky, M. (1980). *Street-Level Bureaucracy: Dilemmas of the Individual in Public Services.* New York, NY: Russell Sage Foundation.

Lipsky, M. (2010). *Street-Level Bureaucracy. Dilemmas of the Individual in Public Services,* expanded ed. New York, NY: Russell Sage Foundation.

Lipton, E., Goodnough, A., Shear, M., et al. (2020). The CDC Waited "Its Entire Existence for this Moment." What Went Wrong? *New York Times,* June 3.

Lipton, E., Haberman, M. & Mazzetti, M. (2019). Inside Ukraine Aid Freeze: An 84-day Clash of Wills. *New York Times,* December 30.

Lipton, E., Vogel, K. & Friedman, L. (2018). EPA Officials Sidelined After Questioning Scott Pruitt. *The New York Times,* April 5.

López, A. (2018). Vocero de AMLO: no desaparecen oficinas de prensa, sólo se reducen. *La Razón,* September 3.

López, C. (2019). En el Gobierno se acabaron los "chapulines fifís," declara AMLO. *La Razón,* February 12.

López, I. (2018). Los "hoyos negros" de la consulta por el aeropuerto en Texcoco o Santa Lucía. *Forbes,* December 31.

López-Ayllón, S. (2019). El memorando y el orden constitucional. *Milenio*, April 17.

López-Obrador, A. M. (2018). Mensaje del Presidente de los Estados Unidos Mexicanos Andrés Manuel López Obrador. Reprinted in *Revista IAPEM*, 101, 155–68.

Lowndes, V., Pratchett, L. & Stoker, G. (2006). Diagnosing and Remedying the Failings of Official Participation Schemes: The CLEAR Framework. *Social Policy and Society*, 5(2), 281–91.

Luce, E. (2017). *The Retreat of Western Liberalism*. New York, NY: Atlantic Monthly Press.

Lührmann, A. & Lindberg, S. (2019). A Third Wave of Autocratization Is Here: What Is New About It? *Democratization*, 26(7), 1095–113.

Lührmann, A., Grahn, S., Morgan, R., Pillai, S. & Lindberg, S. I. (2019). State of the World 2018: Democracy Facing Global Challenges. *Democratization*, 26(6), 895–915.

Lührmann, A., Maerz, S. F., Grahn, S., et al. (2020). *Autocratization Surges – Resistance Grows. Democracy Report 2020*. Varieties of Democracy Institute (V-Dem). Gothenburg. Available from www.v-dem.net/media/filer_public/de/39/de39af54-0bc5-4421-89ae-fb20dcc53dba/democracy_report.pdf

Lührmann, A., Medzihorsky J., Hindle G. & Lindberg, S.I. (2020). New Global Data on Political Parties: V-Party. Briefing Paper #9, October 26 2020. Available from www.v-dem.net/media/filer_public/b6/55/b6553f85-5c5d-45ec-be63-a48a2abe3f62/briefing_paper_9.pdf

Madureira, N. L. (2007). Cartelization and Corporatism: Bureaucratic Rule in Authoritarian Portugal, 1926–45. *Journal of Contemporary History*, 42 (1), 79–96.

Maerz, S. F., Lührmann, A., Hellmeier, S., Grahn, S. & Lindberg, S. I. (2020). State of the World 2019: Autocratization Surges – Resistance Grows. *Democratization*, 27(6), 909–27. https://doi.org/10.1080/13510347.2020.1758670

Mainwaring, S. & Pérez-Liñán, A. (2014). *Democracies and Dictatorships in Latin America: Emergence, Survival, and Fall*. Cambridge: Cambridge University Press.

Mainwaring. S., Bizzarro, F. & Petrova, A. (2018). Party System Institutionalization, Decay and Collapse. In S. Mainwaring, ed., *Party Systems in Latin America: Institutionalization, Decay and Collapse*. Cambridge, MA: Cambridge University Press, pp. 17–33.

Mair, P. (2013). *Ruling the Void: The Hollowing Out of Western Democracy*. London: Verso.

Majer, D. (1987). *Grundlagen des nationalsozialistischen Rechtssystems: Führerprinzip, Sonderrecht, Einheitspartei*. Stuttgart: Kohlhammer.

Majone, G. (2001). Two Logics of Delegation: Agency and Fiduciary Relations in EU Governance. *European Union Politics*, 2(1), 103–22.

Maldonado, M. (2018). AMLO vs. Banxico: jugando con fuego. *El Universal*, September 19.

Maldonado, M. (2019). Crisis en la CNBV; 42 renuncias y contando. *El Universal*, October 7.

Mandavilli, A. (2020). CDC Testing Guidance was Published against Scientist's Objections. *The New York Times*, September 17.

Manow, P. (2018). *Die Politische Ökonomie des Populismus*. Berlin: Suhrkamp.

Manow, P. (2020). *(Ent-)Demokratisierung der Demokratie*. Berlin: Edition Suhrkamp.

March, H. & Ribera-Fumaz, R. (2018). Barcelona: From Corporate Smart City to Technological Sovereignty. In A. Karvonen, F. Cugurullo, & F. Caprotti, eds., *Inside Smart Cities. Place, Politics, and Urban Innovation*. Abingdon; New York, NY: Routledge, pp. 229–43.

Martínez, L. (2018). ¿Qué dice el decreto de la Ley de Salarios Máximos de los funcionarios públicos? *El Economista*, November 5.

Mattei, P. (2007). Italian Democracy Under Threat? The Spoils System in Historical Perspective. In E.C. Page & V. Wright, eds., *From the Active to the Enabling State: The Changing Role of Top Officials in European Nations*. Basingstoke, UK: Palgrave, pp. 81–98.

Mayer, J. (2019). The Making of the Fox News White House. *The New Yorker*, March 4.

Mazur, S. & Hausner, J. (2010). Aparat administracyjny państwa jako agent zmiany. In W. Morawski, ed., *Modernizacja Polski: struktury, agencje, instytucje*. Warsaw: Wydawnictwa Akademickie i Profesjonalne; Akademia Leona Koźmińskiego, pp. 382–401.

Mazur, S. (ed.) (2020). *Public Administration in Central Europe: Ideas as Causes of Reforms*. London: Routledge.

Mazur, S., Możdżeń, M. & Oramus, M. (2018). The Instrumental and Ideological Politicisation of Senior Positions in Poland's Civil Service and its Selected Consequences. *NISPAcee Journal of Public Administration and Policy, Sciendo*, 11(1), 63–89.

McDermott, R. (2002). Experimental Methodology in Political Science. *Political Analysis*, 10(4), 325–42.

Meier, K. J. (1993): Representative Bureaucracy: A Theoretical and Empirical Exposition. In J. L. Perry, ed., *Research in Public Administration*. Vol. 2, Greenwich, CT: JAI Press, pp. 1–35.

Meier, K. J. & O'Toole, L. J. (2006). *Bureaucracy in a Democratic State. A Governance Perspective*. Baltimore, MD: Johns Hopkins University Press.

Mejía, X. & I. González (2019). Germán Martínez renuncia al IMSS; denuncia política de recortes y despidos. *Excélsior*, May 22.

Mele, V. & Ongaro, E. (2014). Public Sector Reform in a Context of Political Instability: Italy 1992–2007. *International Public Management Journal*, 17(1), 111–42.

Méndez, J. L. (1997). The Latin American Administrative Tradition. In J. M. Shafritz, ed., *International Encyclopedia of Public Policy and Administration*. Boulder, CO: Westview, pp. 1254–1261.

Méndez, J. L. & Dussauge-Laguna, M. I. (2017). Introduction. In J. L. Méndez & M. I. Dussauge-Laguna, eds., *Policy Analysis in Mexico*. Bristol: Policy Press, pp. 1–8.

Mény, Y. & Surel, Y. (eds.) (2002). *Democracies and the Populist Challenge*. Basingstoke: Macmillan.

Merino, M. (2013). La captura de los puestos públicos. *Revista Mexicana de Ciencias Políticas y Sociales*, 58(219), 135–56.

Merkel, W., Puhle, H.-J., Croissant, A., Eicher, C. & Thiery, P. (2003). *Defekte Demokratie. Band 1: Theorie*. Opladen: Leske+Budrich.

Metro News. (2016). Raggi: noi facciamo quello che diciamo. *Metro news*, June 14. Available from www.metronews.it/16/06/14/raggi-noi-facciamo-quello-che-diciamo.html.

Meyer-Sahling, J. H. (2011). The Durability of EU Civil Service Policy in Central and Eastern Europe after Accession. *Governance*, 24(2), 231–60.

Meyer-Sahling, J. H. & Jáger, K. (2012). Party Patronage in Hungary: Capturing the State. In P. Kopecký, P. Mair, & M. Spirova, eds., *Party Patronage and Party Government in European Democracies*. Oxford: Oxford University Press, pp. 163–185.

Meyer-Sahling, J.-H. & Veen, T. (2012). Governing the Post-Communist State: Government Alternation and Senior Civil Service Politicisation in Central and Eastern Europe. *East European Politics*, 28(1), 4–22. https://doi.org/10.1080/13523279.2011.635651

Michels, R. (1915). *Political Parties: A Sociological Study of the Oligarchical Tendencies of Modern Democracy*. New York, NY: Hearst Library.

Middendorf, S. (2015). Finanzpolitische Fundamente der Demokratie? Haushaltsordnung, Ministerialbürokratie und Staatsdenken in der Weimarer Republik. In T. B. Müller & A. Tooze, eds., *Normalität und Fragilität: Demokratie nach dem Ersten Weltkrieg*. Hamburg: Hamburger Edition HIS, pp. 315–43.

Miranda, P. (2019). Recortes presupuestales afectan a 3 mil 500 pacientes del Instituto Nacional de Cancerología. *El Universal*, May 24.

Miranda, F. & Guerrero, K. (2020). Gobierno federal desaparece subsecretarías como medida de austeridad ante covid-19. *Milenio*. August 28.

Moe, T. M. (1985). The Politicized Presidency. In J. Chubb & Paul E. Peterson, eds., *The New Direction in American Politics*. Washington, DC: Brookings Institution, pp. 235–71.

Mommsen, H. (1973). Die Stellung der Beamtenschaft in Reich, Ländern und Gemeinden in der Ära Brüning. *Vierteljahreshefte für Zeitgeschichte*, 21(2), 151–65.

Mommsen, H. (2010). *Beamtentum im Dritten Reich*. Munich: Oldenbourg Wissenschaftsverlag.

Monroy, L. A. (2019). Políticas públicas: Transferencias con pies de barro. *Nexos*, September 1.

Morales, A. (2019). Aunque me digan mesiánico voy a purificar el país: AMLO, *El Universal*, January 21.

Morales, A. (2020). AMLO pide a funcionarios "lealtad ciega" al proyecto de transformación. *El Universal*, September 24.

Morales, A. & Zavala, M. (2019). AMLO da estructura a superdelegados. *El Universal*, March 20.

Moreno, D. (2019). Derecho a saber. *Reforma*, January 20.

Morgan, E. P. & Perry, J. L. (1988). Re-orienting the Comparative Study of Civil Service Systems. *Review of Public Personnel Administration*, 8(3), 84–95.

Morlino, L. & Tarchi, M. (1996). The Dissatisfied Society: The Roots of Political Change in Italy. *European Journal of Political Research*, 30(1), 41–63.

Mosca, L. (2014). The Five Star Movement: Exception or Vanguard in Europe? *The International Spectator*, 49(1), 36–52. https://doi.org/10.10 80/03932729.2013.875821

Mosca, L. & Tronconi, F. (2019). Beyond Left and Right: The Eclectic Populism of the Five Star Movement. *West European Politics*, 42(6), 1258–83.

Mounk, Y. (2018). *The People vs. Democracy. Why Our Freedom is in Danger and How to Save It*. Cambridge, MA: Harvard University Press.

Mouritzen, P. E. & Svara, J. (2012). *Leadership at the Apex: Politicians and Administrators in Western Local Governments*. Pittsburgh: University of Pittsburgh Press.

Moynihan, D. P. (2005). Homeland Security and the US Public Management Policy Agenda. *Governance*, 18(2), 171–96.

Moynihan, D. P. & Roberts, A. (2010). The Triumph of Loyalty Over Competence: The Bush Administration and the Exhaustion of the Politicized Presidency. *Public Administration Review*, 70(4), 572–81.

Mudde, C. (2004). The Populist Zeitgeist. *Government and Opposition*, 39 (4), 541–63. https://doi.org/10.1111/j.1477-7053.2004.00135.x

Mudde, C. (2016). *On Extremism and Democracy in Europe*. London: Routledge.

Mudde, C. (2017). *"Populism." Three Conversations about the Rise of Populism in the West*. Background papers prepared for the GAC/POR "Fast Talk" Teleconference on Populism in the West & the International Order.

Mudde, C. (2017). Populism. An Ideational Approach. In C. Rovira Kaltwasser, P. Taggart, P. Ocoa Espejo, & P. Ostiguy, eds., *The Oxford Handbook of Populism*. Oxford: Oxford University Press, pp. 27–47.

Mudde, C. (2019). *The Far Right Today*, Cambridge: Polity Press.

Mudde, C. & Rovira Kaltwasser, C. (2013). Exclusionary vs. Inclusionary Populism: Comparing Contemporary Europe and Latin America. *Government and Opposition*, 48(2), 147–74.

Mudde, C. & Rovira Kaltwasser, C. (2017). *Populism: A Very Short Introduction*. Oxford; New York, NY: Oxford University Press.

Muédano, M. (2019). Gobierno Federal sumó, en siete meses, casi medio millón de despidos. *La silla rota*. October 1.

Müller, J.-W. (2016a). *Was ist Populismus?, Ein Essay*. Berlin: Suhrkamp Verlag.

Müller, J.-W. (2016b). *What Is Populism?* Philadelphia, PA: University of Pennsylvania Press.

Müller, J.-W. (2017). *What Is Populism?* London: Penguin.

Muno, W. (2005). Öl und Demokratie – Venezuela im 20. Jahrhundert. In O. Diehl & W. Muno, eds., *Venezuela unter Chávez – Aufbruch oder Niedergang?* Frankfurt: Vervuert, pp. 11–34.

Muno, W. (2015). ALBA, UNASUR und CELAC. In A. Grimmel & C. Jakobeit, eds., *Regionale Integration. Erklärungsansätze und Analysen zu den wichtigsten Integrationszusammenschlüssen in der Welt*. Baden-Baden: Nomos, pp. 412–431.

Nery, N., Seabra, C. & Franco, B. M. (2011). Cúpula Do PT Defende Controle Da Mídia. *Folha de São Paulo*. Available from www1.folha.uol .com.br/fsp/poder/po0209201112.htm

Neuhold, C., Vanhoonacker, S. & L. Verhey (2013). *Civil Servants and Politics: The Delicate Balance*. Basingstoke: Macmillan.

Niskanen, W. A. (1971). *Bureaucracy and Representative Government*. Chicago, IL and New York, NY: Aldine-Atherton.

Nistotskaya, M. & Cingolani, L. (2016). Bureaucratic Structure, Regulatory Quality, and Entrepreneurship in a Comparative Perspective: Cross-Sectional and Panel Data Evidence. *Journal of Public Administration Research and Theory*, 26(3), 519–34. https://doi.org/10 .1093/jopart/muv026

Norden, D. (2008). Assessing Venezuelan Political-Military Relations Under Chávez. *Nueva Sociedad*, 213(8), 170–87.

Nordlinger, E. A. (1981). *On the Autonomy of the Democratic State.* Cambridge, MA: Harvard University Press.

Norris, P. (ed.) (1999). *Critical Citizens: Global Support for Democratic Governance.* Oxford: Oxford University Press.

Norris, P. & Inglehart, R. (2019). *Cultural Backlash: Trump, Brexit, and Authoritarian Populism.* Cambridge: Cambridge University Press.

Nunes, F. & Melo, C. R. (2017). Impeachment, Crisis Política y Democracia En Brasil. *Revista de Ciencia Política*, 37(2), 281–304.

Nützenadel, A. (ed.) (2017). *Das Reichsarbeitsministerium im Nationalsozialismus. Verwaltung – Politik – Verbrechen.* Göttingen: Wallstein Verlag.

O Antagonista. (2020). Com só 12 inscritos, plano de Aras para a Lava Jato fracassa. *O Antagonista.* Available from www.oantagonista.com/brasil/c om-so-12-inscritos-plano-de-aras-para-a-lava-jato-fracassa/

O'Donnell, G. (1979). *Modernization and Bureaucratic Authoritarianism.* Berkeley, CA: Berkeley University Press.

O'Donnell, G. (2011). Nuevas reflexiones acerca de la democracia delegativa. In G. O'Donnell, O. Iazzetta, & H. Quiroga, eds., *Democracia Delegativa.* Buenos Aires: Prometeo, pp. 19–35.

OECD (2001). *Citizens as Partners. OECD Handbook on Information, Consultation and Public Participation in Decision-making.* Paris: OECD Publishing.

OECD (2017). *Trust and Public Policy: How Better Governance Can Help Rebuild Public Trust, OECD Public Governance Reviews.* Paris: OECD Publishing. https://doi.org/10.1787/9789264268920-en

O'Leary, R. (2006). *The Ethics of Dissent: Managing Guerilla Government.* Washington, DC: CQ Press.

O'Leary, R. (2017). The Ethics of Dissent: Can President Trump Survive Guerrilla Government? *Administrative Theory & Praxis*, 39(2), 63–79.

O'Leary, R. (2020). *The Ethics of Dissent: Managing Guerrilla Government*, 3rd ed. Washington, DC: Congressional Quarterly Press.

Oliveira, M. (2020). Veja a íntegra do abaixo-assinado que questiona nomeação de Aras. *Congresso em Foco.* Available from https://congressoemfoco.uol .com.br/judiciario/procuradores-manifestam-insatisfacao-com-aras-e-promovem-abaixo-assinado/

O'Toole, L. J. (1997). Treating Networks Seriously: Practical and Research-Based Agendas in Public Administration. *Public Administration Review*, 57(1), 45–52.

Olsson, J. (2016). *Subversion in Institutional Change and Stability: A Neglected Mechanism.* London: Palgrave.

Ongaro, E. (ed.) (2006). *Le Agenzie Pubbliche: Modelli Istituzionali ed Organizzativi.* Soveria Mannelli: Rubbettino.

Ongaro, E., (ed.) (2008). *L'organizzazione dello Stato tra autonomia e policy capacity.* Soveria Mannelli: Rubbettino.

Ongaro, E. (2009). *Public Management Reform and Modernization: Trajectories of Administrative Change in Italy, France, Greece, Portugal, Spain.* Cheltenham and Northampton, MA: Edward Elgar.

Ongaro, E. (2010). The Napoleonic Administrative Tradition and Public Management Reform in France, Greece, Italy, Portugal, Spain. In M. Painter & B.G. Peters, eds., *Tradition and Public Administration.* Basingstoke: Palgrave MacMillan, pp. 174–90.

Ongaro, E. (2011). The Role of Politics and Institutions in the Italian Administrative Reform Trajectory. *Public Administration*, 89(3), 738–55.

Ongaro, E. (2018). The Napoleonic Tradition in Public Administration. In W. Thompson, ed., *Oxford Research Encyclopaedia of Politics.* Oxford: Oxford University Press.

Ongaro, E. (2020). *Philosophy and Public Administration: An Introduction*, 2nd ed. Cheltenham and Northampton, MA: Edward Elgar.

Ongaro, E. & Bellé, N. (2010). Réforme de la fonction publique et introduction de la rémunération liée aux performances en Italie: évidence empirique, interprétations et enseignements. *Revue Française d'Administration Publique*, 132(2010), 817–39.

Ongaro, E., Ferré, F., Galli, D. & Longo, F. (2016). Italy: Set Along a Neo-Weberian Trajectory of Administrative Reform? In G. Hammerschmid, S. Van de Walle, R. Andrews, & P. Bezes, eds., *Public Administration Reforms in Europe: The View from the Top.* Cheltenham, UK and Northampton, MA: Edward Elgar, pp. 185–93.

Ongaro, E. & Kickert, W. (2020). EU-driven Public Sector Reforms. *Public Policy and Administration*, 35(29), 117–34. https://doi.org/10.1177/0952076719827624.

Ongaro, E. & Valotti, G. (2008). Public Management Reform in Italy: Explaining the Implementation Gap. *The International Journal of Public Sector Management*, 21(2), 174–204.

Oppelt, R. (2016). Zeptali Jsme Se Opozice, Jak Hodnotí Vládnutí Primátorky Adriany Krnáčové, *Metro.cz*, November 3. Available from www.metro.cz/hodnoceni-adriany-krnacove-ddt-/praha.aspx?c=A161102_231449_praha-metro_lupo

Otto, P. & Thuong Ly, N. (2018). Stavěla Bych, Až Bych Brečela. Ale Nemohu, Říká Primátorka Adriana Krnáčová. *E15.Cz*, March 28. Available from www.e15.cz/rozhovory/stavela-bych-az-bych-brecela-ale-nemohu-rika-primatorka-adriana-krnacova-1344677

Overeem, P. (2005). The Value of the Dichotomy: Politics, Administration, and the Political Neutrality of Administrators. *Administrative Theory & Praxis*, 27(2), 311–29.

Paczocha, J. (2018). *Raport Partia w Państwie. Bezprecedensowa wymiana kadr w administracji rządowej i jej legislacyjne podstawy*. Warsaw: FOR.

Pakulski, J. (2016). Crumbling Elite Consensus and the Illiberal Turn in Poland. In J. Pakulski, ed., *The Visegrad Countries Crisis*. Warsaw: Collegium Civitas, pp. 51–65.

Panizza, F., Peters B. G., & Ramos Larraburu, C. R. (2019). Roles, Trust and Skills: A Typology of Patronage Appointments. *Public Administration*, 97 (1), 147–61. https://doi.org/10.1111/padm.12560

Pantoja, S. (2017). AMLO defiende alianza con el PES y asegura que respeta la diversidad sexual. *Proceso*, December 15.

Pap, A. L. (2017). *Democratic Decline in Hungary: Law and Society in an Illiberal Democracy*. New York, NY: Routledge.

Papadopoulos, Y. (2002). Populism, the Democratic Question, and Contemporary Governance. In Y. Mény & Y. Surel, eds., *Democracies and the Populist Challenge*. Basingstoke: Palgrave-Macmillan, pp. 45–61.

Papadopoulos, Y. (2007). Populizm, demokracja i współczesny model rządzenia. In Y. Mény & Y. Surel, eds., *Demokracja w obliczu populizmu*. Warsaw: Oficyna Naukowa, pp. 86–7.

Pappas, T. S. (2019). Populists in Power. *Journal of Democracy*, 30(2), 70–84.

Pardo, M. C. (2020). El Desdén por la Administración Pública. In Johanna Cilano & Ramiro Sánchez (eds.), *El México de la 4T*. Transparencia Electoral – GAPAC, pp. 147–164.

Paredes, M. (2018). Sectur desparece el Consejo de Promoción Turística de México. *Excélsior*, December 7.

Parker, A. & Rucker, P. (2017). Trump Taps Kushner to Lead a SWAT Team to Fix Government with Business Ideas. *Washington Post*, March 26. www.washingtonpost.com/politics/trump-taps-kushner-to-lead-a-swat-te am-to-fix-government-with-business-ideas/2017/03/26/9714a8b6-1254-11e7-ada0-1489b735b3a3_story.html

Paxton, F. (2020). Towards a Populist Local Democracy? The Consequences of Populist Radical Right Local Government Leadership in Western Europe. *Representation*, 56(6), 411–30.

Penfold-Becerra, M. (2007). Clientelism and Social Funds: Evidence from Chávez's Misiones. *Latin American Politics and Society*, 49(4), 63–84.

Pérez de Acha, L. (2019). El desgobierno de López Obrador. *The New York Times*, May 27.

Pérez-Liñán, A. (2018). Impeachment or Backsliding? Threats to Democracy in the Twenty-first Century. *Revista Brasileira de Ciências Sociais*, 33(98), 1–15.

Perrone, M. (2020). Nuovo Concorsone al Comune Di Roma: 1.512 Posti a Bando in Primavera. *Sole 24 Ore*, 2020. Available from www.ilsole24ore.com/art/nuovo-concorsone-comune-roma-1512-posti-bando-primavera-ACLzlhCB

Perry, J. L., Hondeghem, A. & Wise, L.R. (2010). Revisiting the Motivational Bases of Public Service: Twenty Years of Research and an Agenda for the Future. *Public Administration Review*, 70(5), 681–90.

Peters, B. G. (1988). *Comparing Public Bureaucracies: Problems of Theory and Method*. Tuscaloosa, AL: Alabama University of Alabama Press.

Peters, B. G. (2008). The Napoleonic Tradition. *International Journal of Public Sector Management*, 21(2), 118–32.

Peters, B. G. (2013). Politicization of the Civil Service: What is it and Why do we Care? In C. Neuhold, S. Vanhoonacker, & L. Verhey, eds., *Civil Servants and Politics: The Delicate Balance*. Basingstoke: Macmillan, pp. 12–24.

Peters, B. G. (2018a). *The Politics of Bureaucracy: An Introduction to Comparative Public Administration*, 7th ed. New York: Routledge.

Peters, B. G. (2018b). Comparative Politics and Comparative Policy Studies: Making the Linkage. *Journal of Comparative Policy Analysis*, 20(1), 88–100.

Peters, B. G. (2019). *Institutional Theory in Political Science: The New Institutionalism*, 4th ed. Cheltenham: Edward Elgar.

Peters, B. G. (2020). *Administrative Traditions: Understanding the Roots of Contemporary Administrative Behavior*. Oxford: Oxford University Press.

Peters, B. G. & Pierre, J. (2017). Two Roads to Nowhere: Appraising 30 Years of Public Administration Research. *Governance*, 30(1), 11–16.

Peters, B. G. & Pierre, J. (2019). Populism and Public Administration: Confronting the Administrative State. *Administration and Society*, 51(10), 1521–45.

Peters, B. G. & Pierre, J. (2020). A Typology of Populism: Understanding the Different Forms of Populism and Their Implications. *Democratization*, 27(6), 928–946.

Peters, B. G., Ramos, C. & Alba, C. (Forthcoming). *Handbook of Public Administration in Latin America*. Bingley: Emerald Publishing.

Pettypiece, S. (2020). DHS Faces Coronavirus with Scores of Vacancies and a Leadership Vacuum. *NBC News*, March 16. Available from www.nbcnews.com/politics/white-house/dhs-faces-coronavirus-scores-vacancies-leadership-vacuum-n1160946

Pezzi, M. G. (2019). "Mafia Capitale": Judicial and Symbolic Constructions of the New Italian Corruption. *Journal of Modern Italian Studies*, 24(3), 512–30. https://doi.org/10.1080/1354571X.2019.1576417

Pierre, J. & Peters, B. G. (2004). Politicization of the Civil Service: Concepts, Causes, Consequences. In B. G. Peters & J. Pierre, eds., *The Politicization of the Civil Service in Comparative Perspective*. New York, NY: Routledge, pp. 13–25.

Pierre, J. & Peters, B. G. (2017). The Shirking Bureaucrat: A Theory in Search of Evidence? *Policy & Politics*, 45(2), 157–72.

Pierson, P. (2017). American Hybrid: Donald Trump and the Strange Merger of Populism and Plutocracy. *British Journal of Sociology*, 68(S1), S105–19. https://doi.org/10.1111/1468-4446.12323

PiS (2014). *Program Prawa i Sprawiedliwości 2014. "Zdrowie Praca Rodzina."* Available from http://pis.org.pl/dokumenty

PiS (2019). *Program Prawa i Sprawiedliwości 2019 "Polski Model Państwa Dobrobytu."* Available from http://pis.org.pl/dokumenty

Plumer, B. & Davenport, C. (2019). Science under Attack: How Trump Is Sidelining Researchers and their Work. *The New York Times*, December 28.

Polga-Hecimovich, J. (2019). Bureaucratic Polarization, Partisan Attachments, and the Limits of Public Agency Legitimacy: The Venezuelan Armed Forces under Chavismo. *Latin American Research Review*, 54(2), 476–498.

políticomx (2018). Santa Lucía gana consulta de AMLO: ahí será el NAICM. *políticomx*, October 28.

Pollitt, C. & Bouckaert, G. (2004). *Public Management Reform*, 2nd ed. Oxford: Oxford University Press.

Pollitt, C. & Bouckaert, G. (2017). *Public Management Reform*, 4th ed. Oxford: Oxford University Press.

Popper, K. (1962). *The Open Society and Its Enemies*, 4th ed. London: Routledge.

Postel, C. (2007). *The Populist Vision*, Oxford: Oxford University Press.

Pracodawcy (2018). *Pracodawcy apelują do prezydenta o ratowanie dialogu.* Available from http://konfederacjalewiatan.pl/aktualnosci/2018/1/pracodawcy_apeluja_do_prezydenta_o_ratowanie_dialogu

Pracodawcy, R. P. (2019). *Siedem grzechów głównych stanowienia prawa w Polsce, Edycja III, kwiecień 2018 r. – październik 2019 r.* Available from https://pracodawcyrp.pl/opinie-raporty/raport-siedem-grzechow-glownych-stanowienia-prawa

Pražský deník. (2015). Radní schválili změny na magistrátu. Bude se i propouštět. *Pražský deník*, March 17. Available from https://prazsky

.denik.cz/zpravy_region/radni-schvalili-zmeny-na-magistratu-bude-se-i-propoustet-20150317.html

Pressman, J. L. & Wildavsky, A. B. (1984). *Implementation*, 3rd ed. Berkeley, CA: University of California Press.

Przeworski, A. (2019). *Crises of Democracy*. Cambridge: Cambridge University Press.

Przeworski, A., Alvarez, M., Cheibub, J. A. & Limongi, F. (2000). *Democracy and Development. Political Institutions and Well-being in the World, 1950–1990*. Cambridge: Cambridge University Press.

Puente, K. (2020). Mexico: The Rise of Presidential Populism and the Decline of Congress. In I. Khmelko, F. Stapenhurst, & M. Mezey, eds., *Legislative Decline in the 21st Century*. London: Routledge, pp. 158–69.

Radwan, A. (2018). Zamiast specjalisty dyrektor. To skutek reformy PiS w służbie cywilnej, *"Gazeta Prawna,"* August 27. Available from http://serwisy.gazetaprawna.pl/praca-i-kariera/artykuly/1107652,specjaliste-zwolnic-a-na-jego-miejscu-posadzic-dyrek-tora.html

Radwan, A. (2020). *Kuźnia urzędników wykuwa coraz słabiej. Spada liczba kandydatów do KSAP*. Available from https://forsal.pl/gospodarka/aktualnosci/artykuly/7779738, kuznia-urzednikow-wykuwa-coraz-slabiej-spada-liczba-kandydatow-do-ksap.html

Ramírez, L. (2020). *Efectos de un contexto de erosión democrática en las estrategias de reforma a las instituciones de la administración pública: el caso de la Secretaría de Bienestar, 2018–2020*. CIDE, MPA Dissertation.

Rauch, J. & Evans, P. (2000). Bureaucratic Structure and Bureaucratic Performance in Less Developed Countries. *Journal of Public Economics*, 75(1), 49–71.

Rebentisch, D. (1989). Verfassungswandel und Verwaltungsstaat vor und nach der nationalsozialistischen Machtergreifung. In J. Heideking, G. Hufnagel & F. Knipping, eds., *Wege in die Zeitgeschichte. Festschrift zum 65. Geburtstag von Gerhard Schulz*. Berlin: de Gruyter, pp. 123–150.

Redacción (2019). En materia educativa, López Obrador dice que prefiere la justicia sobre las leyes. *El Economista*, April 17.

Redacción Animal Político (2019a). AMLO otorga el 74% de los contratos por adjudicación directa al igual que EPN y Calderón. *Animal Político*, July 8.

Redacción Animal Político (2019b). Por qué AMLO dice que hay una mafia de la ciencia y cómo impacta en las contrataciones en Conacyt. *Animal Político*, February 15.

Redacción/LP (2019). Recortes a Conacyt pueden colapsar centros de investigación en México: investigadores. *Aristegui Noticias*, May 22.

Reichardt, S. & Seibel, W. (2011). Radikalität und Stabilität. Herrschen und Verwalten im Nationalsozialismus. In S. Reichardt & W. Seibel, eds., *Der prekäre Staat. Herrschen und Verwalten im Nationalsozialismus.* Frankfurt: Campus Verlag, pp. 7–28.

Rein, L. & Philip, A. (2017). Help Wanted: Why Republicans Won't Work for the Trump Administration. *Washington Post*, June 27.

Rein, L., Dawsey, J. & T. Olorunnipa. (2020). Trump's Historic Assault on the Civil Service Was Four Years in the Making. *Washington Post*, October 23.

Report (2019). *Report CG36(2019)13 final 2 2019. April Local and Regional Democracy in Poland.* Committee on the Honouring of Obligations and Commitments by member States of the European Charter of Local Self-Government (Monitoring Committee). David BARO RIBA, Andorra (L, NR) Pascal MANGIN, France (R, EPP/CCE). Available from https://rm.coe.int/local-and-regional-democracy-in-poland-monitoring-committee-rapporteur/1680939003

Reporte índigo (2019). Banco Azteca tendrá manejo de tarjetas del bienestar por invitación de AMLO y sin contrato. *Reporte índigo*, January 17.

Resh, W.G. (2015). *Rethinking the Administrative Presidency: Trust, Intellectual Capital, and Appointee-careerist Relations in the George W. Bush Administration.* Baltimore, MD: Johns Hopkins University Press.

Rey, J. (1976). Ideología y Cultura Política: El Caso del Populismo Latinoamericano. *Revista Politeia*, 5, 123–50.

Rey, J. (2009). *Temas de formación sociopolítica: El sistema de partidos venezolano, 1830–1999.* Caracas: UCAB Publications.

Roberts, A. (2019). Shaking Hands with Hitler: The Politics-Administration Dichotomy and Engagement with Fascism. *Public Administration Review*, 79(2), 267–76.

Rockman, B. A. (2019). Bureaucracy between Populism and Technocracy. *Administration and Society*, 51(10), 1546–75.

Rodríguez, A. (2018). AMLO critica al INAI, INEE y organismos energéticos: son ejemplo de obesidad burocrática. *Proceso*, December 7.

Rodríguez-Pose, A. (2017). The Revenge of the Places That Don't Matter (and What to Do About It). *Cambridge Journal of Regions, Economy and Society*, 11(1), 189–209. https://doi.org/10.1093/cjres/rsx024

Rodríguez-Pose, A., Lee, N., & Lipp C. (2020). Golfing with Trump: Social Capital, Decline, Inequality and the Rise of Populism in the US. *Papers in Economic Geography and Spatial Economics*, Paper No. 14, 1–36.

Rogers, K. (2020). Trump Now Claims he Always Knew the Coronavirus Would Be a Pandemic. *New York Times*, March 17.

Rohr, J. A. (1986). *To Run A Constitution: The Legitimacy of The Administrative State.* Lawrence, KS: University Press of Kansas.

Rosagel, S. (2019). AMLO llama "hampa del periodismo" a columnistas. *El Imparcial*, May 23.

Rosas, O. (2019). Con 18, 147 siervos, AMLO construye un censo bajo sospecha de sesgo. *Expansión Política*. July 24.

Rosenbloom, D. (2008). The Politics–Administration Dichotomy in US Historical Context. *Public Administration Review*, 68(1), 57–60.

Rovira Kaltwasser, C. & Taggart, P. (2016). Dealing with Populists in Government: A Framework for Analysis. *Democratization*, 23(2), 201–20.

Rovira Kaltwasser C., Taggart, P., Espejo, P. O. & Ostiguy, P. (eds.) (2017). *Oxford Handbook of Populism*. Oxford: Oxford University Press.

Rubio, L. (2019). Paso a paso . . . . *Reforma*, October 13.

Rucker, P. & Costa, R. (2017). Bannon vows a daily fight for "deconstruction of the administrative state." *Washington Post*, February 23.

Rucker, P. & Leonnig, C. (2020). *A Very Stable Genius: Donald J. Trump's Testing of America*. New York, NY: Bloomsbury.

Runciman, D. (2018). *How Democracy Ends*. London: Profile books.

Rupnik, J. (2007). Is East-Central Europe Backsliding? From Democracy Fatigue to Populist Backlash. *Journal of Democracy*, 18(4), 17–25.

Sager, F. & Rosser, C. (2009). Weber, Wilson, and Hegel: Theories of Modern Bureaucracy. *Public Administration Review*, 69(6), 1136–47.

Santos, F. & Guarnieri, F. (2016). From Protest to Parliamentary Coup: An Overview of Brazil's Recent History. *Journal of Latin American Cultural Studies*, 25(4), 485–94.

Sassen, S. (2000). *Cities in a World Economy*, 2nd ed. New York, NY: SAGE Publications.

Savoie, D. J. (1999). *Governing from the Centre: The Concentration of Power in Canadian Politics*. Toronto: University of Toronto Press.

Savoie, D. J. (2008). *Court Government and the Collapse of Accountability in Canada and the United Kingdom*. Toronto: University of Toronto Press.

Scheiring, G. (2019). Dependent Development and Authoritarian State Capitalism: Democratic Backsliding and the Rise of the Accumulative State in Hungary. *Geoforum*, Online first. https://doi.org/10.1016/j.geoforum.2019.08.011

Schmitter, P. (1971). *Interest Conflict and Political Change in Brazil*. Stanford, CA: Stanford University Press.

Schmitter, P. (1972). La Portugalización de Brasil. *Estudios Internacionales*, 5(19), 3–55.

Schmitter, P. C. (1975). *Corporatism and Public Policy in Authoritarian Portugal*. London: Sage Publishing.

Scholz-Paulus, S., Strobel, B., Vedder, S. & Veit, S. (2020). *Die Politisch-Administrative Elite der Weimarer Republik am 1. September 1920*.

Randauszählungen zu Elitestudien des Fachgebiets Public Management der Universität Kassel, volume 2. Kassel.

Schröter, E. (1993). Was trennt Bürokraten in einer vereinten Bürokratie? Einstellungen und Werthaltungen (Ost- und West-) Berliner Verwaltungsführungskräfte. In G.-J. Glaeßner, ed., *Der lange Weg zur Einheit.* Berlin: Dietz. S. 247–74.

SDPnoticias. (2018). Critica AMLO altos sueldos y pocos resultados en el INAI. *SDPnoticias,* December 7.

Seawright, J. & Gerring, J. (2008). Case Selection Techniques in Case Study Research A Menu of Qualitative and Quantitative Options. *Political Research Quarterly,* 61(2), 294–308.

Sebők, M., Kubik, B. & Molnár C. (2017). *A törvények formális minősége: Empirikus vázlat.* In Z. Boda & Szabó, A., eds., *Trendek a magyar politikában 2. A Fidesz és a többiek: pártok, mozgalmak, politikák.* Budapest: Napvilág Kiadó, pp. 285–310.

Senado Federal. (2014). Na Câmara, Decreto de Dilma é Chamado de Autoritário e Antidemocrático. *Senado Federal.* Available from www12 .senado.leg.br/noticias/materias/2014/10/29/em-disputa-politica-pos-eleicoes-camara-aprova-derrubada-do-decreto-de-dilma

SGI (2018). *Governance. Sustainable Policies. Democracy. Policy Performance and Governance Capacities in the OECD and EU.* Sustainable Governance *Indicators 2018.* Gütersloh: Bertelsmann Stiftung.

SGI (2019). *Governance. Sustainable Policies. Democracy. Poland Report. Sustainable Governance Indicators 2019.* Gütersloh: Bertelsmann Stiftung.

Shalders, A. (2020). A ofensiva contra a Lava Jato que "une" esquerdistas, bolsonaristas e Augusto Aras. *BBC News Brasil,* August 6. Available from www.bbc.com/portuguese/brasil-53676271

Shaw, R. & Eichbaum, C. (2018). Introduction: Ministers, Minders and Mandarins. In R. Shaw & C. Eichbaum, eds., *Ministers, Minders and Mandarins. An International Study of Relationships at the Executive Summit of Parliamentary Democracies.* Cheltenham: Edward Elgar Publishing, pp. 1–14.

Shepsle, K. A. & Bonchek, M. S. (2007). *Analyzing Politics – Rationality, Behavior, and Institutions,* New York, NY: Norton.

Silberman, B. (1993). *Cages of Reason: The Rise of the Rational State in France, Japan, the United States, and Great Britain.* Chicago, IL: Chicago University Press.

Silva-Herzog Márquez, J. (2018). La tenacidad de López Obrador. El *País,* June 26.

Sina, Y. (2016a). Quattro pilastri per 58 azioni, Roma presenta la sua strategia per diventare resiliente. *RomaToday*, July 18. Available from www.romatoday.it/politica/progetto-roma-citta-resiliente.html

Sina, Y. (2016b). Comune, l'annuncio di Raggi: "Pronta la riforma della macchina amministrativa." *RomaToday*, November 10. Available from www.romatoday.it/politica/riforma-macchina-amministrativa-virginia-raggi.html

Sina, Y. (2016c). Raggi ridisegna il Campidoglio: ruotano i dirigenti, spuntano nuovi dipartimenti. *RomaToday*, December 10. Available from www.romatoday.it/politica/riforma-campidoglio-dipartimenti-diri genti-cosa-cambia.html

Skaaning, S.-E. (2020). Waves of Autocratization and Democratization: A Critical Note on Conceptualization and Measurement. *Democratization*, 1–10, online first. https://doi.org/10.1080/13510347.2020.1799194

Skocpol, T. (1979). *States and Social Revolutions: A Comparative Analysis of France, Russia & China*. Cambridge: Cambridge University Press.

Skocpol, T. (1985). Bringing the State Back In: Strategies of Analysis in Current Research. In P. B. Evans, D. Rueschemayer, & T. Skocpol, eds., *Bringing the State Back*. Cambridge: Cambridge University Press, pp. 3–37.

Sonntag, H. (1988). Estado y desarrollo sociopolítico en Venezuela. *Síntesis*, 5, 97–142.

Sontheimer, K. (1999). Die Kurze Demokratie. *Der Spiegel*, 53(33), 64–73.

Sotiropoulos, D. (2004). Southern European Public Bureaucracies in Comparative Perspective. *West European Politics*, 27(3), 405–22.

Spicer, M. W. (2019). What Do We Mean By Democracy? Reflections on an Essentially Contested Concept and Its Relationship to Politics and Public Administration. *Administration & Society*, 51(5), 724–48.

Sprawozdanie. (2019). *Sprawozdanie Szefa Służby Cywilnej za 2018 rok*, April 4. Available from https://bip.kprm.gov.pl/kpr/bip-kancelarii-prezesa/sluzba-cywilna/sprawozdania/6314,Sprawozdanie-Szefa-Sluzby-Cywilnej-za-2018-rok.html

Sprawozdanie. (2020). *Sprawozdanie Szefa Służby Cywilnej za 2019 rok*, April 8. Available from https://bip.kprm.gov.pl/kpr/bip-kancelarii-prezesa/sluzba-cywilna/sprawozdania/7468,Sprawozdanie-Szefa-Sluzby-Cywilnej-za-2019-rok.html

Stanley, B. (2008). The Thin Ideology of Populism. *Journal of Political Ideologies*, 13(1), 95–110. https://doi.org/10.1080/13569310701822289

Staroňová, K. & Gajduschek, G. (2013). Civil Service Reform in Slovakia and Hungary: The Road to Professionalisation? In C. Neuhold, S. Vanhoonacker, & L. Verhey, eds., *Civil Servants and Politics*. London: Palgrave Macmillan, pp. 123-51.

Statista. (2019). *Einnahmen, Ausgaben und Verschuldung des Deutschen Reichs in den Jahren 1926/27 bis 1932/33 (in Millionen Reichsmark).* Available from https://de.statista.com/statistik/daten/studie/249970/umfrage/staatshaushalt-der-weimarer-republik/ [updated on June 19, 2019].

Steinhauer, J. & Kanno-Youngs, Z. (2020). Job Vacancies and Inexperience Mar Federal Response to Coronavirus. *New York Times*, March 26.

Stoker, G. (2006). Public Value Management: A New Narrative for Networked Governance? *The American Review of Public Administration*, 36(1), 41–57.

Stoker, G. (2019a). Can the Governance Paradigm Survive the Rise of Populism? *Policy & Politics*, 47(1), 3–18(16). https://doi.org/10.1332/030557318X15333033030897

Stoker, G. (2019b). Relating and Responding to the Politics of Resentment. *The Political Quarterly*, 90(S1), 138–51. https://doi.org/10.1111/1467-923X.12576

Stoker, G. & Evans, M. (2016). Evidence-based Policy Making and Social Science. In G. Stoker & M. Evans, eds., *Evidence-based Policy Making in the Social Sciences*. Bristol: Policy Press, pp. 15-28.

Suleiman, E. N. (2013). *Dismantling Democratic States*. Princeton, NJ: Princeton University Press.

Supiot, A. (2017). *Governance by Numbers: The Making of a Legal Model of Allegiance*. Oxford: Hart Publishing.

Svolik, M. (2018). When Polarization Trumps Civic Virtue: Partisan Conflict and the Subversion of Democracy by Incumbents. Available from https://ssrn.com/abstract=3243470

Swan, J. (2020). Trump's Loyalty Cop Clashes with Agency Heads. *Axios*, June 14. Available from www.axios.com/john-mcentee-white-house-trump-a799d519-aa2f-4e3d-b081-601f8193d75d.html

Szuleka, M. & Wolny, M. (2019). *Zagrożenia dla ochrony praw człowieka w Polsce w latach 2015-2019. Rządy prawem zamiast rządów prawa.* Warsaw: Helsińska Fundacja Praw Człowieka.

't Hart, P. & Wille, A. (2006). Ministers and Top Officials in the Dutch Core Executive: Living Together, Growing Apart? *Public Administration*, 84 (1), 121–46.

Taggart, P. & Kaltwasser, C. R. (2016). Dealing with Populists in Government: Some Comparative Conclusions. *Democratization*, 23(2), 345–65. https://doi.org/10.1080/13510347.2015.1076230

Tálos, E. & Manoschek, W. (2005). Aspekte der politischen Struktur des Austrofaschismus. In E. Tálos & W. Neugebauer, eds., *Austrofaschismus. Politik – Ökonomie – Kultur, 1933-1938*, 5th ed. Münster: Lit Verlag, pp. 123–61.

Tarrow, S. (1977). The Italian Party System Between Crisis and Transition. *American Journal of Political Science*, 21(2), 193–224.

Teófilo, S. & Souza, R. (2020). Augusto Aras bate boca com procuradores durante reunião no MPF. *Correio Braziliense*. Available from www.correio braziliense.com.br/app/noticia/politica/2020/07/31/internapolitica,877337/augusto-aras-bate-boca-com-procuradores-durante-reuniao-no-mpf.shtml

Thamer, H.-U. (1992). *Die Deutschen und ihre Nation. Deutschland 1933-1945*, 3rd ed. Berlin: Siedler.

The Economist (2018). Poland's Government Wants to Take Control of Banking. *The Economist*. August 9. Available from www.economist.com/europe/2018/08/09/polands-government-wants-to-take-control-of-banking

The Economist (2019). Why Latin America's Left Loves the Petroleum Economy. *The Economist*, September 19. Available from www.economist.com/the-americas/2019/09/21/why-latin-americas-left-loves-the-petroleum-economy

Tomini, L. & Wagemann, C. (2018). Varieties of Contemporary Democratic Breakdown and Regression: A Comparative Analysis. *European Journal of Political Research*, 57(3), 687–716. https://doi.org/10.1111/1475-6765.12244

Trinkunas, H. (2002). The Crisis in Venezuelan Civil-Military Relations: From Puntofijo to the Fifth Republic. *Latin American Research Review*, 37 (1), 41–76.

Tsebelis, G. (2002). *Veto Players: How Political Institutions Work*. Princeton, NJ: Princeton University Press.

Tullock, G. (2004). *The Selected Works of Gordon Tullock, Volume 1: Virginia Political Economy*. Carmel, IN: Liberty Fund.

Urbinati, N. (2014). *Democracy Disfigured: Opinion, Truth and the People*. Cambridge, MA: Harvard University Press.

Ureste, M. (2018). Trabajadores despedidos del SAT exigen reinstalación o ser liquidados conforme a la ley. *Animal Político*, December 25.

US Government Accountability Office. (2020). *Senior Executive Service. Opportunities for Selected Agencies to Improve their Career Reassignment Process*. Washington, DC: US Government Accountability Office.

Vandenabeele, W. (2009). The Mediating Effect of Job Satisfaction and Organizational Commitment on Self-Reported Performance: More Robust Evidence of the PSM-Performance Relationship. *International Review of Administrative Sciences*, 75(1), 11–34.

Vandenabeele, W., Brewer, G. A. & Ritz, A. (2014). Past, Present and Future of Public Service Motivation Research. *Public Administration*, 92(4), 779–89.

Ványi, É. (2018). Political Predation or Personal Loyalty? The Background of Highly Politicized Senior Civil Servants in Hungary. *Politikatudomány Online*: Special Issue, 1–14: online www.uni-corvinus.hu/alfresco/dokumentumtar/preview/?id=0fe3f7e8-ae70-4b07-983d-9998ed58bbc5;1.1

Veit, S., Fromm, N. & Ebinger, F. (2018). "Nein" zu sagen ist eine unserer wichtigsten Pflichten. Politisierung, Rollenverständnis und Entscheidungsverhalten von leitenden Ministerialbeamt*innen in Deutschland. *der moderne staat – Zeitschrift für Public Policy, Recht und Management*, 11(2), 413–36. https://doi.org/10.3224/dms.v11i2.02

Venezuela. (2020). Misiones. Available from https://web.archive.org/web/20130518025319/http://www.gobiernoenlinea.ve/home/misiones.dot

Verbeek, B. & Zaslove, A. (2016). Italy: A case of Mutating Populism? *Democratization*, 23(2), 304–23.

Villalpando, A. (2019). El combate a la pobreza en la Cuarta Transformación: regalar dinero funciona bien, pero sólo si se hace bien. *Nexos*, February 19.

Villegas, G. (2019). Alegan "fantasmas" … pero no aparecen. *Reforma*, July 7.

Vivanco, M. (2019). Lo que hay detrás del memorándum presidencial. *Nexos*, April 22.

Vladeck, S. I. (2019). The Solicitor General and the Shadow Docket. *Harvard Law Review*, 133, 123–63.

Waldner, D. & Lust, E. (2018). Unwelcome Change: Coming to Terms with Democratic Backsliding. *Annual Review of Political Science*, 21, 93–113.

Waldo, D. (1952). Development of Theory of Democratic Administration. *The American Political Science Review*, 46(1), 81–103.

Wang, X. (2001). Assessing Public Participation in US Cities. *Public Performance & Management Review*, 24(4), 322–36.

Ward, A. (2020). Trump's Purge of Inspectors Generals Continues. It's an Assault on Good Governance. *Vox*, May 2. Available from. www.vox.com/2020/5/2/21245273/coronavirus-trump-inspector-general-fired

Weber, M. (1949). *The Methodology of the Social Sciences*. New York, NY: The Free Press.

Weber, M. (1978). *Economy and Society: An Outline of Interpretive Sociology* [reprint], Berkeley, CA: University of California Press.

Weber, M. (2005). *Wirtschaft und Gesellschaft*. Frankfurt: Zweitausendeins.

Weingast, B. R. (1984). The Congressional-Bureaucratic System: A Principal Agent Perspective (with applications to the SEC). *Public Choice*, 44(1), 147–91.

Weiss, C. (1979). The Many Meanings of Research Utilization. *Public Administration Review*, 39(5), 426–31.

Weitz-Shapiro, R. (2008). The Local Connection: Local Government Performance and Satisfaction with Democracy in Argentina. *Comparative Political Studies*, 41(3), 285–308. https://doi.org/10.1177/0010414006297174

Weyland, K. & Madrid, R. L. (eds.) (2019). *When Democracy Trumps Populism: European and Latin American Lessons for the United States.* Cambridge: Cambridge University Press.

Wilson, J. (1989). *Bureaucracy: What Government Agencies Do and Why They Do It.* New York, NY: Basic Books.

Wilson, W. (1887). The Study of Administration. *Political Science Quarterly*, 2(2), 197–222.

Wise, L. R. (1996). Internal Labor Markets. In H. A. G. M. Bekke, J. L. Perry, & T. A. J. Toonen, eds., *Civil Service Systems in Comparative Perspective.* Bloomington & Indiana, IN: Indiana University Press, pp. 100–118.

Wójcik, K. (2018). Wzrost zatrudnienia w służbie cywilnej, zwłaszcza dyrektorów, "Rzeczpospolita," April 4. Available from www.rp.pl/Urzednicy/304049979-Wzrost-zatrudnienia-w-sluzbie-cywilnej-zwlaszcza-dyrektorow.html

Woldenberg, J. (2018). Consulta Popular. *Reforma*, August 23.

Woldenberg, J. (2019). *En defensa de la democracia.* Mexico: Cal y Arena.

Wright, B., Hassan, S. & Christensen, R. K. (2017). Job Choice and Performance: Revisiting Core Assumptions about Public Service Motivation. *International Public Management Journal*, 20(1), 108–31.

Wybory. (2015). *Wybory 2015: Jak głosowali pracownicy, rolnicy, studenci, emeryci i bezrobotni?* Available from www.wnp.pl/parlamentarny/wydarzenia/wybory-2015-jak-glosowali-pracownicy-rolnicy-studenci-emeryci-i-bezrobotni,1588.html

XIII Komunikat. (2020). *XIII Komunikat Obywatelskiego Forum Legislacji podsumowujący aktywność legislacyjną rządów Zjednoczonej Prawicy, Sejmu VIII kadencji i Senatu IX kadencji (2015–2019).* Forum Idei, Warsaw: Fundacja im. S. Batorego.

Yesilkagit, K. & Van Thiel, S. (2008). Political Influence and Bureaucratic Autonomy. *Public Organization Review*, 8(2), 137–53.

Yesilkagit, K. (2018). *Bureaucracy under Authoritarian Rule: Autonomy and Resilience of Administrative Institutions in Divided Times.* Presented at the Structure and Organization of Government 2018 Conference "Bureaucracy in Divided Times," University of Potsdam.

Yeung, K. (2018). Algorithmic Regulation: A Critical Interrogation. *Regulation & Governance* 12(4), 505–23. https://doi.org/10.1111/rego.12158

Zacka, B. (2017). *When the State Meets the Street: Public Service and Moral Agency*. Cambridge, MA: The Belknap Press of Harvard University Press.

Zakaria, F. (1997). The Rise of Illiberal Democracy. *Foreign Affairs*, 76(6), 22–43.

Zielonka, J. (2018). *Counter-revolution: Liberal Europe in Retreat*. Oxford: Oxford University Press.

Index

Abelshauser, W., 39, 41, 285
Aberbach, J. D., 16, 225, 285
Abutaleb, Y., 170, 285
accomplish, 12, 16, 82, 83, 132
accountability, 6, 7, 13, 17, 31, 32, 49,
    50, 51, 59, 60, 66, 83, 93, 97,
    110, 118, 128, 133, 153, 161,
    163, 167, 168, 171, 172, 176,
    193, 203, 214, 217, 218, 252,
    268, 271, 272, 276, 281, 283
administrative culture, 13, 14, 25, 92
administrative reform, viii, 3, 4, 14, 16,
    17, 18, 21, 23, 31, 33, 37, 43,
    44, 48, 49, 52, 53, 54, 55, 58,
    59, 61, 63, 64, 65, 66, 67, 68,
    69, 72, 73, 74, 75, 76, 85, 116,
    129, 139, 151, 155, 158, 161,
    184, 185, 188, 192, 195, 196,
    197, 198, 205, 213, 251, 258,
    260, 262, 268, 273, 275, 279,
    282, 291, 294, 295, 303, 312,
    315, 320
Agerberg, M., 137
Aguilar-Camín, H., 181, 182, 285
Ahmed, A., 183, 285
Ajuntament de Barcelona 2016, 141,
    144, 146
Alba, C., 276
Albertazzi, D., 58, 127, 256, 267, 268,
    284, 285
Alford, J., 22, 285
Ali, S. B., 5
Amorim Neto, O., 222, 286
Andersen, L. B., 224, 286
Animal Político, 182, 194, 316
Anonymous, 98
Antagonista, 223, 311
Arellano, S., 188, 286
Arenas, N., 215, 286
Arias, L., 191, 286

Arnsdorf, I., 155, 286
austerity, 54, 62, 63, 71, 137, 144, 180,
    183, 185, 188, 189, 190, 192,
    195, 196, 197, 198
authoritarian regimes, 1, 4, 7, 43, 243
autocracy, 2, 4, 19, 42, 98, 200
autonomy, 13, 14, 36, 48, 52, 57, 58,
    62, 63, 65, 67, 71, 81, 85, 86,
    88, 91, 97, 103, 104, 109, 112,
    113, 122, 123, 134, 141, 150,
    186, 187, 204, 210, 212, 215,
    218, 223, 232, 244, 274, 275,
    280, 287, 301, 312, 324
Avelar, I., 230, 286

Babiš, A., 140
Bach, M., 12
backsliding, viii, xi, 1, 2, 3, 4, 5, 6, 7, 8,
    12, 14, 16, 17, 18, 19, 20, 21,
    22, 23, 28, 29, 38, 42, 43, 44,
    76, 77, 79, 100, 127, 128, 129,
    136, 148, 151, 152, 153, 157,
    161, 162, 163, 165, 171, 172,
    173, 175, 176, 177, 178, 179,
    180, 195, 198, 200, 201, 202,
    203, 204, 207, 208, 209, 212,
    214, 217, 218, 219, 221, 222,
    223, 226, 230, 235, 241, 243,
    246, 247, 248, 265, 282, 293
Badell, D., 54
Baekgaard, M., 174, 302
Baker, R., 4
Banfield, E., 107
Barack Obama, 152, 157, 161, 167,
    168, 170
Barcelona, 19, 128, 129, 136, 137, 139,
    141, 142, 144, 145, 146, 147,
    148, 149, 285, 288, 290, 296,
    307
Barr, W., 162, 287

McDonnell, D., 58, 127, 256, 267, 268, 284, 285
McGinley, L., 170, 285
McGraw, M., 168, 291
media, 2, 7, 13, 14, 31, 32, 58, 65, 75, 76, 79, 87, 89, 93, 99, 103, 104, 112, 118, 122, 123, 125, 131, 135, 137, 138, 142, 155, 164, 167, 174, 180, 181, 192, 230, 249, 250, 254, 257, 259, 264, 265, 267, 303, 306, 309
Medzihorsky, J., 174, 306
Meier, K. J., 5, 6, 281, 307
Mele, V., 48, 53, 73
Melo, C. R., 230, 311
Méndez, J. L., 179, 188, 193, 198, 291, 308
Mény, Y., 268, 308, 313
Mercado, A., 188, 286
Merino, M., 179, 192, 198, 308
Merkel, W., 202, 308
Metro News 2016, 140
Metz, R., 78
Mexico, 20, 152, 178, 179, 180, 182, 183, 184, 185, 188, 193, 196, 197, 198, 291, 296
  doublespeak populism, 179
  doublespeak populist, 181, 184, 197, 198
Meyer-Sahling, J. H., 22, 81, 117, 308
Michael Flynn, 162
Michels, R., 10
Middendorf, S., 26, 29, 38
militarization, vii, 11, 45, 85, 92, 97, 166, 168, 200, 204, 206, 214, 215, 216, 217, 218, 219, 222, 230, 231, 268, 270, 288
Miranda, F., 189, 308
Miranda, P., 190
missions (Venezuela), viii, 207, 212, 213, 214, 218
modernization, 1, 4, 52, 101, 135, 205, 258, 312
Moe, T. M., 154, 309
Molnár, C., 79
Mommsen, H., 27, 31, 34, 36, 38, 39, 40, 41
Monroy, L. A., 180, 309
Morales, A., 182, 187, 192, 309
Morales, Evo, 178

Moreno, D., 193, 309
Morlino, L., 54
Mosca, L., 58, 138, 145
Mounk, Y., 2
Mouritzen, P. E., 137
Moynihan, D., x, 19, 151, 154, 155, 159, 309
Mudde, C., 2, 130, 151, 179, 181, 249, 250, 257, 258, 272, 290, 309
Muédano, M., 189, 310
Müller, J.-W., 2, 3, 117, 128, 179, 181, 257, 259, 268, 269, 310
Muno, W., x, 20, 200, 214, 219, 276, 279, 290, 310

Natalini, A., x, 18, 47, 51, 52, 53, 58, 60, 62, 63, 66, 71, 268, 278, 286, 294, 295
nationalization, 104, 105, 123, 216
Nery, N., 230, 310
Neuhold, C., 276, 310, 314, 320
neutrality, 14, 36, 40, 41, 92, 116, 122, 124, 131, 153, 203, 212, 217, 218, 257, 313
Niskanen, W. A., 5, 154, 203, 225, 310
Nistotskaya, M., 42
Norden, D., 215, 311
Norris, P., 2, 249, 272, 311
Nunes, F., 230, 311
Nutley, S., 247, 293
Nützenadel, A., 41

O'Donnell, G., 202, 272, 311
O'Leary, R., 154, 165, 277, 311
O'Toole, 311
O'Toole, L. J., 5, 6, 281, 307
OECD, 65, 66, 247, 254, 259, 311, 319
Oliveira, M., 223, 311
Olorunnipa, T., 158, 160, 317
Olsson, J., 10
Ongaro, E., x, 18, 47, 48, 49, 50, 51, 52, 53, 60, 62, 64, 73, 268, 278, 286, 288, 294, 295, 303, 308, 312
Oppelt, R., 141, 143
opulism, 310
Oramus, M., 105
Orbán, Viktor, 18, 77, 78, 83, 86, 98, 172, 283
Ortiz Lemos, A., 272, 294

For EU product safety concerns, contact us at Calle de José Abascal, 56–1°,
28003 Madrid, Spain or eugpsr@cambridge.org.